THE WORLD REFERENCE
ENCYCLOPEDIA

THE WORLD REFERENCE
ENCYCLOPEDIA

Foreword by Professor J. K. Galbraith

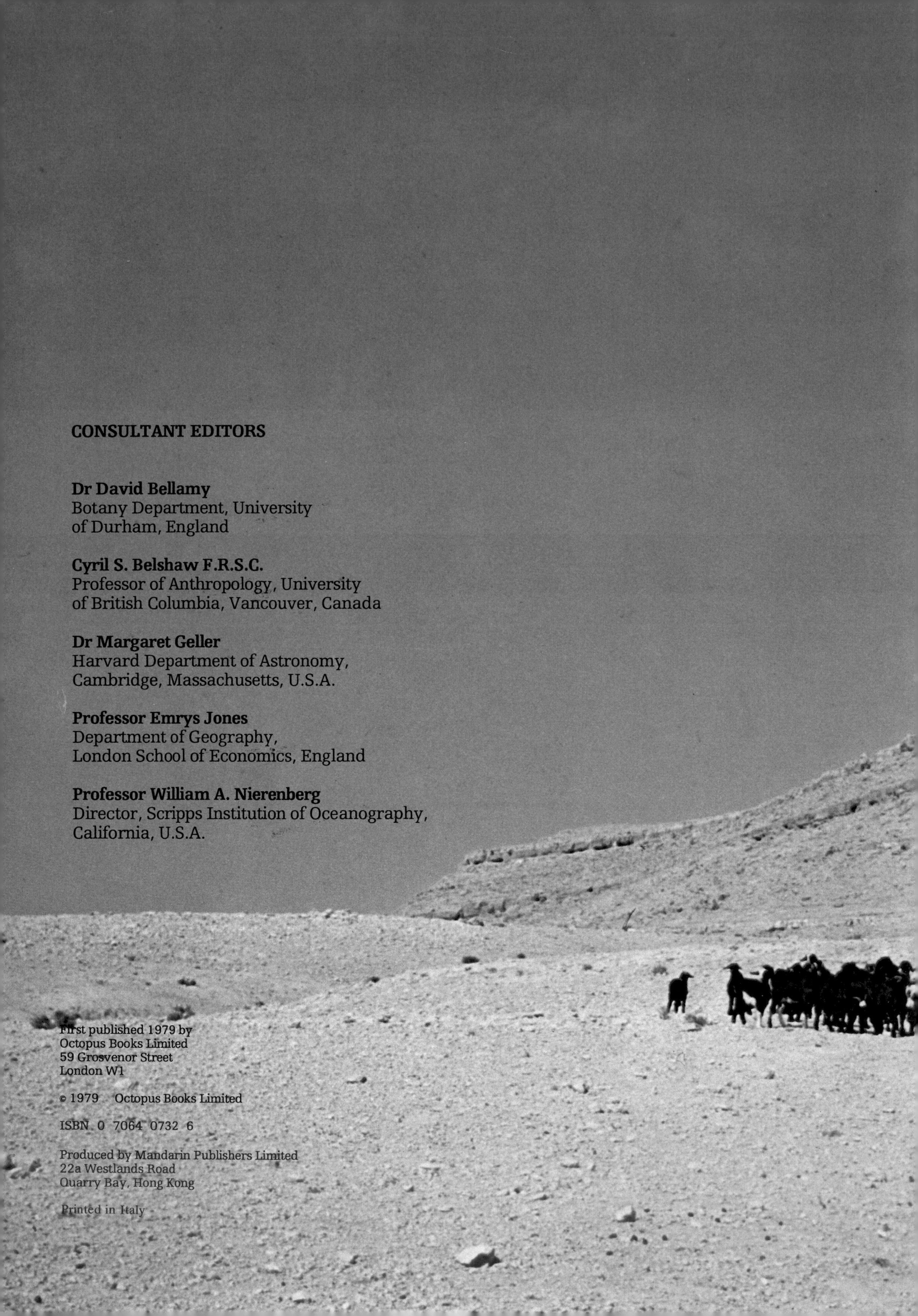

CONSULTANT EDITORS

Dr David Bellamy
Botany Department, University
of Durham, England

Cyril S. Belshaw F.R.S.C.
Professor of Anthropology, University
of British Columbia, Vancouver, Canada

Dr Margaret Geller
Harvard Department of Astronomy,
Cambridge, Massachusetts, U.S.A.

Professor Emrys Jones
Department of Geography,
London School of Economics, England

Professor William A. Nierenberg
Director, Scripps Institution of Oceanography,
California, U.S.A.

First published 1979 by
Octopus Books Limited
59 Grosvenor Street
London W1

© 1979   Octopus Books Limited

ISBN 0 7064 0732 6

Produced by Mandarin Publishers Limited
22a Westlands Road
Quarry Bay, Hong Kong

Printed in Italy

CONTENTS

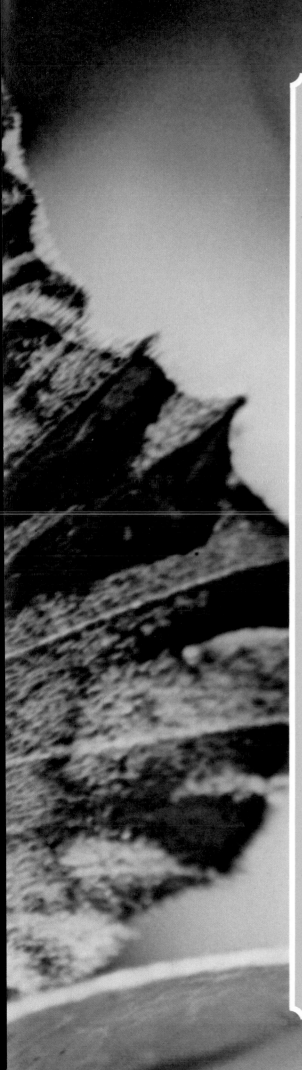

FOREWORD

There should be no doubt in anyone's mind as to why I am writing this introduction. I am an encyclopedia addict. Where I am writing this, up at our old farm in Vermont, I have three encyclopedias, one of them a portable item that I move around with me. In Cambridge where we live, I have an upstairs set and a downstairs set. For years I have been secluding myself in Switzerland where, as in a medieval monastery, one is forced to write as the only available escape from one's own company. I keep an encyclopedia there.

There are three kinds of encyclopedia users. The first, most common and most respectable, are those who use an encyclopedia merely to look things up. By a writer, teacher, student or the like, that is to discover spelling, dates, population, age and other facts relevant to professional need. And in families and between friends, it is to resolve disputes, seldom acrimonious, and to award the proceeds from associated wagers. The second type of encyclopedia user, also reputable, is equipping himself or herself with the requisite information that will allow of conversation or association with a particular subject. 'If we're stopping over in Florence, we should know something about the Medici. Ghiberti too, or was he just a door?'
Finally, there are the people who read encyclopedias to learn things. President Truman was said to have been one. Not having gone to college, he compensated as a young man by reading all that he would there have learned at much less cost, in much less time and without the distractions of sex or intercollegiate football. Curiously this form of self-education has always been thought slightly eccentric, even slightly disreputable. I think I know why. It is greatly unfair competition for those who write books and gives lectures.
This brings me to *The World Reference Encyclopedia*. It is, I must say, quite good for looking things up. The publishers, when preparing it, sent me the Gazetteer along with the other proofs. Eventually I punched a hole in the corner of the long sheets and hung them by my desk. It's the single best rapid reference that I've encountered. I now refer to it daily. But most of all I judge this to be an encyclopedia for straight-through reading in the manner of Harry Truman. It is competent, well-written, terse and, to me at least, extremely interesting.

So I found my education on various matters, both commonplace and arcane, greatly and painlessly advanced from reading these pages. I congratulate the editors and authors and commend their work not alone to encyclopedia addicts but to all who retain an old-fashioned preference for learning by reading.

PROFESSOR J. K. GALBRAITH

THE UNIVERSE

Man's Universe
Astronomy through the Ages

Modern astronomical studies indicate that the planet on which we live is one among at least nine planets orbiting our Sun in the Solar System. Planet Earth is a small, rocky planet; the Sun which dominates our Solar System is a small, rather insignificant star, one among perhaps 100,000 million similar stars which, with other objects make up the Milky Way. But this picture of awesome insignificance on the cosmic scale of things is scarcely half a century old. For thousands of years, man regarded himself as something special, and thought that the Earth he walked must be a very special place in the Universe.

Unprepossessing in appearance, this is one of the most important of all astronomical instruments – Newton's reflecting telescope.

It is hardly surprising that the Sun and Moon, both dominating the sky viewed from Planet Earth, were regarded as gods, and to these early observers of the heavens added the planets, peculiar objects that looked like stars but moved in their own paths against the background of the so-called 'fixed' stars. This religious aspect of the study of the Heavens was the forerunner of astrology. With such a powerful incentive, the study of positional astronomy and of predicting motions of heavenly

bodies on the sky received a great boost both in antiquity and with the revival of science a millenium or more later.

Like the Sumerians before them, Greek astronomers were fascinated by the cycles of repetition of heavenly events which, once recognized, made prediction possible even if the *causes* of the cycles were not understood. At its simplest, we know that night follows day even if we do not know what makes the Sun shine, or how the Earth spins on its axis. The Moon's phases—as the Greeks knew —follow a pattern which repeats exactly after 19 years; the saros cycle, 18 years and $11\frac{1}{3}$ days long, made it possible to predict most eclipses; and even the procession of the equinoxes, which looks from Earth to be a slow drift of the constellations with a cycle 26,000 years long, were known to the Greeks.

Even by modern standards, remembering that they had no telescopes to aid their observations, the achievements of the Greek philosophers are impressive. They deduced correctly that the Moon must be a dark globe lit by the Sun, and that the Earth too must be a globe. They made fairly accurate estimates of the size of the Earth, based on a variety of measurements, and slightly less accurate estimates of the distance to the Moon.

At first, the philosophers failed to ask themselves the question 'Does the Earth rotate?' or, 'Does the Earth move through space?' So their model of the Universe started out with a fixed Earth at the centre, surrounded by, in order, the Moon, Venus, Mercury, the Sun, Mars, Jupiter, Saturn and the 'vault of the heavens' with the fixed stars attached

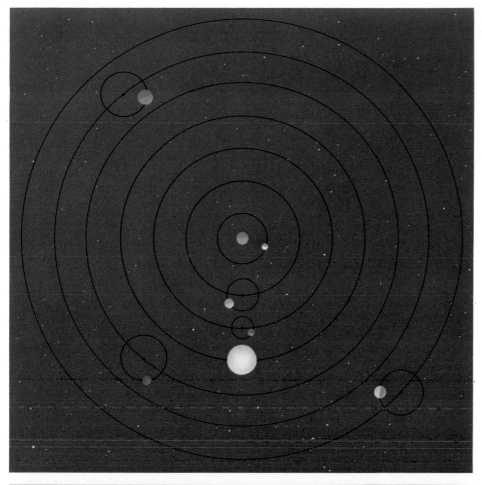

Until the 16th century, models of the Universe always showed the Earth at the centre (left). In 1543, Copernicus published his ideas on a Sun-centred Universe (below). It was not until the 17th century, however, that it was suggested that the planets did not move in perfect circles.

to its inside surface. When some philosophers suggested that perhaps the Earth itself moved in an orbit around the Sun, their speculation was quickly countered and it was the model of an Earth-centered universe that was passed on and accepted unquestioningly for centuries.

After the decline of Greek influence, the light of astronomical study was kept alive not by Christian Europe, but by the Islamic culture. One powerful reason for this was that the Arab astronomers had access to Greek libraries containing records which, because of religious differences and wars, were lost to Europeans for more than a thousand years. In the 15th and 16th centuries, religious dogma still held that the Earth was the centre of the Universe. At first, the rebirth of European astronomy produced no great conflict with this dogma, as astronomers concentrated once again on observing motions of the planets and cyclic repetitions of heavenly events. However, in 1543 Nicolaus Copernicus published his ideas based on a Sun-centered Universe. This failed to gain wide acceptance but the ideas were preserved so that in the 17th century they could be taken up and improved by the astronomers who at last laid the foundations of modern astronomy.

These pioneers were led by Galileo, who invented the telescope and opened up, literally, new vistas in astronomy. Galileo fought unsuccessfully to break the hold of religious orthodoxy on science, but through his fight made it possible for the next generation to shake off this restrictive yoke. Johannes Kepler made the great theoretical breakthrough by suggesting that planets move around the Sun not in perfect circles as Copernicus had thought, but in ellipses and Isaac Newton began to explain why they should move in this way with his theory of gravitation.

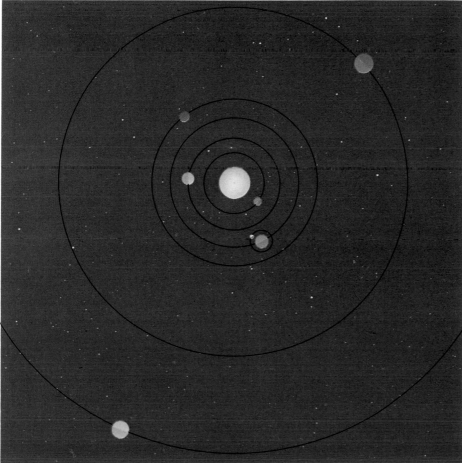

The Inner Solar System

The inner Solar System planets are shown here in their order out from the Sun, with their relative sizes. In reality, wherever you might be in

Including the Earth, there are nine known major planets in the Solar System. These divide naturally into two groups, four small inner planets and four large outer planets, with one 'maverick'—Pluto—the outermost planet of all. It may be that Pluto is not a 'real' planet but an escaped moon which once orbited around Neptune. In any case, because it is so remote, moving between 4.42 and 7.37 thousand million km from the Sun, and so small, probably less than 5,900 km in diameter, Pluto is very difficult to observe and little is known about it except that it exists and takes 247.7 years to complete one orbit around the Sun.

Mercury

Mercury is small (4,880 km diameter) and moves in a very elliptical orbit, taking it between 46 and 69.8 million km from the Sun, and completing one circuit every 87.97 days. For many years it was thought that Mercury always kept the same face towards the Sun, so that one side fried in eternal day while the other froze in eternal night. But when the NASA space probe Mariner 10 made three close passes to Mercury in 1974 and 1975, sending back a stream of photographs and other information, it was discovered that the 'day' on Mercury is actually 58.65 of our days, or two-thirds of the mercurian 'year'. Like our Moon, Mercury has only the most tenuous traces of an atmosphere, and the surface of the planet is pockmarked and battered by the impact of many meteorites.

Venus

As with Mercury, our knowledge of Venus, the next planet out from the Sun, was revolutionized in the 1970s by the Mariner 10 space probe, which passed Venus on its way in towards Mercury. Also, Soviet space probes have landed on the planet in recent years. Venus is almost exactly the same size as the Earth, 12,104 km in diameter, and has a density 5.25 times that of water compared with the Earth's 5.52. It takes 243 days to rotate once on its axis and moves in a very nearly circular orbit at a distance of 108,210,000 km from the Sun, taking 224.7 days to complete each orbit. The 'day' on Venus is actually longer than the 'year'. It has a very thick atmosphere rich in carbon dioxide, which traps heat underneath like the glass of a greenhouse. As a result, the surface temperature reaches a scorching 475°C. The atmospheric pressure at the surface is 91 times that at the surface of the Earth, and the clouds of Venus contain such reactive substances as hydrogen chloride and sulphuric acid.

Earth

Next out from the Sun comes our Earth-Moon system. In a sense, this counts as a double planet, since our Moon is comparable in size (diameter 3,476 km) and probably in structure to Mercury. Other planets have

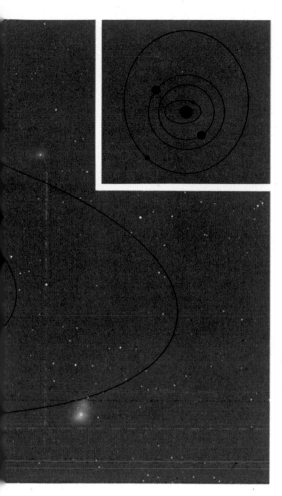

space, you would only see one planet at most as a large disc, the others as pinpoints of light.

meteoritic battering like that of the Moon and Mercury; it also possesses features that appear to be dried up river channels and other signs that liquid—presumably water—once flowed on its surface. It may be that water remains frozen below the surface of the planet as permafrost, and that in the distant future changes in the orbit of Mars may warm the planet sufficiently for the rivers to flow again, and for frozen carbon dioxide to be released, thickening the atmosphere.

Great interest centered on experiments on the two Viking craft designed to test for the presence of life on Mars, in the form of micro-organisms in the soil. As scientists

should, perhaps, have expected, the results of their experiments came out literally like nothing on Earth. Most of the scientists involved in these experiments say that this shows signs of 'unusual' chemistry on Mars, but not of life; a few claim that the evidence may instead be due to life, but not exactly as we know it. It does seem though that certain types of hardy terrestrial organisms, such as lichens from Antarctica, could survive under conditions no harsher than those on Mars today.

Mars, the red planet, is veiled in enigma from a distance, offering a tantalising possibility that it might harbour intelligent life. However, space probes have shown the planet to be a cold, dead desert.

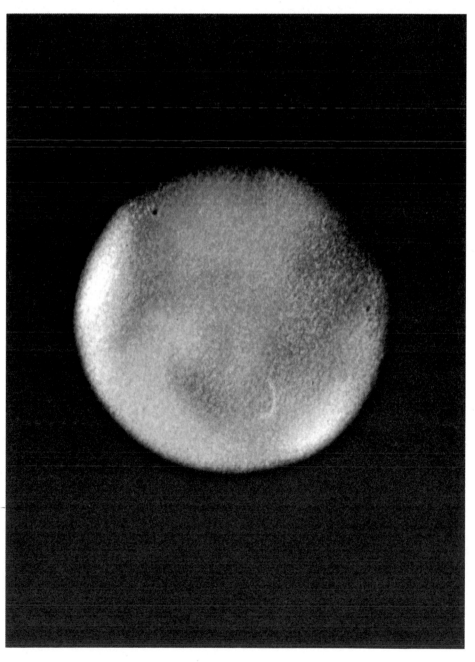

moons which are no more than a few thousandths of their own mass, but the mass of the Moon is a more impressive 1/81st of the mass of the Earth. The Earth is 12,742 km in diameter and averages 149,597,791 km from the Sun, a distance called the Astronomical Unit (AU).

Mars

Mars (6,787 km diameter) moves around the Sun once every 687 days, at an average distance of 227,941,000 km (1.7 AU) and turns on its axis once every 24 hours 37 minutes and 23 seconds—the martian 'day' is almost exactly the same as that of the Earth, although its 'year' is twice as long as ours. A great deal is known about this planet as a result of a succession of space probes, both Soviet and American, culminating (so far) in the landing of NASA's two Viking probes on the surface in 1976. Although the atmosphere today is thin, and the surface of the planet shows ample cratering, evidence of a

The Outer Solar System

Saturn with its dramatic ring system is the most beautiful object viewed through even a small telescope.

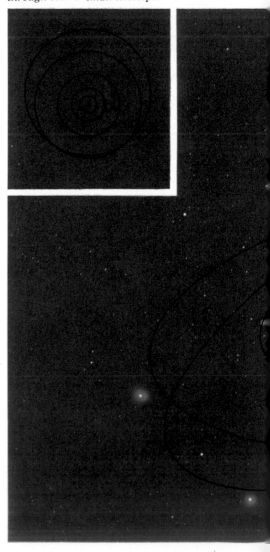

Between Mars and the outer planets there is a belt of cosmic rubble called the asteroids. About 2,500 asteroids have accurately known orbits, 2,000 more (at least) have been sighted on occasions but not tracked for long enough for orbits to be measured, and there must be many more rocks in the belt. Asteroids in the main belt orbit the Sun with periods between 2 and 6 years; they range in size up to a very few with diameters of several hundred kilometres. The idea that these objects mark the debris of a former planet which, somehow, broke up has now been superseded by the theory that when the Solar System formed, an original 'family' of about 30 large asteroids formed between Mars and Jupiter, and that these have since been broken up into smaller pieces by inter-collision.

Jupiter

The fifth planet out from the Sun (4.9 AU) is by far the biggest, with 2.5 times the mass of all the others put together. Its diameter at the equator is 142,800 km. It takes 11.9 years to orbit the Sun once and features we see on the equator show a spin rate for the planet of 9 hours 50 minutes, the fastest of any planet. But this figure should be treated with

caution, since we do not see any solid surface but rather the tops of coloured, banded cloud layers high in the jovian atmosphere. These orange, brown, yellow, red and green clouds form parallel stripes around the planet, dominated by one long lasting feature, the Great Red Spot, which alone is big enough to swallow the entire Earth. Again, our understanding of Jupiter has been transformed by NASA space probes, which have revealed in particular a very strong magnetic field. Its influence stretches across an enormous volume of space, at least out beyond the orbit of the next planet, Saturn. Jupiter is a warm planet, radiating into space more heat than it receives from the Sun. This may be a residue from the formation of the planet, heat released through the slow shrinking of the giant, or it may be a result of some form of nuclear reactions occurring in the interior—Jupiter is so large that it is, by planetary standards, on the edge of being a star in its own right. Whatever its origin, the warmth raises interesting possibilities. The clouds we can see are rich in the chemicals essential for producing the building blocks of the kind of life we know on

Earth. With temperatures reaching about 60°C below the cloud layer, it may very well be that Jupiter possesses some form of life. But Jupiter has no rocky surface like the inner planets. The cloudy atmosphere blends into a very high pressure hydrogen/helium mixture, with perhaps a tiny inner core only 10,000 km across.

Saturn

A gas giant, like Jupiter, Saturn (119,000 km diameter) has at least ten moons, and is distinguished by a beautiful system of rings. The planet moves in an elliptical orbit between 9.01 and 10.07 AU from the Sun, taking 29½ years to complete one orbit. No space probes have reached Saturn yet, although Pioneer II is targeted to fly by in mid-1979 with Voyager 1 arriving near the planet in August 1980 and Voyager 2 in June 1981. As yet all our information about Saturn is based on observations made from the Earth. These observations reveal similarities to Jupiter, although if past experience is anything to go by the space probes will change our image of the planet.

Uranus and Neptune

Even further away and also unvisited by any space probe so far, these two outer giants also seem to be smaller versions of Jupiter. Uranus, about four times the diameter of the Earth, averages 19.18 AU from the Sun, turns on its axis once every 10 hours 49 minutes, and takes 84.01 years to orbit the Sun once. Neptune, slightly smaller (49,500 km diameter compared with 51,800 km), rotates once in 15 hours 48 minutes and takes 164.8 years to orbit the Sun at a distance averaging 30.06 AU. Both planets have moons. Uranus is unique among the known planets in pointing its spin axis almost exactly in the plane of its orbit so that each *pole* has a 42 year 'winter' followed by a 42 year 'summer'.

Comets

The last of the known members of the Sun's family, comets, are small, icy bodies which spend most of their time in the frozen depths of space but occasionally dive in close to the Sun on highly elliptical orbits. When this happens, they heat up, releasing gas and dust to form a hazy 'head' and a streaming 'tail'. Most comets are faint, fuzzy objects visible only with the aid of a telescope; a few provide spectacular displays lighting up the whole sky. Some comets in well known orbits provide regular, predictable displays in the sky. Most famous of these is Halley's Comet, due to return to the inner regions of the Solar System next in 1986, when, unfortunately, it will be badly placed for observation from Earth.

The outer planets of the Solar System are shown here schematically. They would never appear like this to any space traveller, but their relative sizes and the order of their distances from the Sun are indicated.

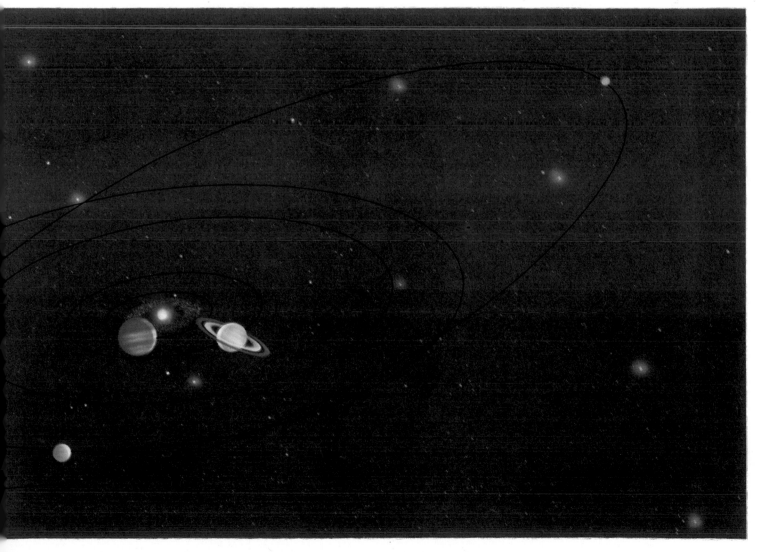

Observing the Universe
Optical Astronomy

Modern astronomy depends on modern instruments. While information about the Universe was limited to that available to the human eye—even the human eye aided by telescopes—man's vision of the Universe was necessarily restricted. Astronomical instruments today extend this vision in two ways. First, they are more sensitive than the human eye. The eye is very rapidly 'saturated' by light, so that if we look through a telescope at a distant star we do not see any change if we look for 30 seconds, or a minute, or half an hour (unless, of course, the star itself changes in brightness). A photographic plate, on the other hand, adds up all the light (photons) falling on it as long as it is exposed, so that simply by adding a camera to a telescope astronomers gain more information. The same star photographed with different exposures will look different, longer exposures generally giving more information.

The second improvement of instrumentation over the eye is in the range of electromagnetic radiation which can be investigated. To either side of the visible spectrum, there is a vast range of invisible, but detectable, radiation—infrared and radio waves at long wavelengths beyond the red end of the rainbow spectrum; ultraviolet, X- and gamma-rays at the short wave region beyond the blue-violet end of the spectrum. Wherever in this range an astronomical object radiates, it can in principle be observed.

Optical astronomy today includes both astronomical photography and instrumentation for studying electronically the visible spectrum. Very few astronomers 'look through' a telescope at the stars or other objects; information is collected by a battery of instruments and analyzed later, often with the aid of modern high speed electronic computers. Even so, the size of telescope used is important. The bigger a telescope, the more light it can gather in to be studied. It is also important to avoid much of the obscuration caused by the layers of the atmosphere.

The first telescopes were refractors, essentially two lenses in a tube, like the mariner's spyglass. Because of the difficulty of making large, perfect lenses and supporting them so that they do not bend under their own weight while in use, such telescopes cannot be scaled up in size indefinitely, and the practical limit was reached a century ago with the 102 cm diameter lens of a telescope at the Yerkes Observatory in the USA. In this century, further progress has been made by building successively bigger reflecting telescopes, in which the 'back' lens is replaced by a reflecting mirror. A mirror can be supported underneath without obscuring the field of view, and the largest now operating is a 6 metre diameter reflector at Zelenchukskaya in the USSR. This is about the practical limit for a mirror which can be turned without distortion as the telescope is pointed at different parts of the sky. A new concept, using several smaller mirrors working together to mimic the power of a giant reflector, is now being tested in the USA.

Among the modern instruments used in conjunction with telescopes for 'optical' astronomy are the spectroscope, which measures the amount of light coming from a star or other object at different wavelengths, and the photometer, which measures brightnesses electronically. Spectroscopy is particularly important because it enables astronomers to deduce the composition of distant objects (since particular atoms or molecules produce characteristic lines at different places in the spectrum). Also, because the movement of a star affects the position of the lines in the spectrum, through the so-called Doppler Shift, spectroscopy provides information about the motion of distant sources.

The giant 200-inch telescope at Mount Palomar in California was for many years the biggest in operation.

Radio Astronomy and the New Astronomies

After optical astronomy became established as a modern science, the next region of the electromagnetic spectrum to be opened up to observation was the radio spectrum. This is because, apart from light and a very narrow infrared 'window', only radio waves in a certain range (roughly 1 cm to 30 m wavelength) penetrate to the surfaces of the Earth. Radio waves from space were discovered in 1931, but rapid progress in the study of these waves came only after World War II, when the techniques developed for use in radar were applied to create a new branch of astronomy.

Radio telescopes include an antenna (aerial) to pick up radio waves, an amplifier, akin to an ordinary radio receiver, and a recorder to preserve the observations, often either magnetic tape or a chart recorder. Because radio waves are roughly a million times longer than light waves, a radio aerial comparable to an optical telescope mirror would have to be a million times bigger to provide the same detailed information (resolution). This is impractical but a great deal about strength and variability of radio sources can be learnt even without high resolution, and it is also possible to link two or more dishes which are far apart electronically, mimicking the behaviour of a giant radio dish antenna and producing very high resolution.

With radio telescopes on different continents linked in this way, resolutions as fine as 0.001 seconds of arc have been obtained. The best optical resolution possible on Earth, limited by the blurring effects of the atmosphere, is 1 arc second; for comparison, the angular size of the Moon viewed from Earth is about 30 arc seconds. With the latest computer techniques, high resolution radio signals can be used to create a 'photograph' of what the sky in a particular region would look like if we had eyes sensitive at a certain radio wavelength.

Probably the single most important discovery made by radio astronomy is the background radiation, a weak radio 'noise' coming from all directions in space, which is best explained as the faint leftover radiation from the 'Big Bang' in which the Universe as we know it began. The best known radio discovery, however, was that of the pulsars, late in the 1960s. These are thought to be very small, dense stars (neutron stars) which rotate very rapidly and send out a beam of radiation like the beams of light from a lighthouse, flicking past the line of sight from Earth to produce the appearance of regular pulses of radiation. Radio studies have also been important in investigating the structure of our Galaxy.

The last great breakthrough in observational astronomy has now come about, with instruments lifted above the atmosphere to make un-impeded observations from space. This is the end of the beginning of observational astronomy, with the whole of the electromagnetic spectrum now open to observation. But it will take many years before the impact of these new observations is fully felt in terms of our understanding of the Universe.

First attempts to make observations of radiation, which is stopped by the atmosphere, involved sending instruments up in the balloons, and later in 'sounding' rockets which go straight up and down, not into orbit. Both techniques are still used and are of great value. But the real breakthrough has come with the ability to put unmanned orbiting observatories into space to monitor the sky for a long period of time at X-ray and other frequencies.

X-ray astronomy has provided a wealth of information about very energetic processes going on in the Universe, including a hint that the exotic 'black holes' may really exist. Ultraviolet radiation, the band of the spectrum between X-rays and visible light, has been studied in particular by the 2½ ton Copernicus satellite, which carried an 81 cm diameter reflecting telescope for ultraviolet observations and three X-ray telescopes, giving it a broad range of observations across the spectrum. Such orbiting observatories are directed from ground stations on Earth, where many astronomers can make use of the facility, and their observations are relayed back to the ground for interpretation and analysis.

An X-ray 'map' bears no resemblance to a conventional 'map' of the stars.

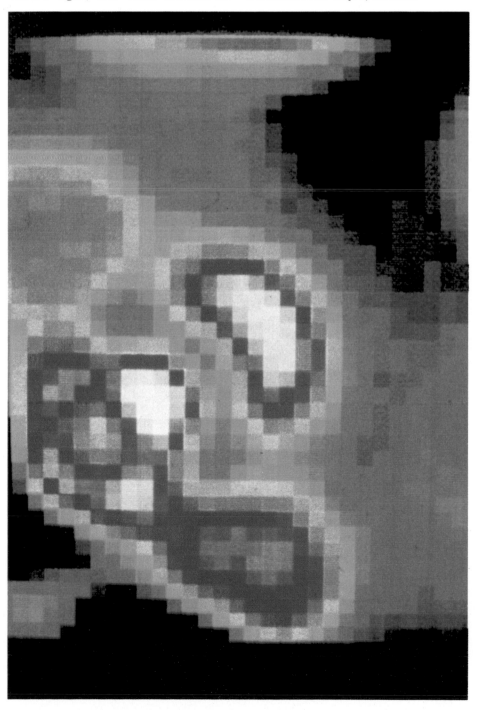

The Sun as a Star
Origin of the Solar System

The Sun contains 99.9 per cent of the mass (matter) in our Solar System, and is the source of almost all of the heat and light in the system. So the Solar System is essentially a by-product of the existence of the Sun, and the formation of the Solar System was intimately linked with the processes by which the Sun formed. It is not yet clear whether solar systems like our own are a common by-product of the formation of stars like the Sun, or whether ours is a rare example. Even if stars like our Sun are generally accompanied by planets, however, such systems are in the minority overall, since only about 15 per cent of the stars in our Milky Way Galaxy are not accompanied by companion stars. About 46 per cent of stars form binary systems and the remaining 39 per cent occupy even more complex systems with three or more stars bound together by gravity. Most

probably, the formation of a planetary system occurs only where the material which gathers to form a star produces only one star and a collection of debris—the planets, comets and so on—rather than two or more stars together.

Stars form from the collapse of clouds of gas and dust in space, and this process continues today. We can see clouds which are in the process of forming stars in, for example, the Orion Nebula. The oldest stars, however, formed when the Galaxy was young, are rather different from both our Sun and stars forming today. This is because at first the material of the young Galaxy contained only gas, chiefly hydrogen with a little helium. Heavier elements—everything else—were only built up by nuclear 'cooking' in these original stars, some of which exploded and spread their material through the Galaxy to make the

dusty clouds from which younger stars, our own Sun included, have formed. With no heavy elements, the oldest stars, even those in isolation, cannot have any Earthlike planets, so solar systems like our own are a phenomenon of the second and later generations of star formation.

Clouds of dust and gas in the Galaxy can remain relatively stable for hundreds of millions of years until a collapse is triggered by outside effects. Once collapse begins, it will continue under the pull of the cloud's own gravity field, with the cloud breaking up into smaller, self-gravitating pieces which collapse down to form stars and, in some cases, solar systems. A collapsing cloud heats up through the release of gravitational energy. At a temperature of about 10 million degrees the pressure of the hot gas is enough to halt the collapse and a star has been born.

Stars Like the Sun
The Sun is an average star. It is kept hot by nuclear reactions in the interior, fusion reactions which are slowly building up heavier elements from a 'fuel' of 90 per cent hydrogen

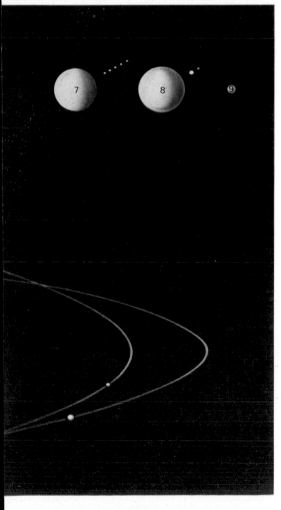

and 8 per cent helium. The reactions keep the centre at about 17 million degrees. The surface is at about 6,000 degrees. Although 1.4 million kilometres in diameter, the Sun's overall density is just under 1½ times that of water. But three-quarters of the Sun's mass is concentrated within about one-third of its radius, just three per cent of the volume, in a much denser core where the nuclear burning takes place. This is typical of stars like the Sun. Energy released in the Sun's core is transported out to the surface. The energetic photons— gamma rays—which start the transport process are bounced around among the atomic nuclei in the core and take some 10 million years to work their way outwards to the regions where energy is transported rapidly by other means. In a sense, then, the surface of the Sun as we see it is the result of conditions in the deep interior as they were 10 million years ago.

Intriguingly, experiments design-

Left The Sun, the planets and their orbits.
Above The Great Nebula in Orion.

ed to detect neutrinos, particles which are thought to be produced in the Sun's interior but travel directly out into space without scattering and through the Earth without this 10 million year delay, have so far proved inconclusive, although the amount of heat now being radiated at the surface suggests that the interior of the Sun should be active enough to produce a flux of neutrinos bigger than that detected. It is possible that in the centre the Sun is, in fact, as much as 10 per cent cooler than the equilibrium that corresponds to the amount of heat now leaving the surface, and that we are seeing a surface corresponding to a state of the Sun's interior which has changed slightly sometime in the past 10 million years.

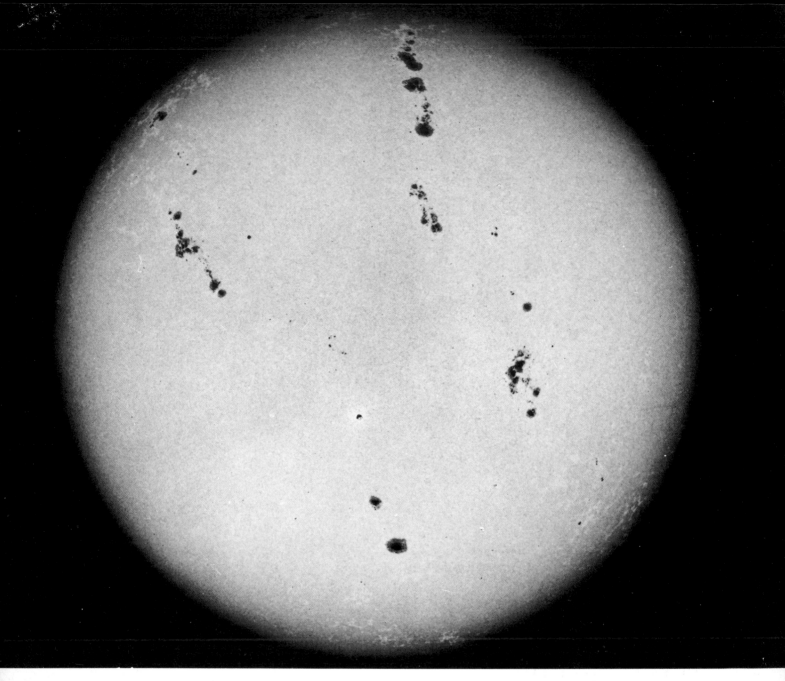

The Surface of the Sun

There is less uncertainty about the surface layers of the Sun where the time required to transport energy does not occur. Convection is an important mechanism in transferring energy. At the surface itself the Sun's heat emerges in the form of electro-magnetic radiation. The surface layers show a pattern of activity which varies over a cycle roughly 11 years long, during which activity builds to a peak and then dies away. The activity takes the form of flares and storms on the Sun's surface which hurl blasts of material outwards. This activity is associated with the presence of dark 'spots' on the solar surface (sunspots) which are themselves associated with chan-

ges in the Sun's magnetic field. However, the spots themselves are merely an outward sign of the important changes. What all this activity tells us is that the Sun is actually a variable star on a modest scale. It seems likely that this too is a common feature of stars like the Sun, but the effects are so small that it has not yet been possible to confirm by observations whether most stars like the Sun do have their own 'starspot cycle'.

The material which streams out from the Sun during flare activity and at other times forms a 'wind' of charged particles which extends well out past the orbit of the Earth to Jupiter and beyond. In a sense, our

The surface of the Sun shows a regular pattern of activity in the form of flares and storms. These are associated with sunspots – dark 'spots' which appear on the surface of the Sun.

planet moves within the outer reaches of the Sun's 'atmosphere'. This streaming of material into space is a common feature of stars; particles from the solar wind, trapped by the Earth's magnetic field, are responsible for the bright aurorae seen at high latitudes.

Evolution of the Sun

When it first forms, a star like the Sun is as much as 50 times as big as the Sun today and 500 times brighter. It takes 30 million years for the further contraction and stabilization which produces steady nuclear burning and a recognizable young star. Once stabilized, however, such a star remains much the same in outward appearance for as much as 10 thousand million years—our Sun is roughly half way through this period of stability. During this time, more and more hydrogen 'fuel' is converted into other elements by fusion, until the core is composed mainly of helium nuclei. The Sun's energy in this phase comes from a thin shell of hydrogen being converted into helium around the inert helium core. With the source of heat much nearer the surface, the Sun will expand its outer layers to about 100 times its present size, engulfing the Earth. But when the hydrogen is all used up, the outer layers will contract again.

Eventually, the core contracts and heats up sufficiently to force the beginning of the next step up the fusion ladder, with helium providing the new fuel. At the same time, the outer layers of the star expand dramatically, perhaps to 400 times the size of the Sun today, with a great deal of material being blown away into space. After this giant phase, the Sun will have exhausted all its helium fuel as well. Since it does not contain enough mass for pressure to build up in the interior sufficiently to force further nuclear burning, it will then settle down into a slowly cooling star no bigger than the Earth, with no remaining source of internal energy. Initially a white dwarf, still radiating stored up heat, it will finally become a dead, cold black dwarf star. By then the planets of the Solar System will have been first roasted by the Sun's giant phases then frozen.

Detail of a large sunspot group. The 'spots' are associated with changes in the Sun's magnetic field and are an outward sign of them.

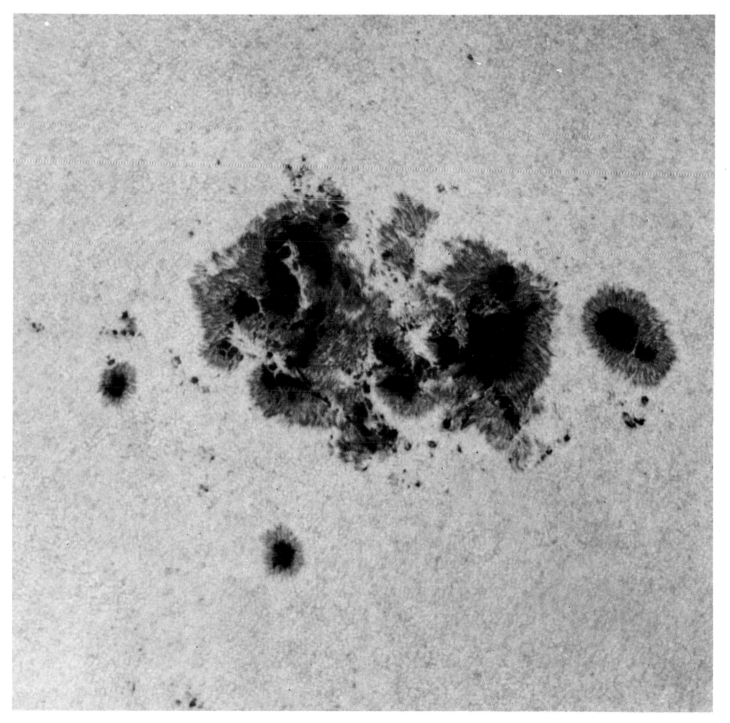

Stars and the Milky Way
The Structure of Our Galaxy

A spiral galaxy similar to our own.

Stars and the Milky Way
The Structure of Our Galaxy

The family of stars to which our Sun and Solar System belong is the Milky Way Galaxy. As well as stars and their attendant planets the Milky Way contains a great deal of cold dust and gas in interstellar space. This can be detected directly by its radiation at radio frequencies, or by its obscuring effect on radio waves, light or other electromagnetic radiation coming from farther away. However, because of their ready visibility to the human eye, it is the band of stars circling the sky, given the name Milky Way by the ancients because of its appearance, which provides the first clue to the nature of our immediate surroundings in space.

The main feature of our Galaxy is that the stars in it form a flattened disc, much greater in diameter than its thickness. The Sun is located in this thin disc, well out towards the edge. This disc of shining stars, viewed from inside, is what we see on the sky as the distinctive band of the Milky Way. We are located about 31,000 light years from the centre of the Galaxy, around which the Solar System circles about once every 200 million years. The whole disc is perhaps 100,000 light years across (although it is hard to define an exact 'edge') and 2,000 light years thick; among the bright stars there are several dark bands of cold material. All of this material orbits around the galactic centre, forming a distinctive spiral structure—viewed from outside, our Galaxy would show clear spiral markings.

Hydrogen gas clouds between the stars provide the best means of 'mapping' the structure of our own Galaxy, because they produce characteristic radio noise at 21 cm wavelength, and this radiation is able to penetrate a long way through the material of the disc, giving us a long range view of our surroundings. This kind of mapping, aided by studies of the distribution of stars, shows the spiral pattern very clearly.

Such studies also show that the disc region is almost entirely made up of *young* stars and other material; it is thought that these have formed —and continue to form—from the gas concentrated in the plane of the disc. Outside the disc, there is very little material left today from which stars can form, and only very old stars, formed during the birth of the Galaxy itself, remain.

The region surrounding the disc forms the halo, a spherical region 500,000 light years across in which the stars are much more thinly spread than in the disc, very old, and concentrated in several hundred tightly knit groups, the globular clusters. Most astronomers believe that these old halo stars mark the volume of the gas cloud from which our Galaxy collapsed 10,000 million years ago. During such a collapse, some stars formed from the primeval hydrogen and helium of the gas cloud to make the old, first generation halo stars. Because of the rotation of the collapsing cloud, however, most of the material settled into a swirling disc in which more stars formed and in which stars continue to form today. These second generation stars contain a wealth of heavy elements which have been produced by the nuclear burning of the original stars, and are mixed in with the interstellar material. Halo stars cannot, on this picture, have planets like the Earth, although they might be accompanied by gas giants like Jupiter.

In the central part of the Galaxy, disc and halo merge in the central bulge of the nucleus, a region about 20,000 by 10,000 light years in size, ellipsoidal in shape. Most of the mass (matter) of the Galaxy is concentrated in this region, where stars crowd together thousands of times more closely than near the Sun. Dense clouds of hot hydrogen gas can be detected blasting outwards from the central region, which is also marked by outbursts of radiation across the spectrum, including high energy X- and gamma-rays. It is possible that all this activity is powered by the presence of a supermassive black hole at the centre of the Galaxy.

The shape of our own galaxy

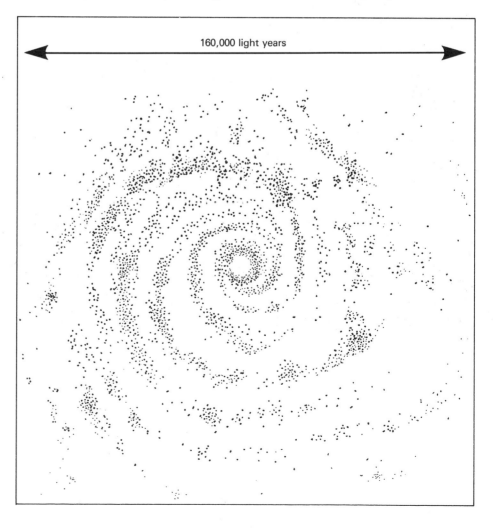

160,000 light years

Stars Unlike the Sun

Gaseous nebula in Serpens.

Although the Sun is a typical member of the Galaxy's population, being very roughly medium sized on the stellar range and about halfway through its life, there are many stars which are very different from our Sun, older or younger, bigger or smaller and so on. The biggest are red supergiants with diameters 1,000 times that of the Sun while the smallest are only a few miles across, perhaps 1/1,000,000 the diameter of the Sun. Bright stars are fast-burning young objects, the lifetime of a quieter star like our Sun may be 10,000 million years or more.

Different surface temperatures produce stars of different colours. Hot, blue stars may have surface temperatures of up to 100,000 degrees; the yellow Sun is rela-

has a luminosity 10,000 times greater, and the largest known stars have 50 times the Sun's mass. These stars have to be much hotter in the centre in order to support their outer layers against the inward pull of gravity. They burn their hydrogen fuel rapidly and end this stable part of their lives after only about 10 million years. After burning hydrogen into helium and helium into carbon and oxygen, the core of a massive star can contract so much under its own gravity that pressure builds up to force the conversion of carbon into magnesium and magnesium into first neon and then iron in further successive phases of nuclear fusion. At each stage, as one fuel is exhausted the centre contracts and heats up to start on the next, while lower temperature fusion processes continue in shells around the core itself.

Once an iron core is formed the process must stop. Iron is the most stable element and although energy can be gained by converting other nuclei into iron, converting iron into anything else uses up energy. Although the details of the process have not yet been worked out in a fully satisfactory form, in outline astronomers believe that this is just what happens next. As the iron core of a supermassive star collapses, with no new fusion reactions ready to step in and hold the star up, the outside layers fall in as well, releasing great quantities of gravitational energy. The result is an explosion so violent that the outer regions of the star are scattered through space, having been converted into a whole variety of elements by the energy of the blast. Left behind there may be the tiny core of the original star, a neutron star which will become a pulsar, or perhaps no 'star' at all but the remnants of the core literally squeezed out of existence, a black hole. It is the material scattered in such supernova explosions that provides the basis for later generations of stars and planetary systems. Apart from hydrogen and helium, literally everything around us, including the material of our bodies and of this book, has been 'cooked' inside stars and spread by supernova explosions.

tively cool at 6,000 degrees; and dim, red stars have surfaces at temperatures below 2,000 degrees. The evolution of the Sun previously described, is typical of the fate of medium mass stars. Smaller stars follow a similar evolutionary path in a more subdued pattern as they burn their limited stocks of hydrogen and

helium fuel. But much more massive stars than the Sun have much more spectacular life cycles, with repercussions on the whole Galaxy, and on ourselves.

In the early stages, such a massive star follows a similar evolution to the Sun, but becomes much brighter. A star with 10 times the Sun's mass

Evolution of the Galaxy

Observations of many stars show that the further away from us a star is, the dimmer it appears, over and above the reduction in apparent brightness caused by distance alone. This is because of the presence of dust between the stars, enough to block out half the light from a star about 3,000 light years away, three-quarters of the light from a star 6,000 light years away, and so on. Because this dust obscures (scatters) more blue light than red light, more distant stars appear reddened. When a star (or stars) is embedded in a dust cloud, the scattered light shows the cloud as a glowing nebula; when a particularly thick, dark cloud lies between us and bright stars we see it as an obscuring dark patch.

Gas in space shows up both through nebulae, like that in Orion, and the hydrogen 21 cm radio emission mentioned above. Dark gas clouds can also be detected because of their effects on light from stars which lie beyond them. These clouds absorb light selectively at certain frequencies to produce a characteristic pattern of dark lines in the spectra of light from the distant sources. Radio studies also reveal the presence of many molecules in these clouds in space, identified by their own characteristic radio spectrum 'signatures' of absorption and emission lines. More than three dozen compounds have now been identified in this way, the most complex containing nine atoms and including many materials that can be regarded as the precursor 'building blocks' of even more complex living molecules.

The discovery of these complex organic molecules came as a surprise to astronomers. It now seems that the conditions in the gas and dust clouds of space inevitably bring about the build-up of such molecules, which must therefore be scattered on planets forming out of such clouds in a new 'solar system'. This may have an important bearing on new theories of the origin of life in the Universe, and in particular it cuts down considerably the time needed for life to evolve on a planet such as the Earth, since many steps up the ladder have already been taken in space before the planet forms.

Very little is known for certain about the way a galaxy changes with age. The most widely favoured theory has for some time been that a galaxy like our own forms from a collapsing cloud of gas in space, with first halo, then disc stars, condensing out of the swirling material of the rotating cloud. As successive generations of stars go through their life cycles and leave behind dead dwarf stars, neutron stars or black holes, on this picture the Galaxy will remain much the same overall while slowly fading into dark, cold old age as fewer and fewer bright young stars are formed and more and more matter is locked away inaccessibly.

But this picture may not be correct. Many galaxies show evidence of very violent activity spreading outwards from their central (nucleus) regions. Our Galaxy is no exception and there is some evidence for an explosion at the nucleus within the past few hundred million years. Today we see an active central region radiating across the spectrum and pushing out clouds of hot gas. This activity may be associated with the presence of a black hole at the galactic centre, or, as a few astronomers argue, it may be a sign that our simple picture of galactic structure is incorrect in some fundamental and not yet understood way. The growing suspicion, either way, is that all spiral galaxies, including our own, undergo repeated violent convulsions during their lifetimes and the picture of a quiet decline from brilliant youth to dim old age may be very far off the mark. The evidence for this new picture is seen by looking at the variety of other galaxies in the Universe.

Irregular galaxy in Ursa Major, NGC 3034, M82. Although galaxies are categorized by astonomers into three main types – spiral, elliptical and irregular – the differences between them are not clear cut. Very little is known about the way a galaxy changes with age so it is not possible to tell, at this time, exactly how and where irregular galaxies fit into the overall pattern and whether they are an unusual stage in the development of the other types.

Other Galaxies
Types of Galaxy

Spiral galaxies
Left (top to bottom) *NGC 1201,
Type SO; NGC 2811, Type Sa; NGC
488, Type Sab.*
Right (top to bottom) *NGC 2841,
Type Sb; NGC 3031 M81, Type Sb;
NGC 628 M74, Type Sc.*

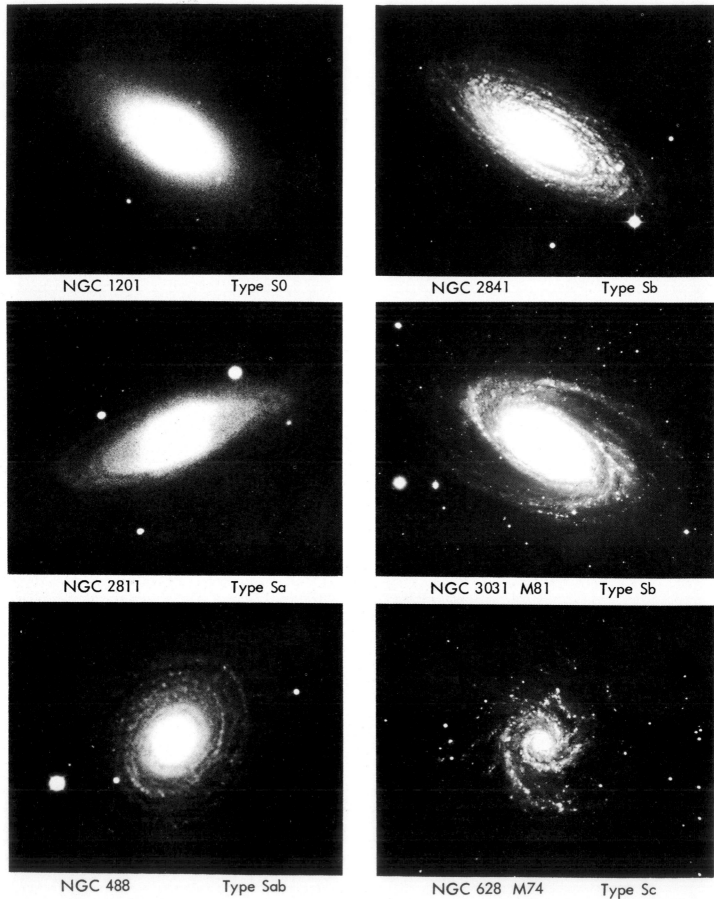

NGC 1201   Type S0

NGC 2841   Type Sb

NGC 2811   Type Sa

NGC 3031 M81   Type Sb

NGC 488   Type Sab

NGC 628 M74   Type Sc

Just as there are many different kinds of stars grouped together to form the Milky Way system—our Galaxy—so there are many kinds of galaxy in the Universe. There must be hundreds of millions of such systems, of one kind or another, and compared with the relative distances between stars inside a galaxy, neighbouring galaxies can be very close together. The diameter of a star like our Sun corresponds to a few light minutes; the gap between stars is hundreds of thousands of stellar diameters, but the gap between neighbouring galaxies can be only a few tens of galactic diameters.

The great variety of galaxies in the Universe is divided into three basic categories by astronomers, although there are objects now known which do not fit into these main categories. There are no clear dividing lines between the categories, however, and there seems to be a continuous range of properties from one extreme to the other. Spiral galaxies, like the Milky Way, have a bright central nucleus, a large spherical halo of old stars gathered together in globular clusters, and a disc of young stars, gas and dust. A typical disc may be 100,000 light years in diameter and 2,000 light years thick, with a spiral pattern of two main 'arms' of bright stars, edged by gas and dust, twisting out from the nucleus. In some cases, the arms start from the ends of a short bar across the nucleus and these are called barred spirals. A typical spiral galaxy has a mass equivalent to a 100,000 million times the mass of the Sun; since the Sun is an average star, this implies that these galaxies contain about a hundred thousand million stars. There is also a proposal that spiral galaxies are embedded in an extensive dark halo (old low mass stars) which may contain up to 10 times the amount of mass we detect by visible light.

Elliptical galaxies present a very different appearance. They have no spiral structure, very little gas and dust, and seem to be mainly made up of flattened ovals, which may look cigar-shaped viewed sideways on by our telescopes. Giant ellipticals can be 300,000 light years or more in diameter, supergiants a hundred

times more massive than the Milky Way, containing a hundred times as many stars. These are the biggest galaxies of all. At the other extreme, the smallest galaxies are ellipticals no bigger than the globular clusters in our own Galaxy, containing perhaps a million stars, or even fewer. These dwarf galaxies are often found as gravitationally bound companions of larger galaxies.

The third category, irregular galaxies, are generally smaller than spirals and fit neither of the other two categories. They contain both young and old stars, but do not show a clear spiral structure; the two Magellanic Clouds, visible in the sky of the southern hemisphere as hazy patches, are irregulars which are gravitationally bound to our own Galaxy, and orbit around it.

Within these categories there are still further variations. In particular,

it is now clear that the behaviour of the central core (nucleus) of a galaxy is as important as its overall outward shape. Some spirals have very bright nuclei, radiating energy at radio and infrared frequencies as well as optical light, which seem to be the sites of violent explosions. Depending on appearance, these are called Seyfert or N-galaxies, although the difference seems to be only one of degree. Many very massive ellipticals are bracketed by extended regions of intense radio emission, and are called radio galaxies. It is possible that this kind of behaviour is something that happens to all galaxies so that Seyferts, for example, may be simply ordinary spirals at an unusual stage in their evolution.

Seyfert Galaxy NGC 4151. Seyferts are one of the types of irregular galaxies. It is possible that, in fact, they represent an unusual stage in the evolution of an ordinary spiral.

Groups of Galaxies

Most galaxies occur in groups, or clusters, which are bound together by gravity. The Milky Way is a member of the so-called Local Group which contains about 30 members including the Magellanic Clouds and the spiral Andromeda galaxy and its companions. Large clusters can include thousands of galaxies of all kinds; in many cases a large cluster occupies a spherical volume of space and surrounds a giant elliptical more or less at the centre.

The galaxies in a bound cluster orbit a common centre of gravity, but this motion across the sky is far too slow to be measured directly from Earth. However, the motion produces an effect on the lines of the spectra from these galaxies, the Doppler Shift, from which it is possible to calculate their orbital velocities. Intriguingly, it turns out that in many cases the velocities correspond to bound orbits only if the cluster contains 10 to 100 times as much matter as the total visible in bright galaxies. Either there is a lot of dark matter—dim stars, gas and dust—in such clusters or the 'missing mass' has some other form, perhaps even one or more black holes.

The Doppler Effect is also important in measuring distances to galaxies and clusters. For nearby galaxies, distances are estimated by measuring the brightness of individual stars, and it is on this basis that we know the distance of the Andromeda galaxy, our near neighbour at 2.2 million light years. Comparing distances of nearby galaxies with Doppler Shifts in the spectra of light from them, astronomers find that, after allowing for orbital motions in clusters, the further away a galaxy is, the greater its Doppler Shift. This rule is then turned around to give us a means of estimating distances to remote clusters by measuring the Doppler Shift in light from them. This relationship is a key to the concept of the expanding Universe: the apparent recessional velocity of a galaxy is proportional to the distance of the object from us. The most distant clusters detectable by our telescopes are some 12,000 million light years away, using the Doppler Shift to estimate their distance. There is some evidence that clusters of galaxies themselves group together in superclusters; our own Local Group, for example, is on the outskirts of a large cluster, the Virgo Cluster, which is centered about 65 million light years away.

The mysterious quasars

In the 1960s, astronomers identified what seemed to be a new class of astronomical object. These appear as star-like points of light, but have redshifts (Doppler Shifts) indicating,

A rich cluster of galaxies photographed by a 200-inch telescope. Each of the fuzzy blobs here is the equivalent of our whole Milky Way and contains thousands of millions of stars.

if the redshift/distance relation derived from galaxies is applied, that they lie well beyond our Milky Way. To be seen at all at such distances, these objects must radiate at least as much energy as a galaxy, but from a very compact region, giving the star-like appearance. The name given to them, quasar, is short for quasi-stellar object. The most distant objects yet identified in the Universe (again assuming the redshift/distance rule is valid) are quasars, so bright intrinsically that they can

be detected by our telescopes at a range where ordinary galaxies are too dim to be seen. At such extreme cases, the redshift is higher than 4.5, meaning that the wavelength of radiation from the quasar has been lengthened 4.5 times by the Doppler Effect.

Like some galaxies, some quasars are associated with strong sources of radio noise, often coming from two lobes on either side of the quasar (or galaxy) suggesting a link with some great central explosion. There are other links with active galaxies, and the spectra of quasars show some similarities to the spectra of N-galaxies (which, in turn, may be related to Seyferts). In the 1970s, astronomers identified another category of active sources, the BL Lac objects, which are definitely galaxies but have extremely active, energetic, quasar-like nuclei. There seems little reason to doubt now that quasars are, in fact, the enormously active central regions of galaxies, and it is likely that there is some more or less

The Andromeda galazy, our large neighbour beyond the Milky Way.

continuous gradation in activity from quasars and BL Lac objects through radio galaxies, N-galaxies and Seyferts to the quiet 'normal' galaxies. It remains a great puzzle, however, to explain how so much energy—as much as the output from a galaxy of a hundred thousand million stars or more—can be produced from a tiny region, perhaps a light year in diameter, at the nucleus of a galaxy.

The Universe at Large
Galaxies and the Expanding Universe

Because the light from galaxies shows a redshift, astronomers deduce that the external galaxies (or rather, clusters of galaxies) are all receding as viewed from our Local Group. The more distant a galaxy is, the greater is the redshift, but this does not mean that we live at the centre of the Universe. Rather, this is exactly the kind of 'law' that applies for a general expansion of the Universe; if *all* galaxy clusters are moving away from all others, with velocity proportioned to distance, then an observer in any galaxy will see the same kind of expansion with all galaxies expanding 'away' from him.

The situation is like a balloon painted with several dots, each representing a cluster of galaxies. As the balloon is inflated, all of the dots move away from each other, and if a microscopic observer on one of the dots could measure this recession he would find just the 'law' we find in the Universe, that the farthest dots (galaxy clusters) recede fastest. Just as in the real Universe, the surface of the balloon has no 'centre'. The difference is that the balloon's surface is two-dimensional whereas our Universe of galaxies occupies three dimensions of space. In this sense, we can regard clusters of galaxies as 'test particles', equivalent to the dots on the balloon's skin, and their recession from one another as an indication of some more fundamental universal expansion, equiva-

A giant elliptical galaxy.

Cosmology and Origins

If the Universe as a whole is expanding, as the evidence suggests, then it must have been in a more compressed state, with the galaxies squeezed closer together, in the past. This is the most obvious conclusion based on our everyday experience of expanding objects, like balloons. But, in fact, the idea has been challenged by proponents of 'steady state' cosmology. They argued that, as the Universe expands, so that galaxies

lent to the stretching of the balloon's skin. This brings us to the study of the nature of space and time and of the origin and evolution of the Universe and everything in it—the science of cosmology.

get further apart, new material is created to fill in the gaps, so that although the Universe always expands it always looks much the same.

The theory has the attraction of removing any problem about how the Universe began—steady state theory says that it always was and always will be, unchanging and with no 'birth' or 'death'. However, there is now evidence that the Universe does indeed change with time, and astronomers have also found radiation from space that may mark the echo of the Universe's birth pangs. So the steady state theory does not seem to be a very good description of the Universe in which we live.

Because light takes a finite time to travel across space, when we observe distant galaxies we see them as they were long ago. So by looking at very remote galaxies we 'see' the Universe as it was long ago, and the indications are that galaxy clusters were indeed more tightly packed in the past. It seems that the Universe did 'begin' in some fashion, best described as a great outward explosion from a single point. By working backwards from the present observed recession of the galaxies we can even compute when the expansion began, and the best estimate today sets this at 18,000 million years ago. But this

was not simply an explosion of matter outwards into an empty void. If we regard the galaxies as test particles carried along in the fabric of expanding space, we see that space itself must have been 'created' in the initial outburst, the Big Bang, and has since carried matter along with it. Indeed, we can go further, with the aid of relativity theory, and say that not just space but time (together as space-time) 'began' in the Big Bang.

What will be the ultimate development of this universal expansion? The key is gravity. If there is enough material in the Universe, gravity will first slow the expansion and then reverse it, so that everything (including the fabric of space-time) eventually squeezes back into another point, or singularity, a kind of universal black hole. If there is not enough matter to do this, however, then the expansion can never be halted and will continue forever, giving a Universe which will become emptier and emptier as galaxy clusters move further and further apart. The best observational evidence today suggests that this continued expansion into emptiness will be the fate of our Universe; but there remains a possibility that new observations will reveal that the Universe is 'slowing down' after all.

The colours of stars of different mass.

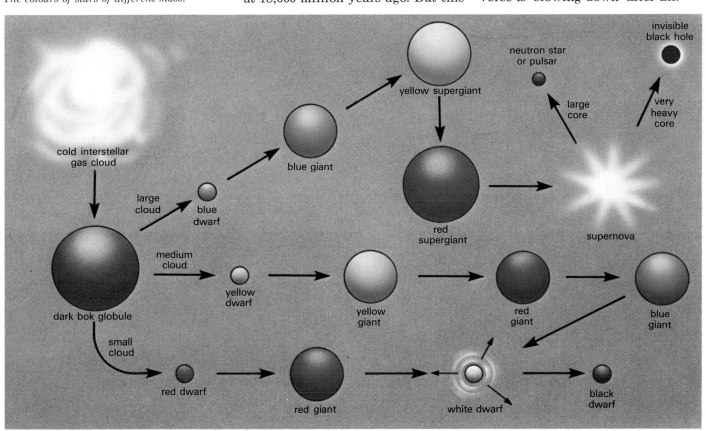

Background Radiation and the Big Bang

One of the most important discoveries ever made in astronomy came in 1965 with the detection of a faint hiss of radio noise coming from all directions in space. Because it comes from all directions and is present as a background to any other radio observations, it is called the background radiation. Although it may seem rather unexciting in its present form as a weak hiss detectable between frequencies of 1 MHz and 500 MHz, it is the echo of the Big Bang in which the Universe as we know it began.

The radiation seems feeble because it has been spread thin by the expansion of the Universe. However, when the Universe was smaller, both matter and radiation were squeezed into a more dense state—which in the case of radiation is equivalent to saying it was at a higher temperature. By calculating the extent to which radiation has been spread out by the expansion of the Universe, we can get a good idea of what conditions were like in the hot Big Bang, immediately after the Universe began its outward expansion, and also of how things have changed as the Universe evolved. The mere existence of the background radiation tells us that there was a big bang and that it was hot. The rest follows from the known laws of physics. Extrapolating backwards in time, and then moving forward from the beginning, the theorists can tell us pretty well how the Universe evolved from the time when it was a hot fireball of tight packed energy, at a temperature of 1 million million degrees. At such a temperature, energetic particles, antiparticles and radiation were interacting continuously in a maelstrom of reactions, obeying the rule that energy and matter are interchangeable in line with the equation $E = mc^2$. As the maelstrom expanded, the temperature dropped, the energy density of the radiation decreased, and things became a little more orderly. The lower the energy density became, the harder it was for particles to be created out of the

radiation energy, with the more massive particles settling out first. At 100,000 million degrees, the protons and neutrons destined to make up the matter of the Universe we know, would already have settled out, although electrons and positrons continued to interact with the radiation of the fireball in annihilation and creation reactions.

At 1,000 million degrees, even the creation of electron-positron pairs required too much energy for the weakening background, and most of the pairs would annihilate themselves. For some reason, there seem to have been a few extra electrons leftover, balancing the presence of protons, rather than anti-protons, that remained from the earlier stages of the fireball. Some protons and neutrons were 'cooked' into nuclei of helium at around 1,000 million degrees, just as nuclear fusion proceeds in the heart of the Sun today. But not until the temperature of the

Universe has fallen to about 5,000 degrees could these nuclei and the remaining protons combine with electrons to form neutral atoms of hydrogen and helium. From here on, matter and radiation went their separate ways, the matter clumping together into galaxies and stars

The shifting neutron-proton balance. *The fraction of neutrons to all nuclear particles is shown as a function both of temperature and of time. The part of the curve marked 'thermal equilibrium' describes a period in which densities and temperature are so high that thermal equilibrium is maintained among all particles. The part of the curve marked 'neutron decay' describes the period in which all neutron-proton conversion processes have ceased, except for the radioactive decay of the free neutron. The intervening part of the curve depends on detailed calculations of weak-interaction transition rates. The dashed part of the curve shows what would happen if nuclei were somehow prevented from forming.*

Tenzias and Wilson, the discoverers of micro-wave background radiation.

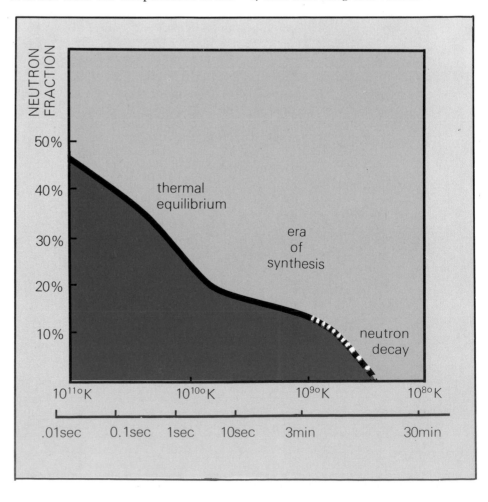

while the radiation spread thinner and thinner with the expansion of the Universe to become the weak hiss we detect today.

In round terms, all of this took place in the first million years of the Universe's history—from the Big Bang to the decoupling of matter and radiation. The 18,000 million years or so since then have all been spent in settling down into the kind of galaxy dominated Universe we now see.

Where Next?

Whenever we stop to take stock of our understanding of the Universe, the picture seems more or less complete. Our 19th century forebears would have thought the same, before the discovery of other galaxies and the expansion of the Universe, and before the new theories of the 20th century, such as relativity. A 16th century citizen might have thought the Universe was pretty well understood, before the telescope came along to change things; and no doubt the Greeks and earlier civilizations were happy with their own ideas. So it would be rash to expect no more dramatic changes in our view of the Universe in future.

Observational Prospects

The key to future observational progress lies in the fact that with the ability to hoist instruments above the atmosphere mankind can now make observations across the entire electromagnetic spectrum. As yet, we have barely scratched the surface of these new possibilities. X-ray

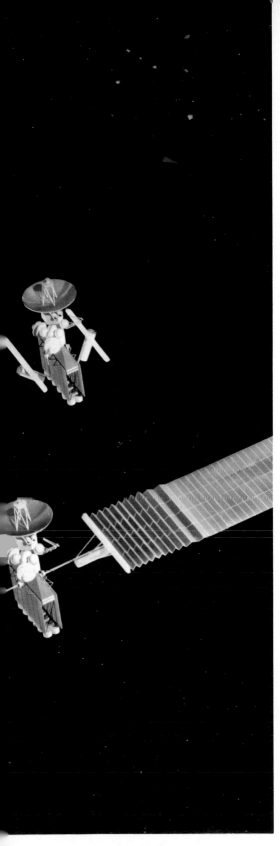

A sequence of illustrations showing how the Shuttle spacecraft can deploy a satellite in orbit. Once clear of the Shuttle, this space probe switches on its own rocket motor to move off into space, spreading solar panels to draw energy from sunlight.

telescopes have been in orbit for only a few years, and we have a long way to go before the equivalent of modern ground based observatories become available in space. Development of the telescope to its present sophistication has taken more than 300 years since Galileo's day, and who can imagine the kind of X- or gamma-ray 'telescope' astronomers will be using in even 100 years from now?

Optical telescopes too may benefit from the space age, since their observations are severely limited by the haze of atmosphere through which they must work today. More information about every kind of object now known in the Universe is certain to flow in; and there can be little doubt that something we do not yet know about will be discovered to rank with the quasars, pulsars and X-ray stars discovered in the past.

We can expect new discoveries closer to home, too, as space probes continue to tell us about the planets of our Solar System. This will include a completely new view of the Solar System when a joint European Space Agency/NASA space probe is launched in 1983 to swing high up out of the plane in which the planets orbit around the Sun, to look 'down' on the Sun's polar regions—all our observations of the Sun so far have been made from a very narrow band, defined by the orbit of the Earth, around the Sun's equator. Who can say what we may then find?

Perhaps most tantalising of all to astronomers today, there is the prospect of detecting radiation from space, the 'waves' in the fabric of space-time itself that are thought to be produced when stars collapse into black holes, or by two close companion stars orbiting tightly around one another. This would be a dramatic development indeed, opening up to observation a 'window' on the Universe quite separate from the entire electromagnetic spectrum.

Theoretical prospects

Investigations of such phenomena as gravitational radiation may provide essential clues for theorists now struggling to explain some of the great mysteries of the Universe, many of which are related to the highly energetic phenomena that ought to be prime sources of gravitational waves. What does go on at the centres of exploding galaxies and quasars? How did the Universe itself begin—what triggered the Big Bang —and is there a link between this universal explosion and the energetic phenomena we see about us now?

Some exciting theoretical progress may come from the continued study of black holes and their links with the rest of the Universe. A black hole is a region where matter has been squeezed out of existence into a singularity, a mathematical point, rather like the outward expansion of the Universe from a point but in reverse. This can happen, according to theory, if the mass of material left over by a dead star is more than the mass of two or three Suns. With no nuclear reactions left to provide heat to hold such a dead star up against the pull of gravity, even the protons and neutrons of such a star would be crushed inevitably and inexorably into nothingness, with the gravitational field at the surface of the collapsing star becoming stronger and stronger as it was squeezed into a smaller and smaller volume. Long before it became a singular point, however, the gravity at the surface would be so strong that nothing, not even light, could escape. This is what gives the name 'black hole' and it means that, tantalisingly, we can never see what does go on as the material is eventually crushed out of existence.

Very massive black holes, containing as much matter as thousands or millions of Suns, may lie at the nuclei of galaxies, producing violent flares of energy as they swallow up more and more material; such violence, perhaps observed with the aid of gravitational radiation detectors, may help theorists to find out how black holes interact with the outside Universe, and provide new insights into the nature of space-time, taking us beyond even the theory of relativity.

All this is speculation. But although relativity theory works well as a description of almost everything that happens in the Universe, it is by no means clear that it can explain the most extreme events, the collapse of matter into a singularity or the beginning of the Universe from a singularity. There are likely to be many surprises in store for us all when we do find out what really goes on at such extremes.

THE
PLANET
EARTH

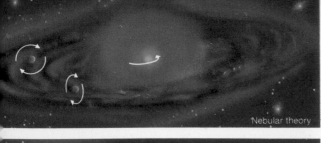

Nebular theory

Accretion theory

Jeans-Jeffreys theory

The origin of the solar system has been the subject of many theories, principally, the condensation of a gas cloud or the gravitational attraction of a passing star.

Origins and Structure

The story of the planet Earth begins more than 4,600 million years ago with the birth of the Solar System—our local family of planets, moons, asteroids, dust and gases, revolving in their near-circular orbits around the Sun. According to the nebula hypothesis—the most widely accepted model for the origin of the Solar System—a vast, tenuous rotating cloud of interstellar dust and gas drifting through the infinity of space began to contract under the influence of its own gravitational field. As the cloud collapsed, the temperature and pressure near the centre rose higher and higher until eventually thermo-nuclear reactions set in. Powered by the atomic fusion of hydrogen atoms into helium a new star—the Sun—began to shine in the Galaxy.

Further from the centre of the rotating disc of dust and gas, localized collapse perhaps initiated by eddies within the cloud, formed the four dense inner planets and beyond them the much larger but very much less dense outer planets. The inner planets—Mercury, Venus, Earth and Mars—are called the terrestrial planets. Formed close to the Sun in a region of relatively high temperatures, they contain very little of the hydrogen and helium which made up the original nebula. In marked contrast the outer planets—Jupiter, Saturn, Uranus, Neptune and Pluto—formed in regions cool enough to allow condensation of the inert gases and, of these distant planets, Jupiter and Saturn still closely represent the composition of the original nebula.

The Age of the Earth

The calculated age of the Earth's crust (4,550 million years) agrees closely with the measured ages of the oldest of the rocks brought back from the Moon (4,600 million years) and with the measured ages of stony meteorites which have survived the fiery passage through the Earth's atmosphere (4,550 million years). And yet the greatest age so far measured in rocks of the Earth's crust is some 3,800 million years: nearly 1,000 million years of our planet's early history are absent from the geological record and must be painstakingly reconstructed from

The oldest rock from the Earth's crust is some thousand million years younger than the estimated age of the Earth. This is due to the constant turmoil of geological activity in the crust.

our knowledge of geophysical and geochemical processes and from the studies carried out by astronomers of processes occurring in distant stars today.

As the primordial Earth grew by condensation of gases and accumulation of dust particles and planetismals its temperature naturally tended to rise, but on a scale insignificant compared to that of the Sun. Indeed, most of the heat energy released by the contraction of the 'Earth' part of the nebula must have been dissipated into space for although water was not present in a free state at this time it was present held in chemical bond in hydrous minerals such as serpentine from which it would have been released at temperatures above about 230° C. This water was held within the contracting cloud and was only released later in the Earth's evolution.

At a critical point some 4,600 million years ago the now dense, compact mass of the contracted cloud had undergone a dramatic change. Internal heating caused by the decay of radioactive minerals had taken over and the Earth was a semi-liquid mass of molten rock still surrounded by an atmosphere of cosmic dust and gas—destined to be swept away by the solar wind during a period of intense activity by the Sun. Within this fluid mass elements combined, separated and re-formed; dense iron-rich compounds became concentrated in the innermost regions forming the core of the primitive Earth while lighter material, rich in silica, formed the first crust. Convection currents driven by radioactive heating kept the fluid interior in motion, aiding chemical differentiation and segregation. The primitive crust was probably basaltic in composition, very like the oceanic crust today, but repeated cracking and re-melting led to further differentiation of the crustal material into basaltic rocks and the even lighter granitic material now characteristic of continental regions.

Era/Period		Time	Events
Quaternary	Holocene	0.01 m years ago	early civilizations
	Pleistocene	2 m years ago	
Neogene	Pliocene	7 m years ago	emergence of Man
	Oligocene	26 m years ago	Age of mammals / flowering plants fully developed
Palaeogene	Miocene	38 m years ago	
	Eocene	54 m years ago	
	Palaeocene	65 m years ago	extinction of dinosaurs
	Cretaceous	135 m years ago	early mammals and birds / early flowering plants
	Jurassic	190 m years ago	Age of reptiles
	Triassic	225 m years ago	first dinosaurs / abundance of marine invertebrates
	Permian	280 m years ago	conifers appear
	Carboniferous	345 m years ago	first reptiles and winged insects / abundant coal forests
	Devonian	395 m years ago	first amphibians / abundant bony fishes
	Silurian	440 m years ago	first land plants / earliest known coral reefs
	Ordovician	500 m years ago	spread of molluscs
	Cambrian	570 m years ago	dominance of trilobites / abundance of fossils
			first multicellular organisms
		c 3000 m years ago	algae well established
		c 3500 m years ago	first unicellular organisms
		c 3800 m years ago	age of oldest known terrestrial rocks
		c 4600 m years ago	formation of the Earth's crust

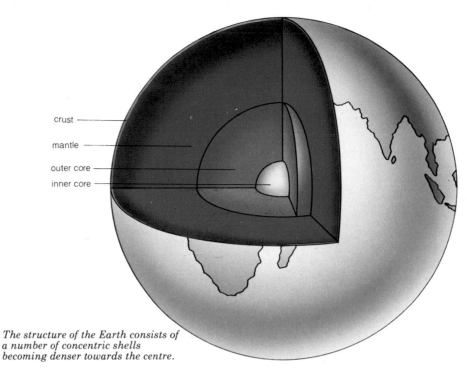

The structure of the Earth consists of a number of concentric shells becoming denser towards the centre.

crust — mantle — outer core — inner core

Free Water

Throughout this period vast quantities of gas and vapour were released into the atmosphere and once the Earth's surface had cooled sufficiently, free water was able to exist on the surface. Small pools would have accumulated—later to swell, merge and eventually develop into the first oceans. The importance of free water on the Earth goes far beyond its role in the chemistry of the Earth's rocks. Almost immediately, running water would attack exposed rocks, eroding them and transporting material down to the primitive seas, there to deposit the first sedimentary rocks. Further, and unique among the planets of the Solar System, the oceans were destined to become the cradle of life on Earth, a story which begins with the first true organisms some 3,300 million years ago.

Inside the Earth

The deepest boreholes driven into the Earth's crust barely scratch the surface, penetrating only about 8 km (5 miles). Our knowledge of the Earth's internal composition is therefore gleaned from the study of the few localities where deep mantle-like rocks appear at the surface; from severe folding and bending; from the outpourings of active volcanoes; from theoretical models of the behaviour of minerals at depth; and from our knowledge of the overall composition of the Solar System.

The Earth's internal structure is rather better understood and results from studying earthquake waves.

The enormous burst of energy released as rocks are stressed beyond their breaking point travels through the Earth as a series of shock waves which are bent and otherwise modified by the physical properties of the rocks through which they are transmitted. The waves effectively 'X-ray' the Earth, revealing a series of concentric shells. A dense inner core of solid iron is surrounded by an outer core of iron in a fluid state, which acts as a dynamo, generating the Earth's magnetic field. Surrounding the core lies the mantle, solid in its lower regions but mobile near its upper limit. Convection currents within the mantle are believed to be the driving force underlying movements of the thin outermost shell— the Earth's crust.

The refraction of earthquake waves as they pass through the various layers of the Earth give clues to their structure.

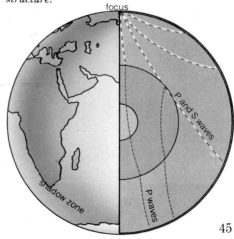

focus — P and S waves — P waves — shadow zone

The Rocks of the Earth's Crust

Geologists recognize three major rock classifications based on the way in which the rocks were formed. Within these classifications the identification of a rock type can be a very complex process. Rock names are largely descriptive and there is no clear-cut definition for each type of rock; for example, a limestone is a rock containing a large proportion of calcium carbonate and a sandstone is one largely composed of fragments of silica. Many rocks contain both and so the distinction between a limy sandstone and a sandy limestone becomes indistinct.

Igneous Rocks

Of the three major rock classifications the most important is the igneous rock group. This comprises the rocks that have solidified out of a melt. They form when molten material, or magma, from deep below the earth's surface migrates upwards and cools. When this magma actually breaks through the surface it pours out in the form of lava or bursts out in clouds of molten droplets or solid particles, building up volcanoes and other surface features. The rocks that are formed on the surface in this way are known as extrusive igneous rocks.

Less dramatic but far more significant in terms of the volume of rock produced are the intrusive igneous rocks. These are formed when the magma comes to rest below the earth's surface and solidifies there. The intrusive masses formed in this way can range from narrow dykes and sills a few metres thick to enormous batholiths many hundreds of square kilometres in extent. Dartmoor, Bodmin Moor and the granite cliffs of Land's End are each protruberances from a single vast intrusive formation of granite underlying most of south-west England and exposed where overlying rocks have been eroded away.

The composition of an igneous rock is very variable and many different rocks can be formed from the same original magma. As the magma travels through fissures in the overlying rock it may absorb large amounts of rock and so change its chemical composition. When it begins to cool certain minerals solidify out first and the newly formed crystals of these may sink to give a rock that is very rich in that mineral at the bottom of the structure. The texture of an igneous rock is largely determined by the speed at which the melt solidifies. Large slow-cooling bodies, such as the batholith in south-west England, consist of coarse rocks with very large crystals. Rapidly cooling lavas give rise to very fine-grained basalt in which it is difficult to detect the individual crystals.

Silica (SiO_2) is one of the most common substances in the earth's crust and so a chemical classification of the igneous rocks is based on the proportion of silica in their composition. An igneous rock containing a great deal of silica, more than 65 per cent, is known as an acidic rock. Such a rock can be recognized by the presence of a large proportion of the mineral quartz in separate crystals and a good example is granite. Rocks containing between 64 and 53 per cent of silica are the intermediate rocks, those containing 53 to 45 per cent silica are the basic rocks and those containing less than this are the heavy, dark and rarely found ultrabasic rocks.

Sedimentary Rocks

The second major classification of rocks, the sedimentary rocks, are those formed by the steady accumulation of particles over a long period. These particles may be derived from the erosion of earlier rocks (producing a clastic sedimentary rock like sandstone), from chemical precipitation in sea water (producing a chemical rock like gypsum), or from the skeletons of once living organisms (producing a biogenic rock like chalk). The particles accumulate in a sediment usually at the bottom of the sea or in a desert and are buried by later deposits. This burial compresses the sediments and percolating ground water deposits minerals between the particles cementing them together to form a sedimentary rock. Such rocks are distinguished

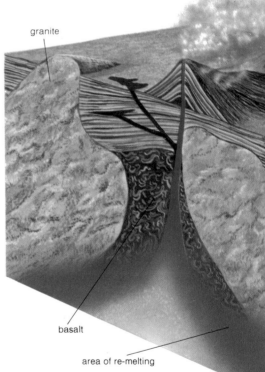

granite

basalt

area of re-melting

from igneous rocks by being formed in layers, called beds, and may contain fossils. The beds may be very thin and alternating with beds of different types or they may be very thick, depending on the conditions under which they were deposited – variable, as in a delta, or stable, as at the bottom of a quiet sea.

Sedimentary rocks are often formed in distinct beds. Here in Utah the sandstones are being eroded and the debris formed will eventually form a new sedimentary rock.

Metamorphic Rocks

The third major classification of rocks is that of the metamorphic rocks. These are rocks that have been altered either by great heat or pressure from earlier-formed igneous or sedimentary rocks. Under certain conditions the minerals in a rock may recrystalize into new mineral types without melting in the process. Two main types of metamorphic rocks are recognized. Thermal metamorphic rocks are those produced largely by the action of heat. These are usually very limited in extent and found only along the side of intrusive igneous rocks where these have been pushed through the earth's crust. They may be very fine grained and have no visible structures, making them difficult to distinguish from igneous rocks. Hornfels is an example of a thermal metamorphic rock.

Regional metamorphic rocks, on the other hand, are formed under great pressure but with little heat involved. They may cover vast tracts of land since they are produced in the heart of mountain ranges as these are forced upwards. Unlike thermal metamorphic rocks they can be easily recognized by their structure and usually show a series of contorted bands of minerals. This is especially true of the more coarse-grained types such as gneiss and schist. As with the other types, metamorphic rocks show a gradation between one extreme of formation and the other.

Members of all three groups can be used as building material. Granite is an intrusive igneous rock and buildings made from it have a characteristic rugged appearance. Limestone and sandstone are extensively used, especially in areas where they are found naturally. Slate is a regional metamorphic rock of a low grade and its deformation structure enables it to be split easily and used as a roofing material. Marble, a metamorphosed limestone, is not very hard wearing but its appearance and ease of working and polishing make it eminently suitable for monumental work.

Above Igneous rocks are formed by the solidification of a melt. Here, off the coast of Scotland, thick lava flows have solidified and cooled quickly forming this characteristic columnar structure. As the rock cooled it contracted and cracked in a series of vertical joints.

The whole of the Earth's continental crust is made up of igneous, sedimentary or metamorphic rocks, all in a constant state of change under the influence of Earth processes.

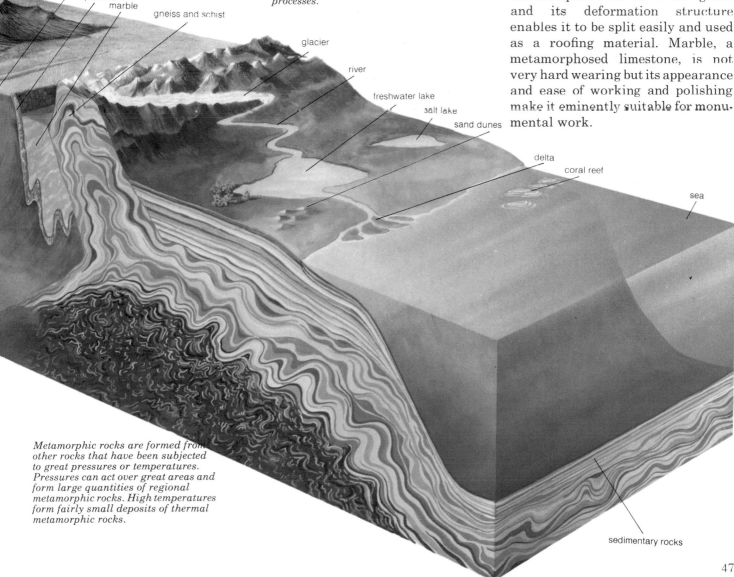

slate
quartzite
marble
gneiss and schist
glacier
river
freshwater lake
salt lake
sand dunes
delta
coral reef
sea
sedimentary rocks

Metamorphic rocks are formed from other rocks that have been subjected to great pressures or temperatures. Pressures can act over great areas and form large quantities of regional metamorphic rocks. High temperatures form fairly small deposits of thermal metamorphic rocks.

Hardness scale	Mineral	Test
10	Diamond	will scratch glass
9	Corundum	
8	Topaz, Beryl, Zircon	
7	Quartz, Garnet, Tourmaline	
6	Feldspar, Turquoise, Rutile, Celsian	can be scratched with steel knife
5	Apatite, Bornite	
4	Fluorite, Malachite, Azurite	can be powdered by scratching with coin
3	Calcite, Argonite, Barytes	
2	Gypsum, Salt,	can be scratched with fingernail
1	Talc, Aluminite	

A mineral can be identified by its hardness, the colour of the mark left when it is scratched against a hard white surface and the way it splits up or breaks.

Rocks and Minerals

Minerals are the building blocks from which the earth's rocks are made. If any rock is examined closely enough it will be seen to be constructed from a few different types of substances, usually in discrete crystals and all growing into one another. These are the minerals and since each mineral usually has a fixed chemical composition the variations found between one rock and another are due to the different proportions of different minerals in them.

When one thinks of minerals it is usually the economic minerals, such as iron ore or gold nuggets, that come to mind. These ore-forming minerals, although very important to mankind, constitute only a small proportion of the minerals in the earth's crust. The remainder are the more mundane rock-forming minerals and these are usually classified by their chemical composition.

Silica

As we have already seen silica is one of the most common substances in the Earth's crust. Consequently a great many minerals have silica in their chemical make-up. Silica has the unusual property of being able to combine with itself in a number of different ways, so that the atoms form pairs, chains, rings, sheets or three-dimensional structures. Atoms of other elements are combined in these structures to give the various silicate minerals. Olivine is one of the silicate minerals that do not conform to the rule that minerals

Cubic—minimum symmetry four 3-fold axes. Examples are fluorite, garnet and diamond.

Tetragonal—minimum symmetry one 4-fold axis. Examples are zircon, calomel and wulfenite.

Orthorhombic—minimum symmetry three 2-fold axes. Examples are barytes, alexandrite (chrysoberyl) and olivine (peridot).

Monoclinic—minimum symmetry one 2-fold axis. Examples are malachite, orthoclase and moonstone.

Triclinic—minimum symmetry none. Examples are sunstone, turquoise and chalcanthite.

Hexagonal—minimum symmetry one 6-fold axis. Examples are emerald, zincite and apatite.

Trigonal—minimum symmetry one 3-fold axis. Examples are calcite, rose quartz and tourmaline.

have a constant composition. The metal component of olivine may be magnesium, giving forsterite olivine (Mg_2SiO_4), or it may be iron, giving fayalite olivine (Fe_2SiO_4), but very often there is some of both and so olivine is regarded as a series of minerals with a general formula $(Mg, Fe)_2SiO_4$. Mica is a silicate mineral in which the silica is arranged in sheets. This is reflected in the crystal of the mineral which can be easily split into thin flakes. Pure silica gives the mineral quartz (SiO_2) in which the silica is arranged in a three-dimensional lattice. This is a very stable arrangement and so quartz is a particularly hard substance.

Igneous Minerals

The sequence of the formation of minerals as a magma cools to an igneous rock is well known. The olivines form first at the highest temperatures and, in doing so, remove some of the silica and practically all of the iron and magnesium from the melt. The crystals so formed are usually well shaped as they have plenty of room to grow. The remaining silica in the melt then combines with the aluminium, calcium, sodium and potassium to form feldspar, $(KNaCa)AlSi_3O_8$. The feldspars may form good crystals if the melt is still quite fluid but not if they are closely surrounded by earlier-formed minerals. In a magma that is particularly rich in silica the magnesium and iron tend not to form olivine but to form

Agate is an amorphous mineral, showing no crystalline structure. It is formed by the deposition of layers of silica in a cavity.

mica instead and, after the feldspars are formed the excess silica crystallizes out into quartz. Often there is some iron left over and this solidifies into tiny grains of magnetite, an iron ore.

Sedimentary Minerals

Minerals formed in sedimentary rocks are quite a different proposition. Very few of them are authigenic (formed at the time of deposition). They are usually the remains of minerals derived from the original rock worn down to give the sediment. The remainder are formed during the lithification process that later turns the sediment into rock, usually by the deposition of the mineral from percolating ground water. The authigenic minerals that do occur are mostly rock salt ($NaCl$), or calcite ($CaCO_3$), substances dissolved in the water in which the sediment was deposited.

Metamorphic Minerals

In metamorphic rocks the crystals found are usually strained and distorted, giving evidence of the great pressures under which they have formed. The metamorphic minerals have the same compositions as the minerals they replace and the extent of metamorphism can usually be determined by the kinds of mineral present. Kyanite and andalusite have the same chemical compositions (Al_2SiO_5) but the former is found in schists formed under great pressure while the latter is found in rocks formed by low heat and only moderate pressure.

Related to the metamorphic minerals are the metasomatic minerals. These are formed by the deposition from hot waters passing through a rock from an igneous body close by. The minerals are emplaced in cavities and fissures in the rock and give rise to veins. Many of the economic minerals are formed in this way including the lead ore galena and the tin ore cassiterite. These are found in the veins associated with the granitic intrusions of Cornwall and Devon.

Identification

As each mineral has a fairly constant composition the atomic structure (the way the atoms are stacked together) is also constant and the

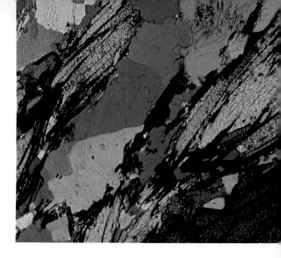

The minerals in a thin slice of rock can show a variety of false colours when seen under polarized light and can be easily identified.

same for every specimen of that mineral. This atomic structure is reflected in the external shape that the mineral forms if it is allowed to grow unrestricted. Such a shape is called a crystal and this can be a valuable aid in the identification of the mineral.

Other aids in the identification of a mineral include its hardness which can be tested by seeing whether or not the mineral will scratch another substance of a known hardness, and the colour of the streak, the mark made when the mineral is rubbed against a hard white surface. The colour in itself is not diagnostic since impurities in the mineral often give false colours, for example quartz may be discoloured by manganese to give the purple amethyst, but the streak is always the same.

To investigate the mineral composition of a rock thoroughly the geologist or mineralogist takes a specimen of the rock back to the laboratory. There he cuts it into a slice so thin that it is transparent and examines it through a microscope. The way in which the various minerals react under different types of light can be seen and from this they may be identified.

Crystals tend to have uniform shapes since they are built up of identically-shaped molecular units. The shape is therefore indicative of a mineral's composition.

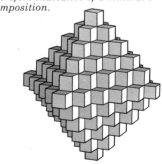

The Deformed Crust

Although sedimentary rocks, as we have seen, are formed from sediments that were laid down in horizontal layers, these same layers, when seen today, are rarely horizontal and often show a great deal of contortion and deformation. Igneous rocks are also subjected to enormous stresses and strains that give the final rock an appearance very different to that presented by the fresh emplacement. Taken to an extreme the Earth movements involved can throw up great mountain ranges, pull continents apart and change vast tracts of underground rock into metamorphic formations. The mechanisms that produce such effects are studied elsewhere but here we deal largely with the results.

Rock is, as a rule, a fairly brittle substance and so it tends to crack when subjected to stress. These cracks, when they appear on an exposed outcrop of rock, are known as joints. They are seen clearly on rocks like limestone and granite where these have been opened up by the erosion of the wind and rain.

Faults

When there is evidence of displacement along a joint, when the rock at one side has moved in relation to that at the other, the joint is known as a fault. The displacement along a fault can be very small, only a few millimetres, or it can be very large indeed.

Obvious deformations of the Earth's crust can often be seen where bedded rocks are exposed, as here in Lulworth Cove in Dorset, England.

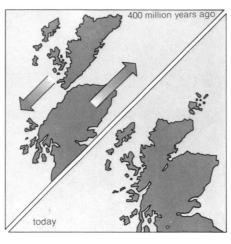

The Great Glen Fault that splits Scotland in two along the line of Loch Ness, Loch Lochy and Loch Linnhe is a massive fault with a displacement of 105 km (65 miles). This is known as a lateral or transcurrent fault as the blocks on each side have moved sideways in relation to each other.

A more common type of fault is the dip slip fault in which one block has moved up or down in relation to the other. When the plane of the dip slip fault is not vertical the fault may be 'normal' if the upper of the two blocks has moved downwards, or 'thrust' if the upper block has moved further up. Such faults are caused by tension and compression respectively. Dip slip faults can be very large as well, the Great Rift Valley of east Africa being a block that has subsided between two parallel faults. Such a subsided block is known as a graben. This may or may not have a valley as a surface feature depending on whether or not erosion has reduced the whole of the surface to a flat plain.

The complementary feature, a block that has been pushed up between parallel faults, is known as a horst. Often the rocks at each side of a fault have polished each other by the movement and the result is a very smooth surface called a slickenside. In other cases the sliding has been accompanied by violent crushing and the fault is filled with fragments giving a locally formed rock called a fault breccia.

Left The disturbance of the Earth's crust may be very large. There is much geological evidence to suggest that, about four hundred million years ago, the area of the north of Scotland was disrupted by a lateral fault and the blocks moved 105 km (65 miles) in relation to one another.

Folds

Often a rock does not crack when subjected to a strain but instead it bends. This bending may seem unlikely for a normally rigid material like a rock but under conditions of great pressure and great temperature the solid may behave in a plastic manner provided enough time is allowed. A bend produced in this manner is known as a fold.

Like faults, folds are of different types. A rock structure that is folded downwards like a length of string supported at each end and sagging in the middle is known as a syncline. An upward fold is called an anticline. Because of the geometry of the folding a series of folded beds tends to be

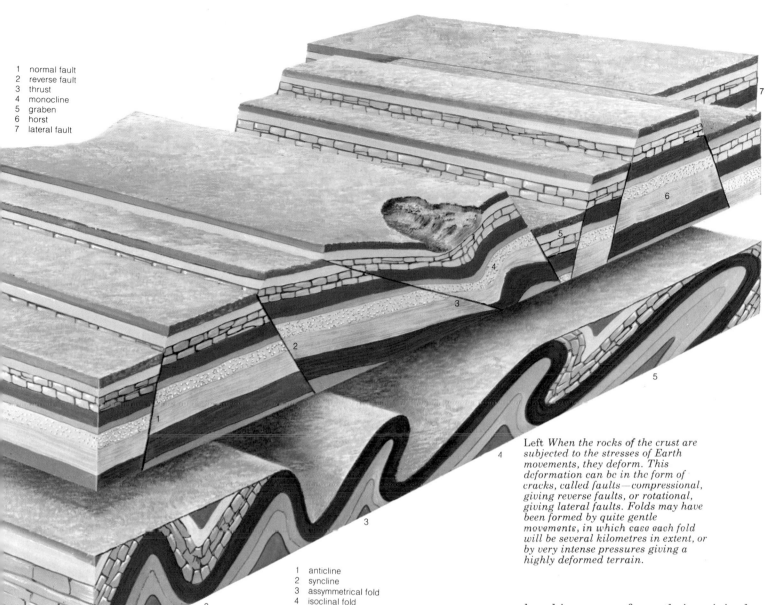

1 normal fault
2 reverse fault
3 thrust
4 monocline
5 graben
6 horst
7 lateral fault

1 anticline
2 syncline
3 assymmetrical fold
4 isoclinal fold
5 recumbent fold

Left When the rocks of the crust are subjected to the stresses of Earth movements, they deform. This deformation can be in the form of cracks, called faults—compressional, giving reverse faults, or rotational, giving lateral faults. Folds may have been formed by quite gentle movements, in which case each fold will be several kilometres in extent, or by very intense pressures giving a highly deformed terrain.

thin on the flanks and thick at the crest. The individual beds may deform easily into this shape, in which case they are called incompetent beds, or they may split into slices that slide about in response to the pressures, and are called competent beds.

When a terrain is subjected to intense and widespread deformation, like that associated with the raising of a mountain chain, all these structures may be found together, producing such a confusing picture of disruption and distortion that it may

be very difficult to determine what the original sequence of beds was like. The Alps are a particularly good example of the large amount of structural deformation that can occur in a mountain chain. Synclines and anticlines are crushed together and then folded into larger scale synclines and anticlines. The limbs of folds may be so tightly packed as to be parallel to each other and appear as one continuous sedimentary sequence—a problem compounded when the crest of the fold has been eroded away or cut off by a fault. Anticlines have formed and fallen over under their own weight,

breaking away from their original sequence and travelling great distances like a crumpled tablecloth sliding down a tilted table. The rocks in these nappes, as they are called, are often found hundreds of kilometres away from their original positions.

Many of these features produced in the same manner but on a smaller scale can be seen in glaciers. Ice, like rock, is usually a rigid material but under the great pressures and stresses involved in the movement of a glacier it may bend and deform like the rocks in a mountain chain. Complex folding can be seen that closely resembles the synclines and anticlines found in sedimentary rock sequences, and cracks and crevasses form that are very similar to joints and faults.

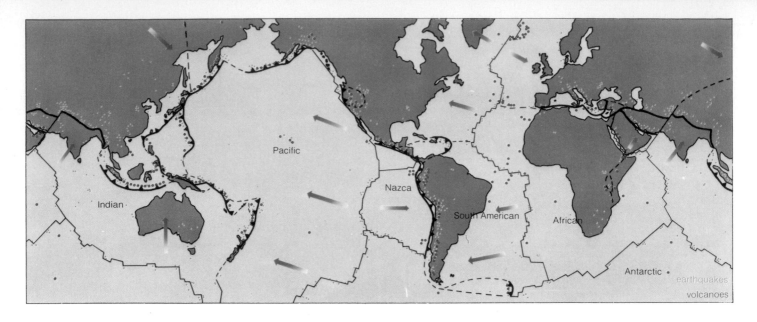

The Violent Earth

Volcanoes and earthquakes are most
often found in the region of plate
boundaries where the movements
associated with plate formation and
destruction are most noticeable.

The faults and folds and the other deformations seen in the rocks of the Earth's crust have, for the most part, been formed by very slow and gentle processes, unnoticed by the instruments or the senses of men. Occasionally, however, geological processes take place with a speed and violence that can be both spectacular and destructive.

Volcanoes

Volcanoes occur when molten magma reaches the Earth's surface and bursts out. On the surface the magma, now termed lava, cools and solidifies around the vent from which it issued and builds up in a cone to form a volcano. The shape of the hill that is formed is largely determined by the nature of the lava.

A very runny lava, one that has a small proportion of silica in its composition, flows for great distances before it cools enough to solidify. The volcanoes formed by such a lava are very low, merely forming lava sheets that spread around a fissure, such as in Iceland, or broad low shield volcanoes like those found in Hawaii.

A number of characteristic structures are found in this type of lava. If it cools as it is flowing the surface wrinkles up to give a ropey appearance known by its Hawaiian name of *Pahoehoe*. If there has been some turbulence in the flow the resulting surface is broken and blocky and called *Aa*. Lava tunnels form when the surface of a lava solidifies and the still molten material in the centre runs out. Tree moulds are produced when a lava flow engulfs a tree. The tree burns away and the lava adhering to the outside is left as a vertical tube. This type of volcanic eruption can be quite destructive of property because of the great areas covered by the liquid lava but there are usually few casualties because the lava runs fairly slowly.

Lava with a slightly higher proportion of silica in its make-up tends to be more viscous, forms steeper and higher volcanoes and produces eruptions that are somewhat more violent. On exposure to air this type of lava solidifies quickly and often blocks up the volcano's neck. The

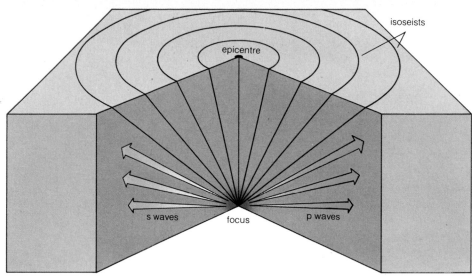

build-up of pressure blasts the obstruction clear from time to time giving thick cauliflower clouds and showers of ash, lumps of lava called bombs and fragments of solid rock. Pompeii, in 79 AD, was buried in ash when Vesuvius erupted in such a manner.

Lava with a very high proportion of silica is very viscous and gives a particularly tall and steep volcano. The eruption of such a volcano can be very violent and destructive. When the vent is blocked by a solid plug the pressure that builds up beneath may force this plug out like a champagne cork, thrusting it up above the summit in a spine. When the lava breaks through it is of a very high temperature and the sudden drop in pressure causes the dissolved gases in it to come out of solution and form millions of bubbles, again like the champagne freed from the pressure of the cork. The resulting mass of extremely hot lava, lubricated by the gas bubbles, then flows down the

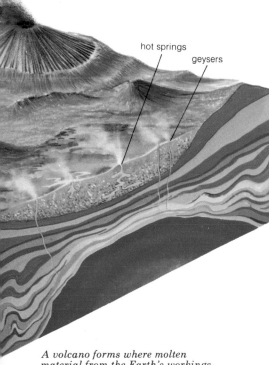

A volcano forms where molten material from the Earth's workings finds its way to the surface through weak spots in the crust in funnels or fissures, and accumulates close to where it is ejected. Volcanic gas contains a large proportion of water, and rains accompany an eruption eroding the unconsolidated material of the volcano's flanks into a distinctive gullied pattern. A caldera forms when a vent becomes empty and the volcano collapses back down it forming a very broad crater.

flanks of the volcano like water, engulfing everything in its path. This feature is known as a *nuée ardente* and one of these was responsible for the destruction of St Pierre in Martinique in 1902 when Mont Pelée erupted at the cost of 30,000 lives. There were but two survivors in the whole town.

Vulcanism in a particular region may last for many thousands or even millions of years. It is thought that the Icelandic and Hawaiian types of eruption are found in the early stages while the Peléan type is found towards the end. Long after the volcanoes of a region are dead the visible activity lingers on in the form of hot springs and geysers that are frequently spectacular.

Earthquakes

Contrary to popular belief destructive earthquakes are not associated with volcanic eruptions. Any earth tremor during an eruption is usually quite small and localized. The major earthquakes are caused by the movements of large masses of the Earth's crust along active fault lines. These occur in regions of the crust that are constantly subjected to great stresses. The stresses build up along the fault line until the inertia of the system is overcome and the blocks jump for several metres relative to one another. This jump may take the blocks past the point of equilibrium and several after-shocks may take place that relieve the stresses. Things will then be quiet until the stresses have built up once more to an intolerable level, perhaps after many years.

The point at which the greatest motion of an earthquake occurs is known as the focus. This is usually situated below the surface of the Earth and the point on the surface

The focus of an earthquake is usually underground, the point on the surface above it being called the epicentre. Isoseists around the epicentre delineate areas in which similar intensities of shock are felt.

directly above it, the point where most damage is done, is called the epicentre. The epicentre can be found by a study of the waves generated by an earthquake. Three types of waves emanate. The first is the primary wave, a wave of compression. The secondary wave has a shaking motion and travels more slowly. The third travels only over the surface of the Earth and is the one that causes the damage. The first two travel through the Earth at a known rate and when these are recorded by an instrument called a seismograph the interval between the arrival of the primary and secondary waves is noted. This interval can be used to determine the distance of the epicentre and when three or more stations are recording the same disturbance the epicentre can be unambiguously pinpointed.

When man's puny edifices are struck by the Earth's mighty movements the result can be total devastation as here at Gibelina in Sicily in 1968.

The Sculpturing of the Land

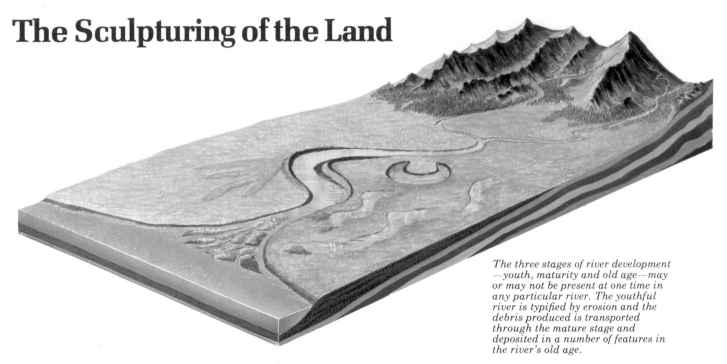

The three stages of river development —youth, maturity and old age—may or may not be present at one time in any particular river. The youthful river is typified by erosion and the debris produced is transported through the mature stage and deposited in a number of features in the river's old age.

Limestone is made up of the mineral calcite. Rainwater dissolves atmospheric carbon dioxide to form weak carbonic acid and this attacks the calcite and dissolves it. The result is the characteristic erosion of limestone giving enlarged joints separating rounded blocks—grikes and clints—on the surface, and caverns underground. Streams dissolve potholes and vanish underground reappearing only where the limestone rests on another type of rock, leaving systems of tunnels and caves behind them. Ground water containing dissolved calcite may seep through to the ceiling of a cave where it evaporates, precipitating tiny crystals of calcite. These accumulate to form stalactites hanging from the ceiling; and any water splashing to the floor similarly builds up stalagmites there.

No sooner have mountain ranges been folded and horst blocks thrust up by the mighty processes beneath the Earth's crust than other forces are brought to bear to wear them down again. It is almost as if there were an equilibrium level of elevation that nature tries to achieve with all landforms. Any high land is worn away and, as a consequence, low lying areas are filled up with the fragments.

Weather

The gentle rain is one of the most potent agents of erosion. Through its action solid rocks are reduced to soil and this soil is washed away. Rain seeping into the ground emerges again as springs, giving birth to streams that merge to form rivers. Rivers run swiftly and erode canyons and valleys in the hills, often bouncing along heavy boulders and other broken rocks to wear away even more material.

When the river reaches a plain its speed slackens and its load of debris is deposited, usually when the river bursts its banks at times of flood, and sediments are built up on a flood plain. On reaching the sea more sediments may be deposited at the river mouth where they may remain to form the distinctive pattern of channels and islands known as a delta, or they may be carried away by sea currents to be deposited somewhere else.

In high mountains or in cold climates the rain falls as snow. The snow may accumulate in hollows where it is compressed by later falls and, under this pressure, turns into ice. The ice under pressure, like rocks under pressure, can bend and flow in a plastic manner. This ice flows out of the hollow in which it formed and moves down the mountainside as a glacier. Valleys are scoured out by the great weight of the ice and are deepened into U shapes, the material torn off being transported by the ice and deposited as mounds of sand and gravel, or vast layers of clay in lowland areas after the ice has melted due to a climate change.

Mountains may be worn by glaciers on each side leaving the intervening ridge as a sharp crest. If a peak has several glaciers originating around it, it is worn back into a sharp pyramid like the Matterhorn. Exposed rocks over which a glacier has passed may be left as streamlined teardrop shapes and may show deep scratches. All of these features are found in various parts of the British Isles, showing that the area has suffered an ice age within the last two million years or so.

Frost itself can have a significant influence on the landscape. When water freezes it expands, as anyone who has had burst water pipes in the winter knows. Water trapped in rock cavities will force the rock open if it freezes. This is why the farmer ploughs his fields in the autumn—to let in the rain and the frost so that the soil is broken up during the winter. Frost shattered rocks tumble down from mountainsides where they accumulate as vast scree slopes, such as those that are so typical of the Lake District.

The rain has a chemical, as well as a physical, effect on the rocks on which it falls. During its passage through the atmosphere it absorbs carbon dioxide gas and becomes carbonic acid. This acid is very weak but in time it will dissolve the mineral calcite ($CaCO_3$) in the rocks. This can have a great effect on limestone which is practically all calcite. The rock is dissolved away especially along joints, widening them into

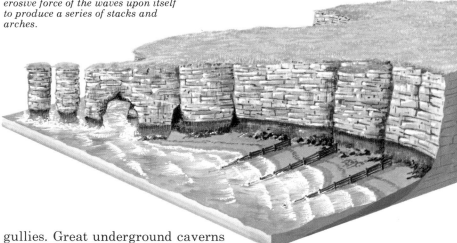

A headland disrupts the wave pattern approaching a shore and turns the erosive force of the waves upon itself to produce a series of stacks and arches.

gullies. Great underground caverns are hollowed out and the calcite in the water is deposited as the characteristic stalactites and stalagmites in the still underground air.

Wind is a powerful erosion agent, especially in arid climates where there is little moisture to hold the soil together. Sand particles are blasted against rocky outcrops producing strange and grotesque shapes, sometimes like mushrooms where the greatest erosion takes place near the ground. Distinctive three-sided rocks are formed, each side polished by the wind. The material eroded away forms even more sand that is deposited in the form of dunes that change shape and travel, still under the influence of the wind. These features are found in the Earth's desert areas but they have also been seen on Mars, attesting to the very dry and windy conditions that must exist on that planet.

The great weight and relentless motion of a glacier produces a deep valley with steep sides. These remain long after the glacier has melted.

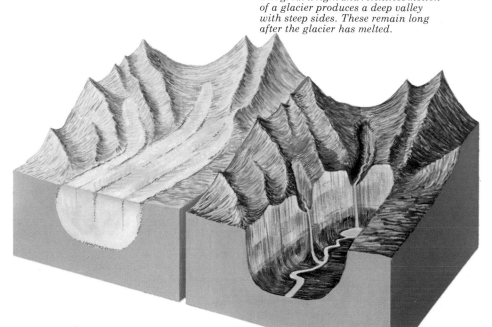

The Sea

Rocks exposed to the constant violence of the seas show very marked erosional features. When an area of high land occurs next to the sea the cliff that forms is subjected to all the destructive force of the waves. Headlands tend to be attacked more swiftly than bays because the waves, as they approach the shore, are deflected towards the sides of the promontories. Sea caves form in the rock, usually along joints, and these are forced open by the pressure of waves thudding into them. Often the pressure is released by a hole being blasted through the roof and a blowhole forms. Two caves cut in from opposite sides of a headland may meet in the middle to form a natural arch and when the lintel of this collapses the offshore section is left standing as a sea stack. This happens whenever headlands protrude into the sea and so the tendency is to produce a straight coastline.

The material worn away, and other debris brought down by rivers, can be carried along by the currents and deposited as a beach. A system of currents that carries this material along a shore is known as longshore drift and its presence can be seen where a beach is continued out across the mouth of a river in the form of a sand bar.

The surface of the Earth is in constant change. The uplands are being slowly worn away by the weather while they are being pushed up by the Earth movements.

The Restless Crust

For many hundreds of years the processes that resulted in the massive forces required to throw up mountain ranges and shake the continents with earthquakes were largely unknown. Only now, with the long and patient piecing together of different fragments of evidence, is there any glimmering of an understanding.

The Supercontinent

The first inkling came in 1858 when Antonio Snider-Pelligrini published maps that suggested that the similarity in shape between the coastlines of South America and Africa was due to the fact that they were once a single continent that had been torn apart at some distant time in the past. Scholars had pointed this out before but Snider-Pelligrini was the first to point out the geological similarities of the two continents as well as just the geometric fit.

The matter was raised again by Alfred Wegener in 1915 and he found similarities between other continents, enabling him to put all the continents together like a vast jigsaw puzzle into one initial supercontinent. The implications of such an idea were so enormous that the whole concept was dismissed as cranky and the situation was not helped when Wegener found himself at a loss to suggest a convincing mechanism for producing such vast movements. Despite this more and more evidence subsequently came to light that indicated that the landmasses of South America, Africa, Antarctica, India and Australia were

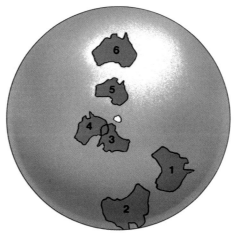

The movements of the continents have been well plotted by estimating the change on the apparent position of the Earth's magnetic poles when rocks of a known age were formed. Australia has moved a considerable distance relative to Antarctica.

The configuration of the supercontinent Gondwanaland is well known from evidence of the distribution of fossil animals and plants and the original continuation of mountain ranges, the remains of which are now widely dispersed.

once one whole. This evidence included the existence of mountain belts of the same age that run continuously across these continents when they are reassembled according to Wegener's reconstructions, the presence of fossils of the same land animals and plants found on each continent, and indications of the ice-caps that covered these continents where there are now subtropical deserts.

Evidence then came to light that suggested that North America was once joined to Europe and north Africa, although the proof of this was not as spectacular as that for the southern continents. Eventually the scientific world had to accept as proven the assumption that the continents had once been joined together and that they had split and moved apart into their present positions. A mechanism had to be discovered to account for this.

Mid-oceanic Ridges

New evidence came to light in the 1960s when detailed studies were made of the mysterious ridges to be found in the ocean deeps, especially the one that runs up the centre of the Atlantic Ocean. It had been found that when a rock is formed any magnetic particles in it align themselves to point to the Earth's magnetic poles. The magnetism of the rocks along each side of the mid-Atlantic ridge was found to point alternately north and south in parallel bands. The distribution of these bands corresponded to the known changes of polarity of the Earth's magnetic field over the last few million years, when the north and south magnetic poles dramatically

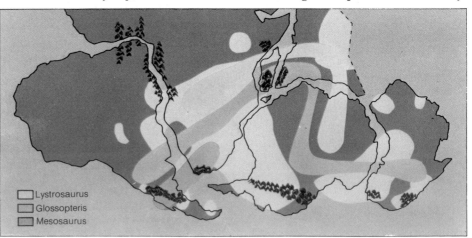

Lystrosaurus
Glossopteris
Mesosaurus

switched places. What was more, the arrangement of bands at one side of the ridge was found to be an exact mirror image of that at the other. The conclusion reached from all this was that the ocean floor was being created at the mid-oceanic ridges and then moving away as if on a conveyor belt.

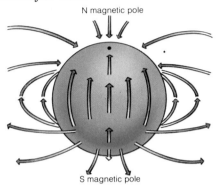

The Earth can be thought of as a giant magnet with lines of force reacing between one pole and the other.

Oceanic Trenches

At other places on the earth's crust these conveyor belts meet. When they do one slides beneath the other and is destroyed. The lines along which this occurs are marked by the presence of deep ocean troughs such as those found all the way around the Pacific Ocean. Confirmation of this constant movement of the ocean floor comes from the dating techniques applied to rocks. Nowhere on the ocean floor are there rocks dating from more than about 150 million years ago. The rocks are created at ocean ridges, they travel, and they are destroyed in the trenches.

The continents are made of lighter rocks than the ocean floors. Consequently they stay on the surface and are carried about rather like logs embedded in ice in a frozen river. When a continent is carried to a trench it is not drawn down and destroyed because it is too light. However it does buckle and deform with the stresses placed on it and so we tend to have great mountain chains along the edges of continents close to ocean trenches.

Crustal Plates

Studies of earthquake waves suggest that there is a soft, almost liquid, region in the Earth's upper mantle below about 100 km (60 miles) on top of which the topmost mantle and the crust ride about like rafts. These

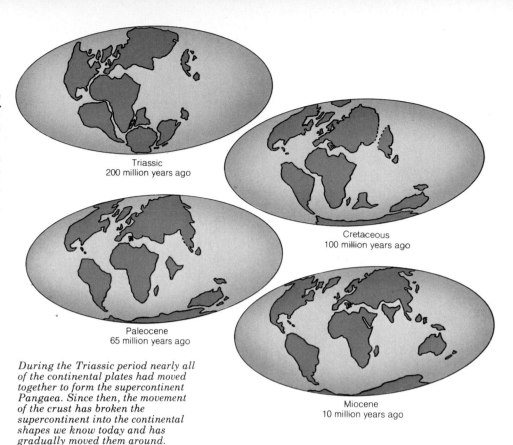

During the Triassic period nearly all of the continental plates had moved together to form the supercontinent Pangaea. Since then, the movement of the crust has broken the supercontinent into the continental shapes we know today and has gradually moved them around.

rafts are called plates (the study of these is known as plate tectonics) and there are about six major ones and several smaller ones in odd corners. The whole system can be compared to a boiling jam pan, with the heat of the boiling supplied by convection from the Earth's interior, the jam moving across the surface represented by the oceanic crust, and the scum and froth that gathers here and there represented by the continents.

A map of the Earth's earthquake belts and volcanic regions will be very similar to a map of the Earth's crustal plates. These violent activi-

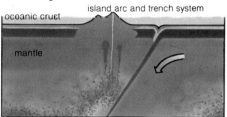

Above *When two plates meet one must slide beneath the other. If both plates are oceanic the resulting volcanic activity forms an island arc. If one plate is continental the edge of the continent crumples up into a mountain chain.*

ties take place almost exclusively along the oceanic ridges or close to the deep ocean trenches. The convection process is constantly active and North America is currently drifting away from Europe at a rate of 2–8 cm (0.8–1.5 in) per year. It is also constantly changing and the rift valley system of east Africa is believed to be the beginnings of another continental split like the one that broke up the super-continents 200 million years ago. In a few million years time Africa may be split into two with a newly formed ocean, complete with ocean ridge, separating the parts.

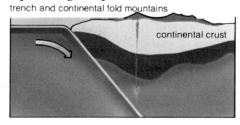

Below *Magnetic stripes are formed in the rocks of the ocean crust as they are created and moved away from the mid-oceanic ridge. This is due to the fact that the Earth's magnetic field is constantly reversing its polarity.*

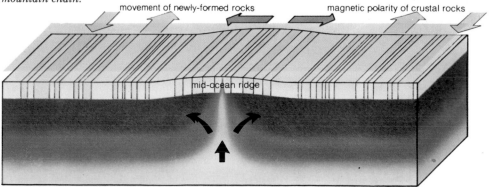

History in the Rocks

The compositions and the structures of sedimentary rocks can tell a great deal about the conditions under which they formed and about the appearance of the landscape at the time.

Composition and Structure
Firstly the nature of the rock itself can give an indication. Sandstone is made of minerals and rock fragments eroded from elsewhere. If the fragments are large and angular it means that they have not been transported far before deposition. If there are fragments of many different sizes it suggests that the deposition has taken place rapidly. If, however, the fragments are small and round and all of one size then the sand that formed it will have travelled great distances and will have been well sorted before being deposited. Such sands are found in desert sandstones.

Other indications from the rock type are more obvious: deposits of rock salt are found in salty lakes, fine grained shales in muddy estuaries and limestones packed with coral fragments in coral reefs.

The structures in sedimentary rocks are good indicators of the conditions under which they formed. In shallow waters near a beach the constant to and fro motion of the waves throws the sand into a series of ripples. The ripples can be preserved in the final rock attesting to the original shallow-water conditions. When wet mud dries out slowly in the sun it shrinks and cracks into polygonal blocks that

Left and right Hundreds of millions of years of Earth's history are recorded in the beds of rock beneath Colorado. These are laid bare for geologists to study in the Grand Canyon.

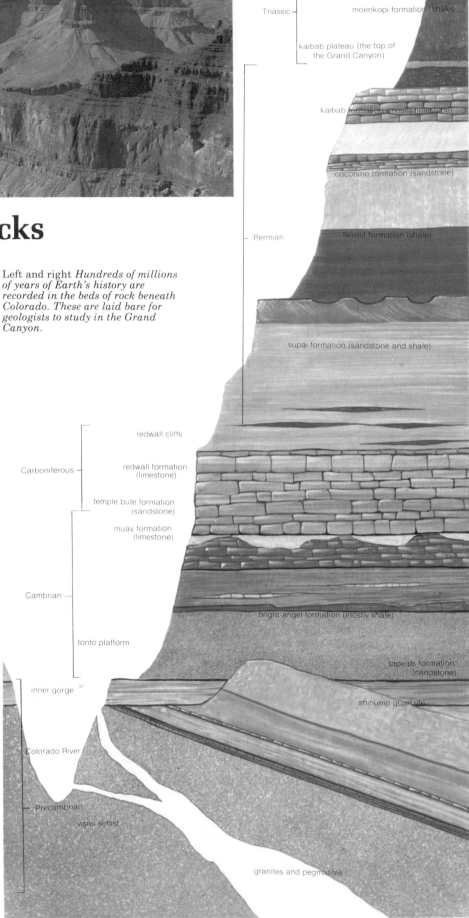

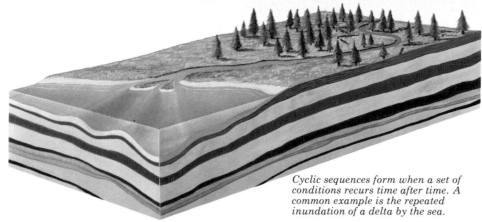

Cyclic sequences form when a set of conditions recurs time after time. A common example is the repeated inundation of a delta by the sea.

may also be preserved. Currents that deposit sand in a river bed do so in short S-shaped beds that are typical of those found in a deltaic sequence. Similar S-shaped beds but on a much larger scale are formed by sand dunes in a desert environment.

One of the most important environment indicators in a sedimentary rock is the rock's fossil content. Basically, marine organisms are found in rocks laid down in salt water, freshwater creatures in those formed in rivers and lakes, and land dwelling animals and plants in terrestrial deposits. Some creatures are known to be very fussy about where they live, for example, the bivalve shellfish *Ensis*, the razor shell, lives only in beaches periodically flooded by the tide. If this creature is found in a rock as a fossil in its living position it can be taken as an indicator of the environment in which that rock was formed.

The phrase 'in its living position' is an important one since any dead shell may be picked up and deposited somewhere else by the current. A fossil assemblage that shows burrowing creatures still in their burrows, bivalve shells still joined together and articulated organisms quite whole is known as a life assemblage and can be used as an indication of the environment. One in which the fossils are broken and disarticulated cannot. An example is the Solnhofen limestone series in Germany. This was deposited in shallow brackish-water lagoons and as well as containing the fossils of the fish and shells that lived there it contains remains of creatures from the different environments nearby.

King crabs and fish entered from a nearby sea area and died when the conditions changed, small dinosaurs and lizards that lived inland were washed in by streams, and birds,

insects and pterosaurs that flew above the water fell in and were buried when they died. Any fossil that, by its presence in a rock, indicates what sort of environment existed when the rock was formed is termed a facies fossil.

Facies

The word 'facies' is a rather vaguely defined term that covers every aspect of a sedimentary rock that suggests something about its history. This includes its composition, grain size, grain shape, internal sedimentary structures and fossil content.

All of these features can be seen in the Carboniferous rocks of the British Isles. These generally show what is known as a cyclic sequence: a bed of shale is overlain by a bed of sandstone, then by one of sea earth, and then coal, to be followed by the shale again. These are typical of the deposits found in a deltaic environment.

The mud brought down by the river is deposited first to give the bed of shale. Then, as the front of the delta approaches, the coarser material is brought in forming the sandstone. The sandstone shows current bedding, proving that it was deposited by a river and giving an indication of the direction from which the current flowed.

The sand bank formed was built up above the level of the water and plants started to grow on it. When this happened the top layer of the sand was riddled with roots and many

of the minerals were leached out, turning it into sea earth, a pale sandstone containing root fragments. The plant growth above was turned to coal and the nature of the vegetation can be seen by examining the plant fragments in the coal. This area was then submerged and the coal buried by fine mud as the delta advanced once more. Occasionally the sea would flood into the system at this stage, giving a bed of limestone with fossils of marine organisms beneath the shale.

By these means the history of the British Isles can be plotted. During the Cambrian, Ordovician and Silurian periods, between 650 and 395 million years ago, the British area lay largely at the bottom of the sea on a moving ocean plate. By the Devonian period the plate had largely been compressed and the area was thrown into a series of mountain ranges with deserts between. Then came the Carboniferous in which the mountains were eroded and deltas covered large areas, giving the coalfields. Mountains and deserts followed again in the Permian and Triassic, giving way to lowlands and seas in the Jurassic and Cretaceous. During the Tertiary the face of the land became gradually more like what it is today and the ice ages of the Quaternary during the last 2 million years put the finishing touches to the familiar landscape.

The coming and going of the ice sheets during the last two million years is an indication of the changing conditions at the Earth's surface.

Fossilization occurs when the hard parts of an organism are buried rapidly. Physical or chemical changes preserve the organism or its shape.

 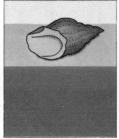  

The Submarine Landscape

Approximately 70 per cent of the Earth's surface is covered by the oceans but, until recently more was known about the Moon's geography than about the features on the ocean floor. Only within the last few decades, with the development of new techniques of underwater exploration and remote sensing, has any headway been made in the mapping of the hidden depths.

The Continental Shelf

The most significant feature of the ocean floor is the abrupt change in slope at a depth of about 130 m (450 ft) around each of the continents. This marks the outer limit of what is known as the continental shelf, the outer edges of the slabs of continental crust. The shelf can be very broad, hundreds of kilometres in some places, or it can be very narrow, especially where the continent is beside a deep sea trench where one crustal plate is being destroyed beneath another.

The nature of the rocks of the continental shelf is the same as that of the rocks of the continent itself. Hence the same deposits and outcrops of fossil fuels and minerals can be expected. Indeed an enormous amount of work has been done in the past few decades in the search for oil here. The sea-level is constantly changing and so the shoreline is continually moving back and forth over the shelf.

Within the last 2 million years ice ages have come and gone, locking up vast quantities of the oceans' water in the ice-caps and lowering the sea-level. The continental shelves of the eastern seaboard of the United States and the North Sea show a number of drowned shorelines with peat deposits, tree stumps and animal remains like elephant's teeth dating from this time.

The Continental Slope

Beyond the edge of the continental shelf the sea-bed slopes abruptly

Above *Lava erupted under water is immediately chilled and a solid crust forms. This crust remains quite flexible and insulates the bulk of the molten material from further cooling. A pillow-like structure results and successions of these from one eruption roll about before they settle and solidify.*

Right *A mid-ocean ridge is the constantly healing scar marking the line of separation between two moving crustal plates. As the plates move apart, new material wells up and solidifies forming the topographic feature and the tensions involved are indicated by the rift valley running along the crest. The Atlantic Ridge is a very good example, running parallel to the edges of both flanking continents. Parallel faults cut the ridge into segments which are staggered along its length—a necessary feature to accommodate the geometry of the separation. Minor ridges on the flanks form a grain running parallel to the rift valley.*

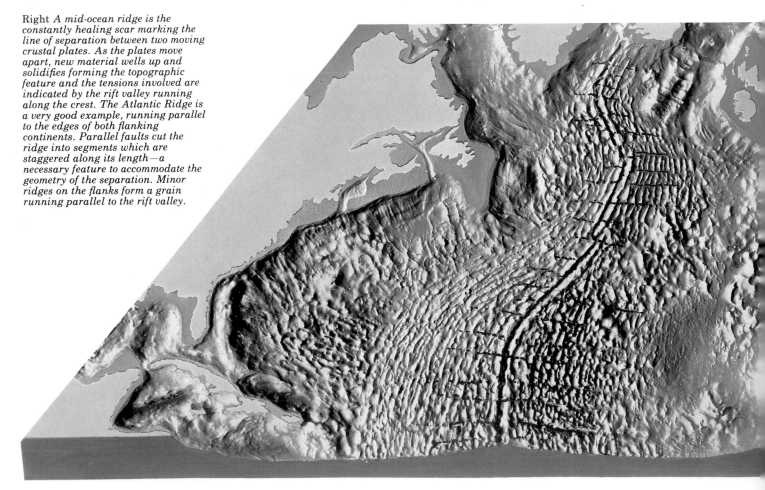

down the ocean depths. This gradient is known as the continental slope and it drops 400 m (12,000 ft) to the floor of the ocean at angles varying between 3° and 20°. The slope is often cut by vast canyons that rival the Grand Canyon of Colorado in size and are often found offshore from the mouths of large rivers. These canyons are made by currents of mud and land-derived debris held in suspension in the water and flowing like a liquid of a greater density than sea water.

The material washed down the continental slope gathers at the bottom to form a gentler slope stretching out more than 600 km (400 miles) across the ocean floor. The sediments here are redistributed from the canyon mouths by deep sea currents. Beyond this continental rise the ocean floor proper begins.

The Ocean Crust

As we have seen, the ocean crust is greatly different in composition and origin from the continental crust. It is constantly being created at ridges that lie along each of the oceans and destroyed in trenches up the sides.

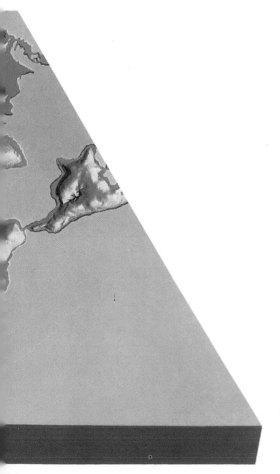

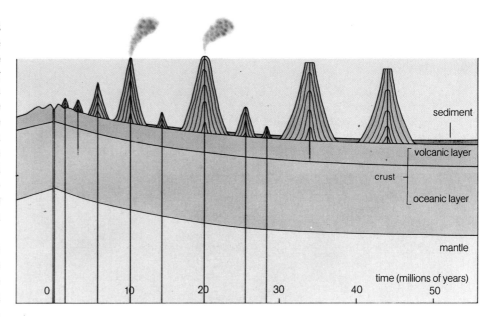

Guyots form when the ridge volcanoes are eroded to sea level and transported to deeper water.

This is reflected by the nature of the surface features and of the sediments. A rift valley is present along the centre of each of the ridges. Such a valley is formed when two plates move away from one another. Vulcanism is seen along the ridges, especially where it reaches the surface as volcanic islands, for example, Iceland and Tristan da Cunha. When lava is erupted into sea water it forms separate mobile blobs that finally come to rest and solidify piled upon one another like pillows. This pillow lava is known from every mid oceanic ridge. Within 1 km (½ mile) of the ridge crest these pillow lavas are obvious and quite clean, indicating how new they are. 5 km (3 miles) away the lava is now several thousand years old and is beginning to be buried by deep sea sediments. 10 km (6 miles) away no such features are visible, everything having been buried by sediment.

The Ocean Floor

The sediment that gathers on the abyssal plain is vastly different from any on the continental shelf or any other environment. They are mostly oozes, muds formed from the shells of microscopic sea creatures, and can consist mostly of calcium carbonate or of silica. In areas where no oozes are found the sediment is a red clay consisting mostly of volcanic dust and meteorite fragments. All sedimentation in these areas is extremely slow, 2 cm (¾ in) in 1,000 years being a typical rate.

Everywhere on the ocean floor, on the top of the sediment, lie spongy lumps of mineral with a high metal content. As big as potatoes (often bigger) they contain large quantities of manganese, iron, nickel and titanium but it is not certain how they form. Manganese nodules, as they are called, are exciting much interest in mining companies which are on the verge of exploiting them, anticipating that land-based ores will become depleted.

Here and there, on the abyssal plain, are dotted flat-topped sea mounts called guyots. These have the appearance of volcanic islands that have been worn flat at the top by wave action, but the tops are at a depth of about 3 km (2 miles) below the surface. The probable explanation is that they were volcanoes that erupted to the surface from the mid-ocean ridge but were later carried away to the ocean depths by movement of the oceanic crust away from its point of origin.

The ocean trenches, the surface expressions of the destruction of the plates beneath one another, are the deepest parts of the ocean, the deepest part yet recorded being the Mariana Trench off the Philippines, being 11,022 m (36,161 ft) deep. At these depths the water is completely dark and strange creatures exist that have only occasionally been sighted from deep sea submersibles and photographed by automatic cameras.

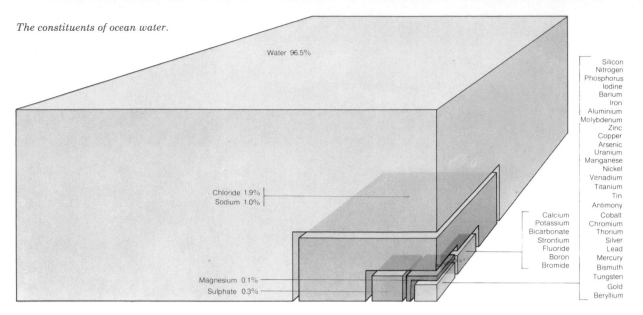

The constituents of ocean water.

Water 96.5%

Chloride 1.9%
Sodium 1.0%

Magnesium 0.1%
Sulphate 0.3%

Calcium
Potassium
Bicarbonate
Strontium
Fluoride
Boron
Bromide

Silicon
Nitrogen
Phosphorus
Iodine
Barium
Iron
Aluminium
Molybdenum
Zinc
Copper
Arsenic
Uranium
Manganese
Nickel
Vanadium
Titanium
Tin
Antimony
Cobalt
Chromium
Thorium
Silver
Lead
Mercury
Bismuth
Tungsten
Gold
Beryllium

The Ocean Waters

The ocean water that covers so much of the Earth's surface is a surprisingly pure substance despite its salty taste and its muddy appearance at certain places. It is about 95 per cent pure water which is a very high purity for a natural substance. The remaining 5 per cent consists of elements dissolved in it. More than three-quarters of this consists of sodium and chlorine, combined to form common salt (NaCl), but most of the other elements are present in some proportion. There is even gold in sea water, some 600 times the amount of gold in man's possession, but despite numerous attempts it is impossible to extract economically due to the high dispersion.

The saltiness of the sea (its salinity) varies greatly from one area to another. Offshore from the mouths of large rivers the salinity tends to be low due to the constant influx of fresh water. The area of low salinity off the mouth of the Amazon stretches halfway across the Atlantic Ocean. In fairly enclosed areas especially in warm or hot climates the salinity will be higher because of constant evaporation of water from the surface. The Mediterranean has a higher salinity than the Atlantic Ocean despite the water brought in by the Nile.

In certain almost totally enclosed basins the salt becomes so concentrated that it is deposited as thick beds of carbonate and rock salt. The inlet is constantly replenished by the water flowing in from the main sea area bringing with it more dissolved salts to be deposited. The gulf of Kara Bogaz off the Caspian Sea is a sterling example of this.

Freezing

Water acts in a rather strange way when it comes to freezing. Most substances contract on cooling. Water, however, although it does contract as it cools, begins to expand again at temperatures lower than 4°C and expands abruptly on freezing. This is why ice floats on the surface of freezing water when all the laws of physics dictate that it should sink. This has a great influence on the state of the globe. If this anomalous property did not exist the polar oceans would freeze from the bottom upwards instead of freezing only at the top and providing an insulation between the cold atmosphere and the warmer waters beneath. The ice in the Arctic Ocean is mostly all sea ice and subject to great variations with the seasons and the currents. Icebergs produced here have mostly broken off valley glaciers where they reach the sea from surrounding land-masses.

In the Antarctic Ocean the ice is largely continental, produced on the Antarctic landmass and moving outwards in vast sheets into the surrounding oceans. Icebergs produced here tend to be huge and flat, some up to 80 km (50 miles) long. Schemes are under consideration for harnessing these great ice mountains and

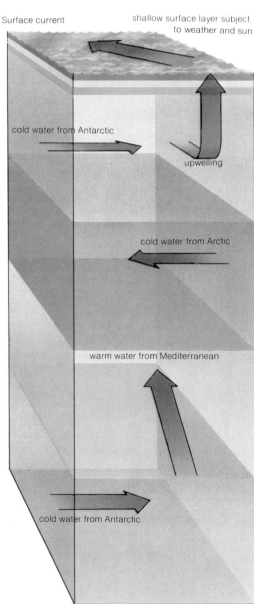

Surface current

shallow surface layer subject to weather and sun

cold water from Antarctic

upwelling

cold water from Arctic

warm water from Mediterranean

cold water from Antarctic

The movement of the water in the Earth's oceans varies a great deal between the surface and the depths. The surface currents are due mostly to the action of the wind and the varying physical conditions of the water. The movement at the surface is complemented at depth by world wide deep sea currents.

towing them to arid coastal areas such as Western Australia or the Persian Gulf to provide water for irrigation. This would be possible as the salt is excluded from the ice as it freezes and so fresh water for parched land would be obtained on melting the iceberg.

Currents

The distribution of the ice, and many other oceanic features, is dependent on the currents. These come about due to the influence of the atmosphere on the topmost layers of the water. Prevailing wind whipping across the water drives the surface waters in a particular direction. This usually results in a vast circular motion of the waters within fairly restricted regions such as the north Atlantic and the Indian Ocean. Every movement of the surface is compensated for by another movement at depth resulting in a worldwide system of deep sea currents that are rarely encountered by man. The average speed of an ocean current is about 10 km (6 miles) per day but some currents may reach more than 160 km (100 miles) per day.

The Tide

The other great movement of the ocean water is that of the tide. As the Moon revolves around the Earth it does not trace out a circle with the Earth's centre as its centre. Rather the Moon and the Earth are linked together and the two revolve around one another pivoted at a point to one side of the Earth's centre. As a result of this the water of the oceans is thrown outwards to one side of the Earth, the side away from the Moon, giving a high tide here. At the same time the water at the other side of the

Earth, beneath the Moon, is gathered up to give high tides here also because of the direct pull of the Moon's gravity.

The system is further complicated by the gravitational pull of the Sun that gives particularly high tides, or spring tides, when it reinforces the Moon's activity and lower tides (neap tides) when it acts against it. In practice the friction of the water retards the movement and the high tides are a little out of step with the positions of the Sun and the Moon. This interaction also results in tidal currents.

The Waves

Much smaller on a global scale but still very important to man is the movement of the water by waves. This, like a current, is usually caused by the winds. The water while exhibiting a periodic motion has no average current. The wave motion transmits energy that can in extreme cases travel thousands of kilometres much like the vibrations on a taut rope. Each water particle involved travels in a circular motion in the

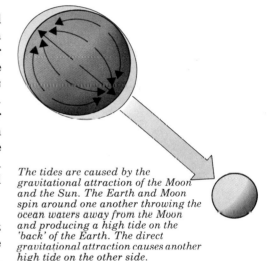

☐ Cold currents
■ Warm currents

The surface waters of the oceans are in constant motion, driven by wind and convection, and modified by the coriolis effect.

The tides are caused by the gravitational attraction of the Moon and the Sun. The Earth and Moon spin around one another throwing the ocean waters away from the Moon and producing a high tide on the 'back' of the Earth. The direct gravitational attraction causes another high tide on the other side.

open ocean but in shallow water this circle becomes more compressed. The result is that the water moving at the top of the circle travels faster than that at the bottom and the wave curls over and breaks near the shore. Very large waves are caused by underwater earthquakes and these tsunamis, also known inaccurately as tidal waves, can cause death and damage as they break on exposed shorelines.

The movements of the ocean waters by currents, tides and waves are now being looked upon as potential energy sources and many schemes are under development to tap them.

The surface of the sea is kicked up into waves by the passage of the wind across it. The vibrations cause waves to travel for great distances and move the water particles in a circular motion.

Earth's Envelope

The Earth's atmosphere, the air we breathe, is in fact the outer layer of the Earth system. It is a very thin covering of gas that stretches from ground level upwards becoming thinner as it goes until it fades away to nothing at the edge of space about 720 km (447 miles) up.

The Troposphere

Unlike the water in the oceans the gas of the atmosphere can be compressed by its own weight. Hence about 80 per cent of the atmosphere is found within 8 to 19 km (5–11 miles) of the Earth's surface, occupying a space of some 5,000 million cubic km (120 million cubic miles).

This part of the atmosphere is known as the troposphere and is the region with which we are most familiar. Most of the water in the atmosphere is found in this zone and most of that near the surface of the Earth. There is a constant cycling of the water by evaporation and condensation between the oceans, the atmosphere and the land but the atmosphere contains only a small fraction of 1 per cent of the Earth's water at any particular time. The temperature of the troposphere decreases with height since most of the warming effect is produced by sunlight reflected from the surface of the Earth.

The Stratosphere

Above the troposphere lies the stratosphere, about 65 km (40 miles) thick and containing only about 19 per cent of the air but occupying a space of some 20,000 million cubic km (480 million cubic miles), four times the volume of the denser troposphere. The lower layers of the stratosphere are constantly in circulation and strong winds blow. For this reason the temperatures are kept fairly constant and low. The temperature begins to rise again towards the top of the stratosphere.

The Ionosphere

Beyond the stratosphere, up to a height of about 400 km (250 miles), lies the ionosphere, cold at the bottom but increasing in temperature with height. This region contains less than 1 per cent of the atmosphere but so rarified is it that it occupies 1,000,000 million cubic km (24,000 million cubic miles), 200

The wind pattern of the globe would take this form if it were not for the irregularities of continents and mountain ranges. The basic north-south movement is produced by convection and the deflection to east and west caused by the coriolis effect.

times the volume of the troposphere.

Above this is the exosphere containing hardly any air and fading away gradually into space.

Radiation

The whole atmospheric system has a role to play in the modification of the Sun's radiation before it reaches the surface of the Earth. Practically all the visible light radiation passes through all layers unaltered. However, in its passage, the shorter waves, those at the blue end of the

The evolution of the Earth's atmosphere is a story of the gradual modification of the primal gases by effusions and biological activity.

original atmosphere of hydrogen, methane and ammonia   water added from cooling rocks   carbon dioxide and sulphur dioxide added by volcanoes   oxygen produced by photosynthesis

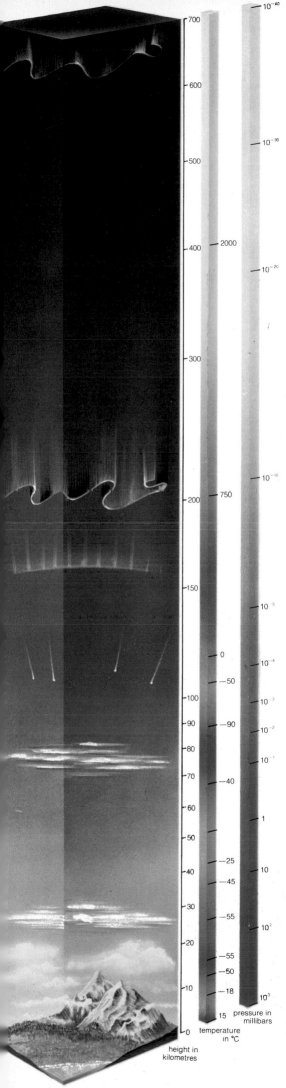

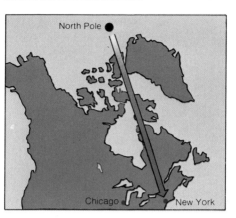

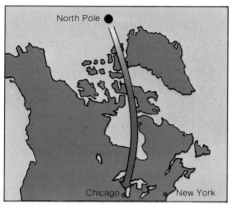

North Pole

Chicago   New York

North Pole

Chicago   New York

spectrum, are scattered to some degree by minute particles of dust. Hence the sky on a clear day is blue from this scattered light, while the longer wavelengths, those at the red end of the spectrum, pass straight through giving the orange appearance of the Sun.

When the visible rays pass through the larger water and ice particles in the clouds of the troposphere and the lower stratosphere all wavelengths are scattered and mixed up giving the white colouration of the clouds and also of the disc of the Sun when it is visible through them. Most of the longer wavelength infrared radiation is bounced back and scattered by the upper layers but some does still filter through to the Earth's surface.

The ultraviolet radiation, that with very short wavelengths and potentially very harmful to life on the Earth, is filtered out almost entirely by a layer of ozone in the lower ionosphere. Charged particles emitted by the Sun react with the layers of the atmosphere and produce startling light displays called aurorae—the Northern and Southern Lights. These particles tend to be caught up in the Earth's magnetic field and only produce this effect over the magnetic poles.

Large solid lumps of rock that enter the Earth's atmosphere from space, the meteorites, experience great difficulty in passing through. The frictional forces that are set up by the atmosphere as the meteorites hit it at their tremendous speeds cause them to burn up, particularly in the denser regions below about 160 km (100 miles). Those that are large enough to penetrate to the Earth's surface without being totally consumed are usually broken into fragments and land as a meteor shower.

The Origins

The origin and history of the Earth's atmosphere is bound up with that of the oceans and of the Earth itself. As the Earth solidified 4,600 million years ago the lighter elements stayed on the outside while the heavier ones formed solids at the centre. The light substances that were formed by this process included hydrogen, methane and ammonia and the Earth's first atmosphere was composed largely of these. Such an atmosphere is to be found today on the larger planets such as Jupiter and Saturn.

As time went by most of the original hydrogen, it being the lightest substance of all, leaked away into space. Great volumes of gas were given off by the cooling rocks as they underwent complex chemical and geological changes. These gases included water vapour, most of which subsequently condensed to form the oceans, nitrogen, sulphur dioxide and carbon dioxide. The first plants that were able to photosynthesize and produce oxygen from carbon dioxide appeared about 3,500 million years ago and ever since then there has been an appreciable amount of oxygen in the atmosphere and this has been the most important factor in the evolution of life on our planet.

height in kilometres

temperature in °C

pressure in millibars

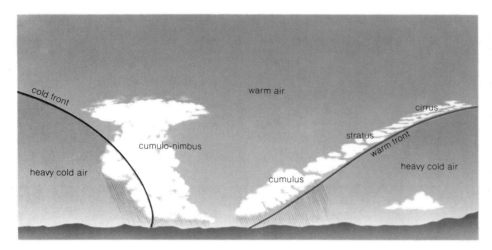

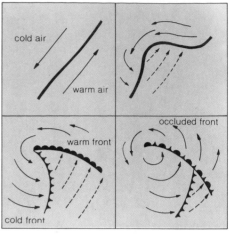

Climate and Weather

The lower reaches of the atmosphere are in a constant state of turmoil as we are all well aware through our everyday experience of the variability of the winds, rain and sunshine. This turmoil is brought about by the influence of the Sun's heat as it warms up certain parts of the Earth's surface and the atmosphere immediately above them. This influences the transportation of moisture from one area to another and hence the global distribution of the climatic belts.

A distinction must be made between climate and weather. As a broad rule climate is what is expected at a particular place while weather is the day to day variation from this expected norm. The climate is determined by studying the weather conditions over a large number of decades and working out a mean from this.

Wind and Air Circulation

The most significant factor in determining the climate is the wind and the air circulation. The Sun's rays exert the greatest influence on the tropical areas. The warmth of the land causes the air above it to rise and spread out in the cooler layers. Once this air has cooled again it descends to the Earth's surface usually at about the latitudes of 30° north and 30° south.

These air masses, as they come down, are very dry and so the great desert belts of the world are found at these latitudes. The air pressure here is usually relatively high and from

these regions the prevailing winds blow outwards, back towards the low pressure areas at the equator. These winds blow from the north east and from the south west and are known as the Trade Winds from their importance in commerce in the days of sailing ships.

From the high pressure areas in the mid latitudes winds are also pushed out towards the north and south resulting in south-westerly warm winds in the northern hemisphere and north-westerly warm winds in the southern. (Winds are always named after the direction from which they blow.)

At the poles the lack of sunshine produces areas of high pressure that cause cold winds to move outwards towards more temperate regions, from the north east in the northern hemisphere and from the south east in the southern.

In this whole global circulatory system the winds do not move directly

The frontal system is caused by the characteristic movement of the boundaries between warm and cold air masses.

Above *Tropical rain forest, such as this in Zaire, is found in hot areas where wet winds blow constantly.*

Below *Deserts like the Sahara, are found where the prevailing winds have lost all their moisture, either because of the distance travelled or because it has already fallen as rain.*

66

northwards and southwards from the areas of high pressure and descending air masses. This is due to the Coriolis effect that deflects the winds, and in fact any north or south travelling object, to one side because of the rotation of the Earth. The actual speed at which the surface of the Earth travels at the equator is greater than that nearer the poles, since the crust here is further from the Earth's axis but still has to get all the way round in 24 hours. Hence anything setting off from the equator to go north or south has already received a kick in the direction in which the Earth is rotating and finds itself going off course as it moves into the slower latitudes. It is of crucial importance in setting the correct trajectory for missiles.

The boundary between the north-easterly polar winds and the south-westerly temperate winds in the northern hemisphere is of particular importance. The boundary is ill defined and can be anywhere in a broad band covering North America, Europe and northern Asia. This is the reason for the very variable weather conditons experienced in these regions. The cold winds in the north and the warm winds in the south slide by one another in different directions. Eventually the friction between them causes them to spiral around one another like water swirling down a plug hole. When this happens a tongue of warm air becomes trapped within the cold mass and as this tongue advances towards the north east its boundaries bring unsettled weather and rain.

The warm air in this tongue is lighter than the cold and so it tends to spread out over the colder masses, lifting with it the rain clouds that it carries. These clouds condense as rain as they rise due to the changes in pressure and temperature encountered. Eventually all the warmer air is lifted clear of the ground and the frontal system, as it is called, is dissipated. The process then starts all over again.

Rain

Air circulation is the major influence on climate but moisture is another. Winds that pass over sea areas are moist and bring rain to any land that

they meet. Winds off continental areas are dry. When a moist wind reaches a mountainous coastline the clouds it carries are forced to rise, like those in the frontal system. This gives wet climates to coastal hilly areas facing the wind. By the time the mountains are crossed all the moisture has dropped and so a 'rain shadow' forms producing an arid climate in lands to the lee of the mountains. The arid plains of Patagonia are an example, being in the lee of the Andes and sheltered from the prevailing north-westerly winds.

The oceans themselves form a gigantic heat trap, absorbing heat slowly from the Sun and dissipating it again slowly in cooler times. Hence areas close to the sea tend to be buffered against extremes of temperature.

The climatic pattern of the world is thus determined by the overall circulation of the atmosphere, the distribution of the land and sea areas and the topography of the continents.

Above *Cirrus clouds* (top left) are formed from ice and found at great heights heralding the approach of a front. *Stratus clouds* (top right) are lower and indicate that a front is close. *Cumulus* (bottom) lie where the front touches the ground.

Below *Windward sides of mountain ranges, as in Nepal, have heavy rain.*

THE LIVING WORLD

Basic Forms of Life
Simple Organisms

All living organisms are composed of collections of chemicals. However, they have one important additional characteristic; they are able to make copies of themselves. It is this ability to reproduce, that distinguishes living organisms from non-living chemical collections. The smallest living organisms have little more structure to them than some of the components for reproduction.

Viruses

These are extremely small, being smaller than one tenthousandth of a millimetre in size and not visible with the light microscope. Their construction is very simple, but they must not be thought of as simple in the same way that a primitive thing is more simple than an advanced one. Viruses are not thought to be similar to the earliest forms of life. Instead, they are considered very specialized because they can only live inside other cells; viruses are a sort of parasite of cells.

Viruses can be variable in shape, rounded, rod-like or in some a geometrical figure such as a hexagon. They consist of an envelope made of protein molecules; inside the envelope are nucleic acid molecules. Nucleic acids are very specialized molecules which all living organisms have. These molecules are long and carry in coded form details of how the organism is constructed. The organism's 'blue-print' is a nucleic acid called deoxyribonucleic acid or DNA for short. Another nucleic acid, called ribonucleic acid or RNA, translates the DNA codes and carries

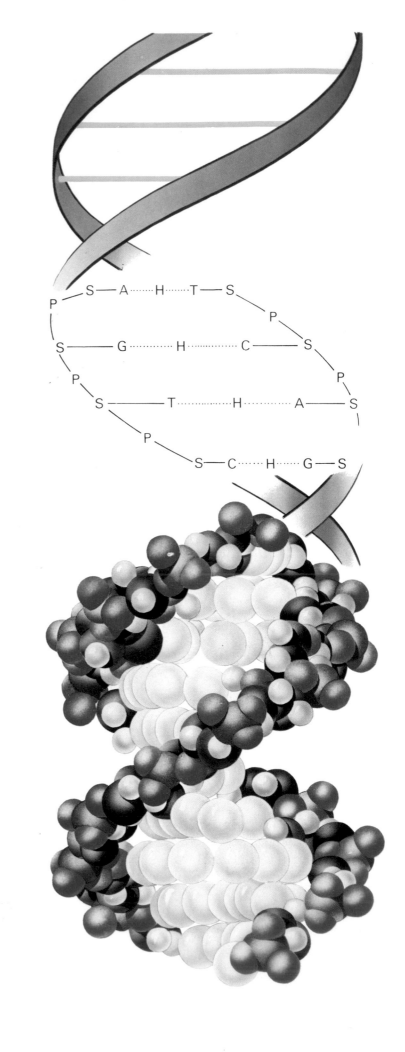

C

H

O

P

Base pairs

Deoxyribo nucleic acid—consists of two strands of molecules connected along their length forming a double helix. The strands are made of several different types of molecules, the most important of which are the bases, two pyrimidines—thymine (T) and cytosine (C)—and two purines— adenine (A) and guanine (G).

In cell division, the DNA molecule unravels leaving the bases unpaired. Unattached bases in the cell protoplasm are attracted to the unpaired bases and so two new DNA molecules are formed. The two DNA molecules are identical.

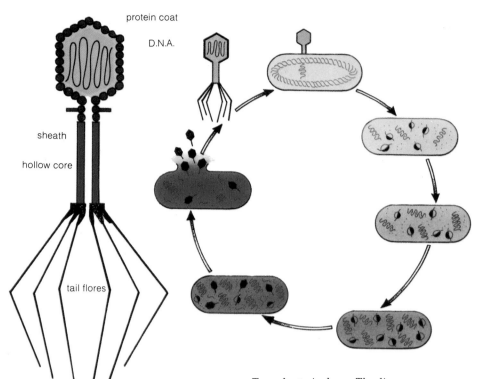

protein coat

D.N.A.

sheath

hollow core

tail flores

T_4—a bacteriophage. The diagram shows the way in which a bacterium is invaded. Bacteriophage DNA is injected into the bacterium where it reorganizes the bacterial DNA to make replica bacteriophages. The bacterial wall then bursts to liberate the newly formed bacteriophages.

the information to structures in the cell which manufacture the cell parts described by the DNA.

Viruses have to live in other cells because they are rather like builders with building plans but no materials. By knocking down other houses they can use the bricks to make houses of their own design. Viruses enter cells and use the DNA instructions to destroy the cell structure and make virus particles instead.

Viruses cause many diseases, both in plants and animals. In man, for example, they cause poliomyelitis, mumps, measles and smallpox.

Bacteriophages

The special viruses which attack bacteria rather than cells are known as bacteriophages. They may be very complex in shape. One bacteriophage which is called T_4 is rather like a hypodermic needle with a bulb on the end. The bulbous part is a protein envelope containing the DNA and RNA molecules. The tail makes a hole in the wall of the bacterium and injects the DNA and RNA molecules. These molecules are then used to destroy the bacterium and create a large number of new bacteriophages.

Bacteria

These are the simplest of the free living organisms. They are very variable in size and shape. Round forms are called cocci and may be as small as eight tenthousandths of a millimetre. Rod-shaped bacteria are called bacilli and corkscrew-shaped ones, spirilla. These may be eight thousandths of a millimetre in length and are easily seen with the light microscope. Some bacteria have long threads, or flagella, which assist the bacteria to move in liquids.

Bacteria are well known for causing a variety of diseases in man, animals and plants. Scarlet fever, pneumonia, whooping cough, diphtheria, tetanus and boils are all caused by bacteria. However, some bacteria also have an extremely important role to play in the circulation of materials in the environment. Bacteria are active in the decomposition of dead organic

The three photographs show spirilla (top), bacilli (centre) and cocci (bottom). Below, the drawing shows some of the structure of a flagellate bacterium, particularly the absence of a nucleus, the thick coat and the flagellum for locomotion.

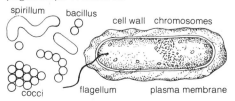

spirillum   bacillus

cocci   flagellum   cell wall   chromosomes   plasma membrane

material. In this process complex molecules are broken down into simpler ones which are absorbed by the roots of plants and used by the plants to build new tissue.

Proteins, used in plant growth, contain nitrogen but plants cannot directly use the biggest nitrogen source, the atmosphere. Leguminous plants, such as peas, beans and clover have nodules on their roots containing bacteria which convert atmospheric nitrogen into compounds which the plant can use.

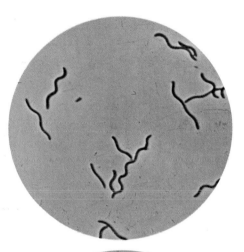

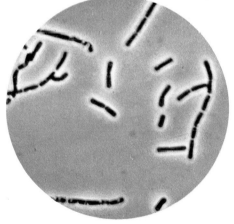

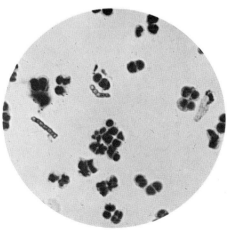

71

The Cell

With the exception of viruses, bacteriophages and bacteria, all living organisms are composed of one or more cells. Cells are highly variable in shape and function, but are all constructed in essentially the same way.

Nucleus

This is the controlling region of the cell. It contains the genetic information of the cell as DNA molecules and also RNA molecules to interpret and transmit instructions to the other cell components. When a cell is about to divide, the long DNA molecules shorten and become fatter. They are then visible with the light microscope and are called chromosomes. At other times the chromosomes are not visible. One or several nucleoli may also be seen as small rounded bodies. These contain RNA molecules.

Mitochondria

These are the powerhouses of the cell. They are complex membranous structures in which energy-containing molecules, such as carbohydrates, are broken down. This breakdown releases energy which is then converted into a form which is usable by the cell. Related to mitochondria are chloroplasts, found in plant cells. Chloroplasts contain chlorophyll which is a molecule capable of trapping light energy. This trapped energy is then available for the cell's use.

Membranes

There are several different types of membrane in the cell. The nucleus is surrounded by a porous nuclear membrane allowing communication between the nucleus contents and the rest of the cell contents. Around the outside of the cell there is a complex two-layered cell membrane. This is an important part of the cell as it regulates what enters and what leaves the cell. It is selectively permeable to materials. The golgi complex is thought to be concerned with the cell's ability to make fatty materials and the endoplasmic reticulum is the framework on which a number of important reactions, including protein manufacture, take place.

Cytoplasm

This slightly jelly-like material forms the bulk of the cell and is held together by the cell membrane. It contains, apart from the structures already mentioned, several different particles or granules. Some of these are for storage, such as starch granules, whilst others are concerned with the manufacture of proteins. These protein formers are called ribosomes and they are often associated with the endoplasmic reticulum. In plant cells, the cytoplasm usually contains a large liquid region called a vacuole, one of whose functions is to act as a water reserve.

Cell Division

Cells are capable of reproducing themselves. They divide into two identical daughter cells which then grow to the size of the original parent cell. This process of cell division is called mitosis. During mitosis, the DNA molecules, which contain the genetic information for the cell, gradually unravel and in doing so create two new DNA strands identical with each other and with the original. This shows up under the light microscope as a breakdown in the nuclear membrane and a lengthwise splitting of the chromosomes.

A generalized animal cell, showing the basic structure. Plant cells are essentially similar.

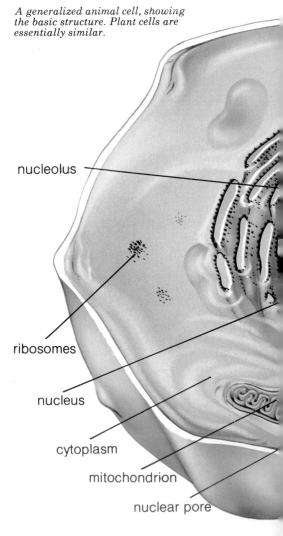

nucleolus

ribosomes

nucleus

cytoplasm

mitochondrion

nuclear pore

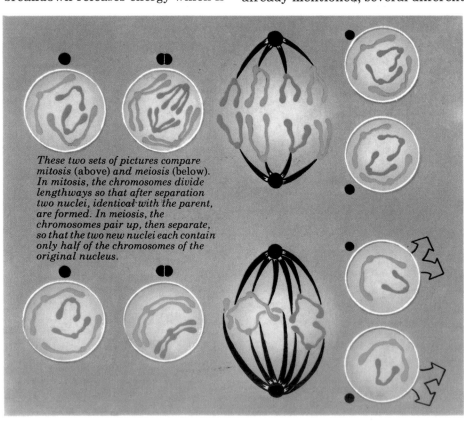

These two sets of pictures compare mitosis (above) and meiosis (below). In mitosis, the chromosomes divide lengthways so that after separation two nuclei, identical with the parent, are formed. In meiosis, the chromosomes pair up, then separate, so that the two new nuclei each contain only half of the chromosomes of the original nucleus.

The two chromosome halves separate and go to opposite ends of the cell. The cell membrane then grows across the cell to divide the cytoplasm into two and a nuclear membrane forms round each group of chromosomes. In this way, two new cells, each half the size of the parent cell are formed, each containing a new, usually identical, nucleus.

Although often very different in size, shape and function, cells are basically similar.

Top row—left to right—Animal cells. The elongate nerve cell has fine extensions along which nerve impulses pass to other cells. Muscle cells are elongate and capable of contraction. Bone cells lie squeezed into narrow spaces in the bone structure. Epithelial cells line the internal structures of animals.

Bottom row—left to right—Plant cells. Flattened epidermal cells from the outer layer of all plant structures. Phloem cells, identified by their sieve elements, transport nutrients, while xylem vessels are associated with water transport and wood development.

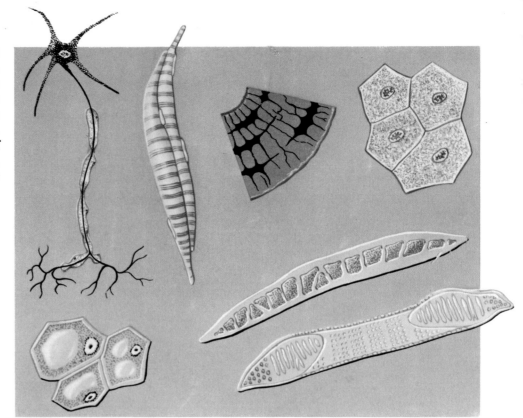

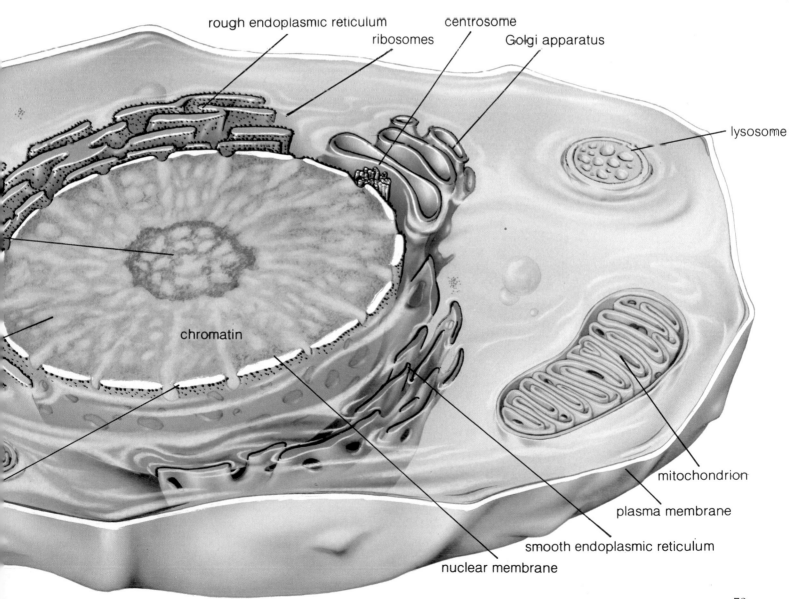

rough endoplasmic reticulum

ribosomes

centrosome

Golgi apparatus

lysosome

chromatin

mitochondrion

plasma membrane

smooth endoplasmic reticulum

nuclear membrane

Evolution
The Beginnings of Life on Earth

For about 1,000 million years, the Earth had no life on it. The atmosphere consisted of a variety of gases including methane, ammonia and carbon dioxide. During this long period, as the Earth cooled down, there were violent thunderstorms and a great deal of heat and gas escaped from volcanoes. It was in this environment that complex molecules and later the earliest forms of life are thought to have formed.

Some evidence of how life may have begun has come from the experiments of the American Stanley Miller. He continuously boiled water in an atmosphere of methane and ammonia whilst passing a spark through the steam and gas mixture. He found a range of compounds called amino acids dissolved in the condensed steam. Since amino acids are the basic units of proteins, it is thought that groups of these compounds came together to form simple cells—in the form of a fatty film enclosing proteins and DNA molecules. These simple cells would need an energy source and it is thought that they obtained their requirements from the soup of compounds which were not organized into cells.

The big breakthrough came when some of these cells developed the molecule chlorophyll which can use the energy of solar radiation to create complex molecules from simple ones. This is the technique used by all green plants today. As a by-product of these reactions involving chlorophyll, oxygen is formed and so, gradually, as the use of chlorophyll increased so too did the oxygen in the atmosphere. Other cells developed methods of using the oxygen in reactions which break down complex molecules to simple ones and in the process release usable energy. So with the development of these two important processes, using the Sun's energy to manufacture energy-rich complex molecules and using oxygen to release the energy contained in complex molecules, the

Time sequence panorama of ancient marine life. This picture shows the development of marine life during the 200 million years from the Cambrian to the Silurian periods.

On the left, the picture depicts a typical marine scene in the Cambrian which started 600 million years ago. There were already at this time several animal groups which are still found today, such as jellyfish, tubular sponges, bivalve molluscs and sea lilies or crinoids. Throughout the

entire period depicted, the most common arthropod was the trilobite. These large animals, vaguely reminiscent of woodlice, became extinct about 300 million years ago but because of their hard exoskeleton there are many well preserved fossils in the rocks.

The central section of the picture shows some of the marine life of the Ordovician period which started about 500 million years ago. During this time other types of mollusc

became common, in particular, the cephalopods. These swimming molluscs are related to the modern day squid and octopus but they still maintained an external shell which was either straight or curled. Other animals present include the corals and the shelled brachiopods looking like flattened molluscs. In the background, the plants are represented by extensive beds of seaweeds.

In the latter part of the Ordovician and in the beginning of the Silurian period (right-hand section) about 440 million years ago, the first fish appeared. The fish shown is Jamoytius which had a curious tail and long lateral fins. The large water scorpion, a eurypterid, is one of the largest artropods ever. They were found during the same periods as the trilobites.

stage is set for the evolution of the plant and animal kingdoms.

Our knowledge of prehistoric life comes from fossil remains. These are preserved bones or impressions of animals and plants in rocks. The age of fossils can be deduced by examining the layering of the surrounding rocks and also by using radioactive dating methods. The oldest fossils known come from rocks in South Africa. They represent different types of bacteria and simple algae and have been dated at about 3,100 million years old. Similar fossils have been found in Canadian rocks about 2,000 million years old. These fossils are, of course, microscopic and so it is not surprising that records of these early forms are scarce. More complex algae have been found in Australian rocks 1,600 and 1,000 million years old.

The oldest fossil animals are also from Australia and have been dated at about 700 million years old but these are already quite advanced and so it is likely that animal origins are quite a bit older.

Development of Life in the Sea

Life started in the sea with the formation of the organic soup from which simple cells are thought to have formed. About 600 million years ago, at the beginning of the prehistoric period called the Cambrian, there were considerable climatic changes on the Earth and these seem to have stimulated the development of a great range of aquatic animals. Particularly well preserved in Cambrian rocks are early shrimp-like crustaceans and trilobites.

By 500 million years ago there were well-developed coral reefs and a great range of different invertebrate types. The first vertebrate fossils come from this, the Ordovician period. These early fish fossils are also found occasionally in the Silurian period (440–395 million years ago) but only become really abundant in the next, the Devonian period (395–345 million years ago). The earliest fish had suctorial mouths without functional jaws. Our modern-day lampreys and hagfish derive from these early forms.

The first jawed fish often looked very ferocious with large armoured

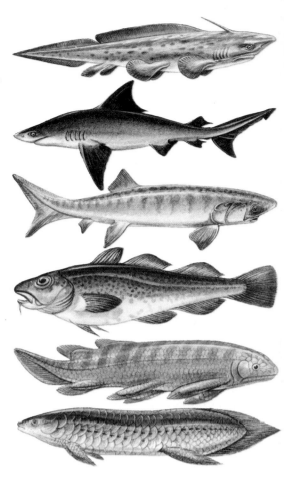

Each pair of fish, one prehistoric and one present day, typifies one of the three main fish groups. The top two, the prehistoric Pleuracanthus and a modern shark, Carcharhinus, are cartilaginous. The centre pair, the prehistoric Chondrosteus and the cod, Gadus, have bony skeletons. The bottom pair, the prehistoric Dipterus and Neoceratodus from Australia are both lung fishes and belong to the lobefins.

heads and wide, sharp, beak-like jaws. From these primitive fish there developed the three main fish types which are recognizable today. The first type included the sharks and the rays which have a skeleton of cartilage rather than bone. Bony fish were the second type, which comprise the majority of present-day fish, and the third group was made up of those fish with their fins on lobes. Present-day relatives of these lobefins are the lungfish and the coelocanth (until 1938 thought to be extinct). The lobe-fins are especially interesting because they are thought to be close to the stock from which the terrestrial animals, amphibians, reptiles and mammals have developed.

75

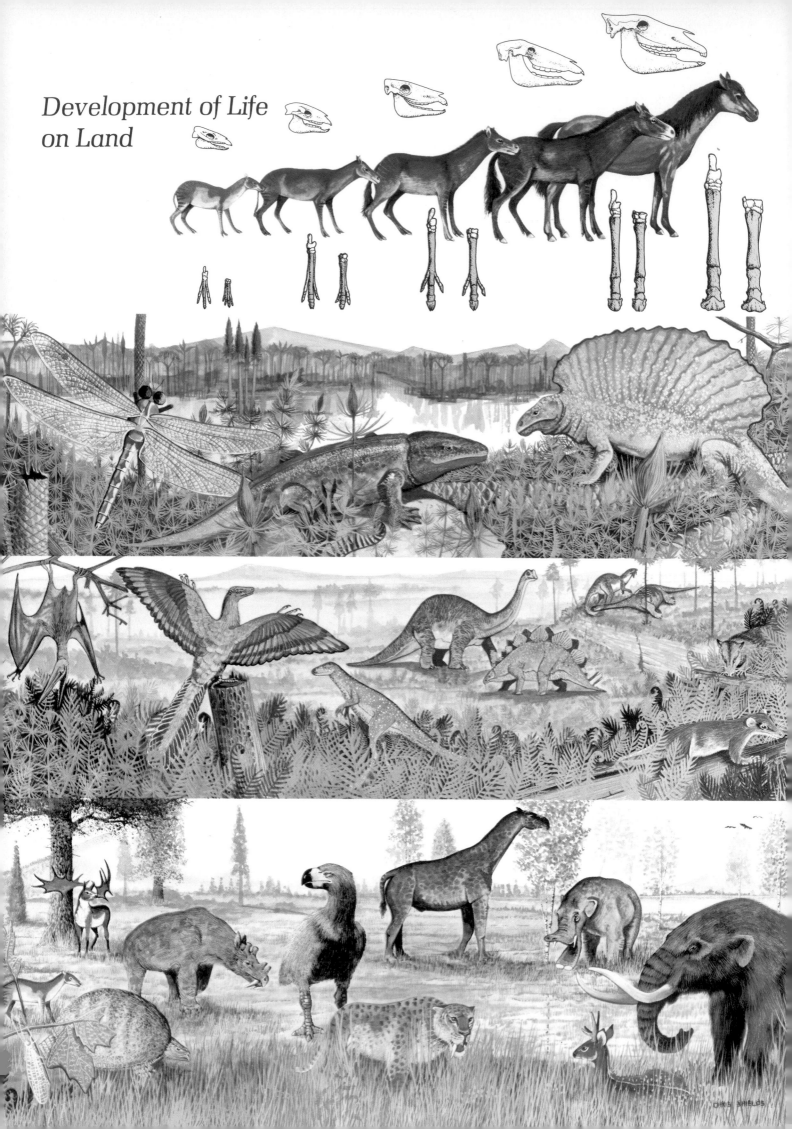

Development of Life
on Land

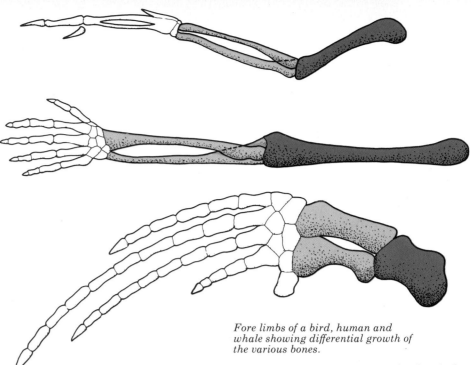

Several major changes in the aquatic animals and plants were needed for them to colonize land successfully. Without the buoyancy of water, the skeletal structures of both plants and animals had to take on the additional role of supporting weight. In the case of animals the lobe-like structures of the lobe-fins extended and strengthened to provide legs.

Another important need was to be able to conserve water. For plants this involved the development of a waxy cuticle and tubes to transport water from their roots to their upper parts. The waxy coverings of insects and hard horny skins of vertebrates also reduced water loss. Respiratory structures had to change. Oxygen enters the body only by dissolving first in the liquid of a moist surface. The large exposed gill surfaces of aquatic forms would dry out too easily out of water. A major step therefore was the development of an internal respiratory system, the lungs of vertebrates and the tracheae of insects. Most other terrestrial animals still have moist exposed surfaces and are therefore restricted to damp habitats.

A final problem concerned reproduction. In plants methods had to evolve so that male and female gametes could meet in the relative absence of water. Pollen is one result of such evolution. For animals, the male sperm swim to the egg. The most successful terrestrial groups have internal fertilization.

It is obvious that plants must have invaded the land before animals thus providing animals with both food and shelter. The first land plants were simple, rod shaped and without

Fore limbs of a bird, human and whale showing differential growth of the various bones.

leaves. Fossils of these early land plants are first found in Silurian rocks about 400 million years old.

Invertebrates were the first animals to invade the land and were very much like present-day forms. Millipedes together with spiders and scorpions were the first and became quite common in the Carboniferous period (345–280 million years ago). At this time part of the land was covered with luxuriant forests which today are preserved as coal measures. Insects also first appeared in this period.

The Carboniferous period saw the development of the amphibians—the first terrestrial vertebrates. They were lizard-like, similar to present-day salamanders, and had functional legs. Like the modern-day amphibians, such as frogs, toads, newts and salamanders, these early terrestrial vertebrates were tied to the water for reproduction and a suitable habitat in which the young could develop.

Reptiles also arose early in the Carboniferous period. They were not tied to water, having internal fertilization and eggs in which the young developed. There followed a great era of reptiles from about 300 million years ago through the Permian, Triassic, Jurassic and into the Cretaceous period about 100 million years ago. During this long period dinosaurs dominated the land and many species reinvaded the sea. This was a time of great evolutionary experimentation and a whole host of bizarre fossils mark its progress.

Two developments in particular led to the birds and the mammals.

It is in Jurassic rocks, about 200 million years old, that the first fossils of flying reptiles (pterosaurs) are found. Insects had colonized the air some 100 million years previously and although the first flying vertebrates probably did little more than glide they gained the advantages of being able to chase the flying insects and of escaping from predatory land dinosaurs. Early pterosaurs had bat-like wings supported by a series of long finger bones. Later, with the change of the reptilian scales to feathers, these flying reptiles evolved to become the ancestors of modern-day birds.

Towards the end of the Cretaceous period almost all the reptiles vanished. Why this happened is still unknown. One suggestion is that the weather became colder and the large reptiles became too cool to operate efficiently. The insulating properties of the feathers of the bird forms gave them an immediate advantage and so too did the fur of the early mammals. Up until this time mammals, which first appeared with the flying reptiles in the Jurassic period, had been overshadowed by the reptiles. With the extinction of the majority of the reptiles the mammals diversified and replaced them. Most of the present-day mammals evolved about 40 million years ago but it was only about 2 million years ago that man-like apes appeared. Compared to the great age of the reptiles man has a very brief history.

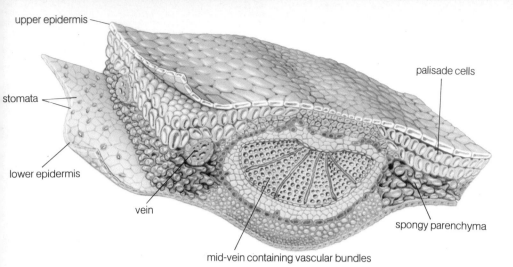

upper epidermis

palisade cells

stomata

lower epidermis

vein

spongy parenchyma

mid-vein containing vascular bundles

The Plant Kingdom
How Plants Function

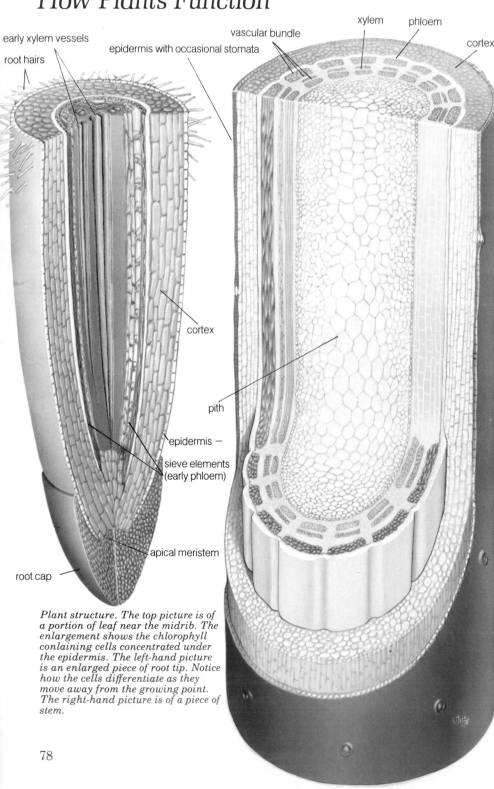

early xylem vessels

root hairs

epidermis with occasional stomata

vascular bundle

xylem   phloem

cortex

cortex

pith

epidermis —

sieve elements
(early phloem)

apical meristem

root cap

*Plant structure. The top picture is of
a portion of leaf near the midrib. The
enlargement shows the chlorophyll
containing cells concentrated under
the epidermis. The left-hand picture
is an enlarged piece of root tip. Notice
how the cells differentiate as they
move away from the growing point.
The right-hand picture is of a piece of
stem.*

Plants are highly variable. A large number of them are small, structurally fairly simple aquatic forms which are wafted about in the surface waters of rivers, lakes and seas as components of the plankton. Larger, more complex aquatic forms tend to be anchored to the substrate with roots or holdfasts. These plants contain strong but flexible elements which enable the plant to bend with the water currents without breaking.

The terrestrial environment poses a support problem for all plants which are more complex than the forms which coat rocks or the soil. Aquatic plants are virtually without weight in water and therefore can grow to a large size without a very strong supporting structure. Plants growing on land do not have the density of water to support them and so they have to produce rigid or semi-rigid structures, both to hold up the plant and to enable it to resist wind action. These supporting structures are sometimes very extensive as is seen in trees, where heights above 60 m (200 ft) are not uncommon. For a tree to reach such massive proportions takes time, often a great deal of time. One of the world's largest trees, the giant redwood (*Sequoia gigantea*) with a height of almost 120 m (400 ft), has been recorded with an age of between 4,000 and 5,000 years old. The bristlecone pine in the Sierra Nevada mountains in the United States also reaches this age. The English oak is a youngster in comparison, living perhaps only 500 years.

The Importance of Water
Water has two major roles to play. If cells lose water, they become limp and floppy. They have lost their rigidity, or turgor, which comes from being fully charged with water. Plants with a water deficit will wilt due to the loss of support offered by turgid cells. Water is also a solvent and as such is a useful medium for transporting materials from one part of the plant to another. When a tall tree is considered, the idea of a force which moves water from the roots to the crown is awe-inspiring. There is no 'plant heart' to work in the same way that an animal's heart circulates blood. Instead, some or all of the

following mechanisms are thought to be important.

Plant leaves are covered with a layer of cells called the epidermis. This layer, particularly on the underside of leaves, is punctuated by myriads of tiny pores. Each pore is surrounded by two guard cells which control the pore size. The pore with its guard cells is called a stoma. Both gases and water vapour can enter or leave the leaf via the stomata. As water vapour passes through the stomata it exerts a suction on water in other parts of the plant, particularly the roots. Water has a high cohesion, that is, the water molecules tend to stick together, and so it is drawn up narrow tubes in the plant stem called xylem elements. Water is thus carried up to the leaves where it replaces that lost by evaporation, and in doing so moves the materials dissolved in it to the leaves. This process of evaporation controlled by the stomata and the transport of materials in the plant is called transpiration.

If the stem is cut on some well-rooted, well-watered plants, sap will ooze from the rooted part for some time. This movement of water, which can generate a respectable pressure, seems to be an active process produced by root cells and may be of use in the spring when the leaves of plants are not expanded.

These two mechanisms, transpiration and root pressure, together with capillarity, move water through the tree on the large scale. At the cellular level, water passes from cell to cell across the cell membrane by a process called osmosis.

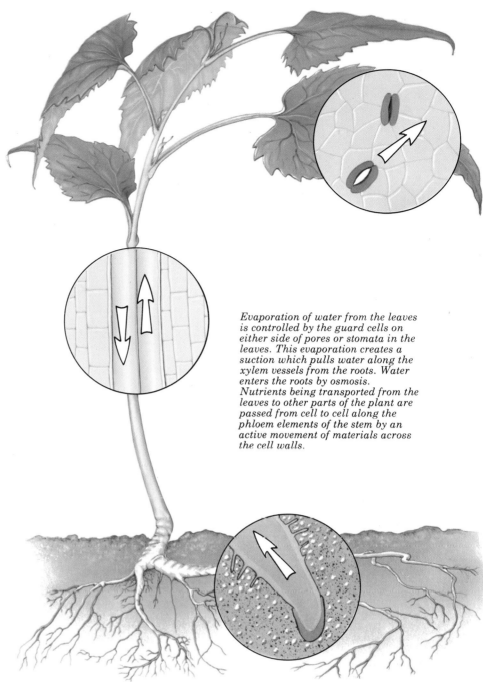

Evaporation of water from the leaves is controlled by the guard cells on either side of pores or stomata in the leaves. This evaporation creates a suction which pulls water along the xylem vessels from the roots. Water enters the roots by osmosis. Nutrients being transported from the leaves to other parts of the plant are passed from cell to cell along the phloem elements of the stem by an active movement of materials across the cell walls.

This is the process whereby water passes across a membrane which is porous to water but not to larger molecules such as sugars. When a situation occurs where two solutions, one weaker than the other, are separated by a semi-permeable membrane then water molecules will pass through the membrane from the weaker to the stronger solution. As a cell loses water, perhaps by evaporation, its cell sap becomes more concentrated. Water enters the cell from adjacent cells until all the cells are at the same concentration. Thus, a chain of cells donating and receiving water can be envisaged joining the stomata to the xylem vessels. Water also passes through the plant via the intercellular spaces.

Marine algae, commonly called seaweeds, often grow to a considerable size. They are able to do this because of the support provided by the water. They are highly flexible and move with water currents.

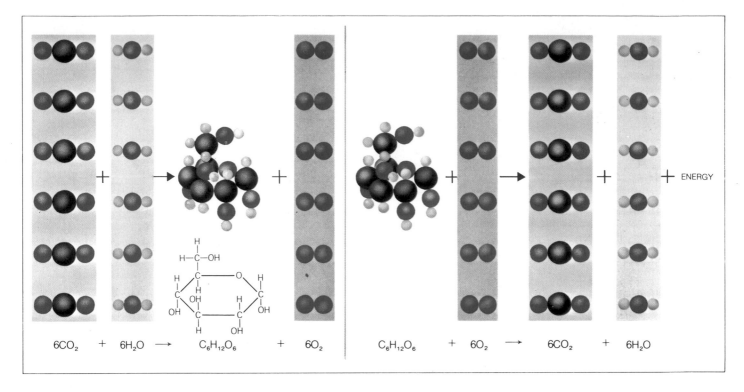

$$6CO_2 + 6H_2O \longrightarrow C_6H_{12}O_6 + 6O_2 \qquad C_6H_{12}O_6 + 6O_2 \longrightarrow 6CO_2 + 6H_2O$$

How Plants Grow

Some plants such as fungi, many bacteria and others such as carnivorous plants can use the complex molecules in plant and animal tissues and convert these to molecules suitable for growth. Green plants, however, are able to use the simple molecules of carbon dioxide and water together with trace elements from the soil or water. The processes of building up and breaking down complex molecules, the general metabolic work of cells, is driven by energy which is stored as special molecular configurations.

Adenosine triphosphate (ATP) is one such molecule. Two of its phosphate molecules are attached by high energy links so that when these links are broken, energy is released and is available for use in the cell. The energy needed to create these high energy storage links is released through a process called respiration which is common to all cells and will be discussed later in the next section on animals.

Although green plants need energy for cellular activity and this is obtained via respiration, they uniquely are able to use solar energy and combine the simple low-energy-containing molecules of carbon dioxide and water to form high-energy

sugar molecules. This process is called photosynthesis. Plants hold a special place in the pattern of life maintenance on Earth because they trap far more energy from the Sun in photosynthesis than they need to use in respiration. This excess energy accumulates as plant growth and is available for fungi, some bacteria and, of course, animals.

Photosynthesis

This vital process is carried out in the chloroplasts of plant cells. The chloroplasts contain a number of special pigments, the most important of which are the chlorophylls. The chloroplasts contain many layers of protein sandwiched between layers of pigments. The pigments capture small packages of light energy and pass these to the protein layer. On the protein layers the captured energy is used to form high energy bonds such as those of adenosine triphosphate. The molecules containing the high energy bonds then pass from the 'sandwich' into the liquid part of the chloroplast where the energy is used to produce sugars from water and dissolved carbon dioxide. Although sugars are the main products of photosynthesis, other materials are also produced, including fats and oils.

The photosynthesis (left) and respiration (right) equations. In photosynthesis, water (H_2O) and carbon dioxide (CO_2) combine to give glucose and oxygen (O_2) in the presence of chlorophyll and light. In respiration, glucose is broken down.

Photosynthesis can only occur in the light. During the night plants rely on stores of energy for their respiratory needs. As light intensity increases, so the energy captured by photosynthesis also increases to the compensation level. This is the level

This Coleus has bent towards the light. Positive phototropism results from concentrations of the plant hormone auxin.

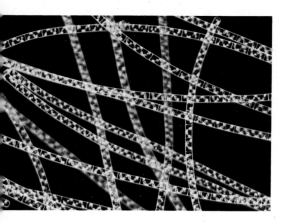

The spiral chloroplast can be seen in these chains of elongate cells.

at which the energy captured by photosynthesis exactly matches that required for respiration. During most of the daylight hours, the compensation level is exceeded and the extra energy stored as plant tissue.

The materials produced in the photosynthetic process are used in respiration and plant growth. This growth is not constant, but varies with both the time of year and with respect to the different plant structures. For instance, growth rate increases during the spring and early summer and at this time the major growth regions are the stems, leaves and, in some plants, the flowers. Later in the year, growth of these structures slows and the photosynthetic products are directed towards flower, seed and storage organ construction. We have seen how growth occurs at the cellular level— by cell division, and this occurs to many thousands of cells during the enlargement of a plant. Growth is normally restricted to specific parts

This picture shows what happens when a potted plant is laid on its side. The root bends towards gravity and the stem grows away from gravity. Differential concentrations of auxin on the two sides of the root and shoot cause these positive and negative geotropisms.

of the plant where cell division proceeds at the greatest rate. Two such areas are the regions just behind the tips of roots and shoots.

Plant growth is coordinated by plant growth substances, sometimes called plant hormones. The two most important of these are auxins and gibberellins. Gibberellins cause increased growth of the plant stem and also induce flowering. Auxins are produced by the terminal regions of shoots and roots and stimulate cell division. In bright light, auxin action on cells is inhibited. If a growing plant is illuminated on one side, cell division on that side will be slower than on the shaded side. This causes the plant to bend towards the light, a process called phototropism. If a plant is laid horizontally, the auxin

becomes more concentrated on the lower side of the shoot and root. The increased concentration on one side of the shoot increases cell growth on that side and the shoot bends upwards. This action is called negative geotropism, growth away from gravity. High concentrations of auxin in roots inhibit cell division so that the underside of the root grows more slowly than the topside, causing the root to bend downwards towards gravity (positive geotropism). Since auxins stimulate budding, they are found in rooting powders to initiate root buds.

The sundew (Drosera) *is a plant of boggy acidic soils. Photosynthesis supplies some of its energy requirements but it supplements this with insect food. The leaves are covered with sticky hairs which trap insects, fold up and digest them.*

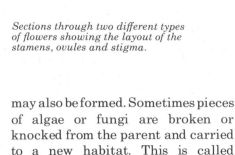

bract

ovary

ovule

style

filament

anther

ovary containing an ovule

stigma

corolla (petals)

stigma

receptacle

calyx

stem

How Plants Reproduce

Virtually all plants have two ways of reproducing—asexually and sexually, although it is usual that for any particular species one method predominates. Asexual reproduction produces individuals which are genetically identical to the parent whilst sexual reproduction serves to create individuals with new genetic combinations, part from the male and part from the female. These new genetic combinations may be more successful than either of the individual parents.

Asexual Reproduction

This is very common in the lower plants. Bacteria usually reproduce by fission—the dividing of one bacterium into two as in cell division. The yeasts use a similar technique but the new cells produced may remain attached to the parent cells as buds. Many algae and fungi produce asexual spores. These are carried by wind and water currents to new areas suitable for colonization. Spores of a different type, produced by sexual reproduction,

may also be formed. Sometimes pieces of algae or fungi are broken or knocked from the parent and carried to a new habitat. This is called fragmentation.

In higher plants there is a wide range of asexual methods of reproduction. One common method is the production of surface runners at the end of which new plants grow as in the strawberry and buttercup. A similar underground method involves rhizomes, as for the iris and grasses. The potato is a special form of runner which forms an underground storage organ—the tuber from which new potato plants develop. Many types of spring and summer flowers are grown from bulbs and corms. Bulbs, for example tulips, daffodils and lilies, are swollen basal buds whilst corms, for example gladioli and crocus, are swollen stems. There are a variety of other asexual methods which are used particularly by gardeners. These include grafting, leaf and stem cuttings and layering.

Sexual Reproduction

This involves the combination of genetic material from two parents. In normal cells there are pairs of identical chromosomes—pairs of DNA molecules with identical arrangements of bases. Such cells are called diploids. In mitosis each chromosome divides so that the new cells have the same number of pairs of chromosomes as the original cell. In sexual reproduction two cells, one from each parent, fuse to form a single cell. If this occurred with two ordinary cells the number of chromosomes in the new cell would be doubled. To prevent this chromosome increase, those cells which are involved in the sexual process, the gametes, undergo a special form of cell division called meiosis. In meiosis the number of chromosomes is halved producing haploids. When combination of two haploid gametes occurs then the result is a diploid cell with half its genetic information from each parent.

In the fungi and algae, sexual reproduction occurs when two different strains come together. In the higher plants there are either male and female plants or both male and female parts on the same plant. In flowering plants the male gametes are contained in the pollen, produced in small stalked structures called stamens and the female gamete or ovule is produced in an ovary. Pollen reaches a receptive structure on the ovary (called a stigma) either by being carried in the wind or by being carried on the bodies of insects such as bees. So that the pollen of the plant does not land on the stigma of that same plant, the male and female components of a flower usually mature at different times. Those plants which are wind pollinated tend to have small, drab green flowers. Insect pollinated plants are brightly coloured and have scents and nectar to increase their attractiveness to the insects.

When the ovule has been fertilized (that is, when the pollen nucleus with its chromosomes has entered and fused with the ovule nucleus to form a diploid cell) it then starts developing into the seed which contains the embryo plant. At the same time other parts of the flower, particularly the ovary, begin enlarging to form the fruit.

Fruits can be of two main types. Dry fruits are those which are dry and brittle when ripe. For example

in the legumes (peas, beans and vetches) the pods are the fruits and when they are ripe, they split open suddenly and fling out the seeds. Fleshy fruits are soft and usually sweet and flavoured. They can be of several forms: berries, for example, grapes, tomatoes, citrus fruits, cucumbers and melons; drupes or stone fruits, for example, cherries, peaches, apricots and olives; druplets are small drupes collected in clusters, for example, raspberries and blackberries; and pomes, for example, apples and pears.

The essential function of the fruit is to disperse the seed to a new habitat. The dry fruits throw the seed to disperse it whilst the fleshy fruits rely on animals to consume the fruit and the seed within. In these cases the seed is resistant to the digestive juices and is passed out, still viable, in the faeces of the animal.

Insect pollinated plants are brightly coloured and usually scented to attract insects which brush against the pollen and thus transport it to other flowers.

Many plants are wind pollinated. Here, pollen is liberated from the male flowers or catkins of a silver birch. It is carried in the wind to the feathery styles of the female flowers.

Asexual methods of reproduction in plants. From left to right—strawberry runners, iris rhizomes, tubers of potato, corm and bulb.

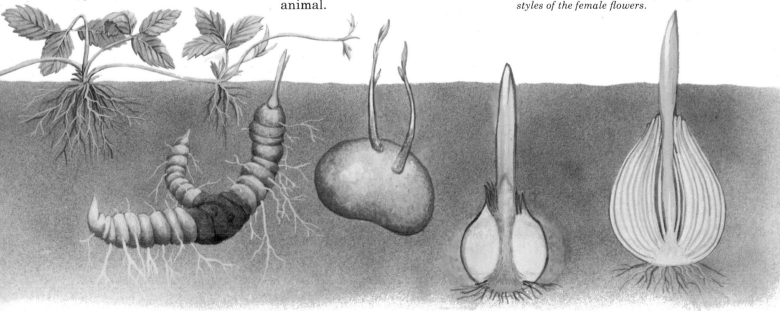

The Animal Kingdom
Animal Movement

Animals display a great diversity of shape and form. Over one million different animal species are known, a large proportion of which are insects. Some of the smallest animals live parasitically inside red blood cells whilst the largest animal, the blue whale, may reach 30 m (100 ft) long and weigh about 100 tonnes (100 tons). The size range in specific animal groups is also impressive: the smallest insect is about 0.2 mm long (1/100th in) whilst some stick insects can reach 60 cm (2 ft) in length. The smallest mammal, the Etruscan shrew from the northern coast of the Mediterranean, weighs between 1.5 and 2 gr (0.05–0.07 oz) and this is to be compared with the blue whale's weight.

Although there are a number of immobile animals, such as barnacles, sea anemones and mussels, most animals are mobile and have well-developed sensory structures to acquaint them with their surroundings. Often certain senses are developed to a greater degree than the rest. In hunting animals, spiders, dragonflies, predatory birds and carni-

The tetrapod pattern of alternate leg movements—hindleg moving with the opposite foreleg—is typical of all walking vertebrates.

In flight, the wings are stretched out on the downstroke and folded on the upstroke. The downstroke forces air downwards and backwards, providing lift and forward movement. Gaps at the wing-tips reduce turbulence.

vorous mammals, the eyes are large and arranged towards the front of the head giving binocular vision which is important in being able to judge distance. Other species have particularly acute senses of smell or hearing. If a sense is not needed, then the structures associated with that sense become reduced or even lost. Some animals live in caves where there is no light, so their eyes tend to be reduced or absent, as in the blind cave fish. Insects, shrimps and spiders living in caves have developed very long legs and antennae so that their fields of touch are increased to compensate for the loss of vision.

The actual method of movement employed by animals depends on the medium in which they live, water or land or in the air. It is usually easy to see which animals have changed from one medium to another by looking at how they move. For example the most successful aquatic form is that shown by the fish, but several other groups have recolonized the water although descended from ancestors which were terres-

Moles are adapted to life underground. Eyesight is poor but they have a keen sense of smell and enlarged forelimbs for digging.

trial. Newts, frogs, turtles, otters and seals all have functional legs, indicating their terrestrial ancestry. Another indication is the method of breathing. Fish, crustaceans, most molluscs and many other aquatic groups use gills to extract oxygen from the water. Animals whose ancestors were terrestrial breathe air. Only some aquatic insects have been able to adapt their terrestrial breathing mechanisms to 'gills' operating in water.

Swimming

This is the method used by animals to move in liquids, the sea, lakes and rivers and also in body fluids. In swimming, one large or a number of smaller structures create waves which push liquid away from the animal. Since the animal is not anchored, this movement causes it to move in the opposite direction. Small single-celled animals have small whip-like threads called flagella which propel them through liquids. Larger animals use a combination of muscle action and outgrowths or fins. For muscles to operate to produce wave-like movements, some stiffening of the body is needed otherwise muscular contraction would merely concertina the body. Stiffening in vertebrates is provided by the backbone and in crustaceans and insects by the tough exoskeleton. In soft-bodied animals, for example worms, a hydrostatic skeleton is used, where the body fluids are pressurized in the same way that car tyres are pumped up hard enough to support the vehicle's weight.

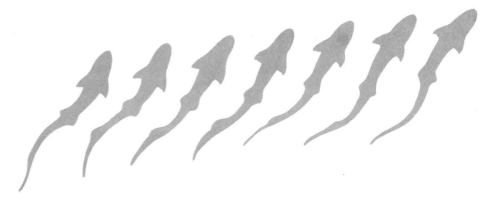

As a fish swims, waves pass backwards down the body. The side of the body and the tail push against the water propelling the fish forwards. This pattern is seen in most swimming animals.

Flight

Only three groups of animals, the bats, birds and insects are able to fly, although several others can glide. These groups have developed one or, in the case of insects, two pairs of wings. These wings not only provide lift but also directional movement. Hovering and even backward flight are sometimes possible.

Insect wings are made of two thin stiff sheets with veins sandwiched between them for support. Bats have skin wings supported by elongated 'hand' bones whilst birds have wings composed of feathers and only a small component of flesh and bone.

Walking and running

Both of these are terrestrial modes of locomotion. The basic principle here is that legs, numbering from 2 in man to over 100 in millipedes, both support and move the animal's body. There is a great variety of form in legs. Short legs give a strong slow locomotion whilst longer legs produce a faster moving animal. All vertebrate land animals are tetrapods, that is, they have four legs and these legs move alternately. Even in humans the basic tetrapod ancestry of alternate limb movements is seen in arm swinging. When the right leg is moved so the left arm swings and vice versa.

The hare has large mobile ears to warn it of possible danger. The ears also have another function. They are well supplied with blood and act as temperature regulators.

Savigny's Eagle Owl (Bubo b. ascalaphus) *shows several characteristics of predatory birds — large forward facing eyes for binocular vision and a strong hooked beak. Owls also have acute hearing which enables them to hunt at night.*

Feeding Methods

Animals have explored a great range of potential food materials, even things as bizarre as vinegar and tar. Different types of food require different handling techniques and the animal kingdom therefore displays a wide range of feeding methods and the type of diet can often be deduced by examining the mouth parts.

Biting and Chewing

This is one of the commonest feeding methods. It is used by most vertebrates although the amount of time spent chewing depends on the food. It is also a common method in crustaceans and insects. Biting mouth parts in invertebrates usually consist of two lateral structures with hardened edges. These are moved from side to side. Such mandibles may be extremely strong: insects have been recorded as being able to cut through tin, copper and silver. Mandibles in vertebrates operate vertically with usually only the lower mandible moving. In birds, tortoises and turtles, hardened beaks derived from the mandible bones are formed. In other vertebrates teeth are developed. The tooth structure varies with the type of food. Where tough plant material forms the whole or part of the diet the teeth at the front of the mouth are sharp and chisel-like for cutting whilst teeth towards the back of the mouth are flattened and used for grinding.

Where the diet is mainly meat, some or all of the teeth are pointed to assist in holding the prey. In mammals the canine teeth are well formed and there may be special carnassial teeth which work with a scissor action to cut meat from the bone. Reptiles and amphibians have

This female mosquito is taking a blood meal. The needle-like stylets can be seen penetrating the skin while the protective sheath is folded back. The abdomen is swelling up with blood. Females need a blood meal meal before they can lay eggs.

These two skulls, a dog (left) and a sheep (right) show major adaptations to feeding on meat and vegetation respectively. The dog has large canines for holding prey and overlapping carnassial teeth for cutting meat off bones. The sheep has large grinding molars to break down plant tissues. A further modification is the strong ridge on the dog skull to which the large jaw muscles are attached.

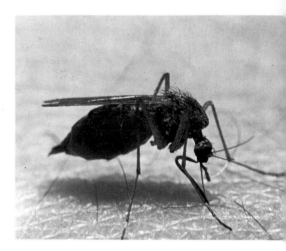

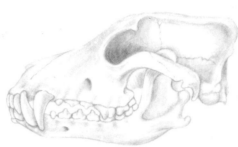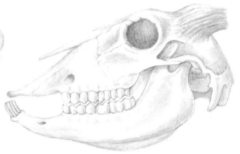

only conical teeth since they swallow their prey whole. Pointed modifications for gripping are also found in carnivorous birds; the hooks on eagles' beaks and the notches on the beak of the fish-eating merganser are examples. Invertebrate carnivore mandibles are also endowed more with spikes than grinding areas. Besides these basic types of feeding, there are a variety of other methods particularly found in the invertebrates.

Fluid Feeding

This is quite common in insects. The mouth parts are modified into long needle-like stylets which are used to pierce plant or animal tissues. These species also have a pump which is

then used to suck up the liquids. Aphids and mosquitoes are examples of fluid feeders. In the vertebrates fluids rarely form the sole food supply. The vampire bat, however, has sharp teeth which it uses to cut into the flesh. The blood which oozes from the wound is lapped up. Also, hummingbirds and sunbirds feed from flowers using their long beaks to reach the nectar.

Filter Feeding

Many aquatic sedentary animals such as certain molluscs, sponges and some worms and protozoa, filter their food. Here water is wafted over

This series of pictures shows the way in which the amoeba engulfs food particles. The pseudopods grow round the object and enclose it.

surfaces sticky with mucus. Minute hair-like structures called cilia beat together to create the water movement. Particles in the water get stuck to the mucus which is also wafted by cilia to the mouth. In a different way the whalebone or baleen whales are also filter feeders. These animals take in mouthfuls of water containing shrimps and plankton. The mouth is then shut and the water expelled through a sieve of baleen which replaces the teeth around the edge of the jaws.

These four birds' heads show the modifications of the beak for specialist feeding. The pelican feeds on fish, the sunbird on nectar in flowers, the eagle on meat and the duck grubs around for aquatic organisms.

The Digestive System

This is essentially similar throughout the animal kingdom. Only some lower invertebrates such as sponges, sea anemones and protozoa have different systems. Essentially, the digestive system or gut consists of a tube running from the mouth to the anus in which food is broken down, the useful components are extracted and the waste is expelled. From the mouth the first part of the gut, called the oesophagus, passes to an enlarged region called the crop or the stomach. The crop is usually only a storage region where food is retained

prior to processing. The stomach is also a storage structure but some digestion occurs there.

The next region of the gut, the small intestine, or midgut in invertebrates, is where digestion is completed and some absorption of useful materials takes place. Associated with this region of the gut are several organs (liver, pancreas) which produce enzymes. Enzymes are important complex compounds which help specific chemical reactions to proceed more easily. Pro-

tease enzymes help the breakdown of proteins, lipases the breakdown of fats.

In birds and many invertebrates where the food is not ground up in the mouth there is a grinding chamber or gizzard between the crop and the midgut. The gizzard of a bird contains swallowed stones and these rub against one another grinding the food.

The last part of the gut, the large intestine or hindgut, is the region where the remaining useful materials are absorbed. The waste is stored in the rectum and periodically voided via the anus.

These two pictures show the digestive systems of the cow (above) and man (below). Compare the very large multi-compartment stomach of the cow, in which micro-organisms assist in breaking down the food, with the much smaller stomach of man where only gastric juices are present.

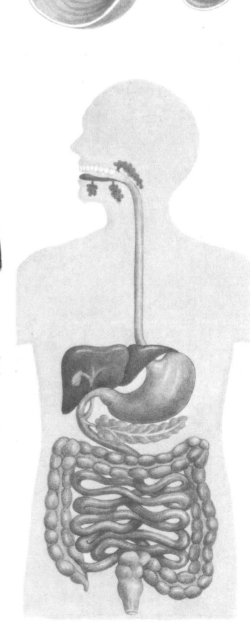

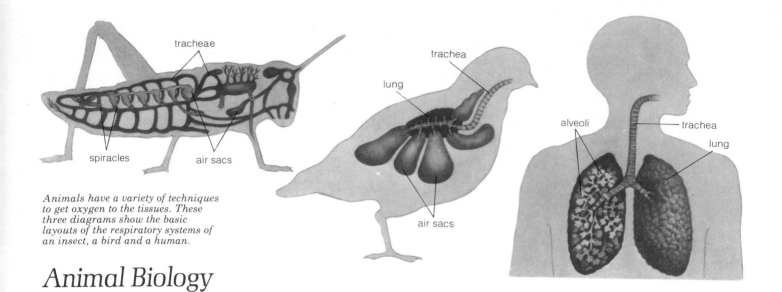

tracheae

spiracles

air sacs

trachea

lung

air sacs

alveoli

trachea

lung

Animals have a variety of techniques to get oxygen to the tissues. These three diagrams show the basic layouts of the respiratory systems of an insect, a bird and a human.

Animal Biology

Animals, like plants, need energy to drive their metabolic processes. As in plants, this involves the breakdown of energy-rich complex molecules. Oxygen is needed for this and carbon dioxide is one of the major waste products. Since animals are generally more active than plants they have a greater need for oxygen.

Diffusion of oxygen from the outside medium to all cells is possible in animals with only one or two cell layers such as protozoa and flatworms. Animals with a more complex body structure must have the oxygen transported from the area where it enters the body to where it is needed.

Oxygen enters the actual tissues of an animal's body by dissolving and then diffusing through the membrane and fluid components of its cells. In aquatic situations the oxygen is already dissolved in the water. In terrestrial animals the respiratory surface has to be moist to that the oxygen can dissolve in the liquid film before diffusing through the cell membranes.

Having diffused into the peripheral cells, the oxygen is then picked up by a carrier pigment, such as haemoglobin in the blood, to be transported to where it is needed. The blood system and its functions are discussed below. Aquatic animals have thin-walled gills containing blood as oxygen receptors. A flow of water is passed over the gills and oxygen diffuses into the bloodstream. Gills are found in fish, crustaceans, molluscs and some insects. Terres-

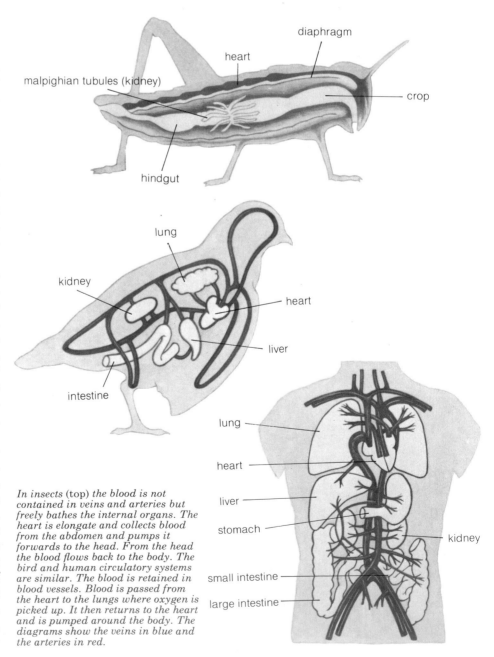

malpighian tubules (kidney)

heart

diaphragm

crop

hindgut

lung

kidney

heart

liver

intestine

lung

heart

liver

stomach

kidney

small intestine

large intestine

In insects (top) the blood is not contained in veins and arteries but freely bathes the internal organs. The heart is elongate and collects blood from the abdomen and pumps it forwards to the head. From the head the blood flows back to the body. The bird and human circulatory systems are similar. The blood is retained in blood vessels. Blood is passed from the heart to the lungs where oxygen is picked up. It then returns to the heart and is pumped around the body. The diagrams show the veins in blue and the arteries in red.

trial vertebrates have lungs. These are internal sacs which have a large moist surface for gaseous exchange. The lungs connect to the outside via the windpipe or trachea. The lung tissue is well supplied with blood vessels. Air is pumped in and out of the lungs by muscle action. In insects a complex series of branching tubes, called tracheae, carry air to all parts of the body and close enough to cells so that diffusion is possible.

Circulation

The blood of animals is usually circulated by one or several pumps or hearts. In most animals the blood is contained within blood vessels (veins, arteries and capillaries) but in the arthropods, such as insects and crustaceans the blood system is open. The organs of arthropods float in blood and the heart keeps the blood circulating by moving it from the posterior to the anterior regions of the body. Blood has many roles including transporting dissolved gases to and from cells and tissues, carrying molecules of digested food to storage organs or to areas where they are needed, protecting the animal by plugging wounds and destroying bacterial and viral infections and carrying waste products to the kidneys for disposal.

Excretion

When complex molecules are used for body-building or energy production, nitrogenous compounds are often left as waste products. These are removed by the kidneys which extract the waste products from the blood whilst retaining the useful components. The way in which nitrogenous compounds are removed varies according to the availability of water. Aquatic animals excrete nitrogen in the form of ammonia. This chemical is toxic and can only be used if it can be continuously diluted to non-toxic concentrations. Many animals, including the mammals and man, excrete nitrogen in the urine as urea. More energy is needed to create urea than ammonia but it is less toxic. When water is at a premium uric acid is used to remove excess nitrogen. This compound is insoluble and forms the white component of bird and reptile droppings.

Reproduction

With the exceptions of the protozoa, sponges and coelenterates, the animal kingdom only reproduces sexually. Male (sperm) and female (egg or ovum) gametes fuse together to form a cell which then repeatedly divides to produce, ultimately, an adult.

The amount of assistance given to the young is very variable. At one extreme, vast numbers of small eggs are laid which hatch into larvae at an early stage of development. These larvae then have to grow in hostile conditions where the rate of survival is low. Only a very few of the thousands of eggs laid actually reach adulthood. This reproductive strategy is common in fish, insects and amphibians. At the other extreme only one or a few young are produced at one time and these young are then cared for by the parents until they are able to look after themselves. This is the reproductive pattern seen in most mammals, the birds and sticklebacks.

Often individuals of the same species are found together in groups which may be loosely knit or highly organized. These social groups give additional protection to developing young as well as to the adults. Such groups are common in mammals and also in insects (bees, ants, wasps and termites) where the social structure is often complex and leads to distinct types of individuals such as workers, soldiers and queens, each of which has a specific role to play in the society.

In this picture of part of a bee colony, the queen in the middle is being attended by workers.

Aquatic mammals have terrestrial ancestors. Whales have to surface to breathe. This need to surface has made them very vulnerable to man.

This series of pictures shows the great similarity of early embryos in different vertebrate groups.

They are, from left to right, a fish, bird, cow and human.

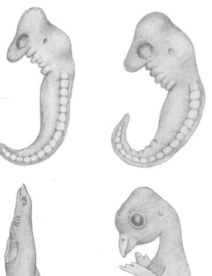
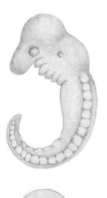

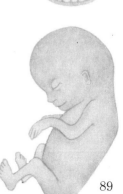

89

Classification
Plants

Prokaryotes

These are organisms without a well-defined nuclear membrane. Reproduction is only by simple division. There are two groups, the bacteria (mentioned earlier) and the blue-green algae. The blue-green algae form minute filamentous structures which are found on rock and plant surfaces.

Eukaryotes

These organisms all have a distinct nuclear membrane and reproduce either sexually or asexually. All the remaining plant groups and the animal kingdom are eukaryotes.

Thallophyta These are plants without roots, stems or leaves. Spores both sexual and asexual are produced.

Algae These are essentially aquatic although there are some terrestrial examples (e.g. *Pleurococcus* which forms the green coating on tree bark). There are a number of different types of algae which are named after the pigments they contain. For example the green algae (Chlorophyta) have chlorophylls, the brown algae (Phaeophyta) have fucoxanthins and the red algae (Rhodophyta) have phycoerythrins. These last two groups embrace most of the common large seashore algae. A large proportion of algae, however, are microscopic.

Fungi These have no chlorophyll at all and therefore have to feed on dead or living plant and animal tissue. They are important in the breakdown of litter. Typically, fungi have thread-like hyphae which grow throughout the substrate. Some species have large spore-producing structures (mushrooms and toadstools). Fungi are important in many branches of industry e.g. cheese production and penicillin manufacture.

The slime moulds are curious organisms, consisting of a mass of protoplasm with a number of nuclei within a membrane. This protoplasm mass, called a plasmodium, is able to flow or creep over the substrate.

Fungi are important in the decomposition of dead plant material. Most of their growth takes the form of threadlike hyphae but the spore-bearing structures are sometimes large and brightly coloured as in this sulphur polypore Grifola sulphurea.

In liverworts, the sexual structures are usually small and only develop into a stalked spore-bearing structure after fertilization. In Marchantia, however, the sexual structures are borne on tall outgrowths of the thallus. The picture shows the female.

After a time movement stops and the plasmodium forms itself into a stalk with a small spore-containing structure at its tip. The spores are liberated and form new plasmodia.

Lichens These are close associations between algae and fungi. The relationship is symbiotic, that is each component contributes to the well-being of the other. Lichens are very variable and can be either flat and encrusting or erect and tufted. They are common on rock and plant substrates.

Bryophyta These are a small group of plants without a root system but having stem and leaf-like structures. They are generally found in damp conditions. There are two generations in the life history—an asexual and a sexual stage—which alternate.

Liverworts Hepaticae, or liverworts, have a fleshy leaf-like thallus which grows over the surface of the soil. They are anchored to the soil with small hair-like processes.

Mosses Musci, or mosses, have a more tufted erect form and consist of stems bearing tiny leaflets. Mosses are often seen with small stalked 'pods'. These are the spore-containing structures.

Fern fronds are spore-bearing structures. On the underside, the spores develop in brown coloured sori. The spores give rise to small thalli which bear the sex organs.

Pteridophyta These plants have a true root system often with a rhizome. Again there is an alternation of generations between a small short-lived sexual form and the much larger long-lived asexual stage.

Ferns Filicinae, or ferns, are moderately sized plants with broad, often dissected leaves growing from an underground rhizome. This well-known structure is the spore-bearing asexual generation. The sexual generation is small and inconspicuous.

Also in this category are a number of fossil groups. The Psilophytales contain the oldest land plants with a simple vascular system. The Lycophytales or club mosses have a

The gymnosperms have cones containing the seeds. As in this example of a Virginia pine, conifers typically have needle-like leaves which are not dropped in winter.

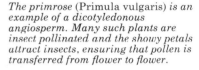

few modern-day representatives but were much more common in the Devonian and Silurian periods and dominated the Carboniferous period. They are the major contributors to the coal deposits. The Sphenophytales were also dominant fossil forms. Modern day horsetails (*Equisetum*) are examples of this group.

Spermatophyta This is the group containing the seed- and pollen-producing plants.

Gymnosperms Those plants where the seeds are not covered by an ovary

The primrose (Primula vulgaris) *is an example of a dicotyledonous angiosperm. Many such plants are insect pollinated and the showy petals attract insects, ensuring that pollen is transferred from flower to flower.*

are known as gymnosperms. The conifers and cycads are the two main groups. The cycads have a long fossil history extending back to the Carboniferous where they contributed to the coal deposits. The conifers also go back to the Carboniferous era and contain many of the largest plants today such as the redwoods.

Angiosperms Plants in which the seed is surrounded by a fruit are known as angiosperms. The group is divided into two depending on how many cotyledons the seed has. Cotyledons are the seed leaves, which contain the food reserves used in the early growth of a seedling.

Monocotyledons have only one cotyledon and usually have narrow leaves with veins which run parallel to the leaf edge. The grasses, sedges, lilies and orchids are all of this type.

Dicotyledons have two cotyledons and broader leaves with rib-like veins. Most of the garden flowers and vegetables fall into this category as do the broadleaved trees.

Animals

Invertebrates

Animals without a bony or cartilaginous skeleton forming a backbone are known as invertebrates.

Protozoa These are single-celled animals with one or several nuclei. Whilst many of them are free living, there are a number of important parasitic species. Some protozoans move using a flagellum (Mastigophora), others have a covering of small hair-like structures called cilia (Ciliata) whilst others creep over surfaces and may have small shells (Sarcodina).

Porifera (sponges) These are almost all marine and grow attached to rocks or corals. They consist of a group of cells which exist together on a protein or mineral skeleton. Water currents are drawn through the sponge structure by flagellated cells.

Coelenterates These have two layers of cells. In structure they are bag shaped with one opening often surrounded by tentacles. They tend to be sessile and fixed to the substrate. The corals build extensive skeletons of calcium carbonate.

Platyhelminthes (flatworms) These are flattened animals which are aquatic or parasitic. They have a mouth for feeding but no anus. Parasitic forms often have hooks and suckers to assist in holding on to the host. Free-living forms have eyes.

Nemetoda (roundworms) These are small to medium sized non-segmented worms with a mouth and anus. Movement is by a side to side lashing. Some forms are parasitic.

Annelida (segmented worms) These have a body divided into segments and often have bristles or other fleshy outgrowths. Leeches have anterior and posterior suckers. Movement is either by waves of extension passing down the body or by swimming in an eel-like manner.

Mollusca These are soft-bodied animals which are typically protected by a shell made of calcium carbonate. In some species the shell is internal or lacking.

Arthropoda This is a very large group of animals with a hard exterior

Some molluscs have no visible shell, such as this squid (Pyrotenthis).

skeleton which is segmented. The segments are connected by flexible membranes so that movement is possible. There are several different groups within the Arthropoda.

Crustacea are primarily marine although there are a number of freshwater forms. They have two pairs of antennae and often have specialized limbs for grasping, walking, swimming and breathing.

Myriapoda are terrestrial and contain the carnivorous centipedes with only one pair of legs per segment and the herbivorous millipedes with segments fused into pairs so that it looks as if there are two pairs of legs per segment.

Insecta are an enormous group of terrestrial animals which have three body sections (head, thorax and abdomen), three pairs of legs and often one or two pairs of wings coming from the thorax.

Arachnida have eight legs and only one or two body sections. Included in this group are the spiders (Araneae), mites and ticks (Acarina), harvestmen (Opiliones), scorpions (Scorpionida) and the pseudoscorpions (Pseudoscorpionida). With the exception of some of the mites, all arachnids are carnivorous.

Echinodermata are all marine and are bottom dwelling. They have a hard internal skeleton which appears to be external because there is only a very thin layer of tissue on the outside. In most cases the skeleton is fused to form a rigid or semirigid box or test.

At this point in the animal classification there are a series of small animal groups which show, particularly in the larval stages, the beginnings of a backbone-like structure.

Above *Typically the starfish have five arms, but in the sunstars* (Solaster) *there are many arms.*

Below *The swallow-tail butterfly* (Papilio machaon) *is a very beautiful example of an insect.*

Vertebrates

These are animals with a backbone which is usually bony. The head is well developed and protected by a skull. There are typically two pairs of appendages.

Pisces (fish) These are totally aquatic. They have a streamlined body shape and propulsion mainly comes from side to side movements of the tail. Fins are used for steering and stability. Sharks and rays have cartilaginous skeletons whilst other fish have bone.

Amphibia This group of imperfectly adapted terrestrial animals have

Toads spend much of their lives on land but, in common with other amphibians, need to return to water to breed.

four functional limbs which are often webbed for swimming. The tadpole larvae must develop in water.

Reptilia The reptiles are truly terrestrial with eggs to protect the developing embryo. They are covered with strong scales. Aquatic forms, such as crocodiles and turtles, come on land to lay their eggs.

Reptiles such as this lizard are completely terrestrial. Their eggs are laid on land, even those of aquatic forms.

Aves (birds) This group and the next maintain a fairly constant internal temperature (warm blooded). They have feathers which are very light, immensely strong and serve as good insulators. The forelimbs are modified into wings and there is a massive development of breast muscle.

Mammalia This is almost totally a terrestrial group (exceptions being whales and porpoises). The embryo develops inside a uterus and they care for the young, feeding them on milk. They are covered with hair and are warm blooded.

Bats are flying mammals which usually feed on insects. Some of the largest bats are the flying foxes.

Nature's Network
The Energy Thread

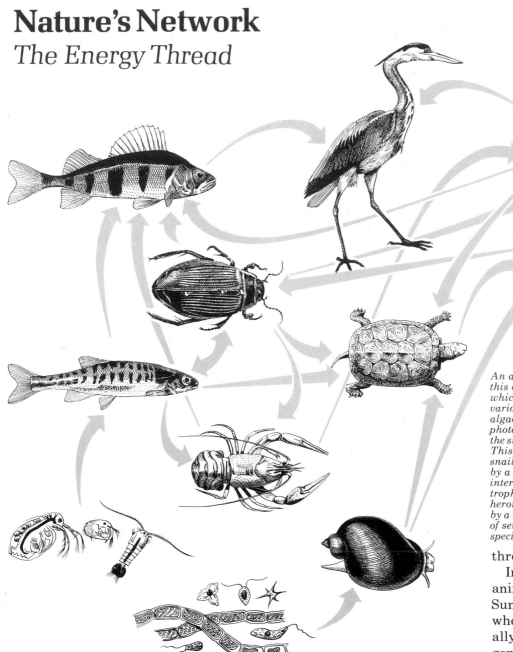

An aquatic food web. The arrows in this diagram indicate the way in which energy flows between the various aquatic species. Microscopic algae, using the process of photosynthesis capture energy from the sun and convert it into algal tissue. This is consumed by plankton and snails which, in turn, are consumed by a range of carnivore species. It is interesting to calculate the number of trophic levels in such diagrams. The heron obtains energy from the algae by a minimum of four and a maximum of seven energy transfers between species.

Living organisms require energy to remain alive. This energy is liberated and used in the process called respiration. The energy required comes from complex molecules but only plants are capable of manufacturing these energy-rich compounds from readily available simple ones (water and carbon dioxide). To do this, most plants use the energy of solar radiation, converting this light energy into chemical energy. All energy used by living organisms therefore originally comes from the Sun.

The Sun provides a considerable quantity of energy to the Earth. Some of it is reflected back into space so that the Earth shines in much the same way that the Moon does. What energy does get through the atmosphere and the clouds is available to plants. Surprisingly, plants use only about 1 per cent of the energy which is available to them to manufacture energy-rich chemical molecules. A large part of the solar radiation warms up the air, soil and water and so provides an environment with a favourable climate for life. Another large proportion of the available energy is used to evaporate water from leaf surfaces and so provide plants with a method of moving sap through their tissues.

In comparison with the plants, animals make much less use of the Sun. They do, however, only exist where the environment is climatically favourable, so they do 'use' the general heating component of the Sun. A few species, notably the reptiles and amphibians make use of the heating effect directly. These species adjust their temperature, and therefore the rate at which their metabolic reactions occur, by basking in the Sun to warm up and moving into the shade to cool down. As far as energy for respiration goes, for animals, it can only come from their food.

Energy is therefore the thing which above all links different species together. Since the energy moves from one organism to the next, as food, these energy links are said to be trophic relationships, trophic meaning feeding. Plants and animals can be categorized depending on how and on what they feed. Plants produce energy-rich materials both for their own respiration needs and the needs of the animals that eat them. These animals are then eaten by carnivores and these in turn are eaten by other carnivores or parasites. Plants and animals are grouped into trophic levels, with plants at the bottom and successive levels of herbivore and carnivore animals above them. Energy moves from one trophic level to the next, through feeding processes.

One important point about trophic levels is that although energy moves from one level to the next, energy is also used by the plants or animals in a particular trophic level. So, although a certain quantity of energy might enter a trophic level not all of that energy would be available for the next trophic level. As an example of this point consider a plant using solar energy to make energy-rich

compounds. If the plant made 100 molecules of these compounds it would need to use the energy in some of them for its own use so that less than 100 molecules could be obtained by a herbivore eating that plant. What actually happens is that only about 10 per cent of the energy that enters a trophic level is available for the next trophic level. As successive trophic levels move further from the plants so less and less of the energy originally captured by those plants is available to animals. This means that there are limits to the numbers of trophic levels which are possible (usually about four or five).

Another way of looking at trophic relationships is as a food chain.

Again the same energy limitations apply because each step in the food chain is another trophic level. Food chains as an idea are rather over-simple because usually more than one species eats a particular food organism. The simple food chain, grass-cow-man, is in practice more complex. For instance man may also feed on deer or rabbits which eat the grass or even on grouse which eat insects which feed on grass. A better idea of the trophic relationships is obtained by considering a food web. Here all the feeding relationships in a particular community are shown. This idea of organisms being closely interrelated is one of the major principles of ecology.

A woodland food web. This diagram illustrates some of the energy pathways in a forest ecosystem. A variety of plant structures are each consumed by different herbivores which are usually insects and these, in turn, are consumed by vertebrate carnivores. This is a simplified web and is by no means a complete picture. For example, spiders have been omitted as have the large range of carnivorous and parasitic insects, all of which feed on herbivores.

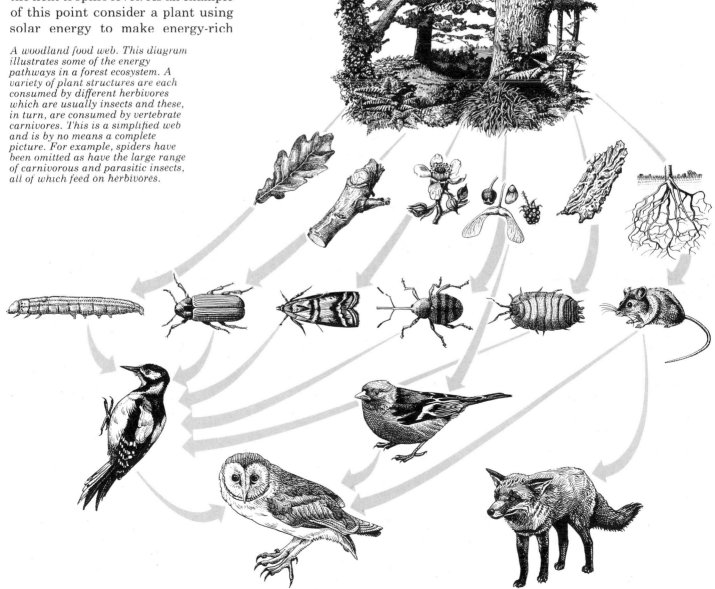

The commensal relationship between
the hermit crab and sea anemones.
The presence of the sea anemones
may be useful in camouflaging the
crab.

The Balance of Nature

The inter-relationships between
organisms can be of three different
types. If two species have nothing in
common, never meet and do not interfere with each other at all, then they
have no effect on each other. Neither
species gains or loses to the other
species. Alternatively one species
may gain from another species. A
parasite gains from its host, a predator gains from its prey and a herbivore gains from the plant species it
feeds on. Finally there is the reverse
of the last examples, where species
lose out to other species. It is the
balance of these three types of inter-
relationship that holds communities
together and allows them to persist
through time without drastically
changing. Some of the more important inter-relationships are described
below.

Predator and Prey

This title can equally apply to animal
feeding on animal or animal feeding
on its plant food. One of the species,
the predator gains whilst the other,
the prey, loses out. It is not however
quite as simple as this. In natural
situations these gains and losses are
balanced. If they were not balanced,
the predators would eat all the prey
and then starve so that both predator
and prey would die out. As the population of a prey species increases so
more food is available to the predators
so their population also can increase.
The increasing predator population
puts a greater and greater predation

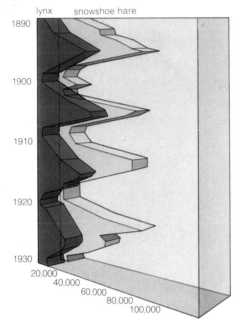

pressure on the prey population so
that the reproduction rate of the
prey population can no longer
replace those of the prey being eaten.
The prey population begins to de-
crease in number and so the food
available to the predators decreases
and becomes more spread out and
difficult to find. Then the predator
population also begins to decline. So
the inter-relationship is not only
gain by the predator, the prey also in
its way contributes to the con-
tinuance of both predator and prey
populations. This pattern of events
has been demonstrated many times
and is especially well seen in the
annual records of pelts by fur companies in Canada. The numbers of
pelts of hares and lynx fluctuate in
exactly the way just described.

Competition

When a particular requirement or
resource is in short supply then
individuals of the same or different
species will compete for that requirement. Food, shelter, territory and
water are all examples of resources

Left *This graph shows how the
population of snowshoe hares and
lynx change together. The processes
which produce these very regular
oscillations are described in the text.
This is a classic example.*

Below *A parasite life cycle. Sheep are
attacked by a liver fluke (Fasciola
hepatica). Eggs of the fluke pass out
of the sheep and are picked up by the
intermediate host, a snail. Here the
parasite multiples and produces the
infective cercarial stage which is
eaten by the sheep during grazing.*

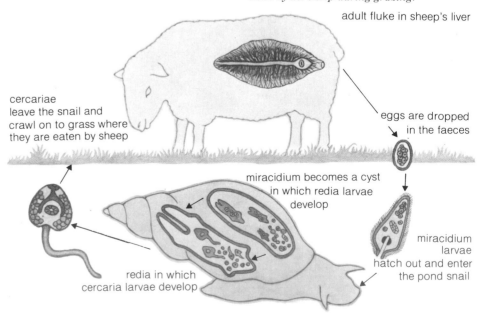

adult fluke in sheep's liver

cercariae
leave the snail and
crawl on to grass where
they are eaten by sheep

eggs are dropped
in the faeces

miracidium becomes a cyst
in which redia larvae
develop

miracidium
larvae
hatch out and enter
the pond snail

redia in which
cercaria larvae develop

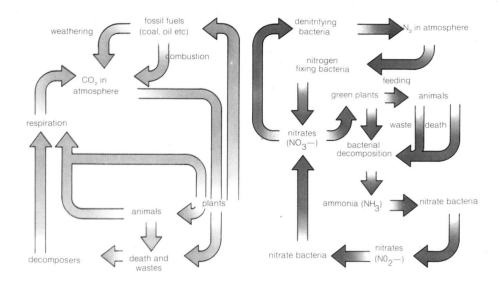

been given scientific names each lichen is in fact made up of two species both of which also have scientific names. The algal and fungal components can be separated and grown in special experimental situations independently. The alga is photosynthetic and provides the fungal part with energy-rich compounds for its own needs whilst the fungus gives the alga a support on which to grow and provides it with supplies of minerals.

No species lives its life totally independent of any other species. Species are interrelated in a number of ways to produce nature's network.

Above The carbon and nitrogen cycles. Unlike energy which has to be constantly replaced mineral nutrients are cycled in the system.

Like energy, they pass along food webs but they are then returned by decomposition to be available to the primary producers.

Below The diagram shows the structure of a lichen thallus with its fungal and algal components. The photograph shows crustose lichens on a gravestone.

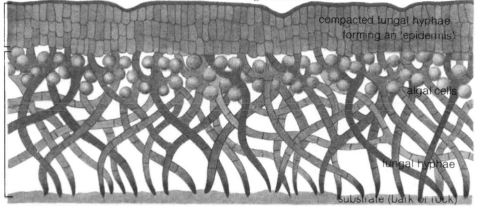

which might be scarce. In a competitive situation the best individuals win and the weak lose. Where two species compete for the same resource one will succeed and the other species will die out.

Parasite and Host

This is a special example of the predator/prey relationship, only here the important thing for the parasite is that it does not kill the host on which it relies for its food and shelter. If the parasite is well adjusted to its host then it gains from the relationship and the host loses but not sufficiently to kill it.

Commensalism

This is a sort of less severe parasite/host relationship. Here one species gains from the relationship but the other is virtually unaffected. An often quoted example of commensalism is that between the hermit crab and a sea anemone attached to the shell in which the crab shelters. The sea anemone has little effect on the crab but the crab, when it feeds, releases tiny scraps of food which waft about in the water and are captured by the sea anemone. So the sea anemone gains a substrate to stick to and also a food supply.

Symbiosis

This relationship is beneficial to both species which are interacting. A good example is found in the lichens. Here, an alga and a fungus live together and produce a distinct growth form. Although lichens have

MAN
AND HIS
PAST

Prehistoric Man
The Emergence of Man

This reconstruction of the skull of the fossil ape Dryopithecus is based on a very complete find made in 1948 by Mary Leakey at Rusinga Island, Kenya. The specimen is perhaps 18 million years old.

By the time Charles Darwin applied his theory of evolution to man in 1871 it had already been realized that our closest relatives in the animal kingdom were the *primates*. This order of mammals includes the lemurs, lorises, monkeys and apes, as well as man. Each species of modern primate is the result of 70 million years of evolution from a tiny shrew-like ancestor which lived at the same time as the last of the dinosaurs at the end of the Cretaceous epoch. The succeeding Palaeocene and Eocene epochs saw the evolution of a tremendous variety of prosimians ('lower primates') in North America and Europe and these already showed the main trends of primate evolution,

many of which are related to life in the trees. These trends included keeping a relatively primitive skeleton including hands and feet with five digits (useful for grasping branches), development of the sense of sight rather than smell, and development of a relatively larger brain than many other mammals. No doubt these early primates were also evolving social systems to provide good care for their litters which were probably smaller in size than those of many other mammals.

By the Oligocene epoch, some 30 million years ago, the ancestors of modern monkeys had evolved from prosimians in America and Africa, and one site, the Fayum in Egypt, has produced fossils of the earliest-known apes. However creatures such as *Aegyptopithecus* (Egypt ape) were more like small modern monkeys than apes in their way of life and appearance. Nevertheless they are regarded as early apes because they can be linked by certain features, particularly in the teeth, with the later fossil apes of Africa, Europe and Asia, collectively known as the Dryopithecines (oak apes). During the earlier part of the Miocene epoch (which lasted altogether from about 25–5 million years ago) extensive tropical and subtropical forests still covered much of the world and this led to the evolution of a tremendous diversity of fossil apes adapted to varying diets and environments. Some were as small and agile as modern gibbons, others were at least as large as modern gorillas. However, during the later Miocene epoch, the Earth's climate gradually deteriorated, leading to the spread of grasslands at the expense of the forests. The Dryopithecines which remained adapted to the shrinking forests are now only represented by their descendants, the gorilla and chimpanzee in Africa, and the orang-utan of south-east Asia.

Other Dryopithecines adapted to the increasing open-country habitats of the later Miocene age and from this group our own zoological

family, the hominids, developed. By 10 million years ago a creature called *Ramapithecus* (Rama's ape) had evolved and lived in Europe, Asia and Africa. Most of the remains known at present consist of teeth and jaw fragments but these show that the creature was short faced with relatively small front teeth and large back teeth with thick enamel. This last feature suggests that *Ramapithecus* may have eaten grass-seeds which would have provided an abundant source of food during the later Miocene. Although there are relatively few fossils covering the late Miocene and early Pliocene (which began about 5 million years ago), it seems probable that *Ramapithecus* evolved into the more advanced hominid called *Australopithecus* (southern ape).

The Australopithecines are represented by abundant fossils from north-east, east and south Africa covering the period 4–1 million years ago. At least two types of *Australopithecus* are known: a larger robust form (*Australopithecus boisei* and *Australopithecus robustus*, also known as *Paranthropus*—near man) which perhaps continued in a specialized version of the grain-eating way of life of *Ramapithecus*, and a smaller 'gracile' species called *Australopithecus africanus* which may have been a scavenger and small-scale hunter. Both the forms of *Australopithecus*

walked upright, but perhaps not in the same manner as modern humans. Their teeth were very distinct from those of apes but whereas the teeth of the gracile Australopithecines were like enlarged versions of modern teeth, the robust Australopithecines had relatively small front teeth and very large back teeth, presumably used to grind their food (since the teeth show heavy wear).

In terms of brain development the Australopithecines had ape-size brains with a volume of less than 500 cc in the smaller forms and up to 600 cc in the bigger specimens (compared with a modern human average of over 1,300 cc). As the gracile and robust Australopithecines probably led a different way of life they were not in direct competition, but the earliest stone tools of the Lower Palaeolithic period (Lower Old Stone Age) are known from Australopithecine sites and were probably made by the more carnivorous gracile forms.

By about 1¾ million years ago a new hominid had evolved from the gracile Australopithecines in east Africa and this hominid has been called the earliest species of true

man, *Homo habilis* (handy man). This is because it was not only larger brained than the Australopithecines (with a brain volume of 600–800 cc) but seems to have been a regular tool-maker and hunter whose skeleton was more like our own, particularly in the parts concerned with upright walking. An increase in body size, a relative reduction in the size of the jaws and teeth, and evidence of the ability to make better stone tools marks the evolution of the more advanced species *Homo erectus* (erect man). First discovered in Java (and formerly called *Pithecanthropus*—ape man), remains of this form of early man are now known from China (e.g. Peking man), Europe and Africa. Some specimens from Java and Kenya have been dated at over 1 million years old. *Homo erectus* was probably the first hunter of big game, and was the discoverer of fire and the inventor of the multi-purpose stone tool called the hand axe.

The South African Australopithecines consisted of at least two distinct types. The more gracile Australopithecus africanus (depicted on the right) may have been a scavenger and small scale hunter. As shown here, these creatures may have used tools, including ones made of bone, wood and stone, to hunt and to defend themselves. The more robust Australopithecus robustus (Paranthropus) was probably more herbivorous, perhaps eating seeds and roots. They too, may have occasionally used tools for digging or for defence, as shown on the left of the reconstruction. There is no direct evidence that the two forms actually encountered one another in South Africa, and, in fact, some of the sites containing bones of gracile Australopithecines may be older than those containing the bones of robust Australopithecines.

	Caucasoid
	Australoid
	Negroid
	Mongoloid
	American Indian

Peopling the Earth

The Pleistocene period during which *Homo erectus* lived began about 2 million years ago. It was characterized by a series of dramatic changes in temperatures which led to periodic spreads of the ice-caps from the north and south poles altering the environments of vast areas of the world. The climatic fluctuations were probably caused by changes in the position of the Earth in relation to the Sun, and will probably continue in the future. But the cooler areas so created and inhabited by man for the first time in the Pleistocene may even have acted as a stimulus for further physical and cultural evolution.

Homo erectus gradually evolved through a further increase in brain size and reduction of the rugged skull, brow ridges, face and jaws into our own species *Homo sapiens* (wise man). Intermediate fossils with different blends of the characteristics of each species are known from sites such as Petralona (Greece), Vértes-szöllös (Hungary), Solo (Java), Salé (Morocco) and Kabwe (Zambia—the skull known as Rhodesian man). With the arrival of *Homo sapiens* there is further evidence of improvements in stone-tool making, the use of wood for weapons such as spears, and the construction of shelters within and outside caves. Language and tribal social systems were probably already well developed. Some of the most significant remains of early *Homo sapiens*, dating from about 200,000 years ago, have been discovered in the European sites of

This skull is that of the 'old man' of Cro-Magnon, found in a rock shelter in the Dordogne region of France in 1868.

Swanscombe (England), Steinheim (Germany) and Arago (France). During the evolution of *Homo sapiens* distinct 'races' seem to have developed in particular areas of the world and by the beginning of the last ice advance in Europe, which began about 70,000 years ago, Neanderthal man (*Homo sapiens neanderthalensis*) had appeared. The Neanderthals (named after the famous German find of 1856) became well adapted to the cold conditions of Europe and western Asia and survived through hunting animals such as the woolly mammoth, woolly rhinoceros, horse,

reindeer and cave bear. The Neanderthals manufactured tools called Middle Palaeolithic (Middle Old Stone Age) or Mousterian (after the French site of Le Moustier), and probably led migratory lives moving from caves to temporary camps in open country.

Elsewhere in Asia and Africa other forms of *Homo sapiens* were evolving and by 40,000 years ago early modern man (*Homo sapiens sapiens*) had appeared in southern Africa, Ethiopia and south-east Asia.

By 35,000 years ago modern man (in the form of the Cro-Magnons named after the French finds of 1868) had taken over from the Neanderthals in Europe. These Cro-Magnons made advanced Upper Palaeolithic (Upper Old Stone Age) tools and were capable workers in materials such as antler, bone and ivory. They are perhaps most famous as the artists of the caves of Europe and the Soviet Union, although their art is also known in the form of sculptures and models found in burials and open camp sites.

About the same time as the Cro-Magnons appeared in Europe, man

The Cro-Magnons made tools from long blades of flint and they were skilful at working ivory and bone.

reached the 'new worlds' of America and Australia for the first time. The ancestors of the American Indians must have entered America across a land-bridge which existed when the sea-level between Asia and Alaska was lower. But the ancestors of the Australian aborigines must have reached their new homelands by the difficult feat of a sea-crossing of 50 miles or so. Once *Homo sapiens sapiens* had spread this widely local differences between populations became accentuated, partly through

the influence of different environments and climates, leading to the development of the modern 'races' of man which were already well established by the end of the last ice advance (and the end of the Pleistocene period) about 12,000 years ago. Soon after this some peoples began to embark on a major change in their way of life—domesticating animals and plants to allow an escape from the limits imposed for 2 million years by the need to hunt and gather their food.

Cave Painting

Prehistorians in the last century found it difficult to believe that primitive hunters such as the Cro-Magnons could have created the beautiful carved bone, antler and ivory sculptures sometimes found in their cave deposits. But even more astonishing were the huge painted galleries of caves as at Altamira in northern Spain and Lascaux in the Dordogne region of France which were discovered later. At first such paintings were thought to be fakes. But the styles and techniques were unusual and the vivid portrayal of extinct animals such as the mammoth and woolly rhinoceros were convincing enough even before their Palaeolithic age was confirmed by other means.

These drawings and paintings, sometimes crude and sometimes beautiful, were not meant to be easily viewed. The Cro-Magnons, even with their oil lamps and torches, could never have seen the total grandeur of their creations and some of their works were buried deep in inaccessible parts of caves. So were the paintings perhaps created as magic to aid hunting, to encourage fertility, to mark tribal territories, or to accompany religious ceremonies? All these suggestions, and many others, have been made in the past but none of them can explain the great variety of magnificent art which was created over a period of 20,000 years in an area stretching from western Europe to the Asian parts of the Soviet Union. Its meaning died with the Cro-Magnons leaving us hardly less puzzled and amazed than the archaeologists of 100 years ago.

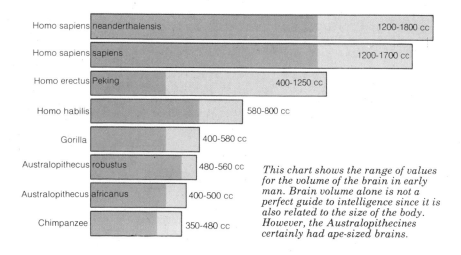

Homo sapiens neanderthalensis	1200-1800 cc
Homo sapiens sapiens	1200-1700 cc
Homo erectus Peking	400-1250 cc
Homo habilis	580-800 cc
Gorilla	400-580 cc
Australopithecus robustus	480-560 cc
Australopithecus africanus	400-500 cc
Chimpanzee	350-480 cc

This chart shows the range of values for the volume of the brain in early man. Brain volume alone is not a perfect guide to intelligence since it is also related to the size of the body. However, the Australopithecines certainly had ape-sized brains.

The Cradle of Civilization
Mesopotamia

The early period of Mesopotamian history is divided into phases, named after the sites where their characteristic features were first identified. These include Hassuna, Samarra, Halaf and Ubaid (*c.*5800–3500 BC). The first three cultures are found mainly in the north and centre of the country; there are no clear-cut divisions, and the three cultures overlap and blend into each other. The Ubaid developed in southern Mesopotamia and later spread north; its earliest stages correspond in time to the Samarran and Halaf. Features of these cultures are settled villages, painted pottery, temple building and the beginning of irrigation.

The succeeding cultures, Uruk and Jemdet Nasr, saw the growth of cities, the development of metallurgy, the introduction of writing and the widespread use of cylinder seals to indicate ownership of property.

During the Early Dynastic period (*c.*2900–2400 BC), city-states flourished throughout the southern part of the plain (Sumer). There was much interstate warfare and cities were often fortified. Sargon of Akkad conquered the Sumerian city-states but the empire that he founded was overturned by the Cutiens, raiders from the east. Their short period of domination was succeeded by the

Third Dynasty of Ur (*c.*2113–2006 BC), under whose centralized government Sumer and Akkad were reunited and a highly organized empire was founded.

The Third Dynasty of Ur was followed by several smaller kingdoms which were political and economic rivals. Hammurabi formed the southern kingdoms into one state (Babylonia). His dynasty was succeeded by the Kassites, who set up a new capital at Dur Kurigalzu (Aqar Quf) and ruled Babylonia for some 500 years.

Meanwhile, in the north, Assyria was developing into a strong kingdom. Both Assyria and Babylonia suffered from the widespread disruptions which occurred around 1200 BC, mainly caused by the movements of Aramaeans in Mesopotamia and the Levant. After this Assyria gradually grew into the predominant power in the area, controlling Syria, parts of Palestine and even Babylonia and Egypt at times. Assyria did not expand unopposed and faced constant rebellions which were for the

Above left The Mesopotamians were especially adept at sculptured reliefs, such as this showing the siege of Hamanu.

Right The Standard of Ur, now in the British Museum London, provides a remarkably clear picture of everyday activities within the community in ancient Mesopotamia.

most part subdued. Eventually Babylonia, the Scythians and the Medes combined in attack, and Nineveh, royal capital of Assyria, fell in 612 BC. Babylonia took over much of the Assyrian empire, capturing Jerusalem and controlling Syria and Palestine.

This period saw the rise of the Medes and Persians and in 539 BC Cyrus, King of Persia, captured Babylon itself. From then until 331 BC Mesopotamia was part of the Persian empire. In that year Alexander the Great defeated Darius III and took over his empire. After Alexander's death Mesopotamia formed part of the Seleucid empire until 140 BC when the Parthians captured Babylonia. They came into contact with the Romans but, because of defeats like Carrhae (53 BC), the Romans usually took the Euphrates as their eastern border. Parthian rule ended in the 3rd century AD and the area was taken over by the Sassian dynasty of Persia.

Religion, literature and the arts

The gods of Mesopotamia were numerous; in Sumerian times each city had its own god, although certain dieties held sway over wider areas and became national symbols. The god of Uruk was Anu, king of heaven; Enlil, god of air, was the deity of Nippur and upon his recognition the kingship of Sumer depended; Enki/Ea, god of wisdom, was the deity of Eridu, the oldest Sumerian city.

Other deities include Nanna/Sin, the moon god; Utu/Shamash, the sun god; and Innanna/Ishtar, goddess of love and war. National gods, such as Ashur of Assyria and Marduk of Babylon, grew in importance with the rise to power of their states. Exorcist priests used incantations and rituals against evil spirits and omen interpretation was practised, often influencing government policy.

The language of Mesopotamia was written with wedge-shaped (cuneiform) signs on clay tablets. The signs are syllabic rather than alphabetic, although some signs are used to convey ideas. The two main written languages of Mesopotamia were Sumerian, used by the Sumerian city-states and the Ur III kings, and in religious texts, and Akkadian, a Semitic language used by the Akkad dynasty which became the main language of Mesopotamia after Hammurabi. There remains a wide body of Mesopotanian literature including the Epic of Creation, Gilgamesh (which contains the story of the Flood), historical inscriptions, law codes, letters and a vast quantity of administrative texts.

In the arts, Mesopotamians were adept at sculptured reliefs (Assyrian reliefs), stone statues (Sumerian worshipper figures), metallurgy (Sargon's head, the Gates of Balawat), jewellery (Pu-abi's headdress at Ur), miniature carving (cylinder seals), and wall-paintings (Mari, Til Barsip). In many periods pottery making was elevated to an art (Halaf, Samarra, Nuzi). Science (astronomy and geometry) was not neglected and in mathematics there was both a decimal and a sexagesimal system. It is from the latter that we get our 60 second minute, 60 minute hour and the division of a circle into 360 degrees.

Ancient Egypt

The prehistoric period of Egypt is divided into four main periods: Tasian, Badarian, Amratian and Gerzean, named after villages nearest to where the main archaeological finds were identified. The first three cultures appear to merge peacefully into each other but there are signs that the Gerzeans were invaders. The Gerzean culture, characterized by its pottery, stone vases and metallurgy, is the ancestor of the historic civilization of Egypt.

The division of Egypt's history by the historian Manetho into numbered dynasties forms a useful

The pyramids at Giza were the tombs of IV Dynasty kings. Each had a Mortuary complex.

framework for its study. At the beginning of the dynastic period Egypt, which had been two kingdoms, Upper Egypt (south) and Lower Egypt (north), was united under one ruler (traditionally Narmer), with its capital at Memphis. The following period (Old Kingdom, Dynasties III–VI, c.2686–21181 BC) was a time of great wealth when the sovereign's power was absolute. It ended with Pepi II, whose 90-year reign was followed by disintegration of the central government. A noble family from Thebes reunited the country but it was not until Dynasty XII (Middle Kingdom, c.1991–1786 BC) that the monarchy regained its former strength. During this dynasty Egypt became an international power, subduing Sinai, Libya, and Nubia to the south. The Middle Kingdom was followed by a period of unrest. Foreigners invaded Egypt and established control over most of the country especially the north (Shepherd Kings/Hyksos), but eventually the nobles of Thebes rebelled and expelled the hated foreigners.

The New Kingdom (Dynasties XVIII–XX, c.1570–1085 BC) was a period of expansion. In Dynasty XVIII, the Pharaohs conquered Palestine and Syria, setting up client kings. Rulers of this dynasty include Queen Hatshepsut, Tuthmosis III, Akhenaten and Tutankhamon. The kings of Dynasty XIX also campaigned in Palestine and Syria. They met with strong opposition. Rameses II had to conclude a peace treaty with the Hittites. Rameses III (Dynasty XX) faced greater threats as invaders ('Sea-People') attacked Egypt itself and land and sea battles were fought around the mouth of the Nile. The Exodus of the Jews from Egypt is usually set in the New Kingdom but the exact time varies.

During Dynasties XXI–XXVI kings from different parts of Egypt established partial control of the country only to be defeated by their rivals. The kings of Ethiopia conquered Egypt but were unable to unite it. During the later part of their reign the Assyrians invaded causing the collapse of Ethiopian rule. Dynasty XXVI was made up of native Egyptians who made attempts to regain control of Palestine. Their efforts were ended by the Persian

invasion. Throughout the Persian rule (Dynasties XXVII–XXX, 525–332 BC), the Egyptians sought to assert their independence, achieving success from 399–343 BC. The Persians regained control for a time until they were defeated by Alexander the Great. After Alexander's death (323 BC) his formidable empire was divided between his generals. One Ptolemy, took Egypt and established his dynasty so successfully that it ruled for 300 years until the Roman army under Octavius (Augustus) defeated Cleopatra who committed suicide (30 BC). After that Egypt became a Roman province.

Religion, literature and the arts
Egypt had numerous gods. Some were originally local gods (e.g. Amon of Thebes) who rose to national importance because of their association with the ruling dynasty. Other gods were associated with Pharaoh (Horus, Re the sun god). The cult of Osiris—the god who dies and is resurrected—belonged both to Pharaoh and to the ordinary people. Isis and Hathor were the main goddesses. The tradition of the mummification of corpses developed from Dynasty III.

The pyramids were built to house the eternal body of the Pharaoh. Dynasty III saw the development of the *mastaba* (a bench-shaped structure built over the tombs of the early rulers) via Zoser's Step Pyramid into the true pyramid. The Giza pyramids (Cheops and Chephren) belong to

Dynasty IV. After the Old Kingdom pyramids were no longer built and kings were buried in elaborate rock-cut tombs. Notable examples of temples are the granite temple of Chephren, the temples of Mentuhotep III and Hatshepsut (Deir el Bahri), and those of Seti I at Abydos and Rameses II at Karnak.

The Egyptian language was written in hieroglyphs, sacred signs of great beauty. The sign values are alphabetic and syllabic and are used as word signs and as determinatives. A less elaborate writing, hieratic, came to be used for secular purposes. This later developed into demotic, a script used into the Christian period.

Although most information about Egyptian civilization comes from tombs, it was not totally preoccupied with death. This is evident from the sculpture which, working within strict artistic conventions, can bring to life the individual (Tuthmosis III, the seated scribe, Nefertiti), in the delicate jewellery (Dahshur diadems), and from the wall paintings and reliefs in tombs which show with vitality scenes of everyday life.

Mediterranean

Buto

Tanis

Giza

Cairo

Saqqara
Dahshur
Memphis

boundaries of Upper and Lower Egypt

El Faiyum

Nile

Hermopolis

Tell el-Amarna

Tasa
El Badari

Red Sea

Abydos

Thebes
Karnak
Luxor

Hieraconpolis

The Empire Builders
The Roman Empire

The history of Rome is the story of the amazing development of a small peasant farming community into an empire controlling almost the whole of the known world. Much expansion took place while Rome was still a republic, from 509 BC, when Tarquinus Superbus was cast out as king, until the arrival of Augustus in 27 BC. The conquest of Italy itself by the middle of the 3rd century BC led to wars abroad around the coasts of the Mediterranean, notably with Carthage, Greece, Spain, Syria, Asia Minor, Gaul and Egypt.

Generally the annexation of provinces in this way in the republican era did not reflect a true imperialism. Provinces were perhaps little more than a 'sphere of administration'. To many they were areas for exploitation. Extortion and corruption were common: there were few checks on the magistrates in pro-consular offices and tax farmers were numerous and hard to restrain.

The Principate
A group of republican diehards led by Brutus and Cassius, fearing the power of Julius Caesar, brought about his murder in 44 BC. This did not secure the republic or peace. In the subsequent clash for power Octavian, Caesar's great-nephew and adopted son, overcame his remaining rival Mark Antony at the battle of Actium in 21 BC.

In 27 BC Octavian became the first emperor of Rome. He took the title Augustus and that of 'Princeps' or leading citizen. Ostensibly Rome remained a republic, for Augustus and his successors retained republican forms of government and titles. Augustus was, however, given pro-consular power in all provinces and this, with the many other titular awards given to him by an acquiescent Senate, brought about a new authoritarian system. In 2 BC he was given the title 'Pater Patriae', Father of the Fatherland. For all practical purposes Augustus was Imperator or Emperor.

The Principate saw the beginnings of a system which gave the empire some 200 years of peace—the Pax Romana. The Augustan Age witnessed the high point of art and literature; it saw the replacement of republican amateur officials by professionals more strictly controlled by the central government; the equestrian order was brought into the ranks of the administration; trade flourished; and a new professional army based on long service was established. The peace made possible the spread of a number of important elements vital to the future of the Western world and still part of its heritage. Among them were the religion of Christianity, the legal system of Rome and the civilization of Greece.

After the death of Augustus the Julian emperors ruled for some 50 years. During this time Britain was annexed to the empire by Claudius. These Julian emperors were followed by others which include some of the greatest of the Roman emperors. Trajan (98–117), a Spanish provincial, added Arabia, Armenia and Mesopotamia to the empire, bringing it to its greatest extent. Hadrian (117–138), a patron of the arts, was a great organizer and the builder of the wall between England and Scotland. Marcus Aurelius (161–180), a Stoic philosopher, consolidated the frontiers of the empire.

Roman Provinces in the 2nd century AD
Urbanization of the provinces did not come about as a result of deliberate imperial policy. It was rather that aspiring provincial officials wished to see the prestige of Rome reflected in their own cities and towns. The towns of the empire strove to be as Roman as Rome itself. Buildings and public works aped those of the capital. All wanted to share in the glory of Rome. Roman citizenship was extended on an increasingly wide scale and Rome was the envy of the barbarians on her frontiers.

Ruled by professional administrators, controlled by an efficient bureaucratic system with men of talent being given the opportunity of reaching the highest offices—these were among the characteristics which cemented the new imperial order and gave it its stability.

The Decline in the 3rd century AD
At the top of the pyramid the ease with which emperors came and went and the influence of the legions and of the Praetorian guard in particular led to the designation of 'barrack emperors' in the 50 middle years of the 3rd century when there were no less than 26 emperors of whom only one died a natural death. Ruinous taxation, requisitions, exactions, tributes and other forms of extortion were demanded in quick succession to provide for each new emperor and his supporters. The army, engaged in emperor-making, was too preoccupied to deal with the barbarians who continually broke through the frontiers.

During a reign of 20 years Diocletian (284–305) commenced a thorough reorganization which Constantine (312–337) completed. The provinces were grouped into four prefectures to ensure greater control and the administration of the western and eastern parts was centred on Milan and Nicomedia respectively—hence the West and East Roman empires. The sole source of authority was the emperor and the new system of government was called the Dominate. After a brief struggle for power following Diocletian's death, Constantine emerged as the victor in the West and in 324 reunited West and East. Two of the most important acts of his reign were the founding of Byzantium (later renamed Constantinople) in 330 and the Edict of Milan for the toleration of the Christians in 313.

The reorganization under the Dominate did no more than defer the fall of the empire, which was divided between his sons by Theodosius (379–395) and from the latter date there were emperors in the West and in the East—a division which became permanent.

The dissolution in the West has no single or simple explanation. The

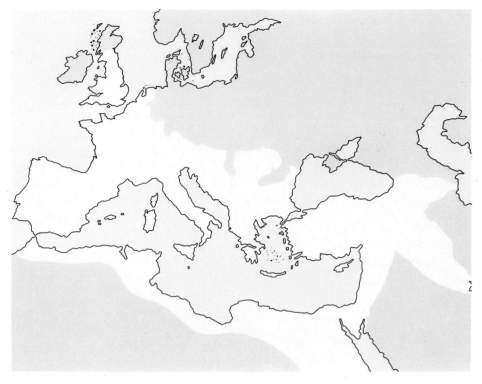

The Roman Empire at its height at the time of the Emperor Trajan (98–117 AD).

great amount of slavery, the mixture of peoples, the weakening of the army, the loss of fertility of the soil, the barbarian invasions and even the establishment of Christianity—all with varying degrees of justification have been given as reasons for the collapse. The migrations of the barbarians, envious of Rome and often themselves recruited into its army, became a force which could not be stemmed. The Goths under Alaric sacked Rome in 410 and in 476 the last Roman Emperor in the West, Romulus Augustus, handed over power to the German, Odoacer. The Eastern empire, however, struggled on for centuries as a Greek more than a Roman survivor, until the fall of Constantinople to the Turks in 1453.

The Roman Army
The Roman legions were a great unifying force supporting the creation and maintenance of the empire. Their success depended on discipline, practice and organization. There were as many as 60 legions at the time of Julius Caesar, each of about 6,000 men, headed by a legatus and organized into cohorts subdivided into maniples. Cavalry was usually supplied by auxiliaries. Reorganized by Augustus on a permanent basis the legions, reduced to about 30 in number, were given permanent duty in the provinces. With this permanent stationing of troops there grew up the practice of recruiting from the provinces so that by the 3rd century the legions were not only mainly provincial but barbarian.

Inevitably the Roman army was a great civilizing force. Not only did it preserve the Pax Romana but it made its own particular contribution in the form of bridges, roads, encampments and aqueducts and, of great importance, the settlements of veterans on the frontiers of the empire.

The Legacy of Rome
The legacy of Roman law is regarded by many as the greatest contribution made by Rome to civilization. The laws of most European countries —and many elsewhere—have been based to a greater or lesser extent on those of Rome. In organized form the law dates back to the Twelve Tables of 449 BC but the most important codification is that of the Byzantine emperor Justinian in the 6th century AD. He reduced a mass of material to orderly form. It badly needed a new declaration for as the empire expanded its judges had been obliged to make use of legal practices and customs acquired from the conquered peoples. Justinian's reorganization took the form of the *Code* which collected and edited existing law, the *Digest* which contained commentaries by Roman jurists, the *Institutes*, a short handbook for students, and the *Novels*, a supplementary publication to the Code. These magnificent contributions to the living law were revived in Italy in the 11th century and came to blossom in the Renaissance of the 15th century.

Rome assimilated the cultural achievements of Greece and to them she gave her own sense of order and discipline, for the Romans were essentially practical people. It preserved this heritage and through the vastness of its empire it passed it on to nearly all the known world. 'The city of Rome as an enduring centre of Christendom, as well as a repository of tradition and culture, has been one of the most influential symbols of all.'

One of the great contributions of Rome to the West – the aqueduct at Pont du Gard, Nimes, France.

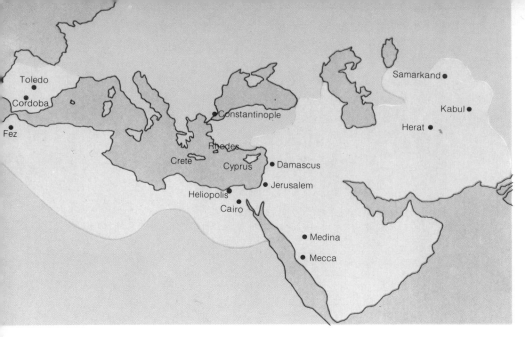

The Islamic Empire

Islam made a contribution to the building of medieval and thereby of modern Europe which is often much underrated. It was the world of the Moslems rather than that of Rome or Byzantium which preserved much of the old classical tradition and which transmitted to Europe ideas in mathematics, medicine and other sciences. Moreover by its overflow into India and the Far East there is today the living survival of its earlier fanatical expansion, for Islam is the second largest religion in the world with a following estimated at over 500 million people.

The beginnings of the present Moslem world were in Mecca in Arabia. Muhammad, declaring himself the true Prophet who had received Allah's revelations through the Archangel Gabriel, was forced to flee to Medina in 622 AD. This is the Hegira (or 'Flight') and the Arab calendar dates from that year. Muhammad established himself as the head not only of a religious but of a political community when in 630 he returned to occupy Mecca and so gained control of most of Arabia. Breaking down the idols on the Kaaba, a shrine of the old religion, he established it as the centre of Islam and into it after his death was placed the *Koran*, the collection of his revelations.

Holy Wars

Muhammad died in 632. The first major expansion of Islam occurred under his immediate successors. The first four caliphs saw the conquest of Syria, Upper Mesopotamia, Persia, Armenia, Egypt, Cyreneica and part of North Africa. The Omayyad caliphate which followed led the Moslems to new victories. During their reigns the caliphs conquered Cyprus, Rhodes, and Sicily and completed the capture of North Africa. A Moslem expedition entered India and annexed Sind; another extended the boundaries to the borders of China. Constantinople was three times besieged although without success. Spain was invaded in 711. The Moslem army then crossed the Pyrenees only to be defeated by Charles Martel at Poitiers (Tours) in 732.

This is a historic battle for it is claimed that it preserved Christianity in Europe by ensuring that Islam would not overwhelm the continent.

These wars are often referred to as the *jihad* or holy war. The caliphs may not, however, have conquered new territory merely to gain converts. Though many among the conquered populations embraced the new faith, there was a marked degree of religious tolerance in the Moslem empire. Nevertheless, whether fighting to defend or extend his empire, the Moslem who was killed in a holy war was assured of Paradise.

The Omayyad caliphate came to an end in 750 and was replaced by the Abbasid dynasty with its new capital at Baghdad. It became Persian in character. Among its great caliphs were Harun Al-Rashid of *Arabian Nights* fame and his son Mamun the Great. This is the era of stability, secure administration, law reform, expanding trade and scholarly translations and other works. Much of the classicism of Greece and Rome was received in the Middle Ages through the work of Moslem scholars of this time.

But the empire was already divided. The Abbasid caliphate was never recognized in Spain and Morocco and the Omayyad dynasty,

The Dome of the Rock at Jerusalem is one of the holiest of places to Moslems

expelled from the East, set up a western empire with its capital at Cordoba. In the East there was a continuing dispute between the Abbasids and the Shiites. One of the leaders of the Shiites, claiming descent from the Prophet's daughter Fatima, founded the Fatimite dynasty in 909 and with Cairo as their capital his successors ruled over Egypt, Syria, Palestine and most of North Africa.

Christians versus Moslems

The West European Crusaders, profiting from the divisions in the Moslem world, managed to capture Jerusalem in 1099 and even advanced as far as Cairo. But the great general Saladin, for a time master of Egypt, conquered Syria and recaptured Jerusalem in 1187. The third crusade with Richard I of England had some initial successes but by 1291 the crusaders were swept from their last footholds.

Constantinople, the seat of the Byzantine empire, continued to resist the tide of Islam. It was not until 1453 that it fell and with it the so-called East Roman empire came to an end. At the other end of the Mediterranean, however, Spain, united under Ferdinand and Isabella, was engaged in driving out the Moors and this may be said to have been accomplished with the capture of Granada in 1492.

The fall of Constantinople encouraged the Moslems to venture further. As with the crusades, the threat from the East drew the countries of Europe closer together in the fight against the infidel. Historical landmarks in the continuing campaigns were the heroic and successful defence of Venice in 1529 and the great naval victory of Don John of Austria at Lepanto in 1571.

The Arabs created the early Moslem empire. The Turks who replaced them built their empire on the ruins of the Abbasid empire. The Seljuk Turks from Central Asia ruled from 1037 to 1109 and were succeeded later by the Ottoman Turks.

The Mongols: Central Asia and India

Genghis Khan from Mongolia began a huge series of conquests in the early years of the 13th century. Overrunning north China, he turned west to establish his authority as far as the Caspian. In India the Delhi sultanate was created in 1204. The Mongols were subsequently converted to Islam and although in a minority in the sub-continent, Islam continued to flourish. Its strength today lies in the now separate countries of Pakistan and Bangladesh.

The Decline

At the beginning of the 18th century there were Moslem empires in India, Persia and Turkey. Moslem rule was also to be found in Egypt and around the shores and islands of the Mediterranean. It was the growing pressure of the European powers which brought about the decline. The Safavid empire in Persia started to

The Christians of the West throw back the Moslem fleet at the Battle of Lepanto, 1571.

crumble under the influence of Russia; in India the Mogul emperors ruled as puppets of Britain until their removal in 1857; the French established themselves in North Africa; the Dutch took Indonesia; the British occupied Egypt and the Sudan and overflowed into Cyprus. By 1900 most of the Moslem world had come under the domination of the colonial powers of Europe. In the homelands the dispossessed Arabs were disputing with their Turkish masters. Following the First World War the Ottoman empire was further divided among the European powers—and Arab hostility was exacerbated by the creation of the Jewish national state.

Modern Islam remains a great religious empire, stretching from the Atlantic Ocean to the Far East. As a force in the world it was a truly wonderful creation. When Christianity came into being it could and did turn for its development to the existing state of the Roman empire and to an existing classical civilization. Islam on the other hand involved the creation of an entirely new state which came to constitute a new empire dominating a vast part of the known world and which, in doing so, preserved much of the beauty of the old order of things and made its own immortal contributions to the lands it won.

The Portuguese and Spanish Empires

With amazing fortitude the Portuguese sailors of the 15th century ventured forth into the unknown Atlantic. Rediscovering the Canaries, the Azores and Madeira, they were encouraged by the capture of Ceuta from the Moors in 1415 to begin the systematic exploration of the west coast of Africa. Their patron and director was Prince Henry the Navigator. As general of the 'Order of Christ' he diverted crusading money and enthusiasm to a series of well-equipped annual expeditions. It was he who prompted the voyages of Bartholomew Diaz to the south of Africa and who foretold the journey of Vasco da Gama round the Cape of Good Hope in 1497–9 to southern India. By 1516 the Portuguese had reached China. Their activities in the East were encouraged by the papal bull of 1493 and by the treaty of Tordesillas of 1494 with Spain whereby the two countries 'divided' the world between them upon a line '370 leagues west of Cape Verde'.

A Great Trading Empire

In 1500 the Portuguese fleet sailing to the East discovered the coast of Brazil on its outward voyage. A succession of voyages established ports on the eastern coast of Africa. In the space of a single decade the Moors were swept from the eastern seas and an empire had been established with its capital at Goa. It was a great trading empire, not an empire of colonies. Huge carracks transported the produce of the East to the West and for a brief time Portugal was the wealthiest nation in Europe.

Spanish Adventurers

Spain was engaged on similar ventures. The most famous of the early voyages is that of Columbus in 1492. Endeavouring to find a route to Cathay westwards across the Atlantic and armed with letters of introduction to the Great Khan, he landed at Hispaniola and Cuba. From the latter island expeditions subsequently ranged into Mexico where Cortes in 1522 conquered the Aztecs and plundered the gold. In 1532 Pizarro with a handful of followers conquered the Incas in Peru and began the export of its silver and precious stones. In 1519 Magellan, Portuguese by birth but in the service of Spain, proved the westerly route to the Spice Islands by rounding Cape Horn and crossing the Pacific to circumnavigate the world.

Above *The Plate Fleets of Spain and Portugal brought wealth from West and East to Europe.*

Below *The departure of Cortes from Mexico.*

He himself was killed in the Philippines which were added to the Spanish possessions.

The Spanish empire sprang from these adventurers and discoveries. The vice-royalties of New Spain and of Peru were established with capitals at Santo Domingo and Lima. The empire stretched from Mexico to Peru and included Panama and the Spanish Main. Two plate fleets each year collected the wealth of the empire for shipment to Spain. The heavy work of transportation was undertaken by negro labour imported from West Africa and this slave trade was jealously guarded by Spain.

While its empire was growing in the West, Spanish troops were showing their strength by victories in France, Italy, North Africa and the Canary Islands. In 1516 Charles, ruler of the Low Countries (now the Netherlands, Belgium and Luxemburg) and a member of the Hapsburg family, became king of Spain. When he succeeded also as Holy Roman Emperor in 1519 he ruled under the two titles of Charles V of that empire and Charles I of Spain. Under his son Philip II the Spanish empire reached

its height. With the conquest of Portugal the Iberian peninsula was united and Philip could pose as the saviour of Europe by his naval contribution to the overwhelming defeat of the Turks at Lepanto in 1571.

The introduction of this new dynasty, however, meant that Spain was drawn to defend a series of Hapsburg interests which were not in its own best interest. Spain's armies were feared throughout Europe for almost a century but a series of wars in France, Germany, the Low Countries and even in defence of Vienna imposed such a burden on Spain that even the great wealth of the Americas could not sustain it. The reign of Philip II (1556–98) marks also the beginning of the decline—and the failure of the Spanish Armada during his reign is symbolic.

The Decline of the Empire

Charles V had left huge debts. Philip II was forced into bankruptcy on two occasions. Taxation was oppressive and the great influx of bullion from the New World pushed up prices to exorbitant levels. The time came when the Spanish armies

were no longer invincible. Portugal asserted its independence in 1640. A series of wars terminating in the War of the Spanish Succession (1701–13) saw Spain lose all its possessions in Europe—the Netherlands, Gibraltar, Milan, Naples, Sardinia, Sicily and Minorca.

The 18th century witnessed conflict with Britain as the two countries challenged each other for colonial power in America. There was some brief success for Spain when, following the successful revolt of the British colonies in America, she obtained Louisiana in 1783; but this was ceded to France in 1800 when Spain was occupied by Napoleon and subsequently sold by him to the United States. In forced alliance with the French emperor Spain lost her fleet in 1797 only to recover and to fail again at Trafalgar in 1805.

The Monroe Doctrine—'hands off' the New World

Following the restoration of the monarchy after Napoleon's defeat in 1815 the overseas empire of Spain revolted. During the war most of the colonies had asserted their independence. Spanish troops mobilized for their reconquest mutinied. George Canning, British foreign secretary, made it clear that the British navy would not allow France to assist Spain in their recovery—a move which led indirectly to the declaration by the United States of the Monroe Doctrine with its opposition to any future intervention by European powers in the New World. By 1825 Spain had lost all its overseas possessions except Cuba, Puerto Rico, some outposts in Africa, the Philippines and Guam. The Spanish–American war of 1898 saw this further reduced.

Portugal's period of 60 years annexed to Spain was disastrous for its empire. It lost almost all its overseas possessions to the Dutch who were fighting for their independence from Spain and declined rapidly to the status of a second class power. Portugal is known in British history as Britain's oldest ally (from 1386) and its partner in the Methuen Treaty of Commerce of 1703—which may be the reason for the popularity of port in Britain!

The British Empire

A small island lying off the coast of Europe became the centre of the greatest empire the world has ever known. At its height, scattered over a quarter of the Earth's surface, it has been truly said that this was an empire on which the sun never set. Today we know it as the British Commonwealth of Nations—a free association of sovereign states, much smaller in size than at its peak, but still acknowledging HM the Queen as titular head.

Among the earliest adventurers were Sir Francis Drake, plundering the Spanish Main and circumnavigating the globe in 1577–80, Sir Humphrey Gilbert with his interest in the New World and the North-West Passage, Sir John Hawkins the 'father' of the West African slave trade and Sir Walter Raleigh, his half brother. Gilbert and Raleigh's ideas of founding an overseas empire in the Americas did not come to fruition in their day but England's oldest colony, Newfoundland, dates back to 1583 and the age of Elizabeth I.

Growing British sea power led to the establishment of trading posts and these came to be protected by the Navigation Acts which restricted trade with the new plantations or colonies to British ships and merchants. The 17th century saw the development of regulated companies which were destined to become world famous—notably the East India Company (1600) and the Hudson's Bay Company (1670).

The American colonies date back to the early 17th century. They reflect a wonderful combination of the efforts of early adventurers (John Cabot) colonizers (Lord Baltimore in Maryland), merchants (Sir Thomas Smith in the East India, Muscovy, Virginia and Levant companies) and a variety of religious dissenters (John Winthrop and the Puritans). By the mid-18th century these colonies enjoyed a remarkable degree of self government and their total population was not far below one quarter of that of the mother country. This first empire terminated with the loss of the American colonies in 1783.

The First to the Second Empire

The year 1763 saw the end of a series of wars in Europe culminating in the Treaty of Paris which saw Britain as a colossal world power. Allied with continental powers concerned with the war on land—and in particular with Austria, the enemy of France—Britain made full use of its sea power to acquire territory and trading stations in India, Canada, the West Indies, Gibraltar and many other parts of the globe which assured Britain of profitable trade. Most of these new acquisitions were at the expense of France and, to a lesser extent, of Spain.

Searching for a Policy?

Commercial policy dominated imperial questions. Overseas acquisitions contributed raw materials or markets to Britain. The colonies were economically dependent on the centre. The revolt of the American

One of the many pieces of Victoriana produced for the golden and diamond jubilees of 1887 and 1897 respectively.

colonies, successful only because of the support of France and Spain, made little change to the thinking of the mother country. Britain did not liberalize her colonial policy. Quite the reverse. The new 'crown colony government' was intended to ensure that no other revolution succeeded. The colonial office controlled all, not least through its appointment of colonial governors who, while acting on the advice of an executive council, had the widest powers.

During the 19th century, however, Britain was uncertain of its colonial policy. Step by step it felt itself obliged to admit local elected members to the inner councils of the colonial governor. And so, almost without realizing it, steps inevitably led to self government with the governor as a titular head.

The Road to Self Government

Napoleon had been defeated by British sea power. Further possessions fell into Britain's lap. The 19th century saw expansion in Africa, Australia, New Zealand and Egypt. The Industrial Revolution put Britain in the position of being the

Kitchener's troops decimate the Mahdi's brave hordes at the Battle of Omdurman. The Mahdi had set up his capital in this town on the left bank of the Nile opposite Khartoum after the death of Major General Charles Gordon and the withdrawal of the British troops. The Mahdi himself did not survive long and contracted a fatal infection about five months after the capture of Khartoum.

leading imperial, commercial and industrial nation in the world. So, away with the Navigation Acts— there was no need for protection, for Britain was the priest of *laissez faire* and free enterprise for all.

Political and commercial motives converged. The foundations of a new empire came about when the colonies asserted their own routes, at first not to independence, but to the taking of decisions which represented at least something of the differences between their feelings and experiences and those of the mother country.

Until the 19th century settlements abroad of British people were limited. During that century they expanded greatly, assisted by the efflux of Irish emigrants. This expansion encouraged the move towards self government. The beginnings can be traced back to the report of the Earl of Durham on Canada in 1839. 'Responsible government' in the colonies may be attributed to him in Canada and to Wakefield in Australia and New Zealand. 'Dominion status', as it came to be called, came into being in Canada in 1867, Australia in 1901, New Zealand in 1907, South Africa in 1910 and southern Ireland in 1922. Loyalty to the Crown, a common citizenship and, later, support with men and materials through two world wars, cemented the relationships even though there was this growing independence. India, though not part of the old colonial system, was controlled by a peculiar admixture of the East India Company and the British government until 1858 when the Indian Mutiny was suppressed. From 1858 India came under the direct rule of the British government, symbolized by the proclamation of Queen Victoria as empress in 1877.

Disraeli, later Earl of Beaconsfield, may be regarded as the prophet of the new imperialism. Control of the Suez Canal, occupation of Cyprus (1878) and of Egypt (1882) coincided with the acquisition of a new tropical empire in the last 20 years of the 19th century. In Africa, Britain added more than 2 million square miles and in Asia, added Malaysia. In South Africa the Boer War marked on the one hand the climax of imperial enthusiasm and on the other a real change of attitude towards the empire.

The New World

The formal independence of the dominions was recognized in the Statute of Westminster of 1931. After two world wars which drained it of men and wealth Britain had ceased to be the predominant industrial and commercial nation it had been in the 19th century. No longer could it be counted among the super powers. Inevitably, since the end of the Second World War Britain has conceded various degrees of independence to its former colonies. Among the countries which have gone so far as to leave the Commonwealth are Burma, Eire, South Africa and Pakistan.

Decisions of this sort have to an extent been forced on Britain. But the influence which she still holds is immense. English is still *lingua franca* in a large part of the world. A vast area of the Earth's surface pays tribute to the democratic ideas and institutions which Britain has exported. In the 19th century Pax Britannica was a pacifying influence —'keep things quiet or else'. Opponents of the policy might talk of it as gunboat diplomacy—a direct reference to the background might of the Royal Navy—but it worked, and to the disadvantage of few.

The modern Commonwealth has seen the export of democracy at least to the extent that heads of government come together to discuss major issues of international affairs. How much they influence international politics is hard to say but it is difficult to believe that they do not. The Commonwealth remains, as it has been for many years, one of the most potent forces for peace and co-operation in the world.

Man and Society
Politics and Philosophy in Ancient Greece

In about 2000 BC, an Aryan people moved into the area which we know today as Greece. They built their settlements between the high mountain ranges of the mainland, on the Aegean islands, and, later, around the coastlands of Asia Minor. The Greeks were farmers and herdsmen, supporting themselves through the cultivation of corn, olives and vines. They also carried out considerable seafaring trade with neighbouring peoples.

Over the centuries, each community developed into a city-state, or *polis*. The states shared a common language and a common mythology but they jealously guarded their independence from one another. In 776 BC the states sent representatives to attend a great athletic festival at Olympia. Subsequently these Olympic Games were held at regular four-yearly intervals and they became a further unifying factor. Appeals were repeatedly made at the Games for a common front against the barbarians (by whom the Greeks meant all non-Greek-speaking peoples). A federation of states was certainly achieved during the victorious war against the Persians (480–490 BC) and shifting alliances were also formed during the periods of savage internal conflict known as the Peloponnesian Wars (459–446 and 431–404 BC). Yet at no time did the states succeed in uniting as a single nation. The independent polis, with its own character and traditions, was the basic unit of life in Ancient Greece.

It is from the word polis that we get the term politics. Civic life within the states was vigorous and competitive. The Greeks experimented with various forms of government, many states passing through successive periods of monarchy, aristocracy and tyranny. By the 6th century BC a unique concept quite new to civilization had emerged—democracy.

Collective decision-making was well suited to public life in the polis, and Athens in the 5th century BC provided the most striking example of democracy at work. By the middle of the century, all free adult males were entitled to take part in a communal assembly where citizens elected their leaders, judges and administrators. Decisions were made by mutual consent. The skills of the orator emerged, as individuals tried to persuade and cajole their fellow citizens to their point of view. With Greek politics came politicians.

Athens was not, of course, a true society of equals. Women and slaves were excluded from the democratic process, and the leaders who emerged tended to come from wealthy and established families. The great statesman Pericles, who dominated public life from 443–429 BC, was a notable example. But, however imperfect, Athenian democracy was a startling innovation.

The habit of reasoned discussion bred new modes of thought. Greek thinkers began to question the nature of man and of the universe outside the framework of religion. The inquiring spirit of one great philosopher, Socrates (469–339 BC), brought him into conflict with the civil authorities. He was condemned to death for his inquiries into the nature of the Good and the True, which, it was said, were corrupting public morals.

Socrates' disciple, Plato (429–347 BC), however, continued in the revolutionary tradition of Greek philosophy. It was he who founded the world's first university—the Academy at Athens. But where Socrates had questioned, Plato attempted solutions. He proposed his own view of the universe, suggesting that behind the visible world there was an unseen world in which the essences of the Good and the True existed as spiritual forms. In his famous work *The Republic* he tried to draw up an outline of the ideal society. In fact, Plato's speculations had taken him far from the relaxed traditions of democratic Athens. His ideal republic was closer in spirit to

Plato's Academy, established on the outskirts of Athens in the 4th century BC. The earliest subjects taught and discussed seem to have been mathematics, dialectics, natural science and political training. The school continued to function until AD 529, and included the great Roman orator Cicero among its teachers.

the authoritarianism of Athens' great rival, Sparta.

Greek thought produced many less speculative philosophers. Plato's pupil Aristotle (384–322 BC) observed and classified the phenomena of the material world, establishing theories in astronomy, biology and meteorology that were not to be challenged for over 1,000

years. Pythagoras (*c*.6th century BC) and Euclid (*c*.300 BC) developed mathematics and geometry. The physician Hippocrates (460–377 BC) founded the modern science of medicine. The roots of almost every 20th-century science can be found in Ancient Greece.

The Greeks, more than any other ancient people, saw the world with eyes unclouded by superstitious fear. In Greek sculpture the human form is represented entirely for its own beauty, and not as an object of religious or magical ceremony. Some sculptors, such as the 4th-century Praxiteles, achieved world fame for their skill, and Greek sculptors seem to have been the first to sign their works.

In poetry and in drama, too, the Greek concern was with the recognizable world. The 8th-century epic poet Homer depicted gods of human proportions, arguing and taking sides in terrestrial disputes. The heroes of Greek tragedy defied the gods of Greek religion, and the heroic characteristic most often celebrated was neither goodness nor obedience, but sheer daring. In literature, as in science, the Greeks explored human potential as never before.

In the 4th century BC, the Macedonian Alexander the Great undertook a campaign of conquest which took Greek culture eastward as far as India. His empire collapsed soon after his death, and in time it was absorbed, with Greece itself, into the Roman empire. But the impact of Greek civilization survived. It has influenced our language, our concepts of beauty, our patterns of scientific, philosophical and political thought. It was a cultural explosion. For the first time, individuals consciously examined, reflected upon and transformed their relationship with the universe and with society.

Europe, partly through the moderating influence of the Church. The warrior kings had parcelled out much of their territory to their lords in holdings known as fiefs or *feuda* (from which the term feudalism derives). Feuda were areas of land to which certain taxes were attached, principally taxes exacted in work and produce from the inhabitants, for coinage was scarce at this time. The landowning nobles held jurisdiction over the inhabitants of their fiefs, and the inhabitants themselves lived under permanent obligation to their lord, often as serfs in conditions of virtual slavery. Between the lord

The medieval knight was more than a military figure. In theory, at least, he embodied the chivalric ideals of honour, loyalty, courtesy and religious devotion. The investiture of a knight became, during the 12th century, an elaborate ceremony involving both sacred ritual (such as the nightly vigil undertaken before the initiation) and acts of secular homage (embodied in the dubbing ceremony). The sword, shield, lance and spurs borne by the Knight of Prato in this picture all had symbolic as well as practical importance.

Knighthood was rooted in the feudal traditions of service and land tenure, but freebooting landless knights began to emerge during the Crusades.

and his 'vassalls' there existed an implicit bond: the master granted land and protection to his men in return for their work, much of the fruits of their labours, and their support in time of war.

In theory, the feudal lord might himself be under obligation to his monarch in a vassal and master relationship. But few feudal monarchs were able to develop central governing bodies to administer their kingdoms. The power of the warrior nobility presented a constant threat to the king's authority and the instability of monarchs was a characteristic of feudal society

Feudalism in Europe and Japan

The barbarian invasions which destroyed the Roman empire in the 5th and 6th centuries AD left a fragmented Europe composed of warring kingdoms and shifting frontiers. For a long period, aptly remembered today as the Dark Ages, the cultural achievements of the Ancient World were lost. Literacy and scholarship survived only in the isolated monasteries of the Christian Church.

With the disintegration of political unity, trade declined and notions of citizenship disappeared. In place of the cosmopolitan Roman civilization, a new pattern of social organization slowly emerged, based on the power of the warrior lord and the physical ownership of land. The system is known as feudalism.

By the 11th century the wave of violent disturbance had died down in

despite the comparative stasis of social life. It was from the 'nobility of the sword', warrior lords living on self-supporting estates, that the great aristocratic houses of Europe evolved, contesting European thrones over a period of many centuries.

Just as the lord's stone castle symbolized supremacy in the temporal world, the stone church, monastery or cathedral symbolized the spiritual and intellectual authority of the Church. Christianity came to monopolize learning throughout most of Europe, and the Church imposed a kind of cultural unity on European civilization as it evolved from the Dark Ages to the Middle Ages. The Church developed vast temporal interests too, becoming a great landowner with jurisdiction over many thousands of vassals.

There were areas of Europe in which feudal vassalage did not exist, and the nature of feudal obligations varied considerably. As trade began to expand in the 11th century, free craftsmen in the growing towns began to organize in guilds, with charters of formal rights as well as obligations. Merchant guildsmen began to club together to build city walls—stone edifices which ranked with castles and churches as symbols of increasing social status. By the end of the Middle Ages, the nobility were beginning to demand constitutional guarantees of their rights in relation to their monarchs. The British parliamentary tradition begins with the Magna Carta of 1215, a document comprising no less than 61 clauses imposed on King John by his barons. In 1238, the Aragon Cortes in Spain made a vow to their monarch which is brutally frank in renouncing respectful homage: 'We, who are as good as you, take an oath to you, who are no better than we, as prince and heir of our kingdom, on condition that you preserve our *fueros* [liberties]; and if you do not, we do not.'

Yet these developments should not conceal the fact that most of Europe's population still lived and worked on the land, in awe of the authority of Lord and Church. Feudalism set the pattern of social life until industrial-

ization revolutionized social relations in the 19th century.

In distant Japan, a system similar to European feudalism also emerged. Until the 8th century Japan had been ruled by an emperor from his court at Kyoto, and power was shared among a number of clans. During the Heian period (794–1185) real power passed into the hands of the Fujiwara clan and it was during this period that the emperor's authority was increasingly whittled away. Lands, with the taxes accruing to them, were granted to clan leaders in return for military support. This development had twin results: successive emperors gradually lost their economic hold over the country, whilst provincial military leaders gained power commensurately. During the Kamakura period (1185–1333) the first of many military directors emerged, ruling under the title of *shogun* in the emperor's name. As in Europe, society became structured around master and vassal relationships; the Lord (*tono*) exacting service (*hoko*) from his vassal (*kenin*) in return for the grant of a fief (*chigyochi*).

Chivalry

Bonds based on relative power were the heart of feudalism, and before the coming of gunpowder the armoured, horse-riding knight represented the acme of military technology. A code known as chivalry developed around the knight, stressing the ideal qualities of courage, courtesy and a willingness to defend the weak. The code of chivalry inspired some of the greatest works of medieval literature, including the romance tales of the *Chanson de Roland*, the *Morte d'Arthur* and *Mio Cid*.

A similar code developed in Japan. It was known as the *Bushido*, the 'Way of the Warrior' which became the moral code of Japan's *samurai* warriors. Like European chivalry, the Bushido paid great attention to the virtues of honour and skill at arms, but whereas chivalry stressed the lord's duty to protect his retainers, Bushido tended to emphasize the retainer's obligations of absolute loyalty to his lord. Heroic self-sacrifice was the most exalted ideal.

The samurai Kumagae Naozane. The samurai class of feudal Japan developed from the earlier bushi warriors who emerged during the 9th century. Notice the bow; archery was an important samurai skill (it played no part in the European knightly tradition).

Feudal society was rooted in the land, and knowledge and education were the exclusive preserve of the Church. But with the growth of towns in the Middle Ages came urban societies in which ideas were exchanged more freely. As early as the 12th century the first universities were set up in Europe, in Paris, Bologna and Oxford. Here scholars rediscovered the works of classical authors with enthusiasm. Subjects forgotten for many centuries were studied again, philosophy, logic and ethics, for example. The Church itself began to incorporate the teachings of Aristotle into its doctrines and Greek philosophers came to be revered almost as pre-Christian saints. At the same time, manuscript illustrators were beginning to include closely observed representations of plants, animals and human figures in their pictures. It was as if, after long centuries of cultural darkness, people were rediscovering the delights of the material world. By the 14th century cultural life was quickening rapidly in a phenomenon known as the Renaissance—the rebirth.

Italy had become the artistic and intellectual centre of Europe, and the state of Florence was particularly rich in cultural activity. Two great poets, Petrarch and Dante, were forging a new literature combining reverence for the Christian Church with a delight in the classical heritage, whilst their contemporary Boccaccio injected new vigour and robust social comment into his tales of the *Decameron*. Humanity, realistically portrayed, became once more a fit subject for art and literature. People were thirsty for knowledge, not only in specialized fields, but throughout the whole range of human experience. No figure displays the breadth of Renaissance man's interests more clearly than Leonardo da Vinci, painter, mechanician and man of science.

The old certainties of the feudal order were being challenged. Flor-

Holbein's The Ambassadors, *surrounded by the trappings of Renaissance culture; maps, books, musical and scientific instruments. Notice the distorted skull in the lower foreground. The omnipresence of death was a recurrent theme.*

ence fell into the hands of the Medici family, bankers rather than landed aristocrats. Niccolo Machiavelli began to analyze how power might be manipulated without concern for morality, causing his name to be associated thereafter with ruthless cunning in politics and diplomacy. The horizons of the human world were extended by Spanish and Portuguese voyages of discovery, culminating in Columbus's discovery of the New World of the Americas.

By the 16th century the Renaissance had become a truly European phenomenon, producing the first giants of English and French literature in Chaucer, Shakespeare, Rabelais and Montaigne; and of Flemish and German painting in Van Eyck, Brueghel, Dürer and Holbein. Ideas were disseminated rapidly through the recent invention of the printed book. A doctrine known as humanism emerged, with the scholarly pursuit of knowledge for its own sake at its core. In place of the monk or cleric, a new image of the educated man arose—the secular man of culture, sceptical, tolerant and cosmopolitan. Erasmus of Rotterdam embodied the ideal.

Humanism was at first tolerated and even sponsored by the Church. But the 16th century brought Luther's revolt against the Pope's authority and thereafter the cultural climate was embittered by religious persecution and intolerance. Protestant zeal was answered by Catholic repression as the Roman Church fought back. The philosopher and scientist Galileo Galilei narrowly escaped execution because his empirical observations of the movement of the stars had challenged the Aristotelian theories which had now been absorbed into Catholic teaching.

The 17th century was a century of bitter strife in Europe, both between and within nations. England underwent a savage civil war as a result of which the monarchy was overthrown, restored, overthrown and restored again on a constitutional basis. The upheaval created a powerful parliament with considerable influence in law-making. A genera-

tion of political philosophers, notably Locke and Hume, tried to redefine the rights of kings in relation to their subjects. According to Locke, the king did not rule by divine right but by an implicit contract with his people. The debate was a critical one at this time for monarchs were beginning to centralize their kingdoms at the expense of the feudal aristocracy. The origins of the modern state, with fixed boundaries and central government, were emerging.

The Renaissance had been above all a cultural and scientific movement. The tradition of secular and rational thought was continued throughout the 17th and 18th centuries in a movement loosely known as the Enlightenment. In France, René Descartes applied the mathematical approach of deductive logic to philosophy and to an understanding of the physical universe. In England, Newton investigated the nature of light and established the law of gravitation, setting out his own laws of motion. The idea that all human experience can be subjected to intellectual scrutiny was expounded by the French *philosophes* of the 18th century, principally Montesquieu, Diderot and Voltaire who collaborated in the *Encyclopédie*, a massive work of reference.

The philosophes argued for freedom of thought and expression. They were not explicitly revolutionary and some argued in favour of 'enlightened despotism' as an alternative to the rule of the feudal lord and the authority of the Church. Yet the ideas of one philosophe, Jean-Jacques Rousseau, were to be political dynamite in France. In the *Contrat Social* of 1762, he suggested that individuals possessed natural rights which ought only to be surrendered in government to the general will of the people.

Society had outgrown the old order. Merchants could no longer tolerate the constraints of feudal tariff boundaries. The aristocracy was falling into eclipse and the moral authority of the Church was no longer universally accepted. The relationship of the individual to society needed radical examination.

A temple at Bhubaneswar, Orissa province, in north eastern India. The great Hindu temples were the focus of all aspects of Indian cultural life.

this far in his campaign of conquest, Islamic invaders subdued the area in the 12th and 13th centuries and the Mogul empire was established here in the 16th. But until the British placed the whole continent under imperial rule in the 19th century, southern India was never brought under full control.

The Golden Age of indigenous Indian culture came under the Gupta dynasty of 320–550 AD. The Guptas fought campaigns throughout the sub-continent though they never succeeded in forming a unified state, and the core of their empire was situated in the north east. This period saw the flowering of Sanskrit, which became the official language and the main mode of literary expression. The works of the poet and dramatist Kalidasa, the epic *Mahabharata* and the mythical *Puranas* date from this period. It was also the time when Indian science and mathematics were developed.

The Indian civilization which developed from the Gupta period onwards was one orientated around the royal courts, and the temples which became centres for pilgrimages, festivals and trade. Hinduism, the principal religion of the sub-continent, left its mark in every walk of life, establishing the principles of social order and of law as well as of religious conduct. At the heart of Hinduism is the belief in *karma*, that an individual's actions produce quantifiable spiritual effects. After death the accumulation of an individual's karma determines his form in his next life. Every individual thus occupies a social position according to his inherited karma, and it was from this belief that the structured caste system evolved, permitting little opportunity for social mobility. The *brahman* (priestly) and *kshatriyas* (noble) castes had distinct roles. Hinduism never became an organized state religion, however, and Hindu culture developed flexibly enough to survive alien rule. It has created an underlying passive continuity in Indian society under differ-

Society in India and China

While European society evolved through the Dark and Middle Ages to the cultural explosion of the Renaissance, the two great civilizations of India and China flourished in the East. Each was to extend its cultural influence beyond its geographical frontiers: India to Indonesia, Java, Sumatra and Borneo, whilst Chinese influence extended to Korea, Vietnam and Japan. The two civilizations were separated by the natural barrier of the Himalayan mountains and developed largely

independently of each other, though the spread of Buddhism (never the predominant religion in either land) resulted in considerable cultural interpenetration, most marked in the border areas of Tibet, Burma and Nepal.

India had always had strong trading connections with the West and the rich trade routes through the north of the continent made the area prone to military invasion and alien cultural influence. For example, Alexander the Great had reached

ent regimes. Only in the areas known today as Pakistan and Bangladesh (where Islam took root) and in Ceylon (where Buddhist colonies were established) was Hinduism supplanted.

Chinese civilization represents a complete contrast. As the empire evolved, the Confucian religion and the structure of the state became inseparably linked whilst, on the social level, family ties provided an underlying cohesion.

It was the imperial bureaucracy which sustained the distinctive character of Chinese civilization. Members of the bureaucracy were selected through a system of competitive public examinations, a procedure which dated back to the 2nd century BC. The examinations were in principle open to all, but the rigours of the examinations meant that only those with the leisure to study were able to join the élite, and these came largely from the landed gentry. The basis of selection was a thorough knowledge of the Confucian classics, of history and philosophy and of the correct style of essay-writing. Army leaders had to submit to similar examinations, although officers were never held in such esteem as the gentlemen scholars of the civil service.

The examination system did ensure that official positions were achieved on merit, but it also promoted an increasing conservatism in cultural life. Chinese artists, for example, became more concerned with perfecting the techniques laid down by tradition than with experiment and innovation. Enormous advances were made in the fields of science and technology, but these were not always developed to transform society as they were in Europe. The Chinese, for example, discovered how to make gunpowder long before Europeans but they did not apply it to warfare. They invented the magnetic compass but did not embark on long voyages of discovery. It is interesting, however, that two innovations, printed books and paper money, were widely applied, perhaps because they better served the interests of the scholarly civil service.

Until the 16th century, Imperial China kept pace with the West in technological advance, but thereafter it was rapidly overtaken. When European traders arrived in numbers in the 18th century, they were confined to restricted areas and forbidden to travel freely. Jealous of its ancient traditions and wary of innovation, imperial China became increasingly inward-looking. A decayed bureaucracy finally succumbed to the advanced technology of the West in the early 20th century. In 1905 the examination system was abolished and with it the whole

Chinese magistrates are examined in the works of Confucius. The great Imperial bureaucracy, based on the examination system, sustained the distinctive character of Chinese culture despite many changes of dynasty.

edifice of Confucian society collapsed.

The collapse of imperial China left a vacuum which was far more susceptible to violent change than that of Hindu India, where society had long been accustomed to political upheavals. Yet cultural traditions have endured in both nations. Mao Tse-tung can be seen as a figure in the tradition of the Confucian scholar-leader, just as Mahatma Gandhi fits into the mould of the Hindu brahman. Both civilizations had to face the challenge of industrialization, but it is important to note that neither was literally feudal; there was no true military aristocracy. In India, personal loyalties were due to the Hindu religion. In China, they were due to the Confucian state.

Liberalism and Socialism

In the first half of the 19th century, a new doctrine of reform spread throughout Europe, finding favour with the growing class of merchants, factory owners and professional men who had come to challenge the landed aristocracy as the figures of importance in society. The doctrine is known as liberalism, and its demands included free trade, the abolition of feudal privileges, and the establishment of self-governing nations. The reforming spirit was also expressed in widespread demands for constitutional government by elected representatives to replace the aristocratic élites of the old order. It is to liberalism that we owe the modern concept of parliamentary democracy; political parties competing in a national assembly and making regular appeals to a wide public for the right to govern. A respect for individual rights and freedoms was central to liberalism, a philosophy inspired by English thinkers like Jeremy Bentham (1748–1832) and John Stuart Mill (1806–73). Its economic bible was *The Wealth of Nations* by Adam Smith (1723–90), who argued that

Scenes from the Paris commune of 1871. When France was defeated by Prussia in that year, Parisian workers took control of the capital for a brief period.

governments should interfere as little as possible in the economy of a country. Under the impetus of liberalism, Britain achieved successive extensions of the right to vote throughout the 19th and early 20th centuries.

The English experience was widely admired, but elsewhere reform came with less continuity. It took the colossal upheaval of the Revolution to overthrow the old order in France. In Germany and Italy, it first took successive wars to unify the fragmentary kingdoms of those countries into two autonomous nation states. Modern states and democratic principles were established in a century of European turmoil which brought new social forces to the surface. Industrialization created a class of workers with increasing need to organize as trades unions in order to defend themselves against trade depressions, low wages and appalling conditions of work. Liberal politicians sometimes allied themselves with these new democratic forces, yet despite the spirit of equality fostered by liberalism, property remained sacred to liberals. The alliance with popular democratic forces did, however, breed a school of thought which was more

fervently egalitarian in spirit—socialism.

Socialists, broadly, demanded that property and the means of production, whether factory or farm, should be owned collectively by the people who worked in them. The early socialists, Robert Owen (1771–1858) and Charles Fourier (1772–1837) experimented with small self-sufficient communities. But memories of the French Revolution also inspired a more aggressive form of socialism, and by mid-century socialist thinking had hardened into revolutionary demands for the transformation of the whole of society. The year 1848 was one of violent insurrection throughout Europe, giving considerable impetus to developments, and subsequently one man in particular, the German Karl Marx (1818–83), came to dominate socialist thought.

Marx witnessed the repeated cycles of trade expansion and depression which came with liberal free trading. Capitalism, he concluded, could not stand the repeated shocks. Sooner or later, the vast and oppressed working class would rise and overthrow the smaller property-owning class. The means of production would come under the collective ownership of the working class; thus, society would pass 'dialectically' from feudalism, through capitalism, to socialism. It was, he considered, the obligation of progressive intellectuals to hasten the coming of this workers' revolution.

Throughout the second half of the 19th century, socialist parties grew in most industrialized nations and most drew inspiration increasingly from Marxism. Two successive international organizations of working men were formed, and, by 1914, the Second International had come to represent millions of working people throughout the world. Yet opinion had become deeply divided between socialists who (like Lenin in Russia and Rosa Luxembourg in Germany) continued to advocate violent revolution, and those 'revisionists' (like the French Jean Jaurès and the German August Bebel) who had

A musical group in Canton, China, performs under the paternal gaze of Chairman Mao. Relations with the Soviet Union reached crisis point during the Cultural Revolution of 1966. Since then, China has pursued her own distinctly individual road to socialism.

come to believe that socialism might be instituted through existing parliamentary channels. After the First World War and the Russian Revolution, the socialist world was bitterly divided between those who adhered to the intransigent doctines of the Russian Bolsheviks (known increasingly as communists) and the moderate socialist parties of western Europe (known generally as Social Democratic parties). Throughout the Depression of the years between the two world wars, the two tendencies remained bitterly opposed, though they did act together in Popular

Front movements to oppose the rise of Fascism and Nazism.

The rift, however, deepened after the Second World War and the communist gains in eastern Europe. Communism seemed to acquire uniform features: state ownership of land and industry, the abolition of parliamentary democracy and the substitution of a single official Communist Party maintained by a bureaucracy taking orders from Moscow. In contrast, Social Democratic parties continued to respect parliamentary forms, seeking to institute socialism through moderate extensions of state ownership and state welfare services.

Time has deepened the complexities of the socialist world. Liberal parties throughout the world have tended to decline, as Social Demo-

cratic parties have taken over much of their electoral support. The emergence of Communist China, hostile to Soviet Russia, has divided loyalties among potential recruits to communism in the Third World, whilst revolutionary Marxist parties adhering to neither Communism nor Social Democracy have proliferated. Recently, the communist parties of western Europe have themselves moderated their unquestioning obedience to Moscow and have won substantial electoral support in, for example, Italy, Spain and Portugal. The prospect of 'Eurocommunism', western European governments combining respect for parliamentary procedures with determined communist programmes, has been suggested as a possibility for the future.

In the long history of mankind, the period of industrialization occupies only a tiny space, little more than 200 years. Yet it has transformed society worldwide. Powered machines and factory production have not only made available a vastly increased quantity of goods, they have shaped our patterns of work and of leisure, our politics and warfare and our social relations. The change has been so abrupt and so startling in its effects that it is aptly described as a revolution.

The industrial revolution began in Britain in the early years of the 18th century. Britain was largely secure politically and socially, and new methods in farming were already producing surplus food for a rapidly expanding population, as well as surplus capital for investment in the proliferating workshops of weavers and metal-workers. Expansion overseas was opening up foreign markets for British goods, and giving access to cheap raw materials from abroad. Accompanying these developments

came a series of scientific and technical inventions which were to transform an agrarian economy into one built around trade and industry.

A variety of ingenious devices revolutionized the textile industry. John Kay's 'Flying Shuttle' (1733) and James Hargreaves' 'Spinning Jenny' (1765) speeded up the production of thread and cloth. Richard Arkwright's water frame (1769) and Samuel Crompton's 'Spinning Mule' (1779) allowed flourishing workshops to expand into large-scale factories.

Revolutions
The Industrial Revolution

The production of coal and iron increased dramatically after Abraham Darby discovered how to make coke for iron-smelting at his Coalbrookdale works in 1709. Coal, iron, and later steel, produced in vast quantities, were to make possible the expansion of railways and the production of steam engines and factory machinery on which Britain's industrial lead was based. But it was steam power itself that drove the wheels of industrialization. Thomas Newcomen invented a steam pump for extracting water from flooded mines in 1712. James Watt built

Machinists at work in a cycle factory, Coventry, England, in about 1895. Women supplied cheap labour for factory production

more powerful engines in the 1770s, and by 1789 steam power was being used in factories. In 1804 Richard Trevithick produced the first steam locomotive for use on rails.

Railways, together with improved roads and canals, made possible the rapid transportation of goods, and also enabled manufacturers to set up factories in areas which had hitherto been sparsely populated. The face of Britain was transformed, and by 1851, the year of the Great Exhibition, Britain's reputation as the 'workshop of the world' was firmly established.

During the second half of the century, however, two new giants came to challenge the British lead—Germany and the United States. It was the railways, and the political unity achieved under Bismarck, that enabled German industry to expand. Here, industrialization was closely associated with military conquest. The wars of unification gave enormous impetus to the arms industry, principally focused on the massive Krupp works at Essen. But in chemicals and engineering, much of the initiative of the later industrial revolution was German too. The engineers Daimler and Benz pioneered the development of motor cars in the 1880s, for example.

Railways and political unity were also the principal reasons for America's dramatic industrial expansion in the late 19th century. Once take-off had been achieved, it was perhaps inevitable that the continent's vast material resources should assure the United States of supremacy in the industrial field. Yet American expansion also owed a great deal to the ingenuity of her inventors, men like Samuel Morse who invented the electric telegraph, and Alexander Graham Bell, who invented the telephone (1876). Modern business methods were pioneered in America by families like the Carnegies who came to dominate steel production and the Rockefellers who dominated oil. It was in America too that mass production techniques were developed, notably by Henry Ford in the motor car industry. Mass production in turn bred mass outlets for goods; chain stores and advertising aimed at a mass public.

The supremacy of Europe and the United States in industrial technology gave them a tremendous advantage over less well-developed cultures, and provided an impetus for rapid colonization. Africa provides a striking example of the pace at which the scramble for overseas territories was conducted. In 1875, only one tenth of Africa had been colonized. About 20 years later, less than one tenth remained independent. Throughout the world, local cultures succumbed to the armour-plated warship and the breech-loading gun. Japan was the sole significant exception, and here only because the Meiji dynasty, restored in 1868, made a determined effort to adapt to western methods. The government gave official subsidies and encouragement to the railways, to industries like shipbuilding, textiles, sugar and glass, and also reformed education to provide the scientists and technologists demanded by industrial growth. Japan's success was dramatically displayed when, in 1905, she was able to defeat Russia in a war won by sheer technical superiority.

Of course, industrialization created appalling social evils, especially in the early years: overcrowded cities, terrible conditions of work, and the callous exploitation of child labour. (Children had worked on landed estates, but only as part of a family unit. The particular evil of the factory system was that children were estranged from their parents and placed under the rigid, often brutal discipline of an overseer.) Yet the very conditions which industrial society created, led to remedies which have advanced the well-being of the working population in the long run. Governments were forced to take on responsibility for such concerns as public health, education, and welfare services in the form of old-age pensions and sickness allowances. A revolution in manufacturing techniques became a social and political upheaval. The small, land-based community, orientated around seasonal change, with local laws and traditions, was superseded by the modern state.

The American Revolution

In 1763 France formally ceded Canada to Britain, and British control of North America seemed secure. Yet within the 13 British colonies of the eastern seaboard, a sense of American identity independent of the mother country was already developing. Separated from Britain by the wide Atlantic Ocean, the colonists saw less and less reason to consider themselves subjects of a distant monarch and a parliament in which they were not represented. Besides, the many German, Dutch, Scots and Irish settlers could not be expected to feel great loyalty to an English king. For some 12 years before open hostilities broke out, a spirit of independence was growing.

There was in Britain itself an awareness of the need to reform relations with the colonies, but British interference of any kind was taken increasingly as a threat to the freedoms which Americans enjoyed. The colonies had their own assemblies, and British officials did not interfere much with their internal affairs. In 1763, however, the British prohibited further emigration to the West because of the dangers posed by a rising of Indian tribes. In 1761 a tax was imposed on sugar, and in 1765 a Stamp Tax applied to certain legal documents in order to raise revenue. The new laws were not in themselves provocative; they represented attempts to reform imperial trade and to ensure that the colonies paid something towards the defence of their territories. But they raised a critical issue—did the British government have the right to legislate in this way, without consulting the Americans?

The taxes caused a wave of riots and protests and the stamp tax was withdrawn. But it was succeeded by further taxes on paint, paper, glass and tea: no real attempt had been made to resolve the constitutional dispute. The cry of 'no taxation without representation' was raised. Five rioters were killed by British troops in an episode known as the Boston Massacre (1770). Alarmed by the strength of the colonists' feeling,

the British again gave way, withdrawing all duties except that on tea. The tea duty became the principal focus of anti-British feeling and in 1773 a small group of American patriots, disguised as Indians, destroyed a cargo of tea in Boston harbour. The British replied with their first offensive moves, closing Boston harbour and imposing martial law on the town.

The situation was now tense. In September 1774 delegates of the states met at Philadelphia to draw up a declaration of rights, and to petition King George III whilst affirming their loyalty to him. The petition was ignored and the British sent extra regiments to America. The colonists replied by collecting arms for the conflict which now seemed inevitable. Hostilities began in April 1775 when a detachment of British soldiers was sent to Lexington to seize an arms cache. Shots were fired and several British troops killed. Just over a year later the states formally declared their independence.

The war that followed was won by the colonists for a variety of reasons. They knew the terrain better than the British, and shrewd leadership kept their ragged army intact during the uncertain months of the early campaigns. The Americans were also able to gain vital support from France and Spain and the battle of Yorktown (1781), won with the assistance of the French, proved decisive. Peace negotiations began and two years later Great Britain recognized the independence of the states at the Treaty of Paris (1783).

The military victory of colonists over Crown was, in itself, an episode of dramatic historical significance. But the constitutional innovations of the young republic were more significant still. The Declaration of Independence opened with words, now famous, which were at the time a startlingly blunt statement of enlightened and democratic principles: 'We hold these truths to be self evident, that all men are created equal, that they are endowed by their

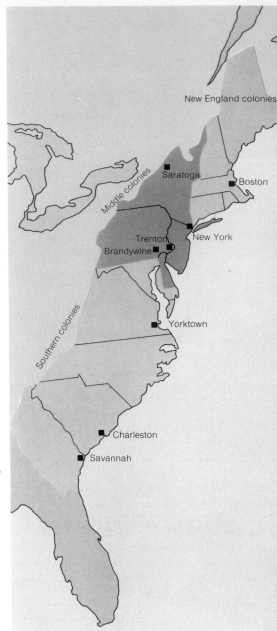

Creator with certain unalienable Rights, that among these are Life, Liberty and the pursuit of Happiness. . . .'

The constitution itself was drawn up in 1787 and its opening words are similarly bold: 'We the People . . .'. A national constitution was being framed around the principle that government derives from the will of the people, in a nation without a king.

Of course, the new United States was as yet weak, and the vast hinterland of the West had not yet been opened up. Democracy was imperfect (as it had been in Ancient Athens) for the growing population of black slaves in the southern plantations were not accorded the rights so boldly proclaimed in the constitution. The full significance of the revolution was only fully recognized elsewhere towards the middle

of the 19th century, as the United States began to take the geographical shape we know today, and as the enormous resources of the continent were exploited. As a major world power, the United States presented a more persuasive argument for the potential of republican government than as the distant federation of rebellious states which came on to the stage of world history in 1783.

The American Constitution

Drawn up in 1787, the constitution embodied many features of English practices. The principles of English common law were adopted, for example. Two chambers, one legislative (the Congress) and one executive (the Senate) were intended as imitations of the two houses of the English Parliament, though there was one important departure—the hereditary composition of the English House of Lords was not copied. Anxious to avoid the tyranny of a central governmental machine, the union was instituted on a federal basis, with the individual states having considerable autonomy. The

George Washington (1732–99).
Modest and largely unambitious, he
accepted the Presidency only with
reluctance.

problems created by the federal approach were not resolved until after the conclusion of the American Civil War (1861–5).

Above all, the American constitution was founded on the principle of republicanism. In place of a hereditary monarchy, the office of the elected president was established. George Washington became the first president in 1789.

The French Revolution

In 1788 France had for over a century been the major power on the European continent. The royal court at Versailles was a model of splendour whose style and manners were imitated in a host of lesser monarchies; the capital city of Paris was the intellectual centre of enlightened thought. Yet France's eminence had been achieved, to a great extent, by borrowing, and during the century of French supremacy the monarchy had acquired a colossal and accumulating debt. Ancient feudal restraints made it difficult to raise taxes from the French nobility, a vast and diverse class with special privileges before the law. The burden of taxation fell more and more heavily on France's poor, peasant and labouring classes. The population itself was growing at an alarming rate, and thousands flocked to Paris seeking work. The rootless and alienated Paris crowd was to provide the insurrectionary impetus of the capital during the years of ferment which were to come.

In 1788, the French government resorted to an ancient institution to solve its fiscal problem: the Estates General were summoned to Versailles. The Estates was a body comprising representatives from the three classes of feudal society—the nobility, clergy and commoners. No such meeting had been held since 1614, and at a time when the educated classes were looking more and more jealously at the constitutional developments in Britain and America, the move was interpreted as a progressive gesture towards representative government. Although the legal powers of the Estates were never closely defined, the expectations it aroused were high.

The first meeting took place on 5 May 1789 and the class of commoners (mostly lawyers and professional men) soon seized the initiative in the debates. In July, thwarted by the two upper estates, they broke away and formed themselves into a National Assembly, whilst in Paris the crowd rioted and sporadic revolts broke

out in the provinces. The revolution was under way. In October, an armed mob made their way to Versailles and forced the royal family and the Assembly to come back with them to Paris.

The Assembly itself was now divided between those (who sat on the left) who demanded sweeping social changes, and those (on the right) who did not. It is a mark of the impact of the French Revolution that the terminology of Left and Right in politics has been used ever since to denote progressive and conservative forces.

It was the Left which triumphed, and during the two years of its existence the Assembly's energy was astounding. Church lands were nationalized. Feudal taxes and privileges were abolished and equality before the law proclaimed. The country was reorganized in 'departments' coming under the control of a centralized representative government. The upheaval inspired considerable opposition both at home and abroad. The new constitution brought France's leaders into conflict with the Pope, and the king, Louis XVI, grew increasingly concerned about encroachments on royal authority. Tension increased in 1792 when France went to war first with Austria, then with Prussia. The revolution was entering a new phase, one of patriotic defence against the threats posed by the old monarchies. With France under siege, the royal family were seen more and more as a possible focus for attempts to restore the old order. In the summer of 1792, insurrection in Paris caused the downfall of the monarchy, and a new assembly was called to draw up a republican constitution. This assembly, known as the Convention, ordered the king's execution in January 1793.

Abroad, the events in France were now viewed with horror by monarchists and aristocrats alike. England joined the alliance of states against the French republic, and this new pressure on the revolution resulted in a savage 'Terror' being instituted

against internal threats. The period saw the rise and fall of Maximilien Robespierre (1758–94), whose ruthless revolutionism provoked his political enemies to coalesce in alliance against him, and to order his execution in July 1794.

The fall of Robespierre brought a relaxation of the Terror. The Convention was succeeded by a Directory in 1795, in which the anti-Robespierre alliance maintained power until it was itself overthrown by a young and successful Corsican general called Napoleon Bonaparte (1769–1821).

The rise of Napoleon in 1799 brought an end to the instability of revolutionary governments, but it did not end the revolution. In time, Napoleon was to adopt the title of emperor, but he was an emperor whose power was confirmed by suc-

cessive plebiscites, and in this sense government remained an expression of the popular will. Many of the structural changes in French society were consolidated during the Napoleonic period, and Napoleon was able to reconcile French Catholics to the state by an agreement with the Pope, known as the Concordat (1801). Church lands, sold during the revolution, remained in the hands of their new owners. As France expanded through conquest, the revolution was exported to new territories and satellite states, particularly in western Germany and Italy. Even the downfall of Napoleon himself did not halt the process which had been set in motion in 1789. Though the monarchy was re-established in 1815, the structural changes in French society were now too deeply rooted to sustain a true return to the old order. Successive revolutions, in 1830, 1848 and 1871 ensured the eventual triumph of republican government in France.

The French revolution was a staggering phenomenon to contemporaries, whether they viewed it favourably or were hostile. It had transformed a whole nation and inspired republican thinkers throughout Europe for generations afterwards. The ancient bastions of feudalism, King, Church and Nobility had been overthrown in the names of Liberty, Equality and Fraternity. Above all, it set up the notion that human beings could order their affairs through the exercise of Reason, rather than Authority and Tradition. Faith in rationalism was exulted in large

Liberty Guiding the People: *Delacroix's representation of the 1830 revolution, when the restored Bourbon monarchy was overthrown for a second time. Republican sentiment and the revolutionary impulse were never finally suppressed after 1789.*

ways and small—sometimes with comic lack of success. Attempts to introduce a new calender, for example, and to develop a cult of the Supreme Being to replace the Christian deity, failed miserably. Other innovations endured—the decimalization of coinage, for example. Finally, the revolution was not as total an experience as it seemed to many at the time. The crowd, which had provided the fuel for revolution, did not profit greatly in the subsequent redistribution of property. Equality before the law was established, but gross inequalities of wealth remained.

The Russian Revolution

Whilst industrialization and democracy gained ground in western Europe during the 19th century, Russia remained an essentially feudal society. The Russian empire, which embraced many different nationalities, was ruled by the Tsar (emperor) from St Petersburg as it had been for centuries. Russia's vast population was still tied to the land, and serfdom itself was not abolished until 1861. Attempts to liberalize the autocratic regime met with repeated rebuffs. By the late 19th century, revolutionism had become for many the only apparent means of bringing about social change.

The Social Revolutionaries comprised by far the largest of the revolutionary groups and drew wide support from the oppressed agrarian population. But around the turn of the century Marxist revolutionaries were beginning to gain ground among factory hands in the first major industrial works in Moscow and St Petersburg. In 1903 the Marxists split into two parties—the moderate Mensheviks, and the Bolsheviks who, under the leadership of Lenin, proposed intransigent revolutionism. As a proportion of the total population, the Bolsheviks were a tiny minority, but they were disciplined and well organized, and powerful in the key cities of St Petersburg and Moscow.

When Russia was defeated by Japan in a war of 1905, unrest came to the surface as revolution. Strikes and demonstrations were widespread throughout the Russian empire, and inside St Petersburg a Council of Workers' Deputies, or *Soviet*, was formed to coordinate strike action. Shaken by events, the Tsar was forced to grant certain concessions to popular feeling. A legislative assembly called the *Duma* was promised, and civil liberties were to be guaranteed. Ferment died down towards the end of the year. The Soviet was disbanded, and the Tsar later withdrew several of his concessions. But successive Dumas were summoned over the following years and although their powers were limited they might have formed the basis of a parliamentary tradition in Russia if the holocaust of the First World War had not intervened.

Military disasters on the Eastern Front undermined the Tsar's authority and a liberal bloc within the Duma pressed for an extension of their powers. The disillusion of defeat spread during the bitterly cold winter of 1916–17; food and fuel prices had risen by 50 per cent since the outbreak of war. In February 1917, strikes, riots and mutinies were rife. A general strike inspired by the Bolsheviks crippled St Petersburg (renamed Petrograd at the outset of the war). Mutinous troops refused to keep order and insurrection spread to the highest levels. In March, Russian generals forced the Tsar to abdicate and a Provisional Government formed by a committee of liberal Duma representatives took office. They did not, however, end the war. By autumn, a second wave of revolution was under way. Real power now lay in the hands of the revived Petrograd Soviet and in soviets established in other major cities. The soviets themselves were now electing Bolshevik leaders, in preference to the slower-moving Mensheviks and Social Revolutionaries, and arming themselves for revolution. On 25 October, inspired by Bolshevik leadership, a crowd of workers and soldiers stormed the Winter Palace in Petrograd. With remarkable ease, they overthrew the Provisional Government.

The Russian revolution, as a social upheaval, extended for many years after the events of 1917. The Bolshevik leaders had won power with the slogan of 'Peace, Land and Bread'. They concluded a treaty with Germany which brought peace, but their position was precarious and, to Marxists, an anomaly. Believing that a true socialist revolution could only take place in a highly industrialized society, they hoped at first for revolutions to sweep the industrialized nations of the West. When these aborted, their isolation became clear. They had to fight both counter-revolutionary armies and foreign intervention, and cope too with the ambitions of millions of peasants who hoped to profit by the revolution in gaining new land. Cherished socialist principles had to be abandoned; after disastrous early attempts to requisition grain from the peasants and to place land under collective ownership, an appalling famine set in. To ensure survival, Lenin launched a New Economic Policy in 1921. Peasants were again allowed to trade privately, to lease land and to hire labour. By the time of Lenin's death in 1924, the NEP was beginning to show results, pro-

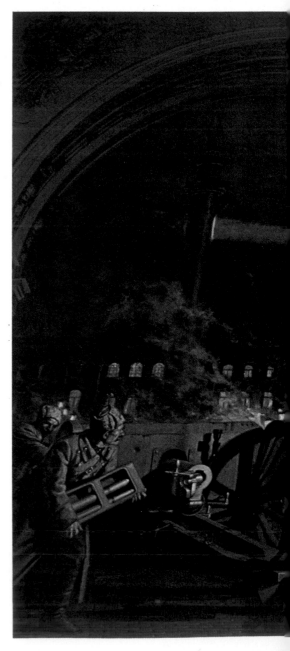

ducing enough grain to feed the starving urban population.

By 1927, Joseph Stalin was firmly installed as Lenin's successor and Bolshevik authority was much less precarious. Stalin was able to examine the peasant question again, and reversed the NEP in the first of several Five Year Plans, instituting forced collectivization of the land and making a determined effort to shift the economic weight of the country from land to industry. The success of his policy was dramatic, but so was the suffering it imposed. Millions of peasants were dispossessed to supply forced labour for new industrial works.

It was also under Stalin that Russian communism developed its most brutal and authoritarian features. Lenin had introduced a single-party state, but considerable argument had been permitted within the Bolshevik party. Under Stalin, the party became little more than the instrument of a centralized bureaucracy. There were successive purges in which thousands of loyal party members and army leaders were executed. The exact figures are not known but it is believed that many millions died in Stalin's determination to make socialism work in one country.

When the Second World War again threw the governments of Europe into confusion, the victorious Red Army brought Russian communism to one after another of the lands of eastern Europe: Poland, Hungary, Rumania, Czechoslovakia and East Germany. Only communist Yugoslavia and Albania avoided submission to the authority of Moscow, despite risings in East Germany (1953), Hungary (1956) and Czechoslovakia (1968). In recent years the rise of communist China had challenged Russian supremacy in the communist world, but for well over half the century the Russian experience has dominated the substance and the mythology of revolutionary socialism.

Red Guards storm the Winter Palace in Petrograd, 25 October 1917. They met little resistance from the Provisional Government: only six people died in the fighting. Yet the successful assault brought the Bolsheviks to power.

Third World Independence

The conclusion of the Second World War ended Europe's domination of world affairs. Power now seemed divided between Russia and the United States. But as the old empires retreated a new presence began to be felt; it has since become known as the Third World.

The term is loosely used to cover all of the underdeveloped areas which are, or have been, under colonial rule. These include much of Asia, Africa, South and Central America as well as fringe territories in Europe such as Cyprus and Malta. Obviously, a term which embraces such a diversity of cultures can have only a limited value.

The concept of the Third World was first formulated at the Bandung Conference of 1955, a meeting of delegates from some 30 of the developing nations. Here, representatives pressed for a united neutralist front against the power blocs of East and West, support for independence

movements throughout the world, and a recognition of the equality of all nations and races. The promise of the Bandung Conference was never fulfilled; the Third World nations have never united as a single cohesive force, for example. Yet their economic underdevelopment and their insistence on the rights of self determination have provided some continuing sense of a common interest.

Among the nations represented at the conference was the newly formed People's Republic of China, a nation whose rise as a world power has been far more successful than any other, to the extent that China is hardly considered a Third World Country any more. The Chinese struggle for independence began in the early years of this century. The last imperial dynasty was overthrown by a nationalist revolution in 1911, and there followed a long period of internal struggle between the ruling

Unita liberation forces training in Angola, 1976, with weapons supplied by China. Angola formerly a Portugese territory, has recently seen bitter fighting between rival factions drawing support from the powers of the East and the West.

nationalists and opposing communist forces. Japan profited by China's disunity by invading Manchuria. The nationalists did agree to form an alliance with the communists against the common enemy, but after Japan's defeat in 1945 civil war broke out. Mainland China fell into the hands of the communists under Mao Tse-tung, and the nationalists were forced to withdraw to the island of Formosa (Taiwan).

Mao confirmed his authority over China in two stages. In the Great Leap Forward of the late 1950s, he introduced the commune system to agriculture and began the war on backwardness and ignorance. The Cultural Revolution of 1966 represented an attack launched against privileged élites, in which Chinese youth was organized on a massive scale in Red Guard units to defend the spirit of the revolution.

Though the Chinese communists had received support from Russia during the early years, a rift between the two had become profound by 1960. China, with its own brand of communism, began to compete with Russia for the allegiance of the emerging nations of the Third World.

In India, the other great Asian sub-continent, the independence struggle had become a mass movement in the years between the two world wars. Mahatma Gandhi led campaigns of non-cooperation and civil disobedience against the British authorities. Though his own approach was non-violent, bitter clashes with the British occurred, and the independence movement also revealed savage hostility between India's Hindu and Moslem populations. In 1947, the British granted independence and the sub-continent was divided into two nations—predominantly Hindu India and predominantly Moslem Pakistan. India subsequently developed good relations with Russia, whilst Pakistan drew support from China. Enmity broke out in the Indo-Pakistan war of 1971, after which East Pakistan was set up as the independent state of Bangladesh.

Whatever India's internal problems, the independence of this, 'the brightest jewel in the British Crown' gave enormous encouragement to nationalist movements elsewhere. One after another, Britain's foreign possessions were granted independence during the following years. Independence was sometimes accompanied by violence, as in Kenya and Cyprus, but Britain's overall policy was to aim for a peaceful transition. This was not the policy of France: Vietnam and Algeria were only ceded after savage warfare.

Predictably, the speed with which independence was granted led in some cases to unstable governments. Coups, civil wars and boundary disputes have troubled almost all of the new African nations, for example. But the ambitions of the major powers have also contributed to the political volatility of the Third World. Far from remaining neutral,

Third World nations have repeatedly been the focal points of international tension, in the Middle East, Cuba, Korea, Vietnam and Angola, for example. Recently freed from colonial rule, many of the Third World nations have preferred to draw support from Russia and China than from the former imperial powers, and many have described themselves as socialist. The term, however, is open to wide interpretation and Western powers have sometimes overreacted in assuming that socialist governments will necessarily be hostile. The position of Tanzania, maintaining strong links with Britain while drawing aid from China, is interesting in this context.

Overt military support is rarely displayed. Economic aid is the main means by which the major powers

Fidel Castro, the Cuban lawyer turned revolutionary leader who in 1959 overthrew the corrupt government of General Batista. Two years later he publicly professed his Communist beliefs.

have tried to secure the allegiance of Third World nations. Russia provided the funds and expertise to build the massive Aswan Dam in Egypt, for example, and China for the Tanzam railway in East Africa. The United States has pumped money into the South American regimes in order to maintain its strategic interests.

In recent years, the Arab oil-producing countries have begun to exploit the enormous power which their reserves of oil confer. Yet here, as elsewhere, the problem of underdevelopment has continued to make Third World countries vulnerable to foreign interference. Advances in medicine have brought rapid increases in population levels, but food and industrial production have not advanced at a similar rate. Hunger and poverty make economic aid a necessity for the survival of many Third World countries. True independence will not be achieved until these have been conquered.

Wars of the 20th Century
World Wars I and II

The first half of the 20th century saw two world wars and the development of atomic weapons, events which changed the face of the world and which colour almost every aspect of contemporary life. During the 19th century the foundations were laid for the war which was to break out in 1914. In Europe, the industrial revolution created the ability to produce weapons of mass destruction and to supply front-line armies comparatively rapidly by means of railways and motor vehicles. Advances in engineering similarly increased firepower at sea, and man's conquest of the air began. The United States established itself as a major power, but development in Russia was slow. In the Far East, Japan emerged from centuries of isolation into a brave new industrial world.

Russo–Japanese War

In the first three years of the new century Japan prepared her revenge for Russian intervention in the Sino–Japanese war of 1894–5. She planned to establish hegemony over Korea by destroying the Russian Far East Fleet, capturing its base at Port Arthur—the only year-round ice-free port available to the Russians on their eastern seaboard—and then destroy Russian forces on land in Manchuria and Korea. Russia's vast army of 4½ million men could not reinforce the troops in the Far East sufficiently rapidly to avoid defeat, since the only supply route was the 5,500-mile Trans-Siberian Railway from Moscow. The Russo–Japanese war was a typical limited conflict but was fought with armies of unprecedented size, and it demonstrated the defensive value of the machine gun as well as the offensive effectiveness of artillery. Japan's navy, which annihilated the Russian fleet at Tsushima in May 1905, won an important moral as well as material victory.

First World War

The First World War (1914–18) was the first example of total war, and involved even larger armies. Tech-

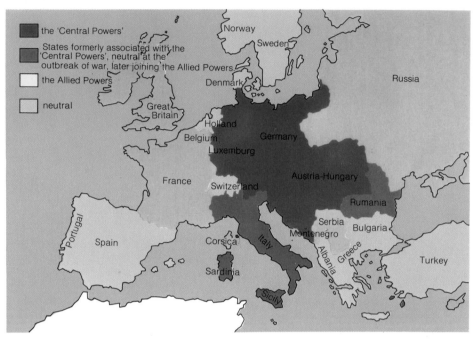

The European powers on August 14, 1914. The central powers were surrounded by potential enemies, with Russia to the east, Italy to the south and France and Britain to the west.

nology made a decisive impact on warfare for the first time: the machine gun, artillery piece, barbed wire and improved construction methods for fortifications sounded the death knell of the cavalry as a shock force, leaving a combination of artillery and infantry as the new tactical element. Poison gas made its appearance, and the tank—which remains a central weapon of the modern army—added a new mobility and firepower.

Gen. Count von Schlieffen, chief of the German General Staff from 1891 to 1906, had evolved a plan to be used in the event of Germany being involved in a war on two fronts with France and Russia. The plan anticipated that France would attack in Alsace-Lorraine upon declaration of war by Germany; this would be met with a feint followed by an encircling move through Holland and Belgium, then round to the west of Paris to trap the French forces. In fact the Schlieffen plan was substantially amended by his successors, and after initial gains the German forces were held by the Allies (mainly Britain and France). The stalemate of trench warfare persisted on the Western Front throughout the remainder of the conflict. In southern Europe,

Italy and Austro–Hungary were at war, and Turkish forces repulsed an attempted Allied invasion of Asia Minor.

At sea, the Royal Navy blockaded the fleets of the Central Powers (Germany, Austro–Hungary and Turkey) and the only major clash between the British Grand Fleet and the German High Seas Fleet, at Jutland in May/June 1916, ended indecisively. Beneath the surface, however, the German navy was bringing submarine warfare to a fine art. Britain depended on seaborne supplies to maintain her war effort, and Germany hoped to affect the course of the war on land by her efforts at sea.

The internal combustion engine, which allowed motor vehicles to assume the roles traditionally carried out by animals, also permitted the development of aircraft. In the early stages of the First World War these were used only for spotting enemy movements, but by 1918 the specialized categories of fighter, bomber and ground-attack aircraft had emerged.

Second World War

The seeds of the Second World War, sown by the Allies' clumsy handling of relationships with Germany after the 1918 armistice, germinated and grew throughout the 1930s. Italy invaded Abyssinia, the only African state which had previously been uncolonized by Europeans, and the Spanish Civil War from 1936 to 1939 gave Italian, German and Russian forces the opportunity of a dress rehearsal for many of the tactics to be employed in the Second World War. In the East, Japan was fighting on the Asian mainland from 1931 and the endless quest for raw materials was to lead almost inevitably to conflict with the United States.

On 1 September 1939 Germany invaded Poland and six years of war began. Using *Blitzkrieg* (lightning war) tactics the all-conquering German forces overran Denmark and Norway in the spring of 1940, followed by Belgium, Holland and France in May and June. Stubborn resistance by the Royal Air Force in the Battle of Britain prevented an invasion of Britain, but from November 1940 the blitz (bombing of British cities) began. Italian forces entered south-eastern Europe and the Middle East.

The European powers in September 1939. The Berlin-Rome axis safeguarded Germany's southern flank in 1939, but the traditional enemies remained to the east and west.

Germany
associated with Germany
friendly to Germany
the Allies
guaranteed by the Allies
neutral

The face of warfare was changed at a stroke in August 1945 with the dropping of atomic bombs on Hiroshima (seen here in March 1946) and Nagasaki. The bombs were tiny by present-day standards.

In mid-1941 Germany turned on her former ally, the Soviet Union, and pushed eastwards in operation 'Barbarossa'. In the Atlantic the wolf packs of 15–20 U-Boats were threatening to disrupt supplies to Europe, and in December 1941 the war spread to the Pacific. The US navy lost a large proportion of its Pacific fleet in the surprise Japanese attack on Pearl Harbor, but the three aircraft carriers escaped and at the battle of Midway in the following June the tide turned, with the Japanese navy losing four carriers.

By the autumn of 1942 the war was moving in favour of the Allies. Montgomery's victory over Rommel at El Alamein in North Africa was closely followed by the landing of US troops in Morocco. The Germans were driven out of Africa and in September 1943, after Sicily had been invaded, Italy surrendered. German forces were suffering crushing defeats in Russia, losing 3,000 tanks, 5,000 motor vehicles and 1,400 aircraft at Kursk in July 1943. By the end of that year, U-Boats were being sunk faster than they could be replaced and the introduction of P-51 Mustang escort fighters allowed German targets to be attacked relentlessly by US bombers during the day as well as by British aircraft at night.

The Japanese navy was finally destroyed as a fighting force in October 1944, four aircraft carriers being sunk during the battle of Leyte Gulf. Allied forces were closing in on two great Axis powers, with US troops island-hopping towards Japan and their counterparts sweeping across France following D-Day in June 1944. The Rhine was crossed in March 1945 and two months later Germany surrendered unconditionally. The war continued in the Far East until September, when atomic bombs were dropped on Hiroshima and Nagasaki, forcing Japan to capitulate.

Post World War II

There have been two major areas of consistent conflict since the end of the Second World War: eastern Asia, where communist forces have opposed non-communist governments assisted by Western powers; and the Middle East, where the struggle between Israel and her Arab neighbours has exploded into active warfare on four occasions. In virtually every major war one side has been supplied by the West, notably the United States, and the other has received aid from the Soviet Union or China. Arms embargoes have been applied and then lifted with bewildering frequency, and often with little discernible effect. Nations differing from their neighbours in political ideology, religion or culture—the traditional mainsprings of warfare—have found one major power or another with a vested interest in the outcome of any conflict and a willingness to supply equipment and expertise.

Korea

At the end of the Second World War the Allies split Korea for the purpose of accepting the surrender of Japanese troops: north of the 38th parallel of latitude they were to be dealt with by Soviet forces, while those south of that line were to surrender to US troops. The 38th parallel became the dividing line between the communist Democratic People's Republic of Korea in the north and the Republic of Korea to the south. On 25 June 1950, Northern forces swept across the border and virtually overran the South within a few weeks. The United Nations responded by landing troops at Inchon in the South. On 25 September the South's capital city, Seoul, was recaptured; less than a month later the Northern capital, Pyongyang, was also overrun by UN forces.

The United Nations armies pushed northwards to the Yalu river which formed the border between North Korea and Manchuria, but aerial reconnaissance beyond the Yalu was prohibited. In the winter of 1950 the North Koreans counter-attacked with the aid of Chinese forces and by January 1951 they had recrossed the 38th parallel. In April General MacArthur, commander of the UN force and of the US forces in the Far East, was relieved by President Truman. He had consistently advocated air attacks on assembly points in Manchuria, the use of nationalist Chinese troops in Korea and support for an invasion of the Chinese mainland by Chiang Kai-Shek's forces.

Fighting continued for another two years before the armistice was signed in July 1953. The ceasefire line coincided closely with the old border, the 38th parallel, but the three years of war had cost the UN forces of 15 states a total of 475,000 killed, wounded or captured. South Korea lost 300,000 troops and 3 million civilian dead, while the North suffered 2 million military and civilian casualties.

Indo-China

The wars further south in Indo-China were also a legacy of the 1939–45 global conflict. The Viet Minh, an assortment of communists and nationalists led by Ho Chi Minh and General Giap, declared Vietnam an independent republic at the end of the Second World War, following support by the Allies in their fight against the Japanese. France was anxious to continue her traditional hegemony over Indo-China, however, and sporadic fighting between French and Viet Minh forces lasted for nearly a decade.

In 1953 the French hoped to crush the Viet Minh finally by concentrating them in an area where they could be destroyed. The village and airfield at Dienbienphu, west of the Viet Minh capital of Hanoi, were fortified and manned by 15,000 troops. General Giap's forces were better trained, armed and equipped than they had been given credit for, however, and after a six-month siege they overran the garrison in May 1954 when the defenders' ammunition was expended. The disaster at Dienbienphu virtually ended French domination of Indo-China.

An international conference sitting in Geneva divided Vietnam along the 17th parallel, with the communists in the north and a non-communist regime to the south. In

The US Government faced opposition to the Vietnam War at home as well as on the battlefields of South-East Asia: students, radicals and draft-dodgers frequently clashed with the National Guard.

1957 the North's guerrilla army, by now known as the Viet Cong, stepped up its actions against the South. The South appealed for US help in 1960, by which time large parts of the country were effectively controlled by the Viet Cong, and in December 1961 US advisors were followed by the first direct military supplies.

In August 1964 North Vietnamese torpedo boats attacked a US destroyer in the Gulf of Tonkin, and President Johnson ordered reprisal air strokes against the North by carrier-based aircraft. The following February the US air force and navy began systematic bombing of North Vietnamese military targets, and the US was well and truly embroiled in the war. By the beginning of 1969 the United States had more than half a million troops in Vietnam, but even the awesome concentration of firepower available from a superpower could not destroy either the military forces of the North or their will to fight. In January 1973 the US ended bombing of North Vietnam and in August all offensive missions in Indo-China were halted. The peace agreement was largely ignored by both the North and South, however, and in the spring of 1975 communist forces overran the South. The Saigon government surrendered on 30 April, and North Vietnam had succeeded in reunifying the country by force.

The Middle East

In the Middle East, war between Israel and her Arab neighbours broke out on 14 May 1948—the day on which the Zionist state was established. Hostilities ended officially the following January, following mediation by the United Nations, but intermittent clashes continued. On 29 October 1956 Israeli forces invaded Egyptian Sinai after fears of an Arab attack. British and French forces invaded Suez, but the United Nations condemned all three aggressors and they were forced to withdraw.

In June 1967 Israel again carried out a preemptive attack on Arab

The Israeli navy (seen here patrolling the Straits of Gaza) has proved more than a match for Arab naval forces since the sinking of the destroyer Eilat *by a missile*

forces. The Israeli air force virtually wiped out Arab airpower and the war lasted only six days. This time the Israelis did not withdraw from their captured territory in the Gaza Strip, Sinai, the west bank of the Jordan River and the Golan Heights. The Six Day War was followed by a three-year War of Attrition before a ceasefire was arranged in 1970.

During the summer of 1973 tension again increased, and on 6 October the Israeli High Command was taken by surprise when Egyptian forces crossed the Suez Canal into Sinai and Syria attacked in the north. The Israeli air force soon gained air superiority, but the Arabs' Russian-supplied surface-to-air missiles took a heavy toll of Israeli fighter-bombers. Thousands of tanks—more than had fought at Kursk in the Second World War—clashed in Sinai and the superpowers were hard put to keep their respective sides supplied. Israel counter-attacked and was moving into African Egypt by the time the final ceasefire came into effect on 24 October. At the time of writing, Israel still occupies most of the territory claimed by the Arabs and a lasting peace is far from certain.

Nuclear Weapons

Nuclear weapons have only been used twice in anger—those dropped on the Japanese cities of Hiroshima and Nagasaki in August 1945. Since then the Soviet Union, Britain, France and China have in turn become nuclear powers. The first nuclear weapons were atomic bombs: they produced a massive flux of energy by a chain reaction in uranium or plutonium. These fission weapons were followed by hydrogen bombs, in which an atomic bomb acts as a detonator for the fusion of hydrogen atoms to form helium. This process releases more energy than can be obtained by fission alone.

As nuclear weapons were made smaller they could be delivered by methods other than giant bombers such as the B-29s used against Japan. Artillery, fighter-bombers and ballistic missiles were added to the nuclear armoury, and the five atomic powers now all deploy both strategic nuclear weapons—delivered by comparatively long-range missiles and bombers—and their tactical equivalents, which in many cases can be interchanged with conventional high-explosive warheads, shells or bombs.

Comparative History Time Chart

4,000–600 BC

4,000–3,000 BC: First Sumerian, Assyrian and Egyptian settlements in the Near East; first written records. Chinese settlements in the Yellow River valley.

3,000–2,000 BC: Sumerian cities founded. Old Kingdom established in Egypt. Rise of Troy and of Cretan civilization in Mediterranean. Rule of emperors established in China. Cities of Indus Valley founded in India.

2,000–1,000 BC: Babylonian Empire founded. Rise of Assyria. Middle and New Kingdoms in Egypt. Hebrew settlements in Canaan. Phoenician cities founded. Rise of Greek civilization; Greeks sack Troy. Writing developed in China; rule of Shang and Chou dynasties. Aryan peoples invade India from Central Asia; Sanscrit developed.

1,000–600 BC: Fall of Assyria. Medes and Persians settle in Persia. Greek alphabet evolved; Homeric literature and Olympic Games. Etruscan settlements in Italy. Foundation of Rome. First poetry in China. Growth of Hinduism and development of caste system in India.

600 BC–AD 1

600–500 BC: Rise of Athens and Sparta. Rome becomes a republic. Confucian teaching spreads in China. Spread of Buddhism in India. Rise of Persia.

500–400 BC: Greeks defeat Persians. Age of Pericles in Athens. Sanscrit grammar in India. Chou Dynasty in China.

400–300 BC: Plato's Academy founded in Athens. Macedonians defeat Greeks. Alexander the Great takes Greek civilization into Syria, Egypt, Persia and India. Mauryan Empire established in India. Hebrew Law collected.

300–200 BC: Punic wars between Carthage and Rome. Defeat of Hannibal; Roman power extends. Rule of Huang Ti in China; Great Wall built. Rule of Asoka in India; *Ramayana,* Indian epic poem composed.

200–100 BC: Rome conquers Greece. Han Dynasty established in China.

100 BC–AD 1: Caesar's conquests of Gaul and invasion of Britain; defeats Pompey in Civil War; becomes emperor; murdered. Octavian defeats Mark Anthony at Actium.

AD 1–500

AD 1–100: Life and teaching of Christ, gospels of Mathew, Mark, Luke and John; missionary work of St. Paul. Persecution of Christians under Nero in Rome. Spread of Buddhism to China.

100–200: Roman Empire at greatest extent under Emperor Trajan. Development of Roman Law. Han dynasty in China. Old Maya civilization develops in North and Central America.

200–300: Origins of Jewish Talmud. Sassanid Empire of Persia.

300–400: Diocletian divides Roman Empire. Christianity adopted as state religion by Constantine; Constantinople founded as Eastern capital of Roman Empire. First Christian monastic communities. Barbarian invasions of Western Europe begin. Flowering of Indian culture under Gupta dynasty.

400–500: Western Europe overrun by Goths, Vandals and Franks. Invasions by Huns under Attila. Capture of Rome by Vandals. Romans leave Britain; Anglo-Saxons invade. Collapse of Roman Empire in Western Europe.

500–1000

500–600: Byzantine art flourishes at Constantinople. Silk manufacture imported into Europe from China. Sui dynasty in China. Arabic poems of *Mu'ullaqat.* Toltec Empire in Mexico. Rise of Peruvian civilization.

600–700: Mohammed and rise of Islam; formulation of *Koran.* Moslem invasions of Persia and Syria.

700–800: Moslem invasions of North Africa, Spain and Southern France. Charlemagne fights barbarians; crowned Holy Roman Emperor. Viking raids begin. T'ang dynasty founded in China.

800–900: Viking raids widespread in Europe. Moslem invasions of Sicily and Southern Italy. First kingdom of Russia proclaimed. First printed book produced in China. Development of feudal system in Europe begins.

900–1000: Viking settlements in Normandy; Viking Leif Ericson discovers America. Kingdom of Poland established. Otto I restores power of Holy Roman Empire. Turks attack Byzantium. First Moslem university established in Cairo. Turks attack Byzantine Empire. Sung dynasty in China.

1000–1400

1000–1100: Norman invasion of Britain. Roman and Orthodox Churches split. First crusade begins. New Maya civilization in America.

1100–1200: Second and third crusades. Papal forces defeat Frederick Barbarossa, Holy Roman Emperor. European universities founded. Growth of banking and trade. Cathedral-building and Gothic art flourish. Genghis Khan establishes Mongol Empire. Development of Aztec civilization in Mexico.

1200–1300: Fourth crusade. Magna Carta signed in Britain. Mongol dynasty in China under Kublai Khan. Travels of Marco Polo. Gunpowder first used in warfare. Yuan dynasty founded in China. Inca civilization develops in Peru.

1300–1400: Hundred Years War between England and France begins. Black Death sweeps China, central Asia and Europe. Italian Renaissance begins in Florence: Dante, Petrarch and Boccaccio. Peasant revolts in Britain and Europe. Turkish Ottoman Empire founded. Russians repel Tartars. Ming dynasty founded in China.

1400–1500

1400–1425: John Huss, early Protestant, condemned and burnt by Church. Giotto introduced perspective in painting.

1425–1450: Portuguese Henry the Navigator encourages voyages of discovery. Van Eyck founds Flemish school of realism in painting. Moveable type invented for printing. Medici family come to power in Florence.

1450–1475: Joan of Arc burnt at the stake in France. Wars of the Roses begin in England. Turks sack Constantinople; Eastern Empire falls. Netherlands absorbed into Hapsburg Empire.

1475–1500: Spain united under Ferdinand and Isabella; Spanish Inquisition set up; France and Spain struggle for control of Italy. Columbus discovers West Indies and South America. Cabot discovers Newfoundland. Da Gama discovers sea-route to India. Savonarola preaches against Church corruption and is burnt at stake in Florence.

1500–1600

1500–1525: Luther begins Reformation revolt against authority of the Pope. Magellan's ship sails around the world. Conquest of Mexico by Cortes. Leonardo, Michelangelo, Raphael flourish.

1525–1550: Catholics launch Counter-Reformation. Pizarro conquers Peru. Ivan the Terrible declared Tsar of all the Russias. Monasteries dissolved in England. Copernicus proposes new theory of the universe. Moghul Empire founded in India. Northern Renaissance flourishes; Erasmus, Dürer, Holbein.

1550–1575: Netherlands revolt against Spain. Spain and Venice defeat Turks at Lepanto. English fleet defeats Spanish. Renaissance now European phenomenon; Shakespeare in England, Montaigne in France, Breughel in Netherlands. St Bartholomew's Night massacre of Protestants in France.

1575–1600: English fleet defeats Spanish Armada. Protestants tolerated in France under Edict of Nantes. British East India Company founded.

1600–1700

1600–1625: Thirty Years War in Europe begins; victory for Catholics under Wallenstein. Pilgrim Fathers sail for America. Richelieu becomes French premier. Invention of telescope. Cervantes writes *Don Quixote*.

1625–1650: Protestant Gustavus Adolphus wins victories in Thirty Years War; war ends with Peace of Westphalia. Civil War in England; Charles I executed, Commonwealth proclaimed under Cromwell. Galileo persecuted by Church. Descartes proposes new philosophy. Rubens, Rembrandt and Velasquez flourish. French drama developed by Corneille, Molière and Racine. Taj Mahal built in India. Japan closes ports to foreigners. Manchu dynasty founded in China.

1650–1675: Anglo-Dutch wars. Monarchy restored in England. Louis XIV becomes absolute monarch in France.

1675–1700: French conquests under Louis XIV consolidated at Peace of Nijmegen; Britain, Netherlands and Austria, Prussia: Grand Alliance against France; English monarchy again overthrown and restored on a constitutional basis. Peter the Great carries out reforms in Russia. Newton sets out his Laws of Motion.

1700–1800

1700–1725: War of Spanish Succession ends with Treaty of Utrecht. Berkeley writes *Principles of Human Knowledge*. Great tradition of German music begins with Bach and Handel (later, Haydn and Mozart).

1725–1750: Frederick the Great comes to power in Prussia; outbreak of War of the Austrian Succession; ends with treaty of Aix-la-Chapelle. 'Flying shuttle' introduced in weaving, begins Industrial Revolution.

1750–1775: Seven Years War in Europe. War between Britain and France for colonial possessions in India and Canada. French *philosophes*, Voltaire, Montesquieu, Rousseau flourish. Hargreaves' 'spinning Jenny' and Arkwright's water frame introduced.

1775–1800: American revolution breaks out; independence declared; British surrender after Yorktown at Treaty of Versailles; Washington elected first President. Outbreak of French Revolution; formation of National Assembly; execution of Louis XVI; Revolutionary wars; Reign of Terror; Directory; Napoleon Bonaparte's seizure of power.

1800–1900

1800–1825: Defeat of Napoleon and restoration of monarchy in France; Congress of Vienna imposes terms of peace, led by Metternich. Greek wars of independence against Turkey. First Atlantic crossing by steamship. First railways opened. Utopian socialism of Owen and Fourier. Philosophy of Hegel. Music of Beethoven.

1825–1850: Mexico defeated by United States. 1848, Year of Revolutions in Europe; French monarchy overthrown. Electric telegraph invented by Morse. Railways spread throughout Europe. Novels of Dickens and Balzac.

1850–1875: Crimean War in Europe. Indian Mutiny against British. American Civil War. Unification of Italy by Garibaldi and Cavour. Unification of Germany under Bismarck. Bessemer develops steel-making process. Darwin's *On the Origin of Species*. Bell and Edison develop electric communications in United States. Spread of Marxist socialism in Europe. Meiji restoration in Japan begins period of westernization. Russian novelists Tolstoy and Dostoievsky.

1875–1900: European colonial expansion. Rise of socialist and trade union movements. Outbreak of Boer War. Pasteur develops medicine. Marconi develops wireless. X-rays developed by Röntgen. Motor cars developed by Daimler and Benz. Philosophy of Nietzsche.

1900–1970

1900–1918: Russo-Japanese War; Russia's defeat leads to outbreak of first Russian revolution. Chinese nationalist revolution under Sun Yat-sen. World War One; concluded by Treaty of Versailles. Russian Revolution; Bolsheviks seize power under Lenin. Aviation developed by Wright brothers. Einstein's *Theory of Relativity* published. Freud develops psychoanalysis. Rise of cinema industry. Development of Cubist and Abstract painting.

1918–1949: Stalin replaces Lenin in Russia. Wall Street Crash and widespread trade depression. Rise of Fascism in Italy and Nazism in Germany. Ghandi's Civil Disobedience. Spanish Civil War. Italy invades Abyssinia. Japan invades Manchuria. Munich agreement fails to halt German territorial ambitions; outbreak of World War Two. War concluded by explosion of First atomic bombs at Hiroshima and Nagasaki. John Logie Baird develops television.

1945–1970: Communist take-over in Eastern Europe. Outbreak of 'Cold War'; Formation of NATO and Warsaw Pact. Communist revolution in China led by Mao Tse-Tung. India granted independence; independence movements successful throughout colonial world. Establishment of Third World concept at Bandung Conference. Suez crisis in Middle East. Six day war between Israel and Arab nations. Vietnam war. Development of space travel results in first landing on the moon.

THE
CONTEMPORARY
WORLD

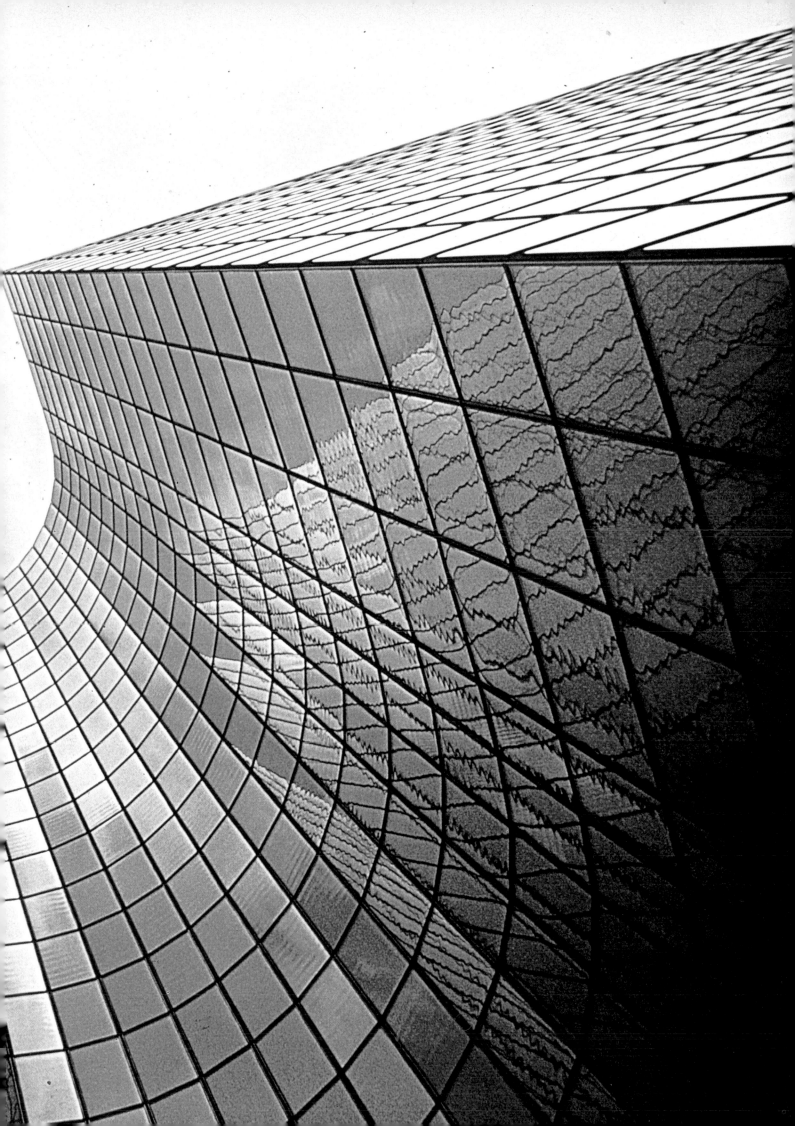

Societies in Action
Types of Society

The term society has many meanings, which depend on how and where you draw the boundary line around a group of people. It can mean a small number of people with similar interests; a village, or town; a country; a culture spanning several countries; and even an international group. However, by types of society we generally mean all those peoples with a distinct national or cultural identity, from the tribal villagers of New Guinea to the inhabitants of North America or modern European countries.

The diversity of social organization is enormous. Among the 'simple' societies alone, anthropologists have described a great variety of ways in which social life—organized around the relationships between relatives or kin—is ordered. Not all tribal societies are alike; nor are all industrial societies. Social scientists have

searched in vain for an agreed classification or 'typology' of all existing societies, based on key aspects of their social organization.

It was once fashionable to put societies on an evolutionary scale, according to their degree of economic, cultural or intellectual development. Sociologists came from Europe, and their countries were put at the top of the scale. The implication that the less 'evolved' societies are inferior is less acceptable now, though classifications based on level of development or degree of complexity are still attempted. But this over-simplified scheme cannot take into account the whole range of societies, nor the many different ways that they react to the pressures of modernization.

Nevertheless, some central themes run through most attempts to classify societies: a) the degree to which the

The towering skyscrapers of Manhatten, New York, have long been a universal symbol of modern, urbanized living. The movement of people into towns has been a major feature of the 20th century.

individual member has been freed from dominance by the tribe, family and closely tied communities b) the degree to which the legal, religious, political, occupational and other institutions have become distinct systems within society c) the extent to which the economy is agricultural or industrial d) the level of urbanization—in other words, what proportion of the population lives in towns. All these themes are linked, and broadly contrast the complex, industrial type of society with the societies of the developing countries. In the former, the majority of the people live in towns, have a range of jobs to choose from, move about, and live in rather loosely linked associations as opposed to close communities. In the latter, jobs and housing are chiefly in rural areas, communities are close, and geographical mobility, movement to find work and housing, is limited.

This sort of classification is suggested both as an historical account of the stages which societies go through in their development, and as a typology of existing societies. You stop the historical timeclock, and say: 'This is the stage they have all reached.' By doing this, you find considerable variations within Europe, in terms of urbanization, the move off the land, the breakdown of communities and so on. But we have to be very careful how we use any generalizations from this grouping.

For example, the great movement of population into towns in Latin America which is now going on is not directly comparable with the move to urban living made in much of

A timeless rural scene in Saudi Arabia. Contrasts between rural and industrial ways of life provides a key distinction between types of society, although oil is transforming the state.

Europe during the years of the industrial revolution. Some of the effects might be the same: slums and shanty towns, for instance. But the economic conditions are different. Industry has not developed to absorb the influx in Latin America as it had in Europe.

Popularly, what is often meant by type of society is the political system under which people live: monarchical, democratic, republican, totalitarian, communist, fascist, and so on. But there are problems with using these terms. They are emotive, and themselves politically loaded. And, though political style is obviously of tremendous importance, particularly for those whose lives are governed by the one system or the other, it is only one of a number of factors affecting social life.

It is interesting to relate types of society to political systems. For instance, both major communist powers—Russia and China—emerged from predominantly rural, peasant societies. Communism has not been established in the earlier

industrialized countries, with the partial exception of Italy. Now, all over the world, in the emergent nations of Africa, the Arab countries, and South America, battles are being fought for the supremacy of one political system or another. Social instability and political immaturity favour some kind of military dictatorship, at least in the first instance. In other words, the *underlying* nature of the society can affect its political fate.

Politics can also, of course, affect social organization. Communist political beliefs, developed partly as a reaction to the hardships working people suffered in the 19th century, have tried to alter the course of modernization. On the other hand, colonial powers—such as the British in India—superimposed democratic political systems on rural peasant societies, not always with success. Political ideas, and the nature of society, are woven together. Classifying societies according to their politics tells us something, but by no means everything, about them.

Social Structure

However much societies differ socially, politically, economically or religiously, they all have some basic features in common. All, whether or not they are literate, have a system of communication, a language. They must have an economic system, however basic. All—or nearly all—known societies have some form of authority by which norms, moral rules defining acceptable behaviour, are enforced. At its simplest level this will take the form of ostracism (making an outcast of offenders) or ridicule (turning offenders into fools). There must be a process of socialization through which each generation is taught the rules of the society by its adult members.

In nearly all societies, too, there is some division of labour, that is, giving individuals specialized tasks to perform, even if this does not go beyond dividing work between men and women. Each individual will have different roles to play—as husband, father, wife, mother, hunter, priest, wage earner, trade unionist, and so on. As individuals grow up in society, their 'coming of age' is generally marked by ceremonies which have been called *rites de passage* (literally, 'passage rites'). Marriage, for example, can be regarded as a *rite de passage*.

None of these aspects of social structure exists in isolation from the others. Terms like 'role' and 'norm' are inventions of social scientists, and members of society do not generally conceive of their behaviour in this way. They see their lives as a whole. Similarly, in trying to understand society, social scientists try to understand the whole social system. By using the term system, they do not necessarily mean that societies always work smoothly according to the rules; the point is that all the parts are connected, and you cannot change one without affecting others.

For example, behaviour which for outside observers of a society might appear irrational, may have its meaning within the social system. A classic instance from anthropology is the *potlach* of North American coastal Indians. During this ceremony, the Indians gave away or destroyed large amounts of their wealth. The Canadian government tried to stamp it out, thinking it stupid wastefulness, but a study of the society showed that *potlach* was supported by an elaborate system of loans and credit, which formed the basis of social organization and status. In modern industrial societies, too, frivolous expenditure can have its social meaning. Thorsten Veblen, the 19th-century American economist, coined the term 'conspicuous consumption' for the buying of useless costly goods by the wealthy to establish their status.

The division of societies into groups with different levels of status, power and wealth—social stratification—is an aspect of social structure which has probably been studied more than any other. This is partly because social equality has become such a widespread political aim. In western, industrialized societies, social stratification is usually referred to in terms of social class, based on people's occupations. Communist countries have in theory abolished social class but inequalities remain. In the modern world, the caste system—unique to India—is the other major form of social stratification. It is a more rigid division

The Jewish Bar Mitzvah to mark the coming of age of boys is a classic example of what anthropologists call rites de passage.

than social class, reinforced by religious ideas of pollution which prevent the mixing of people from different castes, and make social mobility more difficult.

Slavery was a severe form of social division, turning one section of the population into the property of others. The segregation of South Africa's apartheid system—with different laws and opportunities for blacks, coloureds and whites—is a peculiarly severe and rigid form of stratification.

The depth and breadth of social stratification in any society is determined by the degree to which jobs have become specialized, as well as the particular history of that society. The social class divisions of western, industrial societies have been more thoroughly studied than any other types of stratification. But you cannot simply observe social class—it first has to be defined. A person's job is the most common indicator of his position on the social scale, and this method can be used to divide society into two, three, four, five or more social classes, according to the classification used. However, by social class more is meant than the jobs people do: it is a shorthand term for different life-styles within society, which are related to the relative advantage and power of social groups. A person's class will say something about his likely educational prospects, way of voting, beliefs, health, how he spends his leisure time and so on. And there is a difference between subjective social class—the category people put *themselves* in, if asked—and objective social class—the category assigned to them by researchers on some basis such as occupation, financial condition, geneology or education.

Different roles given to men and women in society are not usually looked at in terms of social class; traditionally the woman takes the rank of her father and/or husband. The feminist movement today is not concerned so much with a classless society—though it may seek that as well—as one in which there is no difference in the roles of men and women. The movement has pointed to real inequalities in the opportunities and power of men and women, often upheld by law as well as custom. A society which did not differentiate between the roles of men and women would be an androgynous society.

One of the mysteries of social organization is that despite inequalities societies manage to achieve social and political stability for long periods. There are of course, revolutions, military coups, separatist movements and terrorist activities; all societies have their conflicts. But how do they maintain stability? Some social scientists have argued that it is because a majority agree with certain basic values of society—at a fundamental level there is 'consensus'. Others say it is a matter of coercion: dissenters are held back by force, or hoodwinked into accepting a system which benefits others more than themselves. At any one time, most societies contain a balance of conflict and consensus, opposing forces which respectively threaten to take them apart and serve to hold them together.

Social Institutions

It may seem odd to use the term social institutions for such different components of society as the family, law, property, religion, and bureaucracy. But this is really just another device for taking a closer look at the working parts of social organization, a way of analyzing society. Each social institution, it is often said, has certain functions to perform. For example, the family serves to regulate sexual behaviour, to produce legimate children, to maintain and socialize them, and to play a part in educating them. There is a danger, however, in looking at social institutions in this way. It tends to produce a very conservative view of society, by which all the parts work to maintain stability, uphold tradition and support the *status quo* (the way things are). In fact social institutions can develop in such a way as to break down existing social relations; they might then be regarded as 'dysfunctional'.

Religion, for example, is generally regarded as a conservative force in society, a powerful agency for socialization which serves to reinforce traditional values. But in some circumstances, the church—often sects within an established religious institution—can be revolutionary. A distinction can be made, too, between the 'manifest' functions of an institution—what it is supposed to be doing—and its 'latent' functions—what it actually does. The manifest function of bureaucracy may be to provide an organization expert at handling a mass of complicated decision-making: its latent function may be to bring decision-making to a grinding halt and only to create secure jobs for an enormous number of people.

The family is generally regarded as the most widespread and fundamental of all social institutions. Some would say the nuclear family (husband, wife and immature children) is a universal social institution, upheld by the incest taboo which forbids sexual relations between close relatives. But there are difficulties in making this claim. Where the nuclear family lives in the same household as the wider family of grandparents, aunts, uncles and siblings (brothers and sisters) its separateness as an institution is not always clear. Polygamy (having more than one wife or husband) is still common in some cultures, particularly where a man takes several wives at a time (polygyny). Polyandry, in which a woman has more than one husband, has been known but is rare. Each person in society has two nuclear families (unless they remain single): the 'family of orientation', into which they are born; and the 'family of procreation' which they form with a partner when they marry.

Whether or not the nuclear family is universal, the way the wider family organizes itself, and the extent to which it affects the lives of individual members of it, has many variations in different societies. The small 'independent' family of modern western societies is often contrasted with the kind of extended family network which survives in India, and existed in Japan until the Second World War. Whereas the traditional extended family retains enormous power over its members with regard to property ownership, social welfare, marriage prospects, religious belief and occupation, the more independent, isolated family has given up many of these powers and functions.

In fact the growth of social institutions establish themselves means the gradual adoption of some of the functions of the family by schools, churches, law courts, governments and so on. As these social institutions established themselves they develop their own rules and styles of social organization.

When they become large organizations, all social institutions tend to become bureaucratic: the way they are run is 'routinized' and the power and authority of individuals is hedged about by set rules and established ways of conducting affairs. In theory this can be a very efficient form of organization, because authority is no longer arbitrary, with decisions made at the whim of whoever happens to be in power. But in practice it is often inefficient because bureaucratic institutions respond very slowly to changes in social circumstances. Some aspects of bureaucracy are said to be dysfunctional because they hinder rather than help achieve the aims of an organization.

There is a tendency also for organizations which are supposedly run on democratic lines, with those in power elected by popular vote, to be dominated by a small ruling clique or oligarchy. This is true, for in-

stance, of political parties and trades unions. It has been said that with all such organizations the 'iron law of oligarchy' ensures that they will always come under the control of a small ruling group.

It is possible to list the functions of social institutions, but for the reasons given above this is not very helpful. For instance, the manifest function of educational institutions is to impart knowledge to each generation. Its latent functions might include achieving greater social equality by giving the disadvantaged a better chance to improve their position, or emphasizing inequality thus reinforcing the posi-

tion of those who are better off. Education can instil in children a respect for traditional values, or attempt to break the habits and beliefs passed to children by their families. It is estimated that western Europe, North America and Soviet Russia each have 60 million pupils in schools and universities, and there are 250 to 300 million more pupils in the rest of the world. Educational institutions will not have the same function for all of these.

Social institutions can be studied separately, but, as with all other approaches to analyzing society, they cannot be properly understood in isolation. The power and influence

of the family is related to the relative strengths of other social institutions: the law, religion, education, government, political organization and so on. The family may influence the way a person votes; that vote can ultimately affect political institutions; political action may then alter educational institutions; schools and universities will have an influence on the values of future families; the family will then pass on changed values to a new generation.

It is sometimes claimed that the 'nuclear family' of mother, father and children is a universal feature of societies. But family organization varies a great deal – this Ghanaian farmer is pictured with his six wives and younger children.

Social Change

Societies are always changing. The rate of change varies both within and between societies. In the modern world the most traumatic break with the past experienced by any society has been imposed on isolated tribes —in the Amazon basin of South America for instance—who have been overwhelmed by the destruction of forest and building of roads by their more 'advanced' neighbours. The process of change is less abrupt in most societies, and its analysis extremely complex.

A lament of modern industrialized societies, as well as of those in the developing world experiencing accelerating social change, is the decline of the family. This is said to be happening in two quite distinct ways.

Firstly, the 'extended' family, in which the conjugal pair (husband and wife) live with their in-laws and other relatives is said to have disintegrated. This has created new social problems, for the care of the elderly and the emotional pressure put on the isolated nuclear family, for instance. Secondly, the rising divorce rate in nearly all industrialized

The Trans-Amazon highway, carving a route through the dense forests of the Amazon basin in Brazil, has brought a sudden and brutal change

societies is taken by numerous commentators as an indication of the decline even of the nuclear family itself.

But such judgements on contemporary social problems are often coloured by too rosy a picture of the past. Social historians are now challenging the once widely accepted idea that there has been a simple development from extended to nuclear families as societies industrialized. They point out that there have been many forms of family organization in the past, and there can have been no straightforward shift from large to small households, though the nuclear family itself is smaller because of the lower birth rate.

As for the break-up of the nuclear family, statistics showing a rising divorce rate have to be interpreted carefully. They may tell us more about changes in the law which have altered the grounds for divorce and the ability of people to obtain it, than about real changes in the stability of families. Though it can be argued that making divorce easier *causes* instability in marriage, there is no way of finding out if this is true or not. But it is unlikely, for instance, that the divorce rate of 2.2 per 1,000 marriages in England and Wales in 1910 was a fair indication of the level of marital disharmony. It is much more likely to be a reflection of the costs and legal difficulties of getting a divorce at that time.

The decline of religion is another popular preoccupation of industrialized societies. It is said that there has been a secularization of society, that religious belief has lost its hold on the way people think and behave. This is certainly true if it is measured by church attendance, or the influence of religious institutions on law and morality. But the theory of secularization implies also that people have abandoned their belief in deities (or God) and that they have become more rational. This may be true, but it is difficult to prove. For instance, the decline in churchgoing has been associated with the movement of people from rural village life into large towns, and may be a result of changing life-styles rather than a loss of belief. The claim that modern man is less religious is no more than an assumption which colours our interpretation of behaviour. The relatively high level of involvement in organized religion in North America—compared to Britain—is in the same way attributed not to a survival of religious feeling, but to the social function of the principal religions, Protestant, Catholic, and Jewish, in giving people a sense of 'belonging'. But churchgoing has always had a social aspect to it, and it is maybe this which has declined rather than religious belief. It is almost certainly true that today many more people hold religious beliefs than worship publicly.

Another contentious issue is spelled out in the 'embourgeoisement' thesis, which says that the poorer or working classes in society adopt a middle class life-style as their incomes increase. In other words, greater wealth makes them 'bourgeois'. But a number of studies have shown that rising income does not simply alter people's values and political beliefs. Class and status are much more complex than that, and the better-off in society are usually able to maintain their 'social distance'.

These examples give some idea of the pitfalls involved in trying to measure social change. An even more difficult and intriguing question is: 'How does social change come about at all?' The driving force might be intellectual development which alters people's values and outlook. Or it might be the underlying economic forces—the development of world trade, for instance—which puts pressure on societies to change their values. Marxists claim that economics is the key factor, though societies founded on communist or Marxist principles strive more than any others to mould the economy to their political values and beliefs. Any theory which regards social change as a function primarily of economics or of values will not be able to account for the complexities of the real world.

Modern Indian society provides a classic example of the way in which the values of established social institutions can resist and shape the economic pressures of social change. The caste system ties up labour in mutually exclusive groups; the 'joint family' is incompatible with individual striving; and both caste and family conflict with democratic ideals of equality. Like all arenas of social change India is a battleground between economic pressures, old values and new political ideals.

Population

In 1850 world population was about 1,000 million. By 1925 it had reached 2,000 million. In the last half-century it has doubled again. This accelerating rate of population increase is arguably the greatest problem for international society today. But the population problem is not simply a matter of sheer numbers. Demography, the study of populations, is a much more complicated subject than that, which adds to its interest.

Nobody is certain why the population of first Britain, then Europe and North America, began to rise steadily from the middle of the 18th century onwards. Did more babies survive because of improved medical services —particularly the introduction of smallpox vaccine? Or was it better food and living conditions? There are still arguments about this. But there is no doubt that in this century, large scale health programmes have brought about dramatic falls in the infant mortality rate (the proportion of babies dying) in developing countries. And those who survive infancy have a greater life expectancy (on average they live longer) though starvation and disease still take an enormous toll.

Had the population of industrialized countries continued to rise as it did in the 19th and early 20th centuries the present population problem would be more serious than it is. But it did not: after a time, the birth rate fell as people decided to have smaller families. This began in Britain in the 1870s, the birth rate reaching its lowest point (until recent years) in the 1930s. The pattern of births and deaths had gone through three stages, each with its own demographic characteristics.

Poor rural societies, like pre-industrial Europe and the developing countries up to the second half of this century, have high birth rates and high death rates. The rate of 'natural increase' of population— the numbers added, excluding the effects of migration, when births and deaths are balanced—is slow and fluctuating. Famine and disease will wipe out a population increase following, say, a series of good harvests. The infant mortality rate is high, and expectation of life at birth (the age to which the newborn could on average expect to live) is low. The proportion of children in such societies is relatively high, and of old people relatively low.

In industrializing societies, the birth rate remains high, but the death rate falls, particularly the infant mortality rate. As a result, the rate of natural increase is very high. Because many more children survive, the proportion of them in the population is swelled dramatically. This happened in Britain, Europe and America in the 19th century, and is happening in developing countries today.

Once a society reaches the later stages of industrialization, the pattern changes again. The birth rate

Country	Birth rate per 1,000	Average life expectancy at birth	Natural population increase per 1,000
Ghana	48.8	43.5	26.9
Kenya	48.7	49	32.7
Egypt	35.5	52.7	23.1
South Africa	42.9	51.5	27.4
Canada	15.4	72.8	8
USA	14.7	72	5.8
Jamaica	30.8	64.6	23.6
Peru	41	54	29.1
Chile	26	63.2	17.3
Brazil	37	59.3	28.3
Argentine	23	68.2	13.5
Bangladesh	49.5	35.8	21.4
Hong Kong	19.7	71.1	14.5
Indonesia	42.9	47.5	26
Syria	45.4	56.6	40.6
Denmark	14.1	73.5	3.9
Sweden	12.6	74.8	1.8
UK	13.3	70	1.4
China	26.9	61.6	16.6
West Germany	9.7	70.8	−2.4
Netherlands	13	74.2	4.8
USSR	18.2	69	8.9
Australia	18.4	70.8	9.7
Japan	18.6	73.7	12.1
India	34.6	41.2	19.1
Pakistan	36	51.2	24
Thailand	43.4	56.1	32.6
Greece	15.6	69	6.7
Papua New Guinea	40.6	47.6	23.5
Zaire	45.2	43.5	24.7
Zambia	51.5	44.5	31.2

High birth rates generally mean high death rates, as this table comparing different countries shows. In the developed world, the fall in mortality has historically been accompanied by a fall in the birth rate so that population increase has slowed or stopped.

falls to match the low death rates. The rate of natural increase slows down, and may even reach zero or 'replacement level'. When the birth rate falls, the proportion of old people in society begins to increase, and the proportion of children goes down. The present world population explosion is the result of high birth rates and low death rates in developing countries. If they follow the pattern of industrialized countries, then world population will level out.

But lower birth rates will not be achieved simply by supplying the world with contraceptives. In Britain, the pioneer of smaller families, the birth rate fell long before effective contraceptives were generally available. The contraceptive pill arrived when birth rates were actually *rising* after the 1930s slump.

It is the values, beliefs and customs of people which determine the number of children they want to have. Contraceptives do not lower birth rates, they merely make it easier for people to plan the families they want. Many factors influence desired family size: religious belief, economic circumstances, ideas about status, the wish to have heirs. Age at marriage is also an important determinant of the rate of population growth. If people marry late, the population will increase more slowly than if they marry early, even if the eventual size of family is the same, because the gap between generations is greater.

Those countries which have achieved low rates of natural increase have not solved their population problems. The relatively old age

Advertising and the promotion of contraception has generally been ineffective as a way of stemming population growth. Early education is probably the only answer.

structure which develops—the proportion of old people increases as the birth rate falls—produces social problems now familiar in all industrialized countries. There is an increasing number of elderly who are no longer 'productive', and are more prone to illness and disability than the rest of the population.

Forecasting future population increases is a major task because the planning of schools, health services, housing, and social services is dependent on some estimate of how many people in each age group will be needing them in 10, 20 or 30 years time. Each generation moves through the age structure of a population like a wave: a baby boom now will fill the schools to overflowing in a few years time unless more are built and more teachers trained. A fall in the birth rate will leave classrooms empty. But population projections have always been wrong—whether too high or too low —because to get them right you need to be able to predict human behaviour and that is impossible. We know that a rise in the birth rate now will increase the number of women of childbearing age in 16 years time. But how many children will they want to have? And when will they decide to have them?

Population is not simply a matter of numbers; it is a vital, though sometimes hidden, force in society.

Indigenous Societies
Hunting Communities

Few indigenous societies remain today, and none whose traditional way of life has not been affected, and in most cases dramatically altered, by impact with Western culture.

Europeans have encountered indigenous societies in North and South America, Africa, Asia, and in Australia and the islands of the Pacific Ocean. This confrontation has occurred at different times during history, beginning with the early European explorers who over 500 years ago began to look beyond their own shores, escalating into the greatest period of European exploration in the 18th and 19th centuries, and leading to the present day when the influence of Western-style industrial society has penetrated almost every corner of the globe.

The transforming effect of this contact upon the lives of indigenous peoples has followed a broadly similar pattern all over the world. Technology and the material side of life have always been the first to change: stone and bone implements are replaced by iron tools; imported clothing and ornaments are substituted for traditional forms; and firearms are introduced, together with 'firewater'. Changes of this kind are relatively rapid; less speedy, but nonetheless inevitable, are changes in the traditional social and economic structure, and in religion. Some aspects of the transformation may be welcomed by the indigenous society, some are the result of economic persuasion, and some have been forcibly imposed.

Because indigenous societies have changed so radically, and the change often took place long ago, what is known today about the traditions of these peoples is often fragmentary, and has had to be reconstructed using different kinds of evidence, for example, contemporary accounts written by Europeans, artifacts which may have been preserved in museums and, where possible, the archaeological record. As a result, a

good deal is known concerning the material aspects of life of many of these 'lost' societies, such as the kind of clothes they wore, and the sort of houses they lived in, but far less is certain about their social organizations and religious beliefs. In recent years, however, comparative studies have benefited considerably from the contributions of field anthropologists, who examine the social structures and belief systems of the handful of indigenous societies that have survived into the 20th century.

Indigenous societies, or, as they are also called, 'tribal societies', or 'traditional peoples', are no longer thought of as 'primitive'. It was once popular to look upon European society as the climax of civilization, and to regard people with different lifestyles as inferior, or even 'savage'. But today, with a better understanding of our own and other cultures, it is clear that it is inaccurate and misleading to categorize people as inferior, simply because they pursue a different way of life, which succeeds without what we believe to be basic necessities, such as written records, iron tools, or the wheel.

The crucial difference between our industrialized urban society and indigenous societies, is that ours seeks to dominate and exploit the environment by means of technology, so that continual change in the name of 'progress' is regarded as essential. Indigenous societies, however, adapt themselves to the environment, and having achieved a workable adaptation sustain it through tradition.

Man is the most adaptable of all living species, a characteristic which has enabled him to populate most of the earth. An examination of indigenous societies reveals the variety of adaptations that have been achieved by mankind under widely differing circumstances. These can be divided into two groups on the basis of two major forms of economy —hunting and gathering, and farming. Let us look at the first type.

Hunting and gathering is the oldest and most widespread way of life known to mankind. There are hardly any societies which continue to depend upon this form of indigenous economy, but until relatively recently the entire population of this planet lived in this way, pursuing game, fishing, and gathering roots, berries and seeds. Only during the last 10,000 years have men begun to domesticate plants and animals and live by farming, and the growth of industrial societies like our own has occupied only a fraction of this later period. Those who follow the hunting and gathering way of life can still be found: examples are the Eskimos of the Arctic, the Australian Aborigines, the Bushmen of the Kalahari Desert in South Africa, and the forest Indians of South America. These people have survived until now because they occupy marginal environments which are difficult to live in owing to extremes of climate or topography. But areas which have been ignored hitherto by Western

society are being coveted today, usually for their natural resources, such as oil in Alaska, and timber and minerals in Brazil, which will rapidly be extracted for the use of the modern world, decimating the homelands and traditions of the indigenous peoples in the process.

The Eskimos
Eskimo society is one of several extreme examples of a successful adaptation to difficult conditions, and represents a highly specialized type of hunter-gatherer culture. There is little vegetable food available in their arctic environment, so the Eskimos depend almost entirely upon large mammals, a food source both unpredictable and difficult to obtain. In order to survive the Eskimos are obliged to be nomadic, and they have also evolved a complex technology. Specialized Eskimo forms of dwelling, fur garments, and equipment such as kayaks and harpoons, are justly famous, although today they are increasingly replaced by Western substitutes.

The Aborigines
On the other side of the world the Australian Aborigines are also undergoing changes in their lifestyle. The Aborigines traditionally live in small groups and have to keep on the move owing to the shortage of water and unequal distribution of food supplies. Vegetable foods, which form the major part of their diet, are gathered by the women and children, while the men are expert hunters. Aboriginal life represents to many the classic picture of primitive man existing with only the minimum essential for survival, yet these limits are not entirely imposed by their environment. The Aborigines maintain their way of life successfully with less than they could produce if they wanted to, and many of their implements are multi-purpose—for example, a wooden dish may be a digging tool and a baby's cradle, as well as a food container, and despite their simple material existence, they have evolved a complex ritual life marked by elaborate ceremonies.

In Brazil there are still hunting peoples, like these Xingu Indians, but their lifestyle is threatened with extinction by the modern world.

The Northwest Coast Indians
The lifestyles of the Eskimos and Aborigines appear to justify the view that hunting and gathering societies lead a somewhat precarious existence, but this is not always the case. The Northwest Coast Indians of North America combined with hunting and gathering many features associated with more 'advanced' ways of life, such as settled communities, a complex hierarchical social organization, and a highly developed artistic tradition. They were able to do this because of the abundance of food resources available, both on land and in the sea, which made it possible to store surplus food acquired in the summer for use during the winter, when much time was given to ceremonial dances and the production of the elaborate masked costumes and paraphernalia used on these occasions.

Farming Communities

Many indigenous societies follow a farming way of life and live by tending domesticated plants or animals, although some hunting and gathering activities may also be carried out in varying degrees.

The Fijians

In Fiji, fishing had a place of equal importance in the traditional economy with the cultivation of food crops, and in common with several other Pacific peoples, the Fijians cultivated large areas of paper-mulberry trees for the production of barkcloth which was used for clothing. Like the Northwest Coast Indians of America, the Fijians structured their society according to rank. This contrasts with the customs of most hunter-gatherer peoples, who generally recognized status based upon age and experience rather than

on birth. The Fijians were very warlike, and fought between themselves and with other groups, which is also not a common feature of societies like the Eskimos and Aborigines.

The Masai

Some farmers are highly specialized and concentrate upon a particular food resource. The Masai of Kenya are dependent upon herds of livestock, which in former times they maintained by means of a large army. Despite the example of neighbouring tribes who cultivate plants, or hunt, the Masai themselves do neither and despise anyone who does. Their culture is entirely bound up with their cattle, which they prize not only as a food source, but also from motives of religion and prestige.

It is commonly thought that the farming adaptation represents a 'step up' on a kind of ladder of cultural progress, yet there are societies which have turned away from farming to become hunters. The nomadic buffalo hunters of the North American Plains were once farmers who occasionally banded together to drive a herd of buffalo into an enclosure, or over a cliff, in order to supplement their diet of corn and beans. But the introduction of the horse and the gun into North America by Europeans provided a more efficient method of buffalo hunting, and on this basis the remarkable and shortlived later culture of the Plains Indian developed.

South America

Nonetheless, the farming way of life, because it is a settled existence and can provide a food surplus which frees people from the continual food-quest characteristic of many hunter-gatherer societies, does encourage the growth of larger populations, more complex political and social organizations, and more highly developed forms of art and technology. The ancient civilizations of Mexico and Peru were both sophisticated societies with large farming populations supporting a ruling hierarchy, and highly developed traditions of art and architecture. The culture of Ancient Mexico developed hieroglyphic records, and a complex calendric system, and had a knowledge of mathematics and astronomy. In Peru, Inca engineers constructed bridges and irrigation terraces 500 years ago, some of which are still in use today.

The fabulous empires of Mexico and Peru are lost to mankind as are most other indigenous societies. Today a considerable body of opinion believes efforts should be made to permit the handful remaining to continue their traditions without undue interference; but despite this attitude, and the growth of a feeling of identity among some of the peoples themselves, it is likely that our generation will see their final destruction.

The Masai herders of Kenya have to move with their cattle in search of pasture and water.

157

The Sciences
Nuclear Physics

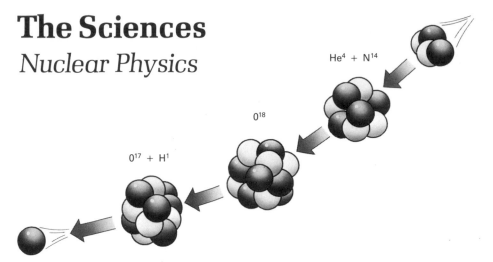

He⁴ + N¹⁴

O¹⁸

O¹⁷ + H¹

Alpha particle hits nitrogen nucleus—result, excited oxygen nucleus; departure of a proton, leaving an ordinary oxygen nucleus: more a rearrangement of nucleons than a 'splitting'.

There are good reasons for calling the first half of this century 'The Atomic Age'. When the century started, scientists had just discovered that atoms were not the smallest pieces of matter in nature; they had no idea just how complex the atom was. Now we know that an atom is hazy, a cloud of tiny particles, called electrons, whirling around a lot of space and a small dense nucleus. The nucleus itself is not simple; we know that a very wide variety of different particles can be released from it. Finally, we have found ways of splitting the nucleus so as to release vast emounts of energy, either violently, in an atom bomb, or under control, in a nuclear power station.

The first particle smaller than an atom to be found was the electron. When J. J. Thompson discovered it in 1897, he thought that electrons were stuck to the atom, like currants to the outside of a piece of cake. He had found that when an electric current passed through a vacuum in a glass tube, rays came from the negative terminal (the cathode) that would make the glass glow with a greenish colour. Thompson found that he could bend these 'cathode rays' with a magnet (it was already known that electric charges would also bend them). This showed that cathode rays were really a stream of tiny particles with a negative electric charge. They were named 'electrons'. Even a small magnetic field bent the rays markedly, so Thompson decided that the particles must have a very tiny mass. Eventually, the mass of an electron was measured and found to be only 1/1,837 of the mass of the smallest atom known, the hydrogen atom. (This latter is 1.675×10^{-24} grams.)

At about the same time, A. H. Becquerel discovered that the element, uranium, continuously sent out rays that would go through solids. X-rays, which did the same, were discovered by W. K. Roentgen earlier in 1895. Elements that gave out rays were named 'radioactive' and it was quickly discovered that radioactive elements gave off three kinds of ray, which were called alpha, beta, and gamma rays. Alpha and beta rays turned out to be streams of particles, and the alpha-particles were used by Ernest Rutherford to make the next important discovery about the atom.

In a long series of experiments between 1906 and 1908, Rutherford sent beams of alpha-particles at thin pieces of metal foil. A piece of photographic film behind the foil recorded the arrival of the alpha rays. Most of the particles went straight through the foil which is what one would expect of this kind of ray. Some, though, were sharply deflected and a very few actually bounced back. What this meant was that the atoms of the metal in the foil had a tiny dense core from which the particles rebounded. The rest of the atom was space, containing only the tiny electrons. The central core, the nucleus, actually has a diameter only 1/100,000 of the whole atom and it is positively charged. The negative electrical charge on the electrons is balanced by its positive charge on the nucleus. The complete atom is neutral.

Rutherford had already named the particles in the nucleus that carry the positive charge: he called them protons. They had the mass of a hydrogen atom, and a single positive charge. Every atom, therefore, was composed of a cloud of electrons surrounding, at a distance, a nucleus containing the number of protons required to balance the electrical charge of the electrons.

There had to be some other particles in the nucleus, because every nucleus had roughly twice the mass that the protons could account for. The solution to this mystery came in the 1930s, when James Chadwick identified another particle. This had the same mass as a proton, but no charge, and was therefore named a 'neutron'.

This short list of particles in the nucleus explained atomic weights and natural radioactivity. But new experiments soon revealed new particles. The particles were produced by a new laboratory tool, technically called the particle accelerator, but commonly known as the atom smaher. The principle behind all these machines is that a charged particle from an atom is attracted by an electrical charge, and moves more and more quickly towards it. In other words, its particle accelerates.

In 1928, John D. Cockcroft and Ernest Walton, for the first time in history, used an accelerator to split an atom. They accelerated protons and split atoms of lithium. Their simple machine was followed by the 'linear accelerator' in which charged particles were accelerated by pulses of electricity, and then the cyclotron, which accelerated protons around a flat spiral. This was in turn followed by even more powerful accelerators for both protons and electrons; scientists found that the beams from these machines drove quite new particles from the nucleus of the atom. The particles can be detected and identified by allowing them to pass into a cloud chamber or a bubble chamber, where they leave recognizable traces, rather like the trails produced by jet planes in the upper atmosphere.

One new particle was produced by 'nature's accelerator'. A steady rain of rays called cosmic rays arrive at the Earth from outer space, sometimes at very high velocities. Because they include charged particles, they are deflected by the Earth's magnetic field and collect near the North and South Poles. In the atmosphere, this produces the aurora: in space they collect as the Van Allen belts that were discovered during the early American exploration of space. Among the particles discovered in cosmic rays was a completely novel one, the positron, a particle with the same mass as an electron but with a positive electrical charge. Positrons arrive in radiation with electrons: if they happen to meet they actually destroy each other, leaving nothing but a flash of very short length light. What has happened is that a particle has met what is called an anti-particle; no matter remains after the collision. Matter has been converted into energy.

A new particle discovered in laboratory atom-smashing was the anti-proton, a negatively charged proton; this would be annihilated in a collision with a proton.

The positron and the anti-proton are two of a long list of anti-particles produced in experiments with the big accelerators. These anti-particles seem a bit odd to anyone who is not a nuclear physicist. They can combine to form atoms of anti-matter, and if an atom of anti-matter meets the corresponding 'normal' atom of matter, both simply disappear, leaving only a burst of energy—of heat and light. It is possible that there are, out in space, heavenly bodies—stars for example—made of anti-matter. If such a star were to meet a normal one of the right size, both would disappear. So far, no such bodies have been detected, but scientists have suggested that large masses of anti-matter have arrived on Earth, producing enormous craters where they landed but leaving no other detectable trace.

One aim of scientists when they investigate the nucleus of the atom is to find the smallest possible particles—the 'bricks' that make up all possible atoms. What they have found is a wide range of different particles, each seeming to have the same claim to being a basic particle as any other. Two physicists, an American, Murray Gell-Mann, and an Israeli, Yuval Ne'emen, showed in 1961 that all known particles could be fitted on to spaces in a chart, and they managed to predict the existence of a particle to fill an empty space. This particle, the 'omega-minus' was discovered a few years later in an accelerator experiment.

Gell-Mann later made another important suggestion. He showed that if there were in nature three new particles, which he called quarks, in theory they could be combined to form every known heavy nuclear particle. The quarks would be the building bricks of at least this group. There would also have to be anti-quarks to account for anti-particles. If these particles do exist, the hope of all scientists that nature really is simple will be justified.

The core tank of a prototype fast reactor is shown here from above with a dummy fuel sub-assembly being lowered into position.

Chemistry

Chemistry is the science that studies the way that the elements combine and recombine. As a scientific subject, as opposed to a rather mystical set of recipes, chemistry dates from 1661, when Robert Boyle in his book *The Sceptical Chymist* defined elements as those substances that could not be split into simpler ones. The major steps after that, before the era of modern chemistry, were the publication in 1789 of the *Traité Elementaire de Chimie* by A. L. Lavoisier, which described accurately, for the first time, what went on when substances burned; and the development of the atomic theory, by John Dalton, explained in his *New System of Chemical Philosophy* (1808).

On these bases, the edifice of modern chemistry was built. Dalton understood that the atoms of differ-

ent elements would have different weights. These cannot be the weights of individual atoms in ounces or grams—an atom of hydrogen weighs only 1.675×10^{-24} grams =

0.000000000000000000000001675 grams: an atomic weight is the weight of the particular atom in terms of the lightest atom known, hydrogen. In round numbers, an atom of oxygen is 16 times as heavy as one of hydrogen, an atom of iron 56 times. Oxygen and iron are therefore said to have atomic weights of 16 and 56 respectively. The simplest atomic weights are found by measuring the densities of elements that are gases, and comparing them with hydrogen. The list is extended from there.

A list of elements written out in ascending order of atomic weights— starting therefore with hydrogen— shows a pattern that is so striking that scientists found it incredible at first: the properties of the elements seem to repeat themselves every eight elements. Sodium, element No. 11 is very like potassium, No. 19: both are light silvery metals that react very vigorously with water. Neon, No. 10 is an inert gas, as is argon, No. 18. What has become the most useful way of recording these similarities is Mendeleev's Periodic Table, shown below.

The pattern that the Periodic Table shows cannot simply be a coincidence. It must be the sign of some pattern in the atoms of the elements themselves. The pattern involved, scientists have learned, concerns the electrons.

Any atom has a centre, the nucleus, that has a positive electrical charge. This is surrounded by negatively charged electrons that whirl about it so rapidly that the electrical attractions (positive charges attract negative ones) are balanced. The electrons do not drop into the nucleus.

The electrons in the outer ring are involved in the chemical reactions of the elements. The gases, helium, neon, argon, krypton, xenon, which are called inert gases because it is extremely difficult to persuade them to form compounds, have in their outer rings eight electrons. Just because these are inert gases, it is reasonable to say that the pattern of their electrons is stable.

This idea makes it possible to understand how chemical elements are bound together. Sodium has one more electron than neon, and chlorine one less than argon. The two elements can easily form a compound in which the chlorine accepts an electron from the sodium, leaving the sodium atom with a positive electrical charge and giving a negative charge to the chlorine. The compound is called sodium chloride (it is actually common salt) and the atoms

1 Hydrogen (H) 1.008		
3 Lithium (Li) 6.939	**4** Beryllium (Be) 9.012	
11 Sodium (na) 22.990	**12** Magnesium (Mg) 24.312	

19 Potassium (K) 39.102	**20** Calcium (Ca) 40.08	**21** Scandium (Sc) 44.956	**22** Titanium (Ti) 47.90	**23** Vanadium (V) 50.942	**24** Chromium (Cr) 51.996	**25** Manganese (Mn) 54.996	**26** Iron (Fe) 55.847	**27** Cobalt (Co) 58.933
37 Rubidium (Rb) 85.47	**38** Strontium (Sr) 87.62	**39** Yttrium (Y) 88.905	**40** Zirconium (Zr) 91.22	**41** Nioblum (Nb) 92.906	**42** Molybdenum (Mo) 95.94	**43** Technetium (Tc) 98.91	**44** Ruthenium (Ru) 101.07	**45** Rhodium (Rh) 102.905
55 Cesium (Cs) 132.905	**56** Barium (Ba) 137.34	**57** Lanthanum (La) 138.91	**58** Cerium (Ce) 140.12	**59** Prasodymium (Pr) 140.907	**60** Neodymium (Nd) 144.24	**61*** Promethium (Pm) 145	**62** Samarium (Sm) 150.35	**63** Europium (Eu) 151.96
			72 Hafnium (Hf) 178.49	**73** Tantalum (Ta) 180.948	**74** Tungsten (W) 183.85	**75** Rhenium (Re) 186.2	**76** Osmium (Os) 190.2	**77** Iridium (Ir) 192.9
87* Francium (Fr) 223	**88*** Radium (Ra) 226.05	**89*** Actinium (Ac) 227	**90*** Thorium (Th) 232.038	**91*** Protactinium (Pa) 231	**92*** Uranium (U) 230.03	**93*** Neptunium (Np) 237	**94*** Plutonium (Pu) 242	**95*** Americium (Am) 243

SODIUM
Atomic No. 11
Atomic Wt. 23

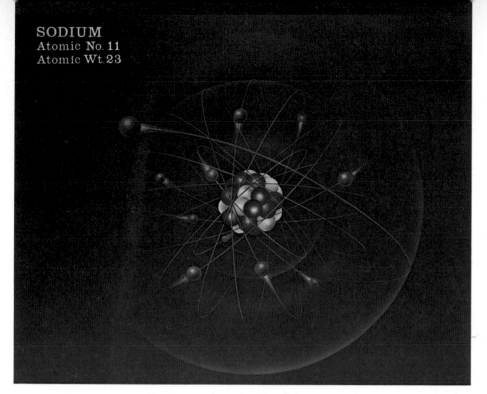

The structure of a sodium atom.

are held together by the mutual attraction of the positive and negative electrical charges. They can be separated by an electrical force, and this is the principle of electrolysis. Compounds in which one element has lost an electron, another gained one are called ionic compounds.

Another way of attaining a full outer ring of electrons gives a differ-

ent kind of compound. In these, called covalent compounds, some of the electrons are shared. Carbon tetrachloride is typical. The carbon shares its four outer electrons with the four chlorine atoms so that each has an 'argon' outer ring. The carbon's own outer ring, with the four chlorine electrons it shares, is the same as neon's. These compounds are held together by the shared

electrons, and cannot be separated by electrolysis. There are also compounds where the shared electrons both come from one atom.

Bonds involving shared electrons —covalent bonds—have fixed positions; the shared electrons have to fit around the nucleus. The formulae of compounds that involve such bonds can be drawn with lines representing the bonds. Further, the fact that the bonds are fixed means that there can often be compounds of the same elements arranged differently in space. The compounds are called stereoisomers; the study of stereoisomers is particularly important in organic chemistry—the chemistry of compounds of carbon. (Its name reflects the fact that it was originally the chemistry of compounds formed by living creatures.) Inorganic chemistry, the chemistry of all other substances, is largely the chemistry of ionic compounds.

The periodic table of the elements. Red areas represent the two rare-earth series, lanthanides and actinides. The lower numbers in the box indicate the element's atomic weight. An asterisk marks radioactive elements. The top numbers indicate the element's atomic number.

						2 Helium (He) 4.003
5 Boron (B) 10.811	6 Carbon (C) 12.011	7 Nitrogen (N) 14.007	8 Oxygen (O) 15.999	9 Fluorine (F) 18.998	10 Neon (Ne) 20.183	
13 Aluminium (Al) 26.982	14 Silicon (Si) 28.086	15 Phosphorus (P) 30.974	16 Sulfur (S) 32.064	17 Chlorine (Cl) 35.453	18 Argon (A) 39.948	
28 Nickel (Ni) 58.71	29 Copper (Cu) 63.54	30 Zinc (Zn) 65.37	31 Gallium (Ga) 69.72	32 Germanium (Ge) 72.59	33 Arsenic (As) 74.992	34 Selenium (Se) 78.96	35 Bromine (Br) 79.909	36 Krypton (Kr) 83.80
46 Palladium (Pd) 106.4	47 Silver (Ag) 107.870	48 Cadmium (Cd) 112.40	49 Indium (In) 114.82	50 Tin (Sn) 118.69	51 Antimony (Sb) 121.75	52 Tellurium (Te) 127.60	53 Iodine (I) 126.904	54 Xenon (Xe) 131.30
64 Gadolinium (Gd) 157.25	65 Terbium (Tb) 158.924	66 Dysprosium (Dy) 162.50	67 Holmium (Ho) 164.930	68 Erbium (Er) 167.26	69 Thulium (Tm) 168.934	70 Ytterbium (Yb) 173.04	71 Lutetium (Lu) 174.97	
78 Platinum (Pt) 195.09	79 Gold (Au) 196.967	80 Mercury (Hg) 200.59	81 Thallium (Tl) 204.37	82 Lead (Pb) 207.19	83 Bismuth (Bi) 208.98	84* Polonium (Po) 210	85* Astatine (At) 210	86* Radon (Ru) 222
96* Curium (Cm) 244	97* Berkelium (Bk) 245	98* Californium (Cf) 246	99* Einsteinium (Es) 253	100* Fermium (Fm) 255	101* Mendelevium (Md) 256	102* Nobelium (No) 255	103* Lawrencium (Lw) 257	

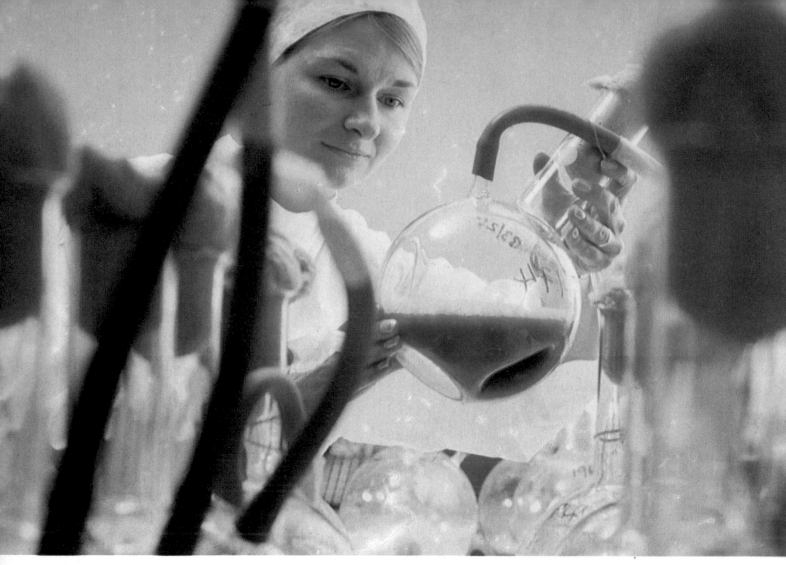

Organic Chemistry

The name 'organic chemistry' reflects the old idea that the chemicals involved in the processes of life are somehow different from those that come from rocks and minerals. These latter chemicals—inorganic chemicals—generally do not burn, and on analysis are often found to consist of only relatively few atoms joined together. Organic chemicals burn and usually contain large numbers of atoms forming complex molecules.

However, it has been known for the last century and a half that organic chemicals could be made from inorganic ones, and the term 'organic chemistry' nowadays simply means the chemistry of carbon compounds, although simple compounds such as carbon monoxide and sodium carbonate are usually excluded.

Organic chemicals are often complicated. A very unusual property of the carbon atom is responsible for this. Carbon has a 'valency' of four (it can link to four hydrogen atoms)

and the 'bonds' to other atoms are usually shown as lines. What is unusual about carbon is that one atom can form bonds with other carbon atoms, giving rings and chains of enormous length, and it can attach itself to other carbon atoms with single, double or triple bonds. This is only the beginning of the complexity. Those carbon valencies that are not used for joining the carbon atoms can attach to hydrogen atoms, or to any of a vast number of alternatives. There is no limit to the number of organic chemicals that are possible, and something like two million have actually been identified.

As soon as people realized that organic chemicals could be synthesized (made in the laboratory) they set out to do this. A story that throws light on many aspects of organic chemistry concerns William Perkin, who at the time (1855) was a 17-year-old student of chemistry in London. His instructor, August von Hoffman,

Advances in chemistry affect our daily lives as, for example, in this laboratory at a pharmaceutical manufacturer. Vaccines, antibiotics and drugs all result from biochemical research.

set him to synthesize quinine, a valuable medicine that occurred naturally in the bark of particular South American trees. Perkin knew how many atoms of hydrogen, carbon, nitrogen and oxygen had to be combined to form a molecule of quinine, but he did not know how the atoms had to be arranged, or even that it mattered how they were arranged. So Perkin hopefully mixed some aniline, a chemical from coal tar that contained hydrogen, carbon and nitrogen, with some potassium dichromate, which he hoped might supply the oxygen that quinine contained. What he actually produced was a black tarry mess. Undeterred, he added alcohol, and produced a beautiful purple liquid. Perkin earned a place in history by seizing his opportunity. He decided that he might have made a dye.

In fact he had made the first artificial dye—the colour was eventually called mauve—and he became very rich. The dyestuffs industry which sprang from his original discovery is a very important part of industrial chemistry and there are now thousands of artificial dyes in use in many industries.

The synthesis of organic chemicals became systematic, and easier, though rarely easy, once scientists had discovered ways of working out how the atoms of a particular compound were arranged. They could then start with a simple, available compound, and build on this molecule to make the one that was wanted. Quinine, which had baffled Perkin, was eventually made by two American scientists, Robert Woodward and William Doering, in 1944.

The long series of chemical reactions needed to make such compounds have one great disadvantage: the ultimate amount of product is very small, because even if you get as much as 90 per cent of the theoretical amount for each reaction in a chain of 20 different reactions, literally tons of raw material will give only a gram or two of final product.

So it is attractive to persuade nature to make your chemicals for you. Fermentation is one valuable technique. The original, natural fermentation is the process that occurs when the yeast on the skin of grapes converts grape juice into wine. It occurs as the yeast cell lives on the sugar of the wine, but the change from sugar to alcohol is actually produced by chemicals, called enzymes, in the yeast. Most of the chemical changes that occur in living creatures are made to happen by enzymes, so that it should be possible to make any organic chemical you want by a carefully arranged fermentation.

One famous chemical originally made in this way is the antibiotic 'penicillin', a drug that acts very powerfully against infection. It is produced naturally by the green mould that is sometimes found on bread. The major problems in making penicillin commercially have been to arrange conditions so that the mould can work easily, and, of course, to purify the product. The penicillin

that is now used comes from a combination of natural and synthetic chemistry: the molecule of the naturally produced compound is altered to make it more resistant to 'antipenicillin' chemicals in the bacteria under attack.

Bacteria themselves make chemicals, like any other living creature, and a very exciting recent discovery is that bacteria can be altered so that, in addition to the chemicals they would make as part of the process of living, they also turn out chemicals needed by industry or medicine. There are risks in changing bacteria—the process is called genetic manipulation—because a new breed of bacteria is made, and this might become a very dangerous, completely new kind. But the process can be made safe, and dozens of chemical companies are looking at the new possibilities.

Strict controls and regulations govern the age-old craft of winemaking and now entail a thorough understanding of the chemical processes involved in fermentation, sterilization, maturing and so on.

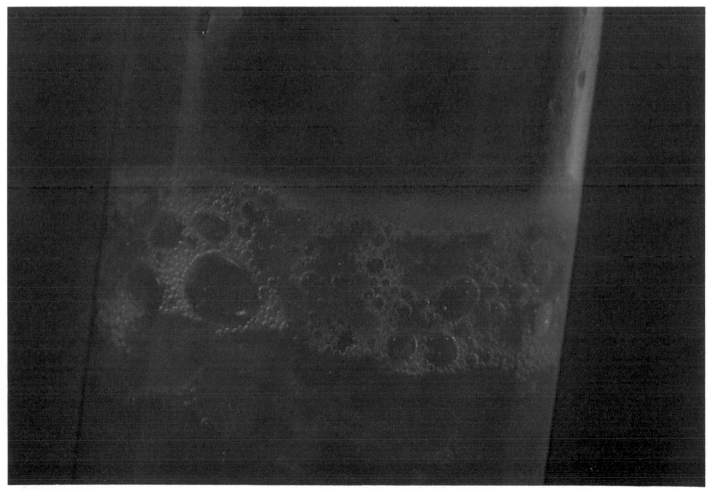

Modern Mathematics

The New Mathematics, as it is known, is a surprising subject because it includes so much that is not normally thought of as being part of mathematics. It is interested in street maps and the characteristics of people, even in strategies of games and war. Its breadth is partly responsible for another surprising fact. The new mathematics is exciting—even exhilarating. Those who learn it in school find it both understandable and attractive, which is more than can generally be said for the old-fashioned kind.

The subject came into being because, particularly in the last 20 or 30 years, we have suddenly found new tasks for mathematics, new problems that we would like it to solve. The development of the computer is the most obvious example. A computer is much more than a marvellous calculating machine. It is a logic machine—a device that can plan landings on the moon and the manufacture of motor cars, for example, and a new kind of mathematics is needed to design and to use a computer.

In a sense, it is not really a new mathematics, and it cannot be if it is to deal with our ordinary world. What it is is an extension of 'ordinary' mathematics and the application of a very broad logic to it.

A very early task of the new mathematics was to clarify what we mean by number. We associate numbers with objects, and it is possible, though not likely, that we first learn that 'Three threes are nine' by noticing that three groups of three objects—pebbles, for example—total nine pebbles. The new mathematics has devised rules for addition and subtraction, multiplication and division that apply, not merely to what are called cardinal numbers, 1, 2, 3, 4, 5 . . ., which can be associated with objects, but also to negative numbers -1, -2, -3 . . . These have no meaning in connection with objects, although they certainly have a meaning in connection with temperatures, and to numbers like the square root of -1, a number that is not 'real'—there is no number that when multiplied by itself comes to -1—and yet is associated with alternating electric currents. Modern mathematics has made the rules for dealing with fractions, such as $\frac{1}{5}$, $\frac{1}{3}$, logical, so that it becomes clear why $\frac{1}{3} \div \frac{1}{4} = \frac{1}{3} \times \frac{4}{1}$.

Quite early, too, mathematics showed how to use unconventional number systems. A computer uses the binary system, where only two digits exist—1 and 0. Thus $1 + 1 = 10$, for three reasons: it is suited to the electronic currents that a computer uses to calculate, it is more accurate, and it is more economical than the decimal system we normally use. Modern mathematics has rules for multiplying, adding and so on in binary, and has put these rules in forms that work for any number system.

Anyone who studies the new mathematics quickly comes across 'sets'. A set is a collection of elements that can be distinguished from one another, and if it is to be a nameable set, the elements will have some aspect in common. The set may be the books of the Old Testament, or the animals with two legs in a zoo, or odd numbers less than 20, to give a few examples. Set theory, like all the new mathematics, can be applied very widely. It can be used as a way of expressing logical relationships. What is the relation between the set of all murderers and the set of all women? The figure shows that they have elements in common. Set theory is important when using machines—a computer is a machine—to attack problems in logic.

As well as tackling problems that can be shown in pictures, modern mathematics looks at problems that actually start from pictures and solid objects. The branch most concerned is called 'topology' and it is about the aspects of shapes that do not change when the shape is distorted. You might think that a distorted map is useless, but most maps of underground railways systems or airlines are grossly distorted. Nevertheless, they show you very accurately where to change trains or planes.

The theory of maps of the underground railways might seem a bit trivial. One of the early problems of topology which might seem even more so shows the study is not trivial at all. Leonhard Euler, a famous 18th-century mathematician, studied a map of the bridges over the River Pregel at Königsberg in Germany (it is now Kaliningrad and in Russia). There are seven bridges, and the problem was: Could you cross every bridge once and once only? You can try it on a map and you will find that it cannot be done. Euler proved this mathematically, and as a result produced two rules for networks such as this one. If you call a junction of 2, 4, 6, . . . paths an 'even vertex' and a junction of 1, 3, 5, 7, 9 . . . paths an 'odd vertex', his laws are that the number of odd vertices must be even, and that only if there are two odd vertices or none can you go through each line of the network once and once only. As soon as you look at a simple diagram of a radio circuit, you can see where these laws might

be useful. A radio circuit is an obvious example of a map that can be distorted and yet be used to make a working radio.

Even topology's favourite surprise, the Möbius band is useful in real life. A strip, given a twist and then joined is called a Möbius band, and it has an odd property. It has only one side. You can show this by imagining a beetle walking along the strip. It can reach any point without having to cross the edge. If you make one of these strips and cut it down the centre you will discover another odd property. But what *use* are the properties of the Möbius band? It turns out that electrical circuits arranged in this way have a lower electrical resistance than others. Modern mathematics is amusing and exciting, but it is also often very useful.

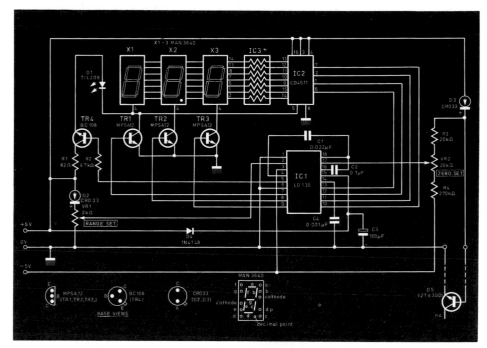

Circuit diagram (top) of digital thermometer (bottom). The diagram is clearly distorted, that is, it bears no resemblance to the actual thermometer in appearance but, of course, is an accurate 'map' for the purposes of constructing the final article.

Relativity

The observer on the pavement sees the stationary tram on the left without distortion. He sees the other two trams tall and thin, because both are moving at high speeds. One tram looks bluer because it is moving towards him; and the other looks redder because it is moving away. The observer in the stationary tram sees the houses undistorted. In the moving tram, he sees them tall and thin.

The picture of the world given by modern science is often unusual, and sometimes seems contrary to common sense. An extremely important theory that has played a large part in building this surprising view of the world is Albert Einstein's Theory of Relativity, first put forward in 1905, when Einstein was employed as a

clerk in the Swiss Patent office.

The theory starts from an attempt to see if anything in the universe can be thought of as fixed. We know that the Earth moves around the Sun, that the Sun is slowly moving around the centre of our galaxy, and that our galaxy is itself slowly drifting in relation to other galaxies. But is

there anything that is stationary, so that we can give some absolute value to, for example, the Earth's movement through space?

In the 19th century, scientists believed that light travelled through a substance they called the aether, roughly as sound travels through the air. The heavenly bodies, including the Earth, also moved through the aether. If a beam of light was sent out through this aether, in the direction the Earth was moving and reflected back, it should seem to travel more quickly because the source would have moved towards its reflector while the light was 'en route'. So if the velocity of the speed of light is measured in different directions, there should be different answers depending on whether the light is travelling with, against, or across the flow of aether across the Earth. The experiment designed to discover the differences was performed by two American scientists, Albert Michelson and Edward Williams Morley, in 1887. They found that the speed of light, in any direction, was always the same. There could be no aether and therefore no fixed point or material in the universe.

What was needed, though, was some explanation of why the speeds were always the same. A physicist, George Fitzgerald, produced an astonishing suggestion. He proposed that a moving measuring device was shorter than a stationary one and that the faster it moved, the shorter it became. As every measuring instrument used to check the original one would also be shortened, the change could not be directly measured.

There might be no way of measuring the 'Fitzgerald contraction' as it was called, but there was a way of measuring a similar effect on electrons. A rapidly moving electron would keep its charge, but should, if the proposal were true, gain in mass if it moved quickly. The ratio of mass to charge could be measured and a Dutch physicist, Hendrik Lorentz, suggested that it should increase in the same way as length contracted. When the equations were worked out, it turned out that the mass of an electron should be infinite at the

speed of light. If the Lorentz-Fitzgerald theories were correct, then nothing could travel faster than the speed of light—there cannot be a mass greater than an infinite one! Experiments with electrons travelling very quickly confirmed these theories.

The ideas of Fitzgerald and Lorentz were put into a complete pattern by Albert Einstein in his Special Theory of Relativity. Einstein held simply that the speed of light in a vacuum was always the same, whatever speed its source moved at. His later General Theory of Relativity extended his ideas from steadily moving objects to accelerating ones. The Lorentz-Fitzgerald equations followed from Einstein's basic idea, and much more besides. As the speed of any object increased, it should get shorter, which was surprising enough: more surprising still was the suggestion that a clock should tick more slowly. Time itself would be slowed.

You can see from this why Einstein's theory is called the theory of relativity. It says that there is no such thing as an absolute time or absolute length or mass. They all alter with the speed of the object, and if we are travelling with the object we cannot detect the change. A stationary observer could.

The effect on time produces the strangest paradox of all. Einstein's theory says that a clock ticks more and more slowly as we travel more and more quickly. Near the speed of light, a clock ticks very very slowly. What this seems to mean is that a space traveller in a very fast space craft will get old more slowly than a friend he leaves behind on Earth. In theory, a space traveller could leave the Earth for a long journey, and return to find his friends 20 years older, while he had aged by only two years. Delicate experiments with atoms confirm this idea, but we shall not know if it is true for living creatures until we can make very much faster space craft than we can now. But if we can, and if the theory is supported by experiment, we could go to the furthest planet in a single lifetime. We would, though, return to find that our friends had died of old age.

Technology
New Materials

We wear skirts and blouses made of nylon, and outer clothes containing Terylene. We look at our television screen through a shield of Perspex when we are not twiddling the plastic knobs on our plastic transistor radios. In our spare time, we might go fishing with a 'fibreglass' fishing rod from our fibreglass sailing dinghy. We truly live in an age of un-natural materials.

At least in part, this is a matter of necessity. The demand for cotton and wool and wood, and for the ability to handle and work with them, has grown so much this century as to outstrip supply. The synthetic materials—the technical name for man-made substances—have become essential to our way of life and it's difficult to imagine life without them.

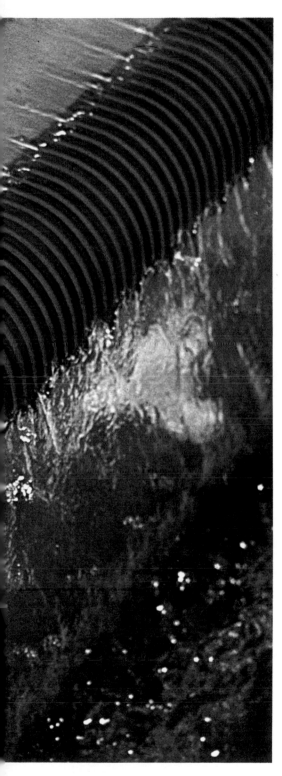

The production of man-made, or synthetic, fibres has become a highly mechanized industry, in the Western world. On their own, or in combination with natural materials, such as cotton and wool, they are found in furnishing and dress fabrics throughout Europe and America.

The first synthetic material, celluloid, actually owes its existence to a deliberate plan to conserve natural supplies. Billiard balls, in the first half of the 19th century, were made from ivory: elephants were killed so that people could play billiards. In the 1860s, a prize was offered to anyone who could produce an adequate substitute for ivory, and it was won by an American, John Wesley Hyatt, who used an improved form of celluloid, a mixture based on camphor and cellulose nitrate.

Cellulose nitrate is made by treating the natural substance, cellulose, which is a major component of wood, and hence of paper, with nitric acid. Camphor is also a natural substance, so that the first plastic was not a genuine synthetic.

Nor was the first artificial fibre—an artificial silk. This also started from cellulose nitrate. A French chemist, Hilaire de Chardonnet, discovered that cellulose nitrate would dissolve in a mixture of alcohol and ether. If the solution were sprayed through small holes, the solvent evaporated, leaving fine strands of highly flammable cellulose nitrate that could be treated to change it into silk-like threads of cellulose.

Neither this artificial silk nor later ones, viscose and rayon, made by dissolving the cellulose itself, rather than cellulose nitrate, were true synthetics. The first genuinely synthetic fibre was nylon, which is still in use.

Nylon was invented in the 1930s by Wallace Hume Carothers, an American chemist interested in ways of persuading simple chemical molecules to join up. He found that some pairs of compounds would link alternately (a . . . b . . . a . . . b . . .) to form long chains, and he eventually made very long chains—long polymers, as they are known—of two fairly complicated chemicals, hexamethylene diamene and adipic acid. The fibre that could be made from this polymer was called nylon, and it was followed by others—Orlon, Acrilan, Terylene, for example, each with their own advantages.

The first synthetic plastic was Bakelite. It was named after its discoverer, Leo Baekeland, who discovered that if he heated two chemicals, phenol and formaldehyde, both of which could be obtained from coal tar, they would, under the right conditions, form a soft resin that could be moulded and then hardened by heating. Bakelite is still used today.

Bakelite is a polymer—a compound formed of a large number of similar molecules joined together. So is a later discovery, polyethylene—also known as polythene. Ethylene is a gas that is usually made from crude oil. Under the right conditions, its simple molecules (it contains only two carbon atoms and four of hydrogen) will combine to form very long chains (polymers) that can be made into sheets and films. A later development was the discovery by Karl Ziegler and Giulio Natta that the pattern of polymerization could be controlled, which in turn gave a way of improving the quality of the polythene. Yet another discovery was a way of producing polymers of a chemical relative of ethylene, tetrafluorethylene, to make the Teflon that coats non-stick saucepans.

Some of the most interesting new materials are hybrids; two materials are used to give a novel substance that has the virtues of both. Plastics, in thin layers, are watertight and can be shaped, but they have no rigidity: it is very difficult to make even small panels for a car body from plastics. But glass fibres are extremely strong. When they are protected from scratches that would weaken them, by a coating of plastic, the result—glass-reinforced polymer (GRP for short)—is a valuable material. It is expensive, at present, to work and this rather offsets its virtues, but once production problems have been solved, GRP will become a widespread substitute for metals.

These polymers don't corrode, they can be formed easily into very complex shapes, and they can be very strong. Indeed polymers—plastics—reinforced with fibres of pure carbon are some of the strongest materials we know. Synthetic materials have become more than substitutes for natural ones. We have managed to improve on nature.

Computers

The computer must be one of the most important technical inventions of the century, because computers expand our mental powers, while other inventions extend only our physical abilities. They were originally invented to solve complicated mathematical problems; computers were superior calculating machines. Nowadays they can make decisions, produce plans of action, or simulate wars. They are machines that seem to think.

The French mathematician Blaise Pascal in 1642 made one of the first working calculating machines, an adding machine that consisted of a series of cogs connected to dials. But neither this nor the slightly later invention by Liebniz of a version that could multiply and divide could really be called a computer. A computer can accept a program (this American spelling is always used in the world of computers) and work its way through a series of operations without any further action by the operator.

The first attempt to make a computer in this sense, dates from 1833 when an English mathematical genius, Charles Babbage, set out to make what he called an Analytical Engine. This was to be a calculating machine that would store results in a temporary memory, compare the results of different calculations, and make decisions that were based on the comparisons. Further, it could store instructions for each stage of its calculations and it could print the result.

Had it ever been finished, the Analytical Engine would have been the first computer. The problem was that it had to work mechanically, through gears and rods and levers, and the engineering of the time was not good enough. It was never finished, although a small part of it is preserved in the Science Museum in London, and it is probably not possible, even today, to make a working mechanical computer.

The first successful computers were electronic; they used radio valves in the part that makes calculations and stores numbers: it is much easier to move tiny electrical currents around than to move a series of cogs and wheels. The US computer ENIAC (Electronic Numerical Integrator and Calculator) was built during the Second World War. It occupied a complete office block and used 18,000 radio valves. A German machine using a similar approach was built at much the same time by an engineer named Konrad Zuse.

The invention of the transistor in 1948 was the first step towards making computers widely available. Transistors are much smaller than valves, more reliable, and use much less electricity. The earliest transistor computers could be fitted into a single large office: the latest, as we shall see, are much smaller still.

All computers must have a device for putting in instructions, and some way of showing the answer to their calculations. They must have memories and they must have what is called an Arithmetic Unit, where the actual calculation is done.

Nowadays, the instructions and the numbers that the computer is to handle are usually put in with a special kind of typewriter, although punched cards on which information is recorded as holes in the card, are still used. Because computers are always electronic, the memories are usually magnetic. The numbers and programs may be stored in the magnetic network of a core memory, or on tape, either in large reels or in the familiar tape cassette. Core memories have rather small capacities, but it takes a long while to work through a tape memory and find the facts you need. A recent development in magnetic memories starts from magnetic discs that rotate constantly past a device for reading the magnetic record: the latest versions use what are called 'floppy disks' and even 'mini floppy disks' so that the stored information can be found quickly.

The output from a computer is nowadays either words, pictures and charts on a specialized 'television' screen called a visual display unit (VDU) or the same answers in a printed form. VDU screens give quick answers and avoid printing material that is wanted only for a few minutes, such as the flight times of aircraft. If a permanent record is needed, then printing is the only way, and there has been a lot of research aimed at developing printers that can keep up with the incredible speeds of the electronic part of the computer.

Computers have become much cheaper and much more widely available since the development of the 'chip'. This is a marvel of modern technology. It is a tiny piece, a chip, of silicone that has been treated with chemicals so that the equivalent of 40 or 50 thousand transistors can fit on to a quarter of an inch square. These chips can be mass-produced and cost very little. They have made it possible to produce computers that are cheap enough to be available in the home for computer enthusiasts or busy businessmen.

Machines of the Future

Machines are devices, such as pulleys and levers, that help us to use our energy more effectively. Alternatively, they may harness non-human energy in the way that steam engines or motor cars do. The history of technology is largely a history of machines, and, these, especially in the period that started with the 18th century in Europe, have enormously altered our lives.

The 18th century saw the begin-ning of the Industrial Revolution, and it can be said that we are still living in it. The Revolution involved the development of agricultural ma-chines—seed drills and combine har-vesters, for example—and industrial machines—which started with ma-chinery for spinning cotton and wool and now includes production equip-ment such as that used in the produc-tion lines for motor cars. These machines have enormously increased

what one person can produce, and as a result, people are nowadays better fed, better housed and travel more freely and easily than any but the few did three hundred years ago.

The signs are that a new industrial revolution is starting now. The basis is the computer, and particularly the tiny computers based on the 'chip'—a quarter-inch square of silicon on which the equivalent of tens of thousands of transistors can be en-

graved. These 'chips' make it easy to control machines, or to build machines that will control themselves, and, in the future, we shall use these machines to do jobs that are dangerous or tedious or unpleasant in some other way.

A remotely-controlled miner, for example, is a real possibility. Mining is a very dangerous and demanding job but it could be made safe overnight if we could invent a machine for mining that could be controlled from a distance. Machines like this are called telechiric machines, and a telechiric coal miner has already been invented by Professor Meredith Thring, in London. It could work continuously underground, under the control of a miner on the surface. It could work three shifts a day and would save enormous amounts of money because there is no need to worry about purifying the air in a mine. A telechiric miner does not breathe.

A telechiric diver does not breathe either and these are actually on the market. There is an enormous need for divers to work on oil rigs at sea. They have to inspect the rigs and repair them and perhaps make adjustments. At present these tasks are carried out either by engineers in submersibles or by divers working from them. Submersibles are essentially miniature submarines that have to be operated from a mother ship. It is convenient to have people working under water, but a remotely-controlled craft such as an SMT 1 made by Sonar Marine, could do many of the tasks as easily, and with no risk to human life. Remotely controlled machines like this one are very much cheaper than submersibles and they are much cheaper to use, simply because the operator does not have to make sure that underwater workers are safe. At the depths at which modern divers work —about 500 feet, for example, in the North Sea—the equipment designed for their safety is very complex indeed.

There are even more fascinating possibilities. A miniature computer can act as a rather simple brain. It can accept messages and control machinery, and the microprocessors, as 'chips' are technically known, can be used to make real robots.

There are already robots working in industry. They do not look like the robots in old-fashioned science-fiction stories, which were really mechanical men. The modern robot is usually designed to do only a few jobs, and the shape is the one that suits the jobs.

The modern robots are used for jobs that are tedious, or fatiguing or unpleasant. Welding steel to make motor car bodies is a job like that. It is a mechanized job as the worker has only to operate an elaborate, almost automatic machine. He has to do this steadily, to play his part in a production line and this can be extremely tedious. Another disadvantage is that the welding machine is so complicated that it is difficult for a manufacturer to change the shape of car body he is producing.

The robot welder used by General Motors welds automatically. It receives steel sheets from other machines and carries out the welding programme that it has been 'told' to do. It is very easy to change its instructions. The operator simply guides the machine around a steel plate, indicating the places that need welding. The robot remembers its instructions and repeats the action automatically.

Microprocessors have been used in more elaborate robots. One of these assembles motor-cycle engines at an experimental factory designed by the Suzuki Company. Some of the jobs are quite complicated. We, as humans, find it fairly easy, to fit a piston into a cylinder. A robot has to be told how to 'feel' which way to push the piston so as to fit it into the cylinder. There are also robots which put nuts on to bolts and tighten them, and which compress springs and fit them. Many of the unpleasant jobs in manufacturing could be carried out by robots like these.

These are machines for industry but there will also be much better 'machines for people' in the future. The most obvious need is better aids for handicapped people. There is already a design for a wheel-chair that will walk up stairs and there are machines which look a bit like space men that handicapped people can operate from inside. There are echosounders so that the blind can at least miss obstacles even if the machine cannot at present actually 'see' for them. Machines have already increased enormously what we can do, and have provided us with a rich supply of food and goods. Machines in the future will go further and will aim at making life pleasant.

Transport

Anyone who has lived through the 20th century has seen the most startling changes in transport that any lifetime could encompass. At the beginning of the century, the only air travel was by balloon: trips were rare and unpredictable. On the surface of the Earth, all travel, with the exception of trains, was limited to a maximum of about 30 miles per hour. Even trains ran only a little faster on their regular trips. By now, many people have travelled at 100 miles an hour on the road and many more at that speed by rail. In the air, 600 miles an hour is commonplace, and space craft travel at tens of thousands of miles an hour. At the beginning of the century, very few people travelled more than a few miles from their home: nowadays, journeys of thousands of miles are commonplace.

The progress in motor cars has been the most predictable. At the beginning of the century, they usually had engines that burned petrol. The engines were at the front, the car was four-wheeled and the engine drove one or both of the rear wheels. Most of the changes since then have been improvements in engineering rather than radical change in the basic design. Even domestic motor cars are now carefully designed to reduce wind resistance to a minimum. The engines have been greatly improved in reliability—the engines

of early motor cars were so unreliable that every driver had also to be a mechanic—and the power they develop is enormous compared with that of the early motor car. Nowadays this power is most frequently transmitted to the driving wheels through a gearbox that changes gear automatically, and the suspension and springing of the motor car is adequate to the high speeds at which these powerful engines can propel the streamlined bodies. Modern cars and lorries are, therefore, able to use to advantage the motorways that have been designed for them.

While modern cars and heavy transport suit motorways, they do not suit cities, and most developed countries are trying to solve the problems of transport in towns. The problem starts from the fact that people buy and use motor cars designed for long-distance travel and these are much larger than a car for towns only needs to be. The immediate results are congestion on the street, an insoluble parking problem, and pollution of the air by exhaust fumes.

The most likely solution in the future is a special 'city car', powered by electricity. The car could be very small and simple, and an electric motor is silent and does not pollute the air. Further, an electric car need use no petrol, which will be important as oil supplies run short

towards the end of the century. The electricity to charge its batteries can come from power stations using coal or nuclear fuel. At present, there are no satisfactory batteries for electric cars, but this problem will certainly be solved.

The main changes in transport by water can be divided into two groups. One has led to increasingly larger cargo vessels: the other to very fast craft, skimming or even travelling above the surface of the water.

There is a third change that has affected the way loads are carried, rather than the speed or size of the ships that carry them. The classical cargo ship loaded its bags of tea, bales of wool, radio sets, coils of cable, soap or whatever directly. The loads were taken to wharves, put aboard as neatly as possible, and unloaded and sorted at the far end. The method was awkward and slow, needed a lot of people to make it work, and the goods could be damaged during handling. Nowadays, increasingly, loads are packed at the factories in standard containers, taken by specially designed 'container lorries' to the ports, and loaded by special hoists. The process is so neat and quick that ports that cannot handle containerized goods, as this traffic is known, are going short of trade.

A major change in shipping has been the development of the bulk carrier. Frequently, what is carried in bulk is oil, and this particular kind of shipping is known as the super-tanker. The thinking behind the design of these is simple. The power needed to drive a ship depends, very roughly, on its area. The amount of oil it can carry depends on its volume. If you increase the size of a ship ten times, you increase its area a hundred times, but its volume a thousand times. The gigantic super-tankers—they can be as large as 500,000 tons—are based on this theory. The disadvantage is that they are difficult to manoeuvre and present great problems if they run aground.

The most original developments in speedy water transport represent two attempts to avoid the resistance of the water. The speed of a ship is limited by friction with the water and by the need to move the water aside to travel through it. Both are avoided if the ship can travel above the water.

One method is to fit the ship with 'wings' below the hull. When the ship travels quickly it will rise on the wings so that the hull is above the water. The first successful hydrofoil, as such ships are called, was designed and built by Enrico Forlanini and demonstrated on Lake Maggiore from 1905 onwards. Eventually, Alexander Graham Bell, the inventor of the telephone, bought a licence to make Forlanini hydrofoils in the United States, but the designs were really rather ahead of the engineering expertise of the time, and interest in hydrofoils lapsed. The first hydrofoil design that solved all the early problems was produced by Baron Hanns von Schertel in 1936.

The aircushion vehicle—the Hovercraft—represents the other method of avoiding the resistance of water to the movements of boats. As the name implies, the ship is supported by a cushion of air. The system was invented by Christopher Cockerel, and was first used on a full-scale craft in 1959. The system used a jet of air in the form of a ring around the edge of the vessel, pointed

downwards. Although this simple system worked, it was very limited until a flexible skirt was added. This skirt was invented by C. H. Latimer-Needham, and enabled the Hover-craft to ride high above the waves. It also rode high above the ground, when necessary, and part of the success of the Hovercraft as a ferry is due to the fact that it is amphibious, and so can drive over sand banks and needs no harbour. In addition, it is very fast, and can travel at some 60–70 knots.

The whole history of successful powered flight falls into the 20th century. The Wright Brothers' Flyer 3, the first practical aeroplane, flew in 1905. Since then, there has been an astonishing development in size, speed and range, and air travel has become widely available.

An important milestone was the development of the jet engine. This was a war-time invention, but the first civilian jet-plane—the de Havilland *Comet*—didn't fly until 1949. It soon became clear that passenger aircraft using propellors were no longer acceptable as jet planes flew faster; they flew so high that they could avoid much of the turbulence of the atmosphere; they were quieter for the passengers; and they were cheaper to operate.

So many people have been attracted by the possibility of jet travel that new shapes of aircraft have been needed. The first of the wide-bodied giant aircraft was the Boeing 747, which can have almost 500 seats. It

has been renamed 'The Jumbo' but is actually very fast—it cruises at over 600 mph. It is also cheaper to operate than smaller passenger aircraft.

Faster still, but very expensive to operate, is *Concorde* which flies at supersonic speeds—faster than the speed of sound. There are special design problems about aircraft that fly at supersonic speeds, as they must take off and land at normal speeds. The development of *Concorde* as a joint enterprise between the British and French governments involved a long history of difficulties and increasing costs. The design difficulties were eventually solved, and there are now regular transatlantic flights by *Concorde* from Paris or London to New York, taking only a little over three hours. The Russians have a very similar aircraft, the Tupolev Tu-144.

A very dramatic development in air transport has produced aircrafts that can take off vertically. Helicopters do this, but they are slow. The Hawker Harrier, though, is a fast aircraft that can take off vertically. The thrust from its jet engines can be directed in any direction. If the blast of air is directed downwards, the aircraft rises; if the blast is directed backwards, the aircraft flies forwards. The Hawker Harrier, which first flew in free flight in November 1960, can even fly backwards.

The Hawker Harrier jet's vertical take-off was a revolutionary development in fast aircraft design

Bridges, Roads and Tunnels

Bridges and tunnels have an interesting place in technology. They include the largest objects man has made—the Verrazano-Narrows Bridge, in New York, for example, has a span of 1,298 metres, and the road tunnel under Mont Blanc is 12 km long. While tunnels are hidden, so that no-one worries very much what they look like, bridges, especially the giant bridges that engineers now know how to build, are very conspicuous, and this is why some of them—for example the Salgina Bridge, near Schiers, in Switzerland—have been designed to be beautiful. These structures, of course, are very important to the modern world. Bridges and tunnels, and the roads they connect, form a vital part of modern communications. New bridges, tunnels and roads make travel easier and quicker than anyone would have imagined a hundred years ago.

The Romans built a wonderful network of roads throughout Europe, but these depended upon the use of slave labour. Modern roadbuilding really dates from the 18th century. Early in that century the French government set up a national authority that was responsible for the roads, but it was two British engineers who made the greatest achievements in road design. One of them, Thomas Telford, built marvellously smooth roads—one survives to this day as part of the road from London to Holyhead. His technique used heavy stones laid on the soil and topped with fine gravel, but it was too expensive for general use. A Scot, John McAdam found a more economical solution which was used extensively for nearly 200 years. He realized that it was the soil that carried the load of traffic, and that the main function of a road was to keep the soil underneath dry. His roads were cambered, so that water drained off them, and covered with rough stones about a couple of inches (5 cm) across. The wheeled traffic of his time had steel tyres and these ground the stones to form a smooth, watertight surface. The building of McAdam's roads was simple and extremely effective.

Unfortunately, the rubber tyres of the 20th century motor traffic picked up the fine particles of rock in McAdam's roads. A binding layer of tar cured this, and 'tarmac' roads, as the new versions were called, are still constructed. Roads designed for very heavy use are built of concrete nowadays.

The great 20th century development in road building has been the freeway or motorway. This is a long, inter-city road with no intersections and with a very limited number of places where traffic can join it. Some of the most visually exciting structures in motorway design are the 'cloverleaf' junctions designed to ease traffic on to and away from freeways. Important links in the chain of these roads are provided by bridges and tunnels. Both have the same function in that they avoid the necessity of taking roads and railways up and down hills, following the slope of the land.

There are three fundamental designs of bridge: beam, arch and suspension. The simplest is a beam bridge, which may be merely planks or stones laid across a river, perhaps supported at intervals by piers. Larger beam bridges often are of cantilever design. In a cantilever bridge, the centres are supported from below: one end is held down so as to keep the other up. Bridges frequently use both simple beams and cantilevers: the Tappan Zee bridge, over the Hudson River, is a good example.

The arch bridge, again, has a long history and there are arch bridges of stone and brick that are still standing a couple of thousand years after they were built. Arch bridges exert a sideways thrust on the ground, as well as the vertical thrust, and the ground must support the load of traffic using the road as well as that of the road itself. Modern arch bridges even have to be designed to carry a heavy moving load. One way of solving this problem is to hinge the bridge, and many of the bridges designed by Robert Maillart, of Switzerland, who designed the Salgina Bridge, use three hinges, one at each end of the arch, one at the centre.

As the name suggests, the roadway of a suspension bridge is suspended; usually, it is held up by cables from towers at the end. Because part of the stress on the towers is a force pulling them inwards, they must be supported. Generally, the cables of the suspension are carried across the towers and anchored to the ground. Suspension bridges can be built economically across very large spans, and they are frequently elegant structures as well.

The alternative method of dealing with uneven terrain involves tunnelling. The technique of tunnelling through hard mountain rock differs, as you would expect, from the one used for tunnelling through soft earth under a river. Both were worked out during the last century and perfected in this. One of the most striking early tunnels through hard rock was started in 1857. French and Italian engineers set out to make a tunnel 12 km long under Mount Cenis. Although the basis of the method has not changed, the tools they had at the time were very limited. They used hand drills to make holes which they filled with gunpowder. Once this had been detonated, the rubble was shovelled out. The engineers travelled less than a foot a day. Fortunately, the hand drills were soon replaced by compressed-air drills, and gunpowder by dynamite, so that the tunnel could be officially opened in 1871.

The Simplon rail tunnel (20 km long) was built during the early years of the 20th century by a similar method, but it had to deal with two particular problems. Firstly, the rock at the southern end where the Italians were working, was so soft that it behaved as a fluid so there was a risk that the tunnel would be crushed. Eventually a lining of steel and timber, with the gaps filled with cement, was used to keep the tunnel

open. Later, the Italians, first, and then the Swiss who were tunnelling from the other end, ran into great springs of hot water. It was a major engineering problem to seal off the springs and drain the water away.

The problem of keeping water away from a tunnel is, naturally, more severe when the tunnel runs under a river. The method that is used now is basically exactly the same as the one that was devised by an engineering genius, Marc Isam-bard Brunel, to tunnel under the Thames in 1825. (He was, incidentally, the father of another engineering genius, Isambard Kingdom Brunel, whose incredibly productive life included the construction of steamships and railways.)

The ground under the Thames is soft—clay and mud—and Brunel invented a shield so as to be able to tunnel safely in this material. Thirty-six men could stand on the frame of the shield. As the earth in front was

One of the longest suspension bridges in the world, the Verrazano-Narrows Bridge has a span of 1,298 metres.

dug away, the shield was moved forward and a brick lining built to the tunnel. The tunnel was built about 150 years ago and is still in use. In those days, the digging and carrying were done by hand. The main improvement in modern times is to use mechanical cutters and conveyor belts: the principle remains the same.

Communications

There has been a great leap forward in the speed, complexity and range of communications during the 20th century, but two of the major developments—radio, and hence television, and high-speed printing—have their roots in earlier times. Printing with moveable type, in fact goes back more than 500 years.

This particular form of printing may actually have run its course, although it will certainly be around for some decades at least. It was invented, so far as Europe is concerned, by Johannes Gutenberg of Mainz, in Germany, and his first practicable printing press was ready in 1450. What made it so important was that he used a separate piece of type for each letter so that words and sentences could be quickly assembled. He printed a German poem, and then turned to printing the Bible. He finished it in 1456, but by then was bankrupt, and printed no more.

The printing of books spread quickly. William Caxton, the first British printer, put out more than 70 books in English in the 15th century. The printing of newspapers, vital to modern communication, soon followed. The first newsheets appeared in the 16th and 17th centuries, but the first step in making them widely available was the introduction of the steam printing press in 1814. This was followed by the rotary presses still used today.

In these early days, type was set laboriously by hand, letter by letter. In 1886, Ottmar Mergenthaler adapted the typewriter principle to typesetting. The operator of his Linotype struck keys, and the machine automatically cast lines of type. Linotypes, and the more recent Monotypes, which cast each letter separately, are still in use, but are threatened by the speed and flexibility of photosetting—the process used, incidentally, for this book.

The most developed version of this uses a computer to link a typewriter keyboard and a screen that is something like a TV screen. The writer, or operator, 'types' what he wants printed. The computer sorts out the length of the lines, puts hyphens in at the proper places and converts the whole into tiny spots of light on a screen. These spots form letters of whatever size and typeface is wanted, that are photographed very rapidly. The sheet of film is used to make the cylinders that actually do the printing. Already this method, with its directness and speed, has enormously helped communication to large numbers of people—photoset paperbacks are remarkably cheap books. Eventually, it is likely to become the main method of setting, especially since the messages from the 'typewriter' can be sent by wire over enormous distances.

Radio and television, the real 20th-century means of communication, began in 1894. Gugliemo Marconi, then only 20 years old, invented a way of sending a message from a Morse key to an electric bell at the other end of his home laboratory. His invention was, of course, an extension of the telegraph—the 19th century system by which messages, in Morse code, were sent along wires, usually beside railway tracks.

Marconi's first wireless was very limited. He sent the messages from a transmitter. This produced powerful electric sparks that set up radio waves. At the receiver, these were detected by a 'coherer'—a glass tube full of iron filings with an electric wire at each end, connected to a bell. When the radio waves reached the coherer, they arranged the filings so that a current would flow and make the bell ring.

As he improved this version, Marconi found that he could send Morse messages across oceans—on 12 December 1901 Marconi, in Newfoundland, received a message from Poldhu in Cornwall, England—but he could not send speech or music. The invention of the radio valve by Ambrose Fleming in England in 1904 was followed by a valve—the triode—that could amplify electric currents, and could 'add' music and sound to the steady note of Marconi's simple transmitter. This was invented by an American, Lee de Forest, and steady improvements led to the first permanent broadcasting station, established in Pennsylvania in 1920. The increased power that could be sent and received using valves meant that eventually people could listen to the radio on loudspeakers, instead of the earphones that the first radio sets had needed.

After the Second World War, transistors gradually replaced radio valves. A valve looked rather like an electric light bulb and had a wire in it that was heated by sending an electric current through it. Valves wasted electricity and got hot, they were unreliable, and they were rather big. A transistor is tiny, uses hardly any electricity, is very reliable, and hardly produces any heat. It is made of solid that has been treated so that it can increase and control electric currents and it was invented by three Americans, John Bardeen, Walter Brattain and William Shockley, who were working for the Bell Telephone Laboratories.

Television was invented by a Scotsman, John Logie Baird, who first transmitted a picture on 2 October 1925. In any television system, the scene that is transmitted is scanned—looked at piece by piece. The transmitter than sends out a radio signal, strong for a light patch, weak for a dark one, that is converted back to light at the receiver and used to build up a picture there. In Baird's system, the camera contained a rotating wheel with holes in that limited the area 'seen' by the camera. As the wheel spun, the whole scene was scanned. The receiver contained a wheel spinning at the same speed, and light through this built up the picture. The system was used by the British Broadcasting Corporation to transmit programmes in 1929 but it was very awkward, and was soon replaced by an American system invented by Dr V. K. Zworykin, who patented it in 1928.

The camera in this system has a screen covered with tiny patches, each of which becomes electrically charged if a beam of light hits it. The patches are scanned electrically, and the pattern of electrical currents

that is produced is amplified and transmitted. At the receiver, this pattern is directed at a screen—the television screen—that glows when the electrical beam strikes it. The beam scans the screen at the same rate as the patches are scanned in the camera, and so a black-and-white picture is transmitted and received. In a colour camera, there are colour filters—like tiny pieces of coloured glass—that make the camera 'look' at only one colour at a time. At the receiver, the radio waves that come from looking at, say, a red patch are converted to a red patch by the chemical coating on the television screen.

Radio signals bounce off layers high in the earth's atmosphere, so that signals can travel around the world. Television signals go straight out into space. Worldwide television is a product of the space age. The signals are sent to satellites apparently hovering in space—in fact,

they are spinning around the Earth at the same rate as the Earth spins. They carry receivers and transmitters, and pick up television signals and beam them to very sensitive receivers on the Earth. The whole Earth is now within reach of television signals transmitted from any other part of it.

These communication satellites are also used in the 20th century's other great development in communications, the telephone. This was invented in 1876 by Alexander Graham Bell, a Scotsman who was brought up in Boston, Massachusetts. He found that a thin metal sheet near a magnet around which wire had been wound, would act as a microphone. A voice would make the sheet vibrate and this would make electric currents flow in the wire. The system would act in reverse as a receiver. In 1876, Bell sent his first message to his assistant, 'Mr Watson, please come here. I need you.' He and the American inventor Thomas Alva Edison set up rival telephone systems which eventually

united. The telephone itself was much improved by the invention of a microphone using grains of carbon, which was invented by David Hughes in 1878.

Telephone messages originally travelled along wires and went across oceans through great cables laid along the bottom. Now they are converted to radio signals and beamed to satellites. These satellites will continue to be used for long distance links, but in the future, telephone messages will no longer travel along wires between cities. They will travel along fine fibres of glass. Scientists have discovered a way of turning the electrical currents from the microphone into pulses of light. These are sent between cities along fine strands of glass, thinner than a human hair, and converted back to electricity at the far end. This method, using fibre optics, is cheaper than the one using wires, and can carry many more messages. The old system simply cannot deal with the enormous number of telephone calls that people wish to make.

Energy
Energy and Industrialization

Steam was the driving force behind the revolution in the 18th and 19th centuries which changed peasant communities into expanding industrial societies with worldwide connections. Britain was in the forefront of this revolution because of her abundant reserves of coal and the enterprise of her inventors.

The key inventions, patented by James Watt in 1769 and 1781, were a new design of steam engine by which steam could be applied more efficiently using a condenser, and a method for converting the up and down motion of a piston into a rotary movement. These innovations were to revolutionize many industries by driving machinery of all kinds. They found their first application in spinning and weaving which had previously depended on water power.

Major advances in transportation were to follow. The Stockton and Darlington railway opened in 1825. Steamships eliminated man's dependence on the vagaries of wind and sail, the first crossing of the Atlantic

taking place as early as 1819. And well before the end of the century the horseless 'steam carriage' had taken to the roads.

The technical progress pioneered in Britain was soon to be exploited by others, notably Germany and the United States—and the world was set on course to a new age of trade and prosperity. Another milestone—no less significant than the harnessing of steam—was the application of electricity in the late 19th century for power and lighting.

Already, however, a new factor was entering the energy equation in the United States—oil was discovered beneath the ground. The first successful oil well was sunk in 1859 at Titusville, at a depth of 21 m (69 ft).

Right *Our dependence on oil as a source of energy has increased dramatically inspite of the growing costs of drilling and refining.*

Below *The immediate availability of electricity in the western world is taken for granted.*

Oil propelled the world into a new era of opportunity and was feverishly sought in many countries. The internal combustion engine and gas turbine applied in automobiles, ships, trains and aeroplanes pushed social advance still further, creating a thirst for oil that has become insatiable in the developed parts of the world.

Today there are four main oil-producing areas: the United States, the Middle East, the countries around the Caribbean Sea, and the Soviet Union. As well as prospecting on land for oil (and natural gas) the oil companies have explored the continental shelves surrounding many sea coasts, which have been found to offer large deposits.

The Fossil Fuels

Our prosperity in the 20th century depends on the reserves of fossil fuels laid down over millions of years in the Earth's crust. We are using up these fuels at a prodigious rate—and they are not replaceable.

Coal is the residue of the great forests which covered large parts of the world in prehistoric times. Oil and natural gas are the products of myriads of small sea creatures and plants buried as sedimentary deposits. Although coal is sometimes found near the surface and can be obtained by strip-mining techniques, much of it lies deep underground. Mining then depends on sinking deep shafts and cutting into coal-bearing seams of rock which sometimes extend for miles.

How oil deposits were formed can be briefly explained. First of all mud settles on the ocean floor burying the remains of sea creatures; the mud then hardens into rock. After millions of years the sedimentary layers have become distorted and oil and natural gas that have formed under high pressure are trapped in pockets. To find the oil it is often necessary to drill through many layers of rock. Before it can be extracted the well-head has to be capped and fitted with 'blowout' preventers; pipes and valves control the flow.

Oil is sometimes found beneath the sea in the continental shelves. Drilling then involves fixing rigs and production platforms to the ocean floor. Divers assist in the placement of the ocean-going platforms and, especially in deep water, undersea robots are used, controlled from the surface with the help of television.

Before the crude oil can be used it must be converted into petrol (gasolene), fuel oil or lubricating oil, and the many chemical by-products used by industry. This is the task of the oil refinery which distils the raw product by a thermal process, separating the lighter and heavier fractions (elements) of the oil.

Atomic Power

There is nothing mysterious about atomic power. It simply means that instead of burning coal, oil or gas in a furnace, heat is produced by the splitting of atoms. Most industrialized countries now have nuclear power stations which, notwithstanding the 'hazards' of nuclear energy, are cleaner, more efficient and less polluting than stations burning fossil fuels.

The principle of nuclear power may be simply explained. Some atoms —including certain types of uranium—break into fragments when a single neutron is added to the central nucleus. The uranium atom splits into two smaller atoms and energy is released, mostly as heat. Two or three neutrons are given off which split more nuclei to continue the process.

For this chain reaction to proceed at a steady rate, the number of neutrons produced must be controlled. This can be done by absorbing the extra neutrons in control rods made of boron. To improve the efficiency of the reaction process it is necessary to slow down the neutrons. This is achieved by a moderator which will slow down the reaction if placed between the pieces of uranium fuel. Some types of moderator are made of graphite; others employ heavy water (the component of oxygen and the heavy isotope of hydrogen).

A nuclear reactor has to be surrounded by a shield to prevent the escape of dangerous radiation (neutrons and gamma rays given off in the reaction process). The heat generated in the reactor is carried away by carbon dioxide gas, water or liquid sodium. This in turn heats water and turns it into steam which is used to drive the turbines of electrical generators.

Britain was first in the field, in 1956, with the Calder Hall type of gas-cooled reactors burning natural uranium. They were followed by advanced gas-cooled reactors (AGRs) which burned slightly enriched uranium. Largely because coal, oil and natural gas were plentiful in the 1950s, America was slower to establish nuclear power stations but in the end produced successful designs which, like the British ones, have been exported to many countries. Russia, too, has established a large nuclear industry and many other countries including Canada, France and West Germany have made important contributions.

The pressurized water reactor (PWR), pioneered in the United States, employs enriched uranium oxide, and water serves both as coolant and moderator. Although it has been criticized as being potentially more dangerous than some other reactors because of the possibility of a defect in the pressure shell, the PWR is claimed to be both safe and economic.

Efforts have been made to raise the efficiency of reactors in new designs. One of the big hopes of the next generation is the Fast Breeder Reac-

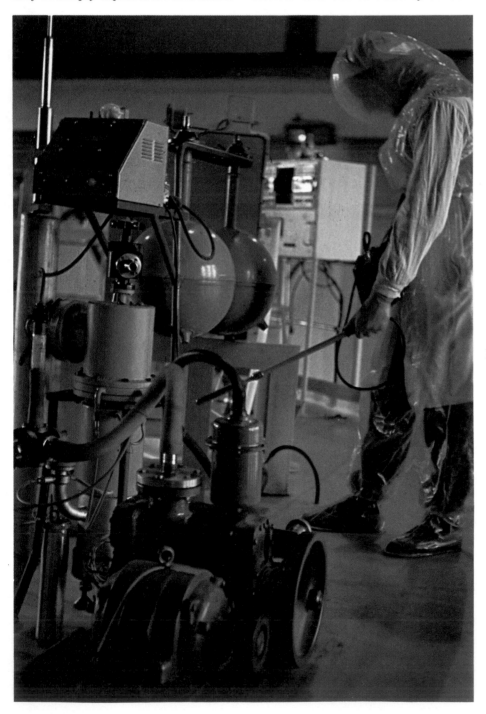

Since the first nuclear reactor, safety has been a major concern for both the public and the authorities concerned.

tor (FBR). Fast reactors burn not only uranium but the plutonium which arises as a by-product of the operation of thermal reactors. They also convert depleted uranium which cannot be burned in thermal reactors, into additional plutonium.

Because it actually produces (breeds) more fuel than it consumes, the FBR has important economic advantages, because uranium is scarce and costly. Fast reactors, which use fuel more efficiently than early types, can produce more than 50 times as much electricity from the same amount of fuel. However, the very process that makes for greater economy is the centre of a growing controversy because of the fear that the extra plutonium produced could end up as atomic bombs.

Another criticism of atomic power concerns the disposal of nuclear wastes, although most of what comes out of a reactor can be re-used and only a tiny part of the used fuel is waste. The highly radioactive liquid waste, most of it from reprocessing fuel so that it can be used again, is concentrated and stored in special tanks until it can be embodied in glass for long-term storage or disposal.

The great hope for the 21st century is that we shall learn to produce *fusion* power—by joining together the nuclei of light elements to form heavier ones. The process is similar to the thermonuclear reaction that drives the Sun. Hydrogen is the lightest element and two types of it, deuterium and tritium, are required for basic fusion power. Deuterium comes from ordinary water. Tritium is made from lithium within the reactor (it 'breeds' in a lithium blanket).

With virtually unlimited energy available from small amounts of common materials—and without the need to reprocess radioactive fuels—we should have a relatively safe and abundant energy supply to fuel a new industrial age. Scientists in Britain, the United States and the Soviet Union believe they are within sight of proving the feasibility of fusion power. But it could take 20 years or more to find a way of applying it commercially.

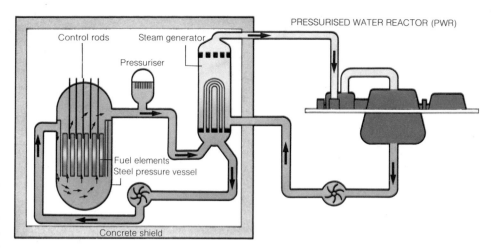

PRESSURISED WATER REACTOR (PWR)

Control rods · Steam generator · Pressuriser · Fuel elements · Steel pressure vessel · Concrete shield

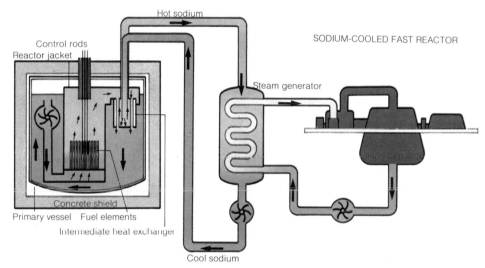

SODIUM-COOLED FAST REACTOR

Hot sodium · Control rods · Reactor jacket · Steam generator · Concrete shield · Primary vessel · Fuel elements · Intermediate heat exchanger · Cool sodium

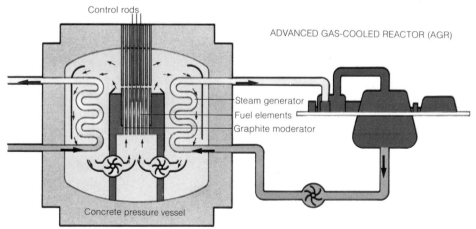

ADVANCED GAS-COOLED REACTOR (AGR)

Control rods · Steam generator · Fuel elements · Graphite moderator · Concrete pressure vessel

To create a fusion reaction the deuterium-tritium fuel must be brought to a temperature of more than 100 million degrees Centigrade; because the fuel conducts electricity it can be heated by an electric current. To handle such enormous temperatures the very hot gas, called a plasma, must be constrained by a magnetic field which holds the plasma away from the walls of the containment vessel.

The Russians proposed a reactor

Types of reactor.
Top *Pressurized water reactor.*
Centre *Sodium cooled fast reactor.*
Bottom *Advanced gas-cooled reactor.*

in the shape of a torus—like a hollow doughnut or tyre—in which the plasma is islolated in the middle. This plan would make it possible to remove heat from the reaction by passing helium gas under high pressure through the lithium blanket which surrounds the reactor. This heat could be used to raise steam to drive turbines.

Alternative Energies

If we fail to provide alternative
sources of energy on a massive scale
before the world's reserves of coal,
oil and gas run out, the outlook for
our civilization is bleak. Industry
will run down, living standards will
fall and famine will become widespread. Armed warfare will be difficult to avoid.

The non-nuclear alternatives—
hydro-power from rivers and the
oceans; wind power; geothermal energy ('hot rocks') and earth-based

solar energy systems—can never
wholly compensate for the loss of our
fossil fuels. It appears that we shall
have to rely heavily upon some form
of nuclear power, but this does not
mean that we should ignore other
potential energy sources.

There is considerable interest, for
example, in harnessing the energy of
the oceans. A small 240 MW tidal
power station has been operating at
La Rance in France since the 1960s.
The tide rushing out from behind a

barrier operates turbines which drive
electrical generators. However, a
tidal power station for the Severn
estuary on the England–Wales border has been estimated to take 20
years to build and cost approximately
£4,000 million.

Research is also going on into the
possibility of generating electricity
from the waves by means of floating
booms and hinged flaps which move
up and down in response to wave
motions.

Another system, already in use in
America, makes use of an electric
power plant fuelled by ocean thermal
energy. In the Gulf Stream there is a
30–40° difference in temperature

Windmills have supplied small amounts of electricity to isolated communities for half a century. Now engineers are trying to perfect new types of windmill, called 'wind turbines', with greatly improved aerodynamic qualities. A huge wind turbine on a mountain in North Carolina (operational in 1979) has blades which span 91 m (300 ft). Designed to operate in average wind speeds of 23 km/h (14 mph), it will generate 2,500 kW of electricity—enough to run 500 homes.

The Sun is our ultimate energy resource for it will last as long as our civilization survives. Solar cells, which power nearly all artificial satellites, convert sunlight directly into electricity. Although present costs are high, these cells are already finding a use in such devices as automatic weather stations and navigational buoys. Possible future applications may involve setting out huge arrays of solar cells in desert areas to serve local agriculture and industry.

The first large-scale direct use of solar energy, however, does not involve solar cells but solar panels fixed to the roofs of buildings. The glass-fronted panels absorb sunlight to heat the air, water or other fluid which flows in the unit.

The ultimate in solar energy may come from city-size satellites in geostationary orbit 35,880 km (22,300 miles) above the equator. Such stations would have immense arrays of solar cells to convert solar energy to electrical power. Huge directional antennae would then transmit the power by microwave beams to special receiving sites on Earth for distribution to homes and factories.

Tidal power station at La Rance, France. A similar scheme proposed for a tidal barrier at Britain's Severn estuary could provide about 3 per cent of the country's energy.

Heliostat solar reflector with a concrete base, mirror and a pressurized dome.

between surface water and water at a depth of 600 m (2,000 ft). This difference can operate heat engines which, in turn, drive electrical generators.

We can also tap 'hot rocks' in the Earth's crust. Most of the heat energy comes from the decay of radioactive elements. One method of extraction involves drilling down to the hot rocks and cracking them open by hydraulic static pressure. Cooled water is sent down one bore hole by a generating station on the surface and hot water taken up through another.

Health and Medicine

We are healthier today than ever before. Even at the beginning of this century man's average life-span was only 46 years, while today life expectancy is about 71 years. Not only do we survive longer, but the threats to our health are quite different. It is the degenerative diseases—coronary heart disease, stroke, osteoarthritis, which kill or cripple us now. A hundred years ago we died, usually of infectious disease, before we had a chance to degenerate. Social improvements, aseptic surgical techniques, have contributed to our better survival rates, but the strongest weapon in our defensive armoury has been the development of effective drugs, beginning with the discovery of the sulfa drugs and penicillin in the 1930s.

What are the hazards to health which face us now? Things are weighted for or against us on our very entry to life. Inherited tendencies to disease, for example, personality and body type may make us more prone to some mental or physical illnesses than others. Sex and marital status both influence longevity—women, on average, live four years longer than men and married people survive better than single. It is healthier to be born into the upper social classes, who tend to live longer, be ill less—factors influenced by

their better housing, nutrition and their employment in less dangerous occupations. Where we live makes a difference too. Many diseases have a geographical variation; multiple sclerosis, for example, is less prevalent near the equator and cancer of the breast is uncommon in Japan. Environment, air pollution and climate all have their effect on health, but undoubtedly the greatest risks of all are the ones we inflict upon ourselves, by eating too much, smoking too much and taking too little exercise.

Obesity is one of the most common and potentially lethal western diseases and it is due, quite simply, to eating more than we need. Fat people throw extra strain on their hearts and weight-bearing joints, they are more prone to coronary heart disease, high blood pressure, diabetes, gallstones and atherosclerosis. *What* we eat can influence our health as well—many doctors think that diets which reduce the cholesterol level in our blood by cutting down on animal fats and replacing them with the 'unsaturated' fats found in vegetable oils may help to reduce coronary heart disease. And because the western diet is a low-fibre diet, with little indigestible residue, it produces a stool too small for the bowel muscle

to propel efficiently. Adding high fibre bran to the diet to increase its bulk has been found to help prevent a good many digestive disorders such as constipation and diverticular disease.

Although tobacco consumption in both Britain and America has fallen slightly since the dangers of smoking were recognized in the 1960s, more than half Britain's adults still smoke, and at least 50,000 deaths per year in Britain in people under 64 can be attributed to smoking. Besides having higher death rates, smokers are generally less healthy too. The main risks they run are from lung diseases, cancer, bronchitis, emphysema, and from coronary heart disease.

Inactivity is not only unhealthy, but can be dangerous. Taking vigorous—and regular—exercise is known to be one of the best protective measures against coronary heart disease you can take.

Many of us lead fairly stressful lives, and although the cause and effect relationship between stress and disease is not a simple one, there is undoubtedly some sort of link between health and happiness. Stresses in an individual's personal relationships, work or financial affairs, for example, have been found to build up in the period preceding a

Life expectancy in various societies and ages.

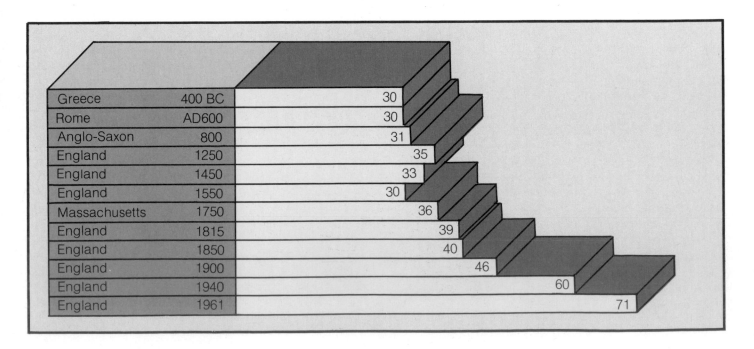

Greece	400 BC	30
Rome	AD600	30
Anglo-Saxon	800	31
England	1250	35
England	1450	33
England	1550	30
Massachusetts	1750	36
England	1815	39
England	1850	40
England	1900	46
England	1940	60
England	1961	71

1876 Great Britain	1976 Great Britain	1976 U.S.A.
1. Tuberculosis	1. Diseases of the heart	1. Diseases of the heart
2. Diarrhoea; Dysentery	2. Cancer	2. Cancer
3. Scarlet Fever	3. Stroke (cardio vascular disease)	3. Stroke (cardio vascular disease)
4. Whooping cough, Cancer	4. Pneumonia	4. Accidents
	5. Bronchitis	5. Pneumonia

coronary attack, and may well pre-dispose him to other illnesses too.

Some of the greatest advances in the last few decades have been in the prevention of disease. Immunization programmes have virtually eradicated smallpox, diphtheria and polio, and milk pasteurization and tuber-culin testing have abolished the risk of tuberculosis. Women are being educated to recognize the early signs of breast cancer for themselves and, where the resources are available, to have regular pap tests for cervical cancer. In addition, programmes of screening (examining apparently healthy people to detect disease in the early, pre-symptomatic stage) have become increasingly popular, especially in America where the businessman's annual check has become almost routine. But it is now believed that to be of any real value such screening should not be hap-hazard but should be concentrated on disease where early diagnosis can affect treatment and eventual out-come and those potentially most at risk can be identified, such as dia-betes. Perhaps more worthwhile are legislative measures such as the clean air legislation which has dramatically reduced the incidence of chronic bronchitis in British cities. Compulsory seat-belt laws in Aus-tralia reduced the road-accident rate by 25 per cent and the drink laws in Britain cut it by 15 per cent in the first year of operation.

Even more important are govern-ment health education programmes such as anti-smoking campaigns. Few medical advances could affect our future health as profoundly as a successful attempt to persuade us to modify our life-styles and reduce the avoidable risks we run.

Above *Foremost causes of death in Britain and America.*
Below *One of the Health Education Council's anti-smoking posters.*

No wonder smokers cough.

The tar and discharge that collects in the lungs of an average smoker.

The Health Education Council

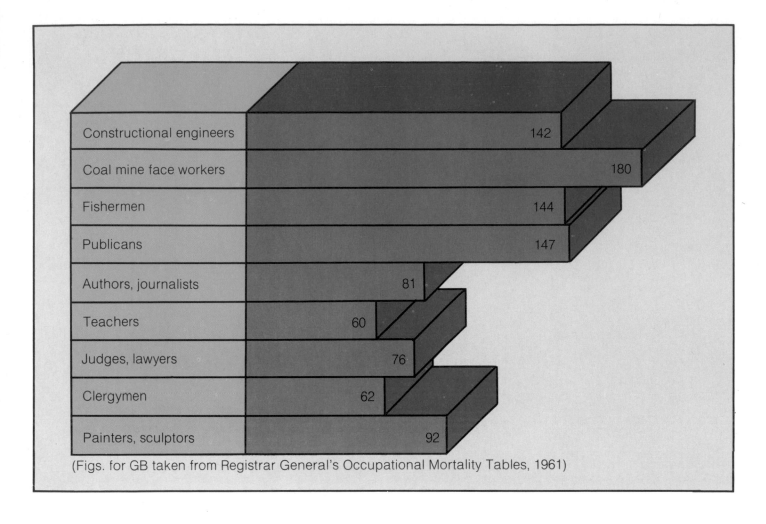

Constructional engineers	142
Coal mine face workers	180
Fishermen	144
Publicans	147
Authors, journalists	81
Teachers	60
Judges, lawyers	76
Clergymen	62
Painters, sculptors	92

(Figs. for GB taken from Registrar General's Occupational Mortality Tables, 1961)

Drugs and Diagnostic Techniques

The Standardised Mortality Ratio gives a measure of the risk of an occupation and is found by comparing the actual number of deaths in a particular group with the number which would be generally expected. An SMR of 100 is 'average'.

A drug is any substance which can alter the structure or function of a living organism. This includes everything from what we think of as the 'hard' drugs of addiction (morphine, heroin) to the nicotine in a cigarette or the caffeine in a cup of coffee.

Drugs which have beneficial effects are used as medicines, and they can act in various ways. They can prevent a disease (the vaccines); fight the invading organisms which cause it (the anti-microbial drugs); alter its course by modifying body processes (anti-coagulants which prevent blood-clotting); relieve its symptoms (pain-killers, cough-suppressants), and they can replace substances which the body cannot manufacture or absorb (insulin in the treatment of diabetes mellitus).

Any new drug is rigorously tested for its effectiveness and safety but there are still risks attached to its use. Besides its main therapeutic effects a drug will always have other, not so useful actions, and the advantages of a particular drug have always to be weighed against its harmful side-effects. Drug treatment is rather like aiming a shot-gun at a can on a shelf of dresden china—you'll probably hit it, but you're likely to do a bit of damage elsewhere.

To be both safe and effective a drug must always be taken in the exact dose and for the exact length of time it is prescribed. Analysis of body chemistry can now be done accurately enough to measure tiny amounts of drugs circulating in the blood so that drug dosages can be adjusted very finely. This is important, for example, in giving the fertility drug and in treating epilepsy where too much medication may cause a fit instead of suppressing it. Special care has to be taken in giving drugs to old people, whose body pro-

cesses may be altered so that a 'normal' dose produces an abnormal effect, to infants and young children who respond much more sensitively to the effects of a drug, and to pregnant women, because the drug may reach the baby's circulation via the placenta and damage its developing organs. Indiscriminate or careless use of some antibiotics, such as penicillin, may allow bacteria to become resistant to the drug, so that new antibiotics have continually to be developed to combat strains resistant to the old ones.

Besides the normal side effects which may affect any user, a few people develop allergic reactions to certain drugs—penicillin can produce these. If two drugs are taken at the same time one drug may modify the action of the other so that they interact, producing adverse effects or rendering one another ineffective. Thus drink and tranquillizers may interact to make you very drunk indeed after only a moderate amount of alcohol.

Many drugs, for example nicotine and sleeping drugs, cause some psychological dependence. Some also cause physical dependence so that 'withdrawal' symptoms such as vomiting, convulsions, confusion, which can be very severe indeed, arise when the drug is suddenly stopped after repeated or prolonged use. Regular use of a drug can produce 'tolerance' to it too, so that larger and larger doses of it are needed to give the same effect.

Some of the most notable recent developments in the drug field include:

The psychotropic drugs whose ability to alter mood and brain-functioning has led to effective treatment of many mental illnesses.

Leva-dopa and amantadine in relieving some of the symptoms of Parkinsons's disease.

The beta-receptor blockers, which slow the rate and force of contraction of the heart-beat and are used in the treatment of angina, high blood pressure and abnormal heart-rhythm.

The contraceptive pill and the 'fertility' drug which have had a marked effect on our reproductive life.

The drug treatment of cancer. Although arsenic was used to treat Hodgkin's disease (an unusual form of cancer) over 100 years ago, modern drug treatment for cancer was not introduced till 1945, and since that time many drugs have been discovered which can damage or kill cancer cells. Unfortunately most of these also attack normal body tissues. But two important advances in cancer chemotherapy have dramatically altered the prognosis for some types of the disease. The first was the realization that large doses of drugs given intermittently—'pulse' treatment—effectively damaged the cancer cells while giving the normal body cells time to recover between doses. The second discovery was that combinations of drugs had a more powerful effect than doses of drugs given singly. The introduction of multiple drug therapy, combined with surgery and radiotherapy, has meant that many more cancer patients can be cured and remissions can be granted for many others. A method recently developed in the USA for growing cells from a patient's tumour in a special strain of mice has meant that the optimum drug treatment for that tumour can be devised without subjecting the patient himself to experimental trial-and-error. The technique is complex and has so far not been tried on a wide scale, but it could represent another significant step forward in the drug treatment of cancer.

Drug efficacy in case treatments.

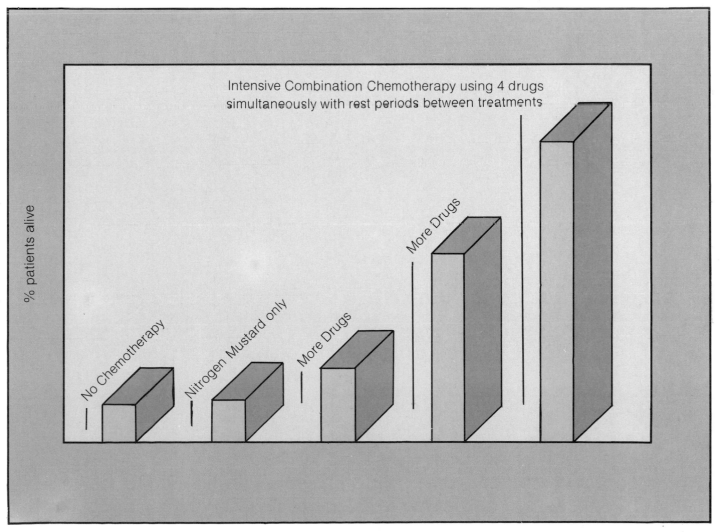

Medical and Surgical Advances

Modern medicine has tremendous resources to fight disability. Artificial limbs (prostheses) are nothing new, but have reached a new level of sophistication. An artificial arm can be moved by miniature motors, or can even use the electrical impulses from the muscles of the stump to initiate movement. Artificial joints within the tissues (implants) present more problems because of the body's tendency to reject any substance foreign to it. Special chemically inert metal alloys and strong polyethylene plastics have solved most of these problems so that now almost any damaged joint within the body can be replaced. Special cements are being developed which will allow the bone tissue to grow into the new material and give the joint added strength.

Many other 'spare parts' are now available. The tympanic membrane and ossicles of the ear can be replaced by man-made components to restore hearing, and artificial lenses are often inserted in the eye after cataract operations. Damaged heart-valves can be replaced and an electric pace-maker can be attached to the heart-muscle to regulate its beat. Synthetic tubes can be used to replace damaged blood vessels. The function of even major organs can, to some extent, be taken over by man-made replacements as it is by the kidney dialysis machine for example, or by the heart-lung machine which enables open-heart surgery to be performed. But it is probably impossible ever to miniaturize organs of this complexity so that they could be carried within the patient's body.

The transplanting of living tissues from one person to another gives rise to even greater problems because foreign protein is usually rejected by the 'host' body. These problems are being gradually overcome by the use of immuno-suppressive drugs, and by advances in 'tissue-typing' to assess the compatability between donor and recipient tissues. These advances have made the transplanting of human kidneys relatively satisfactory—a kidney transplant may last over ten years—but so far transplants of other major organs have achieved no more than temporary success.

The development of the cardiac catheter, a slender tube which can be pushed into the heart via a blood vessel in an arm or leg, has been a major step in diagnosing and treating heart disease. Radio-opaque material can be injected through the tube into the blood stream so that its passage through normal or abnormal channels in the heart can be traced by taking X-ray pictures. Blood samples can be withdrawn from different parts of the heart to measure their oxygen content and so assess lung and heart function directly. Catheterization can also be used to dilate coronary arteries which have become narrowed or blocked. Coronary by-pass operations, in which part of an obstructed coronary artery is replaced, usually by a piece of vein taken from the

Left *If diagnosed sufficiently early, it is possible that cancer can be completely cured. This table demonstrates 5-year survival rates – showing no signs of cancer five years after treatment – of patients whose cancer was diagnosed early against those diagnosed late.*
Above *Direct heart transplant.*

patient's leg, are being increasingly used in the treatment of coronary artery disease.

Simple X-ray techniques are a long-established method of diagnosis but their use has become more sophisticated. Arteriography, as used to outline the vessels of the heart, enables X-ray pictures to be

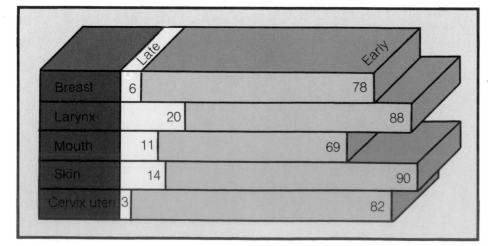

	Late	Early
Breast	6	78
Larynx	20	88
Mouth	11	69
Skin	14	90
Cervix uteri	3	82

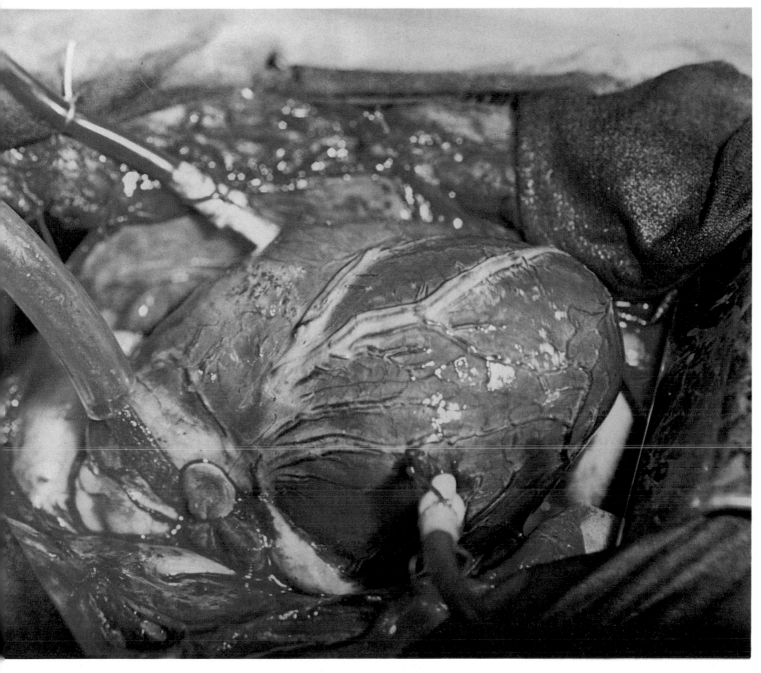

taken of the blood supply to most internal organs. Alterations in the pattern of blood vessels can indicate early cancerous tumours. Another special X-ray technique, mammography, can be used to identify cancer of the breast.

Over the last few years medical diagnosis has been dramatically affected by computer technology. Computerized body-scanning with X-rays (Computerized Axial Tomography, CAT) has proved a major diagnostic advance. Different body tissues absorb X-rays in different amounts, and a tumour in an internal organ will have an absorption pattern different from the normal tissue

surrounding it. Scanning of a particular area will produce an absorption pattern which can be computer-analyzed to plot out the internal structure of the organ. Computers are also used to analyze recordings of the electrical impulses from the brain (EEG waves) and to build up a 'computer profile' showing brain response.

Any X-ray examination has the draw-back that the high-energy radiations can damage body-tissues. Ultrasound diagnosis, developed from war-time radar, is a new and safer technique which can often be used in place of radiological examination. A body area is scanned with

pulsed, high-frequency sound-waves which give an 'echo' when they strike the interface between two body tissues. The echo pattern is analyzed to build up a picture of the area being scanned. Ultrasound scanning can be used to study the heart in action if abnormalities of function are suspected, and—particularly important—in pregnancy to look at the unborn child, because X-ray examination may damage the baby. Sonic radar detectors can also be used as an aid to blindness. The device used sends out a beam of ultrasonic sound waves which is reflected back from surfaces, the change in pitch reflecting distance.

Pregnancy and Birth

Pregnancy and birth are safer now, for both mother and baby, than they have ever been. This is partly because of a greater awareness of the dangers that may threaten the safe development of the unborn child and partly because of the ante-natal care and diagnostic facilities that are available so that a potential threat to a pregnant woman or her baby can be anticipated and if possible, forestalled. Rhesus disease for example (incompatibility of the baby's blood with his mother's), which used to be responsible for the deaths of many babies and for brain damage to many others, has been all but eliminated by modern medical techniques. Even if a baby is affected, his damaged blood can be exchanged for healthy blood and a severely affected baby can be given such an exchange transfusion while still in the uterus. German measles (rubella), formerly a common cause of birth defects, should be a danger no longer, as a result of a recently introduced vaccination programme. But almost every pregnant woman still runs some avoidable risks—smoking, taking drugs or medicines, heavy drinking, X-rays—all these are factors which can damage the developing foetus and which it should be well within

Below *It is sometimes necessary to obtain a 'picture' of the developing foetus or the position of the placenta as, for example, in the case of twins or because of some malfunction. An ultrasound scan is a completely safe way to do this.*

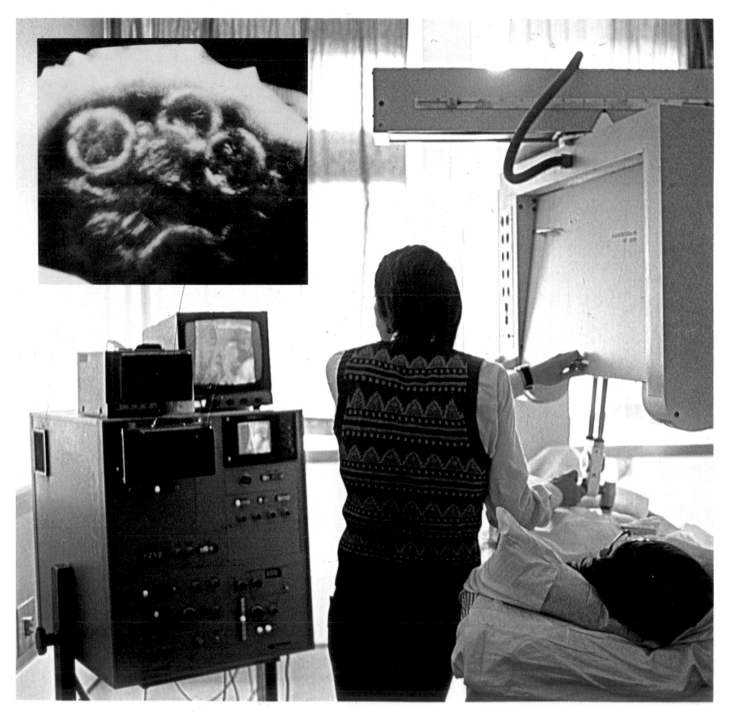

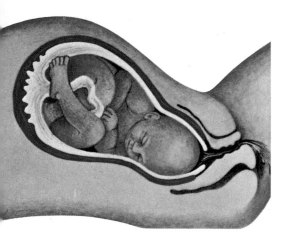

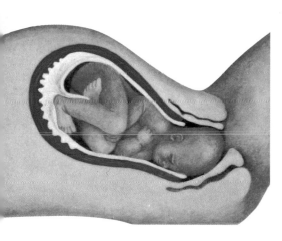

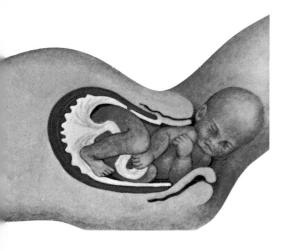

Top *During the first stage of labour the uterine muscles contract to dilate the cervix.* Centre *When it is fully dilated the second stage begins with the birth of the baby's head.* Bottom *The rest of the body follows easily after the head and shoulders.*

our power to control.

Many foetal abnormalities can now be detected before birth by the technique of amniocentesis, which involves drawing off a sample of the fluid surrounding the baby by inserting a hollow needle through the woman's abdominal wall. Loose foetal cells floating in the fluid can be examined microscopically to detect spina bifida, some sex-linked disorders such as haemophilia, chromosomal abnormalities like Down's syndrome (mongolism) and various disorders of body chemistry. The severity of Rhesus disease can also be assessed by amniocentesis and it can even be used to determine the baby's sex, although it is too complex a procedure to be used for this purpose alone. Should a severe abnormality be diagnosed, the mother can be offered an abortion which, with the modern vacuum aspiration method, is virtually risk-free provided it is carried out within the first three months of pregnancy.

Ultrasound scanning can be used to 'map' the placenta, either to indicate the safest place for an amniotic puncture, or to detect placenta praevia (a condition in which the placenta develops low in the uterus, partly or completely blocking the entrance to the birth canal). Ultrasound scanning can also be used to monitor the growth of the baby, to assess its maturity if there is some doubt as to when the pregnancy began, and to confirm the presence of twins.

With the introduction of epidural analgesia (introducing anaesthetic into the space surrounding the spinal cord), the ideal of painless labour for the mother can at last be realized. For the baby, a difficult labour need no longer be a source of potential danger; his condition can be continually assessed by monitoring his heart-beat and measuring the oxygen level in samples of blood taken from his head as he lies in the birth canal. A lengthy labour causing foetal distress can be speeded up using a hormone drip, and if Caesarean delivery proves necessary, improved surgical techniques have made the operation so safe and simple that it is performed relatively often in

preference to a complicated vaginal delivery. Hormone drips are also used to induce labour artificially either because the baby is overdue or because some medical condition in the mother makes induction desirable. Should the baby be born prematurely, the availability of special premature-baby units where he is kept in an incubator at a constant warm temperature and in a controlled atmosphere greatly increases his chances of survival.

Fertility and Family Planning

With the development of the contraceptive pill, which provides an almost 100 per cent effective method of birth control, and the availability of safe and acceptable male and female sterilization techniques, a couple now stands a good chance of having the number of children they want at the intervals they feel most desirable. For the 25 per cent of couples who are below normal fertility, specialized clinics are available and advances in drug-treatment and micro-surgery have improved their chances of conception.

The use of hormonal preparations (the fertility drug) to stimulate ovulation in women who produce too little of the hormone, gonadotrophin, which controls ovulation, has brought about a tremendous improvement in the treatment of female infertility. The risk of multiple pregnancy can be cut by rigorously controlling the dosage of the drug, but about one woman in four having the treatment is likely to produce twins. A few women who fail to ovulate because they have an abnormally high level of another hormone, prolactin, are being treated successfully with a different drug, bromocriptine. About 20 per cent of infertile women have blockages in their Fallopian tubes, and these can often be successfully treated surgically.

Even the test-tube baby is now a reality. Micro-surgical techniques make it possible to extract a ripened egg from the woman's ovary so that it can be fertilized in the laboratory with her husband's sperm: much more difficult, although it can be done, is to implant the fertilized egg in the woman's uterus where it can develop normally.

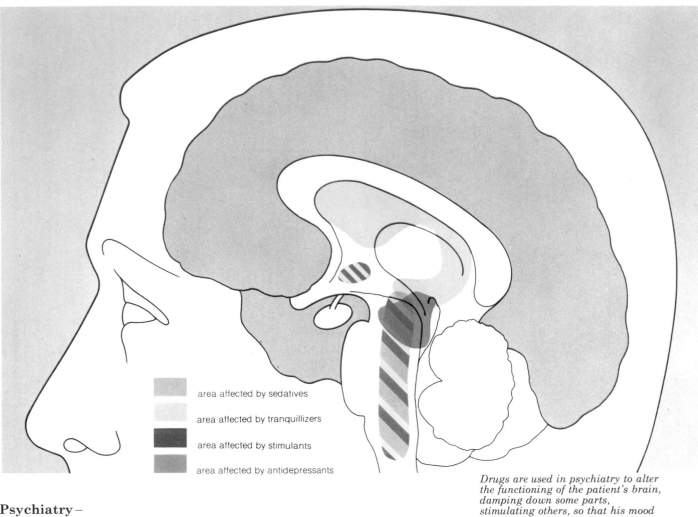

area affected by sedatives

area affected by tranquillizers

area affected by stimulants

area affected by antidepressants

Drugs are used in psychiatry to alter the functioning of the patient's brain, damping down some parts, stimulating others, so that his mood and the way in which he sees the world are modified.

Psychiatry –

Treatment of mental illness can be directed towards modifying symptoms or behaviour by physical means (drugs, ECT, behaviour therapy) or by attempting to analyze the patient's emotional life-history (psychotherapy) so that by recognizing and understanding his early fears and conflicts he may come to terms and be able to cope with his present problems. Most psychiatrists now are eclectic in their approach, using whatever combination of methods seems most appropriate for a particular patient.

There is little agreement about the cause of most mental illnesses, but there does seem to be increasing evidence that they may be due to changes in brain chemistry caused either by emotional factors or by metabolic disturbance within the brain (e.g. schizophrenia or depression), or by brain damage (e.g. in childhood autism).

Drug treatment is probably the most widely used and effective way of relieving the symptoms of mental illness, by normalizing brain chemistry. The main groups of drugs used are:

The tranquillizers
i) major tranquillizers (phenothiazines) used in serious illnesses e.g. schizophrenia, hypomania.
ii) minor tranquillizers (fluorazepam, diazepam) used to treat anxiety.

The anti-depressants
i) the tricyclic compounds (imipramine, amitriptyline) introduced in 1958 and in nearly every case the drug of choice for 'lifting' mood.
ii) the monoamineoxidase (MAO) inhibitors, little used now because of their adverse effects.

The sedatives
Used to produce a calming effect without sleep. The minor tranquillizers (see above) are the most widely prescribed drugs for this purpose.

The hypnotics
Sleep-inducing drugs (e.g. the barbiturates), now seldom used as they alter sleep patterns and produce dependence.

Electroconvulsive therapy (ECT) is not as widely used as it used to be, but short courses of the treatment can be very effective in selected cases of severe depression which do not respond to any other treatment. During ECT the patient is under general anaesthesia and an electric current is passed through the brain, producing the bursts of disorganized brain over-activity which we call a fit and which results in the normalizing of brain chemistry.

Behaviour therapy sets out to discourage undesirable behaviour by giving the patient disagreeable associations with it, while more 'normal' (i.e. desirable) responses are rewarded so that a new behaviour pattern is learned—a combination of the stick and the carrot.

Alternative medicine
Most of the people who try un-

orthodox methods of medicine do so because, in their cases, conventional medicine has failed to work. Many of these fringe practices are much older than modern drug-based (allopathic) medicine, but because they rely on methods which cannot be scientifically assessed, the medical establishment has always been reluctant to accept them. Much of the current popularity probably springs from the fact that their practitioners still tend to treat people rather than disease or symptoms, giving the special attention that the busy doctor may not always have time for but which has, whoever is giving it and for whatever reason, an indisputably beneficial effect.

Most alternative medicine is practised by laymen, some by cranks or quacks, but a few doctors have begun to investigate and even to use these more esoteric forms of treatment. Some doctors recommend meditation or relaxation to their patients, several doctors—and dentists—use hypnosis, and there are a few who practise herbalism and faith healing. Homeopathy (the giving of such minute quantities of drugs that no physical response can be identified) probably has more medical adherents than most other branches of alternative medicine and may owe some of its relative medical respectability in Britain to the fact that the Royal Family have a homeopathic physician.

The methods which seem to have most to offer as adjuncts to conventional medicine are osteopathy, biofeedback and acupuncture. Osteopaths and chiropractors whose treatment involves bone manipulation, get the bulk of their work from back-sufferers—it has been suggested that if orthodox medicine could find a cure for back-ache, osteopaths would go out of business overnight.

Acupuncture, the old Chinese method of healing by inserting needles through the skin at predetermined points, is being tried out in the West with varying degrees of success. It does not work on every patient (about 5 per cent is one estimate) but in some cases has been found effective in controlling pain, arthritis and migraine.

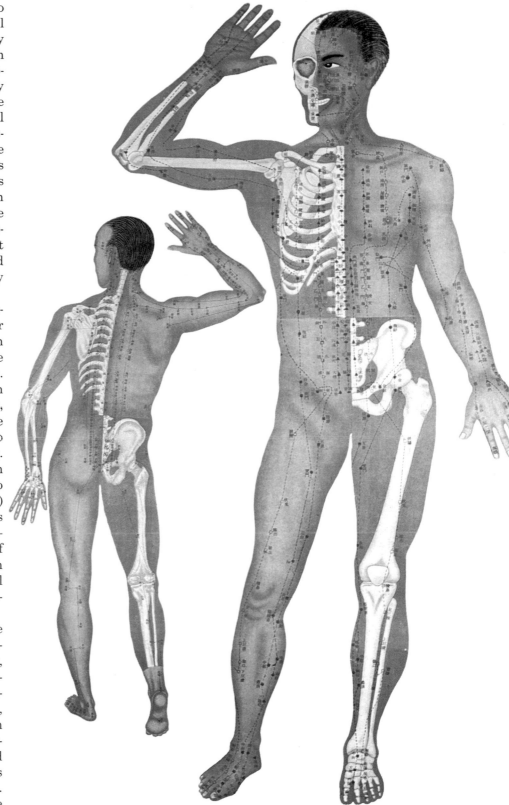

Biofeedback is a relatively new system whereby the patient is wired to a machine which monitors his body's reactions and feeds back the information in the form of visual or auditory signals. He can then try to modify a bodily function, such as heart-beat, which is not normally under his control, getting feed-back

The acupuncturist inserts various needles at one or a series of 365 predetermined points on the surface of the body.

on his success from alterations in the signals. Good results have been claimed for use of the technique in stroke, hypertension and anxiety states but it is still too soon to assess its full potential.

Feeding the Hungry
Food for All

Whatever else people want, they must have food. One of the major problems today is that of enabling everyone in the world to have enough to eat.

Most of man's food comes from agriculture with a relatively small amount from fishing, although this may be important in certain areas. Usually, in the rich countries, we only hear about hunger when a particular famine hits the news headlines. But a continuing lack of food, or famine, is a fact of life for over 10 per cent of the world's population. The Food and Agriculture Organization (FAO) of the United Nations has estimated that about 460 million people are permanently malnourished. Of these, some 200 million are children. Malnutrition for babies and children can mean that they are stunted for life and never able to reach their full potential.

The precise number of people hungry is difficult to determine because statistics are not easily available. The actual figure, however, give or take 100 million, is not critical—the fact remains that there are still a horrifying number of our fellow human beings suffering. The hungry are not evenly distributed over the world but are found largely in the developing countries of Africa, Asia and Latin America. Most are in the rural areas, where the majority of the population lives, but a considerable number are in the shanty towns around the cities.

Nutrition problems are also found in the rich industrialized countries. Only a relatively small but significant percentage of their populations are hungry but many more suffer health problems from overeating. Those who go hungry, though, have one thing in common—poverty.

It is because poverty is at the root of what has become known as 'the world food problem' that, despite all the technical advances this century, there are still many who go hungry. World food production has been rising for decades and has, by and large, kept pace with or been just ahead of population growth. But this does not solve the problem: those who go hungry do not have the land to grow food themselves or the means to buy food grown elsewhere, so the fact that more food is being produced does not help them.

Many small farmers in the developing countries have too little land to support themselves and their families given the type of agriculture they practise. Most would be willing to change their farming practice if it would improve their lives but are unable to do so because of the risk involved. When a family's life depends upon the next crop it is not likely to change from the ways it knows since the failure of a new approach could mean starvation or loss of the land altogether if it cannot produce enough to pay the rent.

The other large group that cannot get enough to eat are the landless labourers and the unemployed in the towns. They do not have enough money to buy the food they need and may have to spend 80–90 per cent of their income on food.

Increased production of food, which appears to be physically possible, is not the basic problem in ending hunger. It has to be accompanied by, or preceded by, social and economic changes that will enable poor farmers, landless labourers and unemployed people to acquire the wealth or resources they need to enable them to feed themselves properly. The problems of hunger and malnutrition are part of the broader question of social and economic development both nationally and internationally.

As a whole there is enough food in the world at present to feed everyone, with a little left over to spare. But we do not live at a global level, and what there is is not evenly distributed. Sometimes, those rich countries with surplus food use it as aid to help meet the food needs of the poorer countries. However, food aid from the rich to the poor countries is not a long-term answer to food shortage problems as it is not reliable, is difficult if not impossible to transport in the quantities likely to be needed, and may be politically unacceptable to both donor and

recipient. The poor countries cannot buy the food they need because they cannot afford it. For them the solution is most likely to come from growing more food at home and distributing it effectively. The developed countries can help in this by transferring some of their wealth, either through direct transfers or through revised terms of trade, to the poor nations to enable them to develop.

Wealth by itself does not mean an end to hunger as is shown by the presence of hungry people in even the rich countries. It does, however,

For most people in the world, it is a struggle to obtain enough food.

alleviate the problem without solving it. For example, in the United States alone in 1977 about $5,000 million was spent on providing food stamps for some 17 million people reckoned to be in need of food.

Increasing Food Production

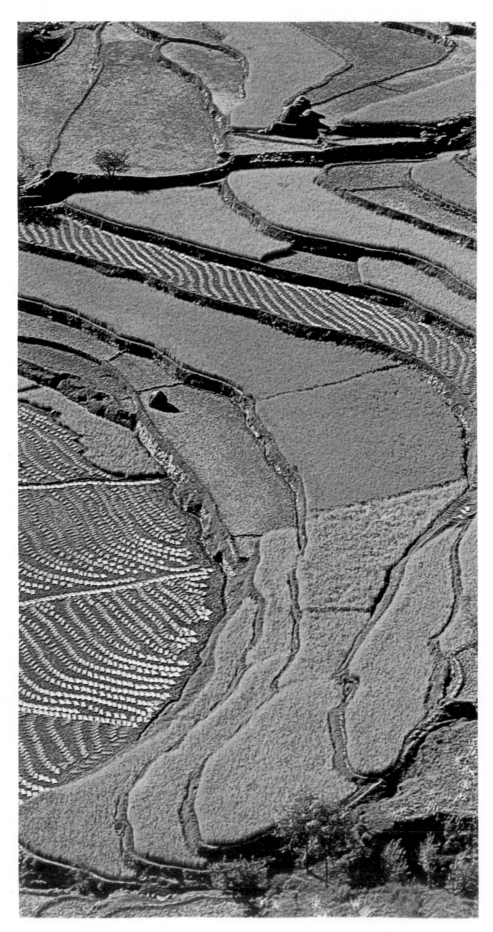

One of the most remarkable achievements of the last quarter of a century has been the way in which food production has more than kept pace with population growth although there are signs that it may now be falling behind. Production of non-food crops such as coffee and tea has increased even more quickly than that of food crops. Food production can be increased in two basic ways. First, the area of land under cultivation can be extended and, secondly, more productive use can be made of land already under cultivation.

Several studies have shown that a considerable area of the world could still be brought under cultivation. The precise amount varies from continent to continent, the least being in Asia and the most in Africa and Latin America. To bring land into production a mixture of capital, labour and technology is required. Often, in the developing countries, people form a vast resource which if tapped, as in China, can increase both the amount of land used and the productivity per acre.

The second approach requires use of the same mixture of factors. The introduction of irrigation, for example, may enable a second crop to be grown and greatly increase the productivity of the land. New varieties of crops can be introduced which yield more than traditional ones but these probably require a greater input of fertilizer and pesticides, both of which are expensive. Improved organization and intensive use of labour can also increase productivity.

Government policies also affect the ability of people to increase food production. Governments may determine the price levels or affect the availability of credit, both of which affect what is produced. Many governments in developing countries will need to pay greater attention to agriculture and rural development. Food production as opposed to cash crop production may have to be singled out for special help.

To increase production often means increasing the productivity of existing land. With rice, for example, it may mean irrigating to obtain two or three crops a season, instead of one.

One way of increasing food production is through what has become known as 'the green revolution'. A closer look at this shows that, despite the technological developments, producing more food does not automatically mean that fewer people will go hungry.

The term green revolution is used to mean the use of high-yielding varieties of crops which give an increased production per acre. Most of the early work in this field concentrated on wheat and rice, but now many more crops are being tested and new varieties developed. The problems arise because no technology can be applied in isolation from the social and economic environment, nor will it develop without being influenced by that environment.

When offered a new variety of wheat, say, which he is told will yield two or three times as much as his present variety, it may seem obvious to an outsider that a farmer should take it—but it is by no means that simple. First there is the problem of risk. If the farmer's family is totally dependent upon next year's crop for the bulk of its food supply then it will be reluctant to leave what it knows to try a new variety which, even if said to produce more, is a great, even life and death, risk. Once it is decided to try it the problems are not necessarily over.

New varieties tend to be more expensive than existing ones. New seed is needed every year because the new varieties are hybrids and seed produced from the crop will not have the same characteristics as the original hybrid. The high yielding seeds also make more demands on the environment in which they are grown. They need a good supply of water at the right time which usually means irrigation has to be provided. They also require the application of expensive fertilizers. They require, in fact, a change in the methods practised by the farmer and in the number and cost of the inputs required.

All this costs money and this is just what the hungry have not got. The poorest farmers, who most need the food, may be unable to afford the new varieties; they will probably not

be able to get the credit necessary to buy them. Only the larger farmers will have the money or access to credit to enable them to increase yields by planting the new varieties. These farmers are then able to expand their income and expand more by taking over smaller farms. They may be helped in this by the smaller farmers falling into debt through borrowing to bridge the gap between harvests or even through trying the new varieties themselves. When they cannot pay their debts, because they have no reserves, they may have to sell what little land they have—usually to the larger farmers.

Thus the amount of employment is reduced and the number of landless labourers increases. The larger farmers tend to mechanize their farming and require fewer people to work the land. So, even though the amount of food increases, there may well be more landless and unemployed who cannot afford to buy the extra food and more can go hungry than before the new varieties were grown. Many who are displaced will go to the cities but are unable to find work and live there in squalor.

If not enough people can buy the foods produced the farmers may change to producing more expensive, luxury foods which the wealthier people in the towns and the rich

Too often mechanisation can replace people without there being any alternative work for them to earn money for food.

countries want and can afford to buy. This change is made at the expense of the basic food crops the poor need but cannot afford.

So, simply introducing new techniques is not enough. A simple transfer of the kind of technology the rich nations have developed can have devastating consequences upon the poor and hungry. The technology of the rich has largely been developed to replace labour but unless some kind of rural industry is created for those losing land or jobs they will not be able to buy the extra food produced by others—they will lack what the economists call 'effective demand' even though they might have dire needs.

Measures to increase food production have to be accompanied by other social and economic measures if the hungry are to benefit. These will depend upon the circumstances of each country and may include land reform, rural development schemes, credit schemes or whatever is appropriate to the local situation. This is assuming, of course, and it can be a big assumption, that the government in question wishes to help the poor and hungry.

The Food System

Very few people consume exactly the same as they produce. In the poor countries, where most people live in rural areas, the difference between the food consumption and production pattern is small: farmers produce much of what they need and for the rest sell or barter some of their produce locally or at a market. The link between producing food and eating it is short and the two activities are closely connected.

However, most people in the towns and cities and in the rich countries generally have little direct connection with the production of the food they eat and have to rely on the market for it. Here the system by which they get food is much more complex, with agriculture playing only a small part. Many different people are involved in the process of seeing food to the table in rich countries. Agriculture in these countries employs only a small proportion of the working population,

ranging from about 2 per cent to a little over 20 per cent. Many of the people who used to work on the land now work in industries which supply the farmer and process, distribute and market what he produces; others make entirely man-made foods.

Modern intensive agriculture uses many inputs. These range from the powerful and sophisticated machinery used on the farm and in the farm buildings to the fertilizers and pesticides used on the crops. These inputs are made in vehicle factories and chemical works. The basic raw materials for both fertilizers and machinery may already have involved many different people in the world in their mining, transporting and refining.

Once the food has been grown on the farm it still has a long way to go before it enters most people's mouths. On the way it may be considerably transformed from the basic grain, vegetable, fruit or animal produce

grown on the farm. Some food, particularly fruit and vegetables, will be taken to wholesale markets and redistributed, largely in the form it left the farm, to shops or local markets. Most food will be taken to factories, mills or abattoirs where it will be processed to varying degrees. Wheat is milled into flour and may be used to make bread, biscuits and cakes or pasta. Foods that do not keep, like fruit and vegetables, are preserved by canning, freezing or drying. Increasingly, since the Second World War, processing has not stopped there but has gone on to make the basic foodstuffs into packaged foods that can be eaten with the minimum of home preparation. In Britain, for example, this has led to over 20,000 items now being available on the supermarket shelves, compared to 1,500 in the 1950s. Many of them are variations on a theme, for example, different ways of turning meat into stews, pies, savouries, and other varieties of food.

As well as processed foods originally grown by the farmer or caught by the fisherman, some new products are entirely man-made from a mixture of chemicals and sometimes modified foodstuffs to give tastes and textures that people like, for instance instant desserts, soups and some snack foods.

The number of people involved in food growing, processing, and supply and distribution—from the tractor maker to the shopkeeper—is huge and food remains the largest single economic activity as well as human necessity.

All these activities now tend to be carried out not by lots of independent small farmers, companies and individuals but increasingly by large companies often active in many parts of the world. These companies are constantly attempting to develop and sell new products or enter new markets. They employ many people in research and development and spend much money in advertising their wares. One company may be involved in all aspects of the food chain—from growing oilseed in a developing country to transporting, crushing, refining and marketing it in the rich countries. A company may contract farmers to grow particular crops in specified ways, for example using certain amounts of fertilizer and pesticide at certain times, so that the crop produced meets the demands of the production process, be it freezing, canning, or packing for a supermarket chain.

As well as involving a lot of people and big business in the rich countries the food system also involves the poor farmers in the developing countries. This is partly for historical reasons. When the European powers expanded to colonize most of what is now the developing or Third World they influenced the agricultural practices there. Emphasis was placed on crops which the Europeans wanted, such as tea, coffee, sugar, cocoa, rubber and, as transport technology improved, tropical fruits such as bananas and pineapples. Much of the scientific research expended in these colonies went into these crops and

the locals were left to carry on growing their own food crops in their own way.

When the developing countries gained their independence this pattern of production and trade was well established and they had little choice but to carry on with it. Large parts of some developing countries are still devoted to these cash crops which are exported to the rich countries of Europe, North America and Japan. When the people of these countries eat and drink their tea, coffee, and bananas they are linked to the developing countries in a long food chain.

The food system by which most of the better-off eat is complex with many links. Change in one part of it may affect some people never considered in making that change, be they small farmers in the Third World or van drivers delivering bread in Europe.

Intensive battery egg production requires a high output of technology and energy. It also requires high protein chicken feed which may include crops from the developing countries.

Diet and Health

There are a wide variety of diets in the world. Before there was much trade the people of each region or country had a diet based on the basic food that could be grown or caught in the area. With the expansion of various empires and the spread of trading networks new foods were introduced which led to changes in the diet. The potato, to take a comparatively recent example, is native to South America and was introduced into Europe in the late 16th century. It became a staple part of

the diet in Europe and in some parts formed the major part of the diet—so much so that a poor potato harvest could mean starvation and in Ireland in the 1840s, after several poor potato harvests, several million people starved to death or were forced to emigrate.

FAO (the Food and Agriculture Organization of the United Nations) divides the world up into nine different basic food regions: animal foods; animal foods/wheat; animal foods and cereals other than wheat; wheat;

rice; mixed cereals; millet; maize; animal foods/roots/cereals/pulses. Even in the same regions the eating habits and the way similar basic foods are used are quite varied. In Britain, for example, most wheat is consumed as bread, biscuits and cakes but in Italy wheat is more often consumed as pasta. At an individual level, a diet is what a person eats over a period of time.

Whatever is eaten, the diet should provide enough of the essential nutrients for a healthy life. Most foods contain a mixture of some of the essential nutrients: protein, carbohydrates, fats, vitamins and minerals. Generally speaking, provided

Too much of the wrong kind of food is the problem for most people in the rich, industrialized countries. Fat, sugar, meat and refined food consumption is high. This increases susceptibility to many diseases.

enough food is eaten to meet an individual's energy needs, the essential nutrients, and in particular protein, will be adequately supplied. The main exception to this is in some parts of Africa where starchy root crops which contain very little protein are the staple food and protein deficiencies occur, especially in children. It was once thought that the greatest problem for food production was producing protein but this is now recognized not to be the case,

except in the special circumstances mentioned. If a correct balance of the essential nutrients is not obtained from the diet, deficiency diseases like scurvy and rickets occur.

Poverty, as we have seen, leads to hunger and deficiency diseases. Affluence, however, is no guarantee that a good diet will be obtained. The problems arising from affluence are not those of too little but of too much food. An excessive or poorly balanced intake of food can also lead to health problems and early death. There is increasing evidence that the diets of the affluent are partly responsible for the disease patterns they suffer from. As people's incomes have increased in the industrialized countries the amount and type of food they can buy has changed. This has been accompanied by a way of life which involves little physical effort for most.

Affluent diets tend to be rich in fats, refined carbohydrates, animal products and processed foods, and have been implicated in the development of many degenerative diseases that characterize rich societies. These include coronary heart disease, certain types of cancer, bowel troubles, diabetes and tooth decay.

Some experts feel that modern farming and food processing methods may not be desirable in the long term. Many different chemicals are used in the farming industry. Traces of these can build up in the food chain and eventually in man. The small quantities usually found appear to be innocuous but large quantities can be harmful and the long-term effects are not known.

This problem was illustrated when the pesticide DDT was used to spray crops and spread through the whole world via the food chain. It can now be found in the bodies of most Americans and the rest of the human population. Although it did help to reduce crop losses the potential dangers of it to wildlife and people through long-term accumulation led to it being banned. DDT is only one of the many chemicals used in intensive farming and the ecological consequences of this type of farming make its long-term viability questionable.

Recently, too, there has been an increase in the amount of processed food consumed in the rich countries. This stems from the nature of the food system at present, with large companies preserving, processing and manufacturing foodstuffs which are distributed nationally or even internationally. In order for the industrial processing of food to work, and for the finished products to keep until they are sold and for them to look the way the advertisers suggest they should, a large number of additives may be added to foods during processing. Depending upon the regulations of the country where they are made or sold, up to about 2,500 additives may be used. The effects of these in the long term, and an average person may eat about 1 kg (2–3 lbs) a year, again is uncertain.

Human requirements for food differ and can be met from a variety of foodstuffs. This makes it impossible to prescribe one diet which will be ideal for everyone. Some general guidelines can be given about diet, however. If the diet provides enough energy (usually measured in calories) then in general it will provide enough protein. Energy requirements vary from individual to individual and there is some tolerance within which the body can adjust. If the food intake exceeds the tolerance level then weight is put on; if it is below this level, weight is lost. If it is chronically below requirements then starvation begins. Age, sex, and activity influence the amount of food needed.

There are four basic food groups from which the diet should be built. They are milk and dairy products; meats, poultry, fish, eggs, legumes or nuts (or any combination); fruits and vegetables; and breads and cereals. A wide range of different diets can be built up from this selection as the various peasant cuisines from round the world show. In general, highly refined foods, such as white flour and sugar, should be kept to a minimum. The fat content of the diet should be less than 35 per cent or, preferably, 30 per cent. Meat is not essential; a basic healthy and tasty diet with little or no meat in it can provide all the essential nutrients.

Future Developments

At the U.N. World Food conference in 1974, the then US secretary of state, Henry Kissinger, called for a goal of no-one going to bed hungry by 1985. Unfortunately, this goal is unlikely to be met, as even the director of the FAO said at the time. This is largely because of the complex technical and socio-economic nature of the problem of feeding people. Barring war and major natural disaster the population of the world will increase between now and 2000 AD to between 6,000–8,000 million people.

The increased population means that food production will have to increase. This is partly a technical matter and, with the application of present knowledge and the promise held out by new lines of research, will probably be technically possible. But increased production will not mean an end to hunger because the root cause is poverty, the solution to which is a social, economic and political problem related to these broader areas. It involves changes in societies and challenging the power of those who have so that those who have not may obtain what they need.

Food aid may continue to alleviate suffering to a limited degree, but the main thrust must come from growing more food in the countries where it is needed. There are now 11 international agricultural research centres and three associated centres which are developing new strains of crops to give higher yields. They are now dealing with most of the crops grown in the developing countries, including those which form poor people's food. Adoption of new varieties, particularly if the kind of problems which can arise in the green revolution are avoided by relevant social and economic policies, will lead to higher food production. The first work was on high yielding varieties of wheat and rice and from 1965/66 to 1974/75 the area planted to high yielding varieties in Asia alone rose from 9,300 ha to 15,741,300 ha for wheat and from 49,000 ha to 21,565,500 ha for rice.

Increasing food production will require considerable investment in agriculture in the developing countries. One outcome of the world food conference has been the setting up of an International Fund for Agricultural Development with an initial capital of $1,000 million to aid agricultural advancement in the developing countries. The World Bank, whose main activities are to promote economic development, has placed the emphasis on rural development programmes, which include agricultural development programmes, aimed at helping the poorest people in the world. National governments will also have to place a greater emphasis on food production and improving conditions in the countryside.

One important area of scientific research which may come to fruition before the end of the century is that on nitrogen fixation. Some plants, for example, peas, beans and legumes generally, are able to transform the nitrogen in the atmosphere into a form of nitrogen that can aid plant growth. They do this in their root system, where bacteria live in little nodules on the roots and play an important role in the transformation.

Nitrogen is one of the major fertilizers used in the world and is quite costly to produce as the industrial process to change atmospheric nitrogen to fertilizer nitrogen requires high temperatures and pressures. Two lines of scientific research are under way which may remove the need for nitrogen to be produced industrially in this way. The first is concerned with trying to breed other species of plants, for instance cereals, which have the ability to fix nitrogen from the atmosphere. The second is seeking a way to imitate what the plant and bacteria do when they transform the nitrogen at normal temperatures and pressures and to use that process industrially.

Another development likely before the end of the century is that involving the production and use of new protein sources produced industrially from single-cell organisms or fungi grown from paraffin, oil, some

As yet, this field of soya beans has little to do with feeding the hungry. By and large the high protein beans will be crushed, their oil extracted and the high protein pulp used in animal feeds. Increasingly ways are being sought to process the bean's protein directly and market it as a meat substitute.

other chemical feedstock or waste products. This is likely to be important in the rich world as the type of food produced will be too expensive for the hungry. It is basically a development in the food manufacturing industry and may be used to feed animals or be processed, textured and flavoured for human consumption as imitation meat.

Although there are fewer people in the rich than in the poor countries,

the rich make far greater demands on the world's resources. The American people, for example, account for only about 6 per cent of world population yet consume about 30 per cent of the resources used annually. Despite this, poverty persists even in the USA. Future development probably requires a fairer distribution of resources so that the basic needs of the bulk of the world's population can be met. Only when this is done are the birth rates likely to fall, population levels stabilize and the need for increased food production to feed extra people diminish.

In an unjust situation, increased production will not benefit those who need the food most. It may be that land tenure arrangements have to be changed, political power given to the mass of rural people, and real transfers of resources take place from rich to poor both within and between countries. At an international level, the difficulties are already proving hard to overcome. It is proving difficult to give any meaning to a new, more equitable, international economic order. The establishment of an insurance measure in the form of an international food reserve system has not been achieved three years after the world food conference called for it as a matter of priority.

Some developing countries may wish to move away from cash crop production in order to increase food production. This will be affected by terms of trade and internal policies and will affect the consumption pattern of the rich. The changes could come with confrontation or co-operation, depending upon how the rich respond to the call for higher and more stable prices for the products of developing countries, and for help for them to diversify their economies.

Whether the hungry will be fed will depend upon the outcome of these different factors. It will obviously be difficult. More difficult than going to the moon but for millions upon millions of human beings much more worthwhile.

The Arts
The Beginnings of Modernism

Modernism was essentially the child of the Symbolist movement which had immediately preceded it, even though leading modernists denounced their symbolist predecessors as worn out and effete. The first emergence of a truly modern way of painting dates from 1905, when Matisse and his followers exhibited as a group in the Paris Salon d'Automne, and were promptly labelled 'Fauves' or 'wild beasts' for their pains.

At this period Matisse's work shows radical simplification of outline, combined with the use of emotive rather than descriptive colour. These characteristics are present in his masterpiece of 1909–10, *La Danse*. The figures whirling in their endless round owe much to the Tahitian paintings of Gauguin, and try to put over the same atmosphere of instinctive, primitive joy.

A similar feeling of revolt against over-complication motivated the Futurist movement, founded by the Italian writer F. T. Marinetti. The First Futurist Manifesto was published in a French newspaper in 1909. Futurism is important in several respects. First because, unlike Fauvism, it was an organized attempt to destroy the past. Second because it introduced the worship of the machine which was to be typical of one branch of modernism. And third because it was the first kind of modern art to catch the attention of a wide audience, thanks to Marinetti's skill in manipulating the press and in organizing newsworthy events.

One of the young artists who joined Marinetti's group was Giacomo Ballà, and his painting of a racing automobile is a response to a famous phrase in the First Futurist Manifesto: 'A racing automobile is more beautiful than the Victory of Samothrace.' This painting is also an attempt to make use of scientific advances made in another field—that of photography. As long ago as 1882 the Frenchman Etienne-Jules Marey had devised a way of making successive images showing different phases of the same movement on a single photographic negative. The futurists were influenced by these photographs when they tried to find a way of rendering what they called 'simultaneity'—the totality of an event which might incorporate several different phases of movement.

It might seem as if Cubism, which made its appearance at about the same time as futurism, was an attempt to do much the same kind of thing. Certainly the cubists—their leaders were Braque and Picasso—were interested in trying to render a three-dimensional totality on a flat surface. But their real inspiration was not photography but the paintings of Cézanne, who had already gone a long way towards a solution.

Analytic cubist pictures, like Picasso's famous portrait of his friend and dealer, Daniel-Henri Kahnweiler, show a multiplicity of faceted, overlapping plates which makes them difficult to interpret. The hermetic nature of cubism, emphasized by the leaders' reluctance to exhibit during their most experimental phase, put it at the opposite extreme from futurism.

The key issue—elitist hermeticism versus a wish to democratize art and make it accessible to everyone appeared even more clearly in Russia, in the years just before and just after the Revolution. While Russian artists were acutely aware of the new developments in Paris, they owed the existence of an organized modern movement largely to Marinetti's efforts as a propagandist.

The movement towards pure abstraction, in particular, was pioneered by Russian artists, whether domiciled abroad, like Kandinsky, or resident at home like Kasimir Malevich, the Suprematist.

Suprematism, which was the expression of mystical and transcendental beliefs, was in turn opposed by another movement, Constructivism. The constructivists, who were among the most enthusiastic supporters of the political revolution, also believed in abstraction, but thought that easel painting must eventually be abolished, as something which had no place in the collective society they wished to create. Their architectural projects, street decorations for revolutionary festivals, and designs for the stage were the first attempts made by modern art to step down from its pedestal and into real life.

Art and Technology

It was natural that modern art, which came to birth at a period of rapid technological change, should identify itself with the alterations technology imposed. It was also natural that it should use technology as a weapon against symbolist nostalgia.

Marinetti's worship of the machine was taken up not only by his own immediate followers in Italy, but throughout the world of art. American painters were especially enthusiastic about industrial subject-matter, which seemed to them to typify the special qualities of American experience. Amongst the most striking images produced by the pioneering American modernists are Joseph Stella's paintings of the great span of Brooklyn Bridge, which also inspired the poet Hart Crane.

Artists were not content merely to celebrate the new technology, they wanted to participate in it. The constructivist sculptor Naum Gabo was perhaps the first to think of using machines to power sculpture, and as early as 1921 devised a piece in which a small motor powers a vibrating rod. However, painters and sculptors tended to be limited in their response to technological possibilities not only by lack of knowledge of engineering, but by the fact that the right opportunities were not always available to them to bring art and technology closer together.

The true beneficiaries of the new epoch were the architects. While most of the techniques which were to give modern architecture its character had already been devised in the 19th century, notably the use of steel framing and of reinforced concrete, it took men like Mies van der Rohe and Le Corbusier to discover a vocabulary of forms which expressed the nature of the materials they were using.

Mies, who was originally associated with the Bauhaus, the famous German art school which throughout the '20s tried to find new and logical means of expression for the modern arts, did some of his most

spectacular work when he emigrated to the United States after the Nazi takeover. His Seagram Building in New York (1958) is the apogee of what had come to be called International Style. The bronze and grey-glass tower rises to a height of nearly 160 m (520 ft), and its regularity and symmetry echo the modular nature of its design.

Nevertheless the Seagram Building is a structure of a kind which only a rich, as well as a technologically advanced society could have produced. The Barcelona chair, designed by Mies in 1929 for a pavilion at an international exhibition, is an even more striking instance of sheer luxury disguised as industrial necessity, as, for all its cleanness of line, it is not an object which can be mass produced. An opposite approach is exemplified by Le Corbusier's buildings for the new city of Chandigarh in India (1950–57). Here reinforced concrete has been adapted to the capabilities of local workmen.

The new technology, nevertheless, has more often led to elaboration than it has to the radical simplicity it was once supposed to promote. Thus, for instance, the ideal modern theatre building, such as the recently completed National Theatre in London, finds itself equipped with a plethora of elaborate, often computer-controlled, stage machinery, which may enlarge the possibilities open to a director, but which does not fundamentally alter the principles of stage presentation which in their most basic form have survived since Shakespeare's time.

Yet one can perhaps say that technology has made fundamental differences to the visual arts in three different spheres of activity. The first and rarest is when it has actually made new materials available for artists to use. The coated glass used by American minimal sculptor Larry Bell was developed as part of the space research programme.

The second is where an individual artist, or group of artists, has made use of scientific progress to produce

an effect which could not previously have been obtained so precisely. Bridget Riley's optical paintings rely on a knowledge of the mechanisms of sight which was until recently unavailable.

The third is where lavish technological resources (rather than research as such) make possible things no previous generation could have experienced. The popular film *Star Wars* (1977) is basically a simple-minded romance, a fairy story transposed to an imagined future. The brilliant special effects which have delighted audiences are in this sense irrelevant to the structure of the entertainment. But they do make it possible for us to enjoy the illusion of new kinds of physical experience, and they show that the romantic appeal of technology is as strong as ever.

In fact, this third aspect extends across the entire range of the cultural spectrum. In the sometimes rarified world of dance, new technology has also had a major impact in the works of such leading modern dance choreographers as Twyla Tharp, Merce Cunningham and Alwin Nikolais. Nikolais, in particular, has experimented with many technological possibilities and his standard backstage equipment includes a computer-like console controlling still and moving lights, and projected images and photographs. Both Twyla Tharp and Merce Cunningham have experimented with video with varying degrees of success, the latter during a project spanning a number of years. He has also become closely involved with the technological possibilities of music using multi-tracked recordings which can be played backwards or forwards at random in a wide variety of different combinations. He is very interested in the music of John Cage.

The Seagram Building in New York is a spectacular example of the impact of 20th century technology on architecture. Designed by Mies van der Rohe in 1958 it represents the finest achievement of the International Style created earlier in the century.

Inner Space

Where the modern arts most clearly take leave of their predecessors is in their psychological rather than their technological content. The discoveries made by Freud about the workings of the unconscious mind have had a profound effect on artists and writers. It is impossible, for instance, to imagine a book like James Joyce's *Ulysses* coming into being before Freud had made his impact on the European creative consciousness.

In the realm of the visual arts, the Freudian current is particularly associated with the development of surrealism. Paradoxically enough surrealism began as a literary movement, and its precepts were only afterwards applied to painting. The surrealist art most typical of the late '20s and early to middle '30s, when the movement was at its height, is in some ways unexpected, since, while its imagery is the freely generated product of the unconscious, its technique is the very opposite of free.

The leading surrealist painters, among them Salvador Dali, Tanguy and René Magritte, seemed determined to abandon the technical liberties which had been won for art by the Fauves and their successors, in order to revert to a painstaking academic manner. Dali's phantasmagoric landscapes are technically indistinguishable from the work of a leading 19th-century academic painter such as Meissonnier.

After the leading surrealists fled en masse to America during the Second World War, this situation began to change. The Surrealist Movement in exile came into contact with, and deeply influenced, American artists such as Arshile Gorky and Jackson Pollock. But these Americans returned to fundamental surrealist principles. In particular, they looked again at the technique called 'automatic writing' which the surrealist poets had used. From freely handled calligraphic swirls of paint they made pictures which reflected the flux within themselves. Pollock, a leading figure in what

came to be called Abstract Expressionism, developed a technique of freely dripping paint, rather than putting it on with a brush in conventional fashion. Sometimes these 'drip paintings' are entirely abstract, sometimes, however, they contain figurative imagery. Pollock had made a close study of Jung, and was also acquainted with American Indian myths and legends. These studies undoubtedly influenced the kind of painting he produced, despite the fact that it was supposed to be free of all conscious control.

One striking thing about the American painting of the immediate post-war period was the large claims it made for the individual. Abstract expressionist canvases act out private fantasies on a heroic scale, and the painter is as interested in getting at some form of truth about himself, or in achieving a kind of self recognition, as he is in communicating.

A similar privacy marks the dramatic output of Samuel Beckett, who is James Joyce's most obvious heir and successor. A brief play like *The Mouth*, a virtuoso piece for a single performer, consists entirely of an apparently freely associated monologue, in which subjective fears and terrors are revealed. The nature of the piece is deliberately emphasized by the way in which it is presented. The performer is shrouded, and only the mouth of the title is exposed.

One especially striking characteristic of this and other plays by Beckett is the fact that they are clearly intended as rituals rather than narratives. This ritual element can be found in a great deal of contemporary art, most obviously in the happenings and performance art which are already closely connected to Beckett's ideas as a dramatic author, but also in things like the strange groups of life-like figures made by the young English sculptor John Davies. Especially when grouped together, as they often are, Davies' figures, sometimes masked but quite often not, seem frozen in the midst of some inexplicable but

Autumn Cannibalism – Salvador Dali, Tate Gallery, London. Dali returns to traditional perspective in order to transcribe a completely private and subjective vision.

obsessive task. Though they offer none of the difficulties to a mass audience that pure abstraction has

been supposed to do, it is difficult to characterize either Beckett's plays or Davies' sculptures as being in any way 'popular'.

The artist's search for his own individuality, and his need to exorcise the demons he carries within himself, are so typical of modern art as to be one of its most readily identifiable characteristics. But they are also the things which make it seem difficult, or even totally inaccessible, to a potential audience which has been greatly enlarged by the growth of modern means of communication, the chief among which is now television. The conflict between the content of the work, and the means of its dissemination, is indeed one of the great problems facing all the arts in the late 20th century.

Art in the Future

Since the middle of the present century, artists have become increasingly conscious of the gap which has opened between themselves and the audience they would like to reach.

Perhaps the most immediate result of their unease was the birth of Pop art at the beginning of the '60s. Pop, which was largely an Anglo-American phenomenon, was a celebration of the consumer-culture which had grown up in the wake of prosperity, a prosperity itself based on immense technological advances.

The celebration was always ironic and ambiguous. Roy Lichtenstein, a leading American Pop artist, made his reputation with paintings based on blown-up frames from popular comic strips. All the mannerisms imposed by the cheap printing process were faithfully reproduced on a giant scale in his canvases—the hard outlines, crude areas of flat colour, and areas of coarse shading rendered by dots. But the compositions were subtly adjusted to bring them into line with an instinctive classicism peculiar to the artist himself and by no means inherent in his material.

Later, Lichtenstein was to use the same techniques to make paraphrases of earlier masterpieces of 20th-century painting, for example cubist compositions by Braque. The implication was that he was more interested in ways of rendering reality than he was in the actual substance of popular culture. Much Pop art is as aloof and aristocratic as anything that has preceded it.

Of course, there has been interaction between popular forms of artistic expression and the 'high art' which still dominates most of our artistic thinking. Often this interaction takes place in a context which is typical of no other century but this. The Kustom Kars typical of California owe their exuberant decoration to ideas borrowed from surrealism (via science fiction) and even to Pop art. But they appeal to strictly popular taste. Less self-conscious still, as a means of artistic expression, are the gaudy neon signs which line the Strip at the Nevada gambling resort of Las Vegas. Here again we find the influence of modern art and modern design, but translated into a new and accessible idiom.

Neon and the automobile are commonplaces of our society, technological marvels so familiar that they have lost the capacity to inspire wonder. Not so things like the Architecture Machine (1970), a computer programmed to assist architects in the depiction of both architectural and urban planning models. This machine, which can project any set of architectural plans in fully three-dimensional form, should theoretically remove any remaining barrier to the user's creative imagination. But it is no substitute for the imagination itself.

A similar situation exists with the newest technological toys to come into the hands of artists—the laser beam and the holograms which laser photography has made possible. Lasers have already made an impact in the world of popular entertainment, and holograms (the word means 'whole image') with their fully three-dimensional re-creation of objects which apparently materialize out of empty space have drawn huge crowds wherever they have been shown. But those artists who have tried to use them, among them the durable Salvador Dali, seem curiously tentative in their approach.

The conclusion must be that the future of the modern arts is impossible to predict because they have not as yet caught up with the possibilities offered by the present.

Art and television

Television is now the most powerful and universal means of communication, and it is therefore important to look at its uneasy relationship with modernism.

Two things have taken place. One is that television, in a rather tentative fashion, has become the means whereby high culture is disseminated to the mass. Lord Clark's series *Civilization* was a celebrated example of this. But artists have not been content to use television merely as a means of spreading information about what has been achieved in other media. They have wanted to turn it into a means of artistic expression in its own right.

The result has been the growth of

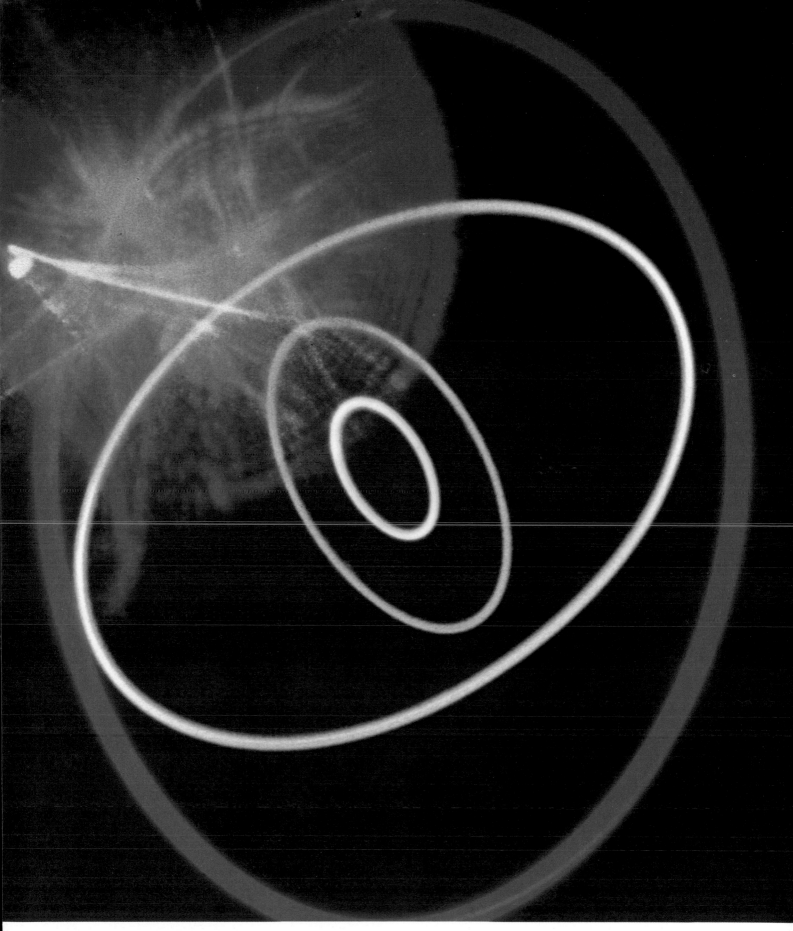

so-called Video Art. Often this, suffering from the hermetism which seems to afflict all forms of modernist activity, has been confined to the art gallery. But very occasionally, like Douglas Davis's noteworthy Videotape Event for the Boston Symphony Orchestra, it has achieved parity with other kinds of television programming. The results, however, have usually been to deprive television of precisely that popular accent which is the essence of its success.

Laserium. Image from the laser concert created by Laser Images Inc., California. Spectacular displays of this kind have been used chiefly in connection with rock music, but recall the attempts made to combine light and sound made before the First World War by the Italian Futurists and also by Russian composer Scriabin.

GAZETTEER

ABYSSINIA:
See Ethiopia.

AFGHANISTAN
Official name: Republic of
Afghanistan. Location:
Southern Asia. Area:
647,497 sq. km (250,000 sq.
miles). Form of government:
Military-civilian junta.
Estimated population
(1976): 19,580,000. Official
language: Pashto; Dari
Persian is also spoken.
Official religion: Islam.
Monetary unit: The
afghani = 100 puli. Principal
towns and their estimated
population (1976): Kábul
(capital) 587,650; Kandahár
115,000; Herát 62,000;
Gardez 46,000; Jalálábád
44,000; Mazár-i-Sharif 40,000.

ALBANIA
Official name: People's
Republic of Albania.
Location: Eastern Europe,
on west coast of Balkan
peninsula. Area: 28,748 sq.
km (11,100 sq. miles). Form
of government: Communist
republic. Estimated
population (1976): 2,432,000.
Official language: Albanian.
Official religion: None but
about 70 per cent Moslem.
Monetary unit: The lek =
100 qindars. Principal towns

*Republic of Afghanistan:
Afghanis in a village settlement
in the northern part of the
country.*

and their estimated
population: Tirana (capital)
175,000; Durrës 57,000;
Skhodër 55,000; Vlona
51,000; Korcë 47,000.

ALGERIA
Official name: Democratic
and Popular Republic of
Algeria. Location: On
Mediterranean coast of
North Africa. Area:
2,322,160 sq. km (896,590 sq.
miles). Form of government:
Socialist republic.
Estimated population (1974):
16,300,000. Official language:
Arabic and French. Official
religion: Islam. Monetary
unit: The dinar = 100
centimes. Principal towns
and their estimated
population: Algiers (capital)
943,000; Oran 325,500;
Constantine 240,700;
Annaba (formerly Bône)
150,000; Sidi-bel-Abbès
87,000; Sétif 88,000; Skikda
(formerly Philippeville)
61,000.

ANDORRA
Official name: The Valleys
of Andorra. Location:
Pyrenees, southern Europe.

Area: 470 sq. km (180 sq.
miles). Form of government:
Independent co-principality.
Population (1975): 26,558.
Official language: Catalan.
Official religion: Roman
Catholicism. Monetary unit:
The French franc (= 100
centimes) and the Spanish
peseta (= 100 centimos).
Capital: Andorra-la-Vella
(estimated population
10,200).

ANGOLA
Official name: State of
Angola. Location: West
coast of Africa. Area:
1,246,700 sq. km (481,351 sq.
miles). Form of government:
People's republic. Population
(1970 census): 5,673,046.
Official language:
Portuguese. Official religion:
Roman Catholicism.
Monetary unit: The escudo
= 100 centavos. Principal
towns: Luanda (capital,
population (1970) 346,763);
Huambo (formerly Nova
Lisboa) is the designate
capital; Lobito.

ARGENTINA
Official name: Argentine
Republic. Location:
Occupies most of southern
South America to the east of
the main Andean divide,
which separates it from
Chile to the west. Area:
2,776,900 sq. km (1,072,200
sq. miles). Form of
government: Military junta.
Population (1970 census):
23,360,000. Official language:
Spanish. Official religion:
Roman Catholicism.
Monetary unit: The peso =
100 centares.

*Argentine Republic: Wool is
both exported and used locally
for weaving in traditional
patterns and colours.*

Principal cities and their
estimated population (1970):
Buenos Aires (capital)
2,972,500; Rosario 807,000;
Córdoba 791,000; Mendoza
471,000; La Plata 391,000;
Tucuman 366,000; Santa Fé
245,000; Bahía Blanca
182,000.
    Land and climate:
Enormous physical
contrasts, varying from
lowland in the north, the
Pampas to the south, and
the Patagonian plateau in
the far south, with the
whole country fringed on
the west by the Andean
chain. The western half of
the country is arid; rainfall
is concentrated in summer
months in the north east,
but spread throughout the
year in the Pampas.
    Economy: One of the
world's largest exporters of
beef, with important sheep
farming and wool
production; processing of
agricultural products,
particularly meat freezing
and packing, provides the
most important industries,
but there is a developing
consumer industry.
    Recent history: President
Perón, who died in 1974, was
succeeded by his wife Maria
Estele (Isabel) de Perón.
She imposed a state of siege,
but outside pressures led to
a bloodless coup in 1976,
and she was overthrown by
a three-man junta, a
member of which was
sworn in as new president.

AUSTRALIA
Official name: Common-
wealth of Australia.
Location: Island continent
in southern hemisphere,
remote from all other
continents except Asia.

Australia: Ayers Rock in the Northern Territory is a traditional site of magic and mystery.

Area: 7,686,900 sq. km (2,970,900 sq. miles). Form of government: Federal parliamentary state. Estimated population (1975): 13,502,300. Official language: English. Official religion: None, but about 90 per cent of the population is Christian. Monetary unit: The dollar = 100 cents.

The people: About 2 million people emigrated to Australia from Europe in the 20 years following the Second World War, mostly from Britain. Today there are about 40,000 full-blooded Aborigines and a further 40,000 of mixed blood.

Political divisions: Australia is divided into six states, each with its own parliament: Victoria, New South Wales, Queensland, South Australia, Western Australia and Tasmania. In addition there are two territories: the Northern Territory and the Australian Capital Territory (Canberra).

Principal cities and their estimated population (1975): Canberra (federal capital) 210,600; Sydney (capital of New South Wales) 2,922,760; Melbourne (capital of Victoria) 2,661,400; Brisbane (capital of Queensland) 958,800; Adelaide (capital of South Australia) 899,300; Perth (capital of Western Australia) 787,300; Darwin (capital of the Northern

Territory) 40,000.

The land: The western part (about three-fifths of the total area) is a low plateau; the rest of the interior is mostly desert, broken by some high ridges. On the eastern side the Great Dividing Range rises in the south, and rivers flowing to the coast from here are mostly small. The continental shelf includes the outlying islands of Tasmania in the south, Guinea in the north, and also supports the Great Barrier Reef, stretching 2,000 km (1,250 miles), 16 km (10 miles) to 240 km (150 miles) off the north-eastern coast.

Climate: Most of the area is arid or semi-arid, only one-tenth of Australia having over 100 cm (40 in) of rain a year. Summer rains are of monsoon character in the north, whereas the southern coastal area has a Mediterranean climate. Tasmania in the extreme south has rain at all seasons. In the interior temperatures of over 38°C (100°F) are common.

Natural resources: Although only 4 per cent of the area is cultivated, the economy of Australia still depends largely on pastoral industries, including dairy products, wool and mutton, beef, wheat and sugar. Other crops include maize, groundnuts, cotton and grapes (especially for wine).

The country is rich in a variety of minerals, including precious metals,

and it is one of the world's largest producers of lead; there are also large deposits of copper and bauxite. Aluminium and steel are important industries, while there are large reserves of uranium and nickel ores which are not yet fully exploited. The continent also has large reserves of coal and oil, and hydro-electric schemes are being developed.

Industry and exports: Agricultural produce is still the main export, but the proportion of minerals is increasing, and in 1976, for the first time, coal overtook wool as Australia's most valuable export. Most manufactures are in the south east, which has two-thirds of the population, most of the coal and water resources, and better transport facilities. There is both light and heavy engineering, including shipbuilding, locomotives and automobiles. Textile, paper, food and chemical industries are also being developed. Japan is the chief market for exports, followed by Britain and the United States.

Recent history: The Labor Party came into power in 1972 under Gough Whitlam, but after a controversial dismissal of the Labor government by the Governor-General, a general election in 1975 resulted in the formation of a coalition government of the Liberal and Country parties. The coalition government won even greater support in the 1977 general election, and Whitlam resigned as leader of the Labor Party.

AUSTRIA

Official name: Republic of Austria. Location: Central Europe, bounded by Switzerland, Liechtenstein, Germany, Czechoslovakia, Hungary, Yugoslavia and Italy. Area: 83,850 sq. km (32,375 sq. miles). Form of government: Federal republic. Population (1971 census): 7,456,403. Official language: German. Official religion: None, but about 90 per cent of the population are Roman Catholic. Monetary unit: The

schilling = 100 groschen.

Principal cities and their population (1971 census): Vienna (capital) 1,614,841; Graz 248,500; Linz 202,874; Innsbruck 115,197; Salzburg 128,845.

Land and climate: Austria is essentially a mountainous country: the Alps cross the area from east to west, covering the southern and central parts. A large part of the country drains to the Danube river, which collects the rivers flowing north from the Alps. Summer temperatures reach over 26°C (80°F) although the numerous valleys create considerable local differences; rainfall is about average, but less plentiful in the eastern part.

Economy: Although arable land is limited, the forests (which occupy 37 per cent of the area) provide important wood-based industries. Magnesite is the main mineral mined, and there are also deposits of graphite, lead and zinc. Light industries include the manufacture of electrical machinery and appliances. The tourist industry is one of the country's most important sources of income.

Recent history: Austria was re-established as a republic in 1945, but occupation by the Allied powers (Britain, USA, France and USSR) continued until 1955, when a treaty restored the prewar frontiers. The country formally regained sovereignty in 1955 and declared perpetual neutrality. Elections since then have usually created a coalition between the People's Party and the Socialist Party; if an absolute majority has been achieved it has always been very slim.

BAHAMAS

Official name: Commonwealth of the Bahamas. Location: Archipelago in the West Indies, Caribbean Sea. Land area: 10,070 sq. km (3,890 sq. miles). Form of government: Parliamentary state. Estimated population (1975): 204,000. Official language:

English. Official religion: None; the largest religious denominations are the Baptists, Roman Catholics and Anglicans. Monetary unit: The dollar = 100 cents. Capital: Nassau (1974 estimated population 112,000).

BAHRAIN

Official name: State of Bahrain. Location: South-western Asia, off the west coast of the Arabian Gulf. Area: 660 sq. km (255 sq. miles). Form of government: Monarchy (emirate). Estimated population (1975): 248,500. Official language: Arabic, but English is widely spoken. Official religion: Islam. Monetary unit: The dinar = 1,000 fils. Principal towns and their estimated population (1975): Manama (capital) 94,700; Muharrq Town 44,600.

BANGLADESH

Official name: People's Republic of Bangladesh. Location: Southern Asia, almost entirely surrounded by India. Area: 142,775 sq. km (55,125 sq. miles). Form of government: Presidential regime enforcing martial law. Population (1974 census): 71,316,517. Official language: Bengali. Official religion: None, but the principal religion is Islam; a small minority is Hindu. Monetary unit: The taka = 100 paisas. Principal towns and their population (1974 census): Dacca (capital) 1,310,972; Chittagong 416,733; Chalma 436,000.

BARBADOS

Official name: Dominion of Barbados. Location: Caribbean Sea, north east of Trinidad. Area: 430 sq. km (165 sq. miles). Form of government: Parliamentary state. Estimated population (1974): 265,000. Official language: English. Official religion: None, but the principal religion is Christianity. Monetary unit: The dollar = 100 cents. Principal city: Bridgetown (1970 population 8,789).

BASUTOLAND:

See Lesotho.

BECHUANALAND:

See Botswana.

BELGIUM

Official name: Kingdom of Belgium. Location: North-west Europe, bounded by the Netherlands, Luxemburg, Germany and France. Area: 30,510 sq. km (11,780 sq. miles). Form of government: Constitutional monarchy. Estimated population (1975): 9,813,152. Official languages: Dutch (Flemish), French and German. Official religion: None, but the population is overwhelmingly Roman Catholic. Monetary unit: The franc = 100 centimes.

Principal towns and their estimated population (1975): Brussels (capital) 1,050,800; Antwerp 209,200; Ghent 142,550; Liège 139,350; Bruges 119,700; Ostend 71,800.

Land and climate: The Meuse river and its tributary, the Sambre, on the edge of the Ardennes divide the country into two distinct regions: to the west level and fertile; to the east a plateau mostly of poor soil reaching a height of 694 m (2,276 ft). The climate of the lowland is relatively mild in winter with rain well

Kingdom of Belgium: The beautiful Brussels lace is still highly valued although now the major exports of the textile industry are man-made fibres.

distributed throughout the year; the higher altitudes of the Ardennes give a cooler summer and a more severe winter.

Economy: Over half the country is under intensive cultivation and stock rearing is also intensive. Dykes along the coast have recovered an area of 500 sq. km (193 sq. miles) of otherwise unproductive land. The traditional industry of textiles, now including man-made fibres, is still important. Between Liège and Antwerp many new factories have been built by international companies to supply other members of the European Economic Community.

Recent history: Belgium has suffered in recent years from the frenzied split over language and also from a controversy over education between socialists and Catholics.

BELIZE

Official name: Belize (formerly British Honduras). Location: Caribbean coast of Central American isthmus. Area: 22,966 sq. km (8,867 sq. miles). Form of government: Parliamentary democracy. Estimated population (1975): 150,000. Official language: English; Spanish is also widely spoken. Official religion: None. Monetary

unit. The dollar = 100 cents. Principal towns and their estimated population (1975): Belmopan (capital) 5,000; Belize (former capital) 45,000.

BENIN (formerly Dahomey)

Official name: People's Republic of Benin (formerly Republic of Dahomey). Location: Narrow strip in West Africa flanked by Nigeria and Togo. Area: 112,620 sq. km (43,483 sq. miles). Form of government: Military revolutionary government. Estimated population (1972): 2,869,000. Official language: French, but each tribe communicates in its own language. Official religion: None; the majority follow their own beliefs and customs. Monetary unit: The franc = 100 centimes. Principal towns and their estimated population (1974): Porto-Novo (capital) 100,000; Cotonou 175,000; Abomey 30,000.

BERMUDA

Official name: Colony of Bermuda. Location: Isolated group of small islands in western Atlantic Ocean. Area: 53 sq. km (20.5 sq. miles). Form of government: British crown colony. Estimated population (1976): 53,500. Official language: English. Official religion: None. Monetary unit: The dollar = 100 cents. Capital: Hamilton (estimated population 3,000).

BHUTAN

Official name: Kingdom of Bhutan. Location: Himalayas, southern Asia. Area: 47,000 sq. km (18,000 sq. miles). Form of government: Hereditary monarchy. Estimated population (1974): 1,100,000. Official language: Dzong-Kha. Chief religion: Lamaism (Tibetan form of Buddhism). Monetary unit: The Indian rupee = 100 paisa. Capital: Thimphu.

BOLIVIA

Official name: Republic of Bolivia. Location: Inland state in South America. Area: 1,098,600 sq. km

(424,170 sq. miles). Form of government: Military-civilian dictatorship. Estimated population (1975): 5,638,800. Official language: Spanish; Quechua or Aymará is spoken by Amer-indians. Official religion: None; Roman Catholicism ceased to be the official religion in 1961. Monetary unit: The peso = 100 centavos. Principal towns and their estimated population (1973): La Paz de Ayacucho (administrative capital) 697,500; Sucre (legal capital) 88,050; Cochabamba 245,250; Santa Cruz de la Sierra 263,300.

BOTSWANA

Official name: Republic of Botswana (formerly known as Bechuanaland). Location: Southern Africa, bounded by the Republic of South Africa, Rhodesia and South-West Africa (Namibia). Area: 569,800 sq. km (220,000 sq. miles). Form of government: Presidential democracy. Population (1971 census): 630,380. Official language: English; Tswana also used. Official religion: None; the chief religion is Christianity. Monetary unit: The South African rand = 100 cents. Principal towns and their

Republic of Botswana: A group of bushmen and women rest in the large and arid Kalahari Desert.

estimated population (1976): Gaborone (capital) 30,000; Selebi-Pikwe 20,600; Francistown 25,000; Lobatse 12,000.

BRAZIL

Official name: Federative Republic of Brazil. Location: Has a common border with all countries in South America except Chile and Ecuador. Area: 8,512,000 sq. km (3,286,500 sq. miles). Form of government: Military-civilian dictatorship. Estimated population (1975): 107,145,200. Official

language: Portuguese. Official religion: None, but over 95 per cent of the population is Roman Catholic. Monetary unit: The new cruzeiro = 100 centavos.

Principal cities and their population (1970 census): Brasília (capital) 271,570; São Paulo 5,924,615; Rio de Janeiro 4,251,918; Belo Horizonte 1,235,030; Recife 1,060,701; Salvador 1,007,105.

Land and climate: Plateaux and hills cover more than half the area; plains extend over the remaining land, of particular importance being the alluvial plain formed by the Amazon river which flows eastwards into the Atlantic in the north. The Rio Grande and other rivers to the south rise near the Atlantic and flow westwards across the plateau into either the Paraná or Uruguay rivers.

Most of the country lies within the tropics; annual rainfall is almost everywhere over 100 m (40 in), but may be twice that in parts of the Amazon lowlands where temperatures may reach 37°C (99°F). Sea breezes cool some coastal areas, and the mountainous areas are also cooler.

Economy: Agricultural production is more valuable than the total output of

Federative Republic of Brazil: This Suya Indian wears traditional body decoration, including the large plate inserted in his pierced bottom lip.

mining and manufacturing, the main crops being coffee, sugar, cocoa and tobacco. There are rich mineral resources, particularly of precious stones, iron ore and manganese ore, but as yet they have not been fully exploited.

Recent history: An army revolt deposed President João Goulart in 1964 and he fled into exile. Thereafter presidents were chosen by the army until 1974 when an electoral college was instituted.

BRUNEI

Official name: State of Brunei. Location: South-eastern Asia, on the north-east coast of the island of Borneo. Area: 5,765 sq. km (2,226 sq. miles). Form of government: Self-governing sultanate under British protection. Estimated population (1975): 162,400. Official language: Malay; Chinese is also spoken and English widely used. Official religion: Islam. Monetary unit: The dollar = 100 sen (cents). Capital: Bandar Seri Begawan (1971 population 72,481).

BULGARIA

Official name: People's

Republic of Bulgaria. Location: South-eastern Europe, in the Balkan peninsula. Area: 110,911 sq. km (42,823 sq. miles). Form of government: Communist republic. Estimated population (1975): 8,730,000. Official language: Bulgarian. Official religion: None; the majority adhere to the Bulgarian Orthodox Church. Monetary unit: The lev = 100 stolinki. Principal towns and their population (1975): Sofia (capital) 965,728; Plovdiv 309,242; Varna 251,588; Ruse 163,012.

BURMA

Official name: Socialist Republic of the Union of Burma. Location: Uppermost region of South-east Asia, between Tibetan plateau and Malayan peninsula. Area: 678,034 sq. km (261,789 sq. miles). Form of government: One-party Socialist republic. Estimated population (1970): 27,584,000. Official language: Burmese. Official religion: None; three-quarters of the population are Buddhists. Monetary unit: The kyat = 100 pyas. Principal towns and their estimated population (1970): Rangoon (capital) 3,000,000; Mandalay 401,700; Moulmein 172,600; Bassein 136,500; Pegu 125,000.

BURUNDI

Official name: Republic of Burundi. Location: On Lake Tanganyika in the heart of Africa. Area: 27,834 sq. km (10,747 sq. miles). Form of government: Military junta. Estimated population (1976): 3,800,000. Official languages: French and Kirundi. Official religion: None; over half the population is Roman Catholic. Monetary unit: The franc = 100 centimes. Principal towns and their estimated population: Bujumbura (capital) 100,000; Kitega 10,000.

CAMBODIA

Official name: Democratic Kampuchea; formerly Khmer Republic. Location: South-eastern Asia, bounded by Thailand and Laos to the north, Vietnam to the east. Area: 181,035 sq. km (69,898 sq. miles). Form of

government: Vietnamese-occupied communist republic. Estimated population (1971): 6,968,000. Official language: Khmer. Official religion: Theravada Buddhism. Monetary unit: The riel = 100 sen (cents). Principal towns: Phnom-Penh (capital); Battambang.

CAMEROON

Official name: United Republic of Cameroon. Location: West coast of central Africa. Area: 465,054 sq. km (179,557 sq. miles). Form of government: Presidential democracy. President: Ahmadou Ahidjo. Estimated population (1976): 7,800,000. Official language: English and French. Official religion: None. Monetary unit: The franc = 100 centimes. Principal towns and their estimated population (1976): Yaoundé (capital) 178,000; Douala 250,000; Nkongsamba 71,000.

CANADA

Official name: Canada. Location: Occupies most of the northern half of the North American mainland between the Pacific and Atlantic Oceans, with the Arctic Ocean to the north and the United States to the south. Area: 9,221,000 sq. km (3,560,240 sq. miles). Form of government: Federal parliamentary state. Population (preliminary census 1976): 22,598,016. Official languages: English and French, both of which are used in parliamentary debates. Official religion: None; there are about 10 million Roman Catholics, but other important denominations are the United Church of Canada, the Anglican Church of Canada and the Presbyterian, Lutheran and Baptist Churches.
The people: Before the First World War immigration was chiefly from Britain, but substantial immigration since the Second World War was composed of nearly twice as many from other European countries. The bulk of the population of Quebec Province is of

French descent. There are about a quarter million Amer-indians and the Eskimo population is estimated at 18,000.
Political divisions: Canada is divided into ten provinces, each with its own separate parliament and administration: Newfoundland, Prince Edward Island, Nova Scotia, New Brunswick, Quebec, Ontario, Manitoba, Saskatchewan, Alberta and British Columbia. In addition there are two territories: the Northwest Territories and the Yukon Territory, governed by commissioners.
Principal cities and their metropolitan population (1976 preliminary census): Ottawa (federal capital) 668,853; Montreal 2,758,780; Toronto

Canada: Wood is the basis for major industry in Canada, particularly export of newsprint. Here logs are collected for transport on the Gatineau River.

2,753,112; Vancouver 1,135,774; Edmonton 542,845; Calgary 457,828; Hamilton 525,222; Winnipeg 570,725; Quebec 534,193.
The land: There are six main structural regions: the Laurentian Shield, which occupies nearly half the country from the Hudson Bay, mostly lowland but rising steeply from the St Lawrence estuary and up to the Labrador coast, and with the southern margin corresponding roughly with the northern shores of the Great Lakes; the Canadian Appalachian Region which includes the maritime provinces and Newfoundland, consisting mostly of bays, lowland and ridges; the St Lawrence–Ontario lowlands, which are generally of low relief; the western plains which rise in the steps of the Red river valley to the foot of the Rocky Mountains, and in which flows the Mackenzie river; the

western cordillera which rises between the western plains and the Pacific Ocean, and includes the Rocky Mountains rising to heights of over 3,350 m (11,000 ft); and the Arctic Archipelago which consists of islands resembling the Laurentian Shield. Vegetation consists mostly of tundra in the north, but farther south is a forest zone that covers most of Canada, and towards the Rocky Mountains is a large area of good quality grassland.

Climate: There is little moisture in the interior, but an annual rainfall of 300 cm (120 in) on the coastal slopes of the Cordillera. Average rainfall elsewhere is between 75 cm (30 in) and 100 cm (40 in), though slightly more along the Atlantic coast. The Pacific coastlands have milder winters and cooler summers than similar latitudes inland and on the east coast. Winter temperatures in Winnipeg can be as low as $-40°C$ ($-40°F$) and there is normally 1 m (4 ft) of snow a year.

Natural resources: The output of grains fluctuates considerably according to climatic conditions, but it is still one of Canada's most important products; the largest area of farmland is in the Prairie Provinces, the Ontario Peninsula and the St Lawrence valley. The country is the third largest producer of minerals; they include iron ore, copper, gold, nickel and uranium. Lead and zinc are also mined in quantity as well as small quantities of silver and platinum. Coal resources are limited, although large quantities of oil and natural gas have been discovered and are being exploited. Canada also has some of the world's finest hydro-electric stations, particularly along the St Lawrence river and on the mountainous Pacific coast. Other important resources are fishing, particularly cod and herring, in the Newfoundland Banks, and salmon on the west coast, and fur trapping in the northern areas.

Industry and exports: The largest group of industries is based on wood, particularly newsprint, most of which is exported. Ontario and Quebec have flourishing food processing industries, and the wheat crop supplies a world market, particularly to western Europe and, in more recent years, even to China when the Chinese harvest has failed. Cheap hydro-electric power has helped industrial development, particularly in the chemical and aluminium industries. Iron ore and coal are brought to Hamilton on Lake Ontario by the St Lawrence Seaway and the iron and steel industry has been developed there. Heavy engineering (locomotives) is important in Montreal, and both Montreal and Toronto have attracted many light industries, mostly for consumer goods.

Recent history: Pierre Trudeau, a young and controversial French-Canadian, came to power as prime minister in 1968 following, the resignation of Lester Pearson, and this did much to placate French interests in Quebec Province where there is a strong secessionist movement. There has been less emphasis on traditional links with western Europe and the United States under his administration, but a closer relationship with Far Eastern countries.

CAPE VERDE ISLANDS

Official name: Republic of Cape Verde. Location: Archipelago in central Atlantic facing coast of western Africa. Area: 4,033 sq. km (1,557 sq. miles). Form of government: Popular republic. Estimated population (1976): 360,000. Official language: Portuguese. Official religion: Roman Catholicism. Monetary unit: The escudo = 100 centavos. Capital: Praia.

CENTRAL AFRICAN EMPIRE

Official name: Central African Empire. Location:

Heart of equatorial Africa. Area: 622,577 sq. km (240,378 sq. miles). Form of government: Military dictatorship. Estimated population (1971): 1,637,000 (excluding refugees from neighbouring countries). Official language: French; the national language is Sangho. Official religion: None; nearly half the population is Christian. Monetary unit: The franc = 100 centimes. Principal towns and their estimated population (1970): Bangui (capital) 300,000.

CEYLON:
See Sri Lanka.

CHAD

Official name: Republic of Chad. Location: Landlocked state in north central Africa. Area: 1,284,000 sq. km (495,800 sq. miles). Form of government: Military dictatorship. Estimated population (1973): 3,869,000. Official language: French; Arabic is also widely spoken. Official religion: None; about half the population is Moslem. Monetary unit: The franc = 100 centimes. Principal towns and their estimated population (1973): Ndjaména (capital, formerly Fort Lamy) 192,950; Sahr (formerly Fort Archambault) 43,900.

CHILE

Official name: Republic of Chile. Location: Along Pacific coast of South America. Area: 756,945 sq. km (292,257 sq. miles). Form of government: Military junta. Estimated population (1974): 10,405,150. Official language: Spanish. Official religion: None; over 80 per cent of the population is Roman Catholic. Monetary unit: The escudo = 100 centésimos. Principal towns and their estimated population (1972): Santiago (capital) 3,700,000; Valparaíso 296,000; Concepción 178,000; Viña del Mar 155,000.

CHINA

Official name: People's Republic of China. Location: Vast area of eastern Asia bounded by

Mongolia, the Soviet Union, Pakistan, India, Nepal and South-east Asia. Area: 9,560,900 sq. km (3,691,500 sq. miles). Form of government: Communist republic. Estimated population (1976): Over 800 million. Official language: Mandarin Chinese; local dialects of Chinese are spoken in the south. Official religion: None; the traditional religions and philosophies are Confucianism, Buddhism and Taoism. Monetary unit: The yüan = 10 chiao = 100 fen.

The people: Nearly all Chinese people belong to the Sinitic group, a division of the Mongoloid race. A small proportion belong to other Mongoloid groups such as Manchus, Tibetans and Uigurs.

Political divisions: The country is divided into 21 provinces, five autonomous regions and two cities (Peking and Shanghai). The five autonomous regions are: Sitsang (Tibet), Sinkiang-Uighur, Inner Mongolia, Ningsia-Hui and Kwangsi-Chuang.

Principal cities (over 1 million inhabitants): Peking (capital); Shanghai; Tientsin; Shenyang (Mukden); Wuhan; Canton; Chungking; Harbin; Lü-ta; Nanking; Sian; Tsingtao; Chengtu; Taiyuan; Fushun.

The land: The North China Plain, the original homeland and still the core of China, lies between shallow seas to the east and high plateaux to the west. The vast alluvial plain is covered in parts by fertile soil. To the north and west of the North China Plain are open grasslands. South-west China is protected by high ridges and deep valleys, while in the west lies the high barren plateau of Sitsang (Tibet), mostly 4,575 m (15,000 ft) above sea-level. On its southern margin are the peaks of the Himalayas. Two of the world's longest rivers, the Yangtze and the Hwang-Ho rise in the mountains of the Tibetan plateau and flow eastwards to the Yellow Sea; the Si Kiang is the only

People's Republic of China: Crowds gather with flags, balloons, flowers and streamers to welcome a foreign visitor to the capital city of Peking.

large river in southern China.

Climate: As would be expected in such a vast area the climate varies from the sub-tropical in the far south to an annual average temperature of below 10°C (50°F) in the north, and from monsoon conditions in the east to extreme aridity in the north-west.

Natural resources: China ranks among the world's leading agricultural nations. Rice is by far the most important crop, grown in the Yangtze valley and everywhere to the south, but wheat is also grown extensively in areas where rainfall is insufficient for rice. The most important root crop is sweet potatoes and the chief commercial crop, cotton. Coalfields are known to exist in most provinces, but limited demand and shortage of transport have restricted output. Oil has been found only in limited amounts, and iron ore is widely distributed. The country is rich in non-ferrous metals, particularly tin, and is one of the main producers of antimony.

Industry and exports: Industry and agriculture

are almost fully occupied in supplying the country's own needs, so that foreign trade plays a relatively small part in the economy. Among exports are raw silk and minerals, which earn foreign currency to import specialized machinery, chemical products, and, in years of poor harvests, large quantities of wheat.

The engineering industry is being expanded to produce transport equipment and machinery, and this has been greatly aided by a marked improvement in the internal transport, including major bridges across the Yangtze river.

Recent history: From 1966 to 1969 China experienced the 'Cultural Revolution' in which communist youths took over the country with the support of the Red Guard in the name of Mao Tse-tung. In 1971 the country was at last admitted to the United Nations, and took over one of the five permanent seats on the Security Council. Diplomatic relations with many countries in the West were re-established, and China also showed some interest in underdeveloped countries. There was considerable confusion when Mao Tse-tung died in 1976; his widow and others

were accused of an attempt to seize power.

CHINA, REPUBLIC OF:
See Taiwan.

COLOMBIA

Official name: Republic of Colombia. Location: North-western South America, with the Caribbean Sea to the north and the Pacific to the west. Area: 1,138,914 sq. km (439,737 sq. miles). Form of government: Presidential democracy. Estimated population (1976): 26,400,000. Official language: Spanish. Official religion: Roman Catholicism. Monetary unit: The peso = 100 centavos. Principal towns and their estimated population (1972): Bogotá (capital) 2,978,000; Medellín 1,269,000; Cali 1,077,000.

COMORO ISLANDS

Official name: Comoro State. Location: Three small islands between African coast and Madagascar. Area: 2,236 sq. km (863 sq. miles). Form of government: Republic. Estimated population (1972): 252,000. Language: The majority speak Kiswahili; French and Arabic are also spoken. Religion: The majority are Moslems. Monetary unit: The franc = 100 centimes. Principal towns: Moroni (capital); Fomboni.

CONGO (BRAZZAVILLE)

Official name: People's Republic of the Congo. Location: Equatorial Africa on western bank of Congo and Oubangui rivers. Area: 342,000 sq. km (132,000 sq. miles). Form of government: Military junta. Population (1974 census): 1,300,020. Official language: French. Official religion: None. Monetary unit: The franc = 100 centimes. Principal towns and their estimated population (1976): Brazzaville (capital) 289,700; Pointe-Noire 141,700; Jacob 30,600: Loubomo 29,600.

CONGO (KINSHASA):
See Zaïre.

COSTA RICA

Official name: Republic of Costa Rica. Location: Central American isthmus. Area: 50,900 sq. km (19,650 sq. miles). Form of government: Presidential democracy. Population (1973 census): 1,871,780. Official language: Spanish. Official religion: Roman Catholicism. Monetary unit: The colón = 100 centimos. Principal towns and their population (1973 census): San José (capital) 228,302; Alajuela 34,957; Puntarenas 30,664; Limón 27,349; Heredia 24,240.

CUBA

Official name: Republic of Cuba. Location: Largest island in Caribbean, 145 km (90 miles) from Florida coast. Area: 110,922 sq. km (42,827 sq. miles). Form of government: Socialist republic. Population (1970 census): 8,553, 395. Official language: Spanish. Official religion: None; the population is predominantly Roman Catholic. Monetary unit: The peso = 100 centavos. Principal towns and their estimated population (1972): Havana (capital) 1,760,000; Santa Clara 332,000; Santiago de Cuba 295,000.

CYPRUS

Official name: Republic of Cyprus. Location: Island in eastern Mediterranean about 100 km (60 miles) off Turkish coast. Area: 9,251 sq. km (3,572 sq. miles). Form of government: Republic. Estimated population (1975): 639,000. Official languages: Greek (four-fifths of population) and Turkish (remainder). Official religion: None; the Greek-speaking population adheres to the Greek Orthodox Church while most of the Turks are Moslems. Monetary unit: The pound = 1,000 mils. Principal towns and their estimated population (1973): Nicosia (capital) 115,800; Limassol 79,700; Famagusta 39,000; Larnaca 19,800.

CZECHOSLOVAKIA

Official name: Czechoslovak Socialist Republic. Location: Central Europe. Area: 12,876 sq. km (49,373 sq. miles). Form of government: Federal Socialist republic. Population (1974): 738,377. Official languages: Czech and Slovak, which are mutually understandable. Official religion: None; about 70 per cent of the population is Roman Catholic. Monetary unit: The koruna — 100 haléřů. Principal towns and their estimated population (1975): Prague (Praha) 1,161,000; Brno 336,000; Bratislava 333,000; Ostrava 293,000; Košice 169,000; Plzen (Pilseň) 155,000.

DAHOMEY:

See Benin.

DENMARK

Official name: Kingdom of Denmark. Location: Scandinavian country in north central Europe. Area: 43,069 sq. km (16,629 sq. miles). Form of government: Constitutional monarchy. Estimated population (1976): 5,065,300. Official language: Danish. Official religion: Evangelical Lutheran Church. Monetary unit: The krone = 100 øre.

Principal cities and towns and their population (1973): Copenhagen (capital) 1,317,891; Aarhus 244,840; Odense 167,772.

Land and climate: The country consists of the Jutland peninsula and about 500 islands including Zeeland and Funen; in addition the large outlying island of Greenland became a Danish county in 1953. Denmark itself is low-lying, with a maximum altitude of 173 m (568 ft), but the landscape possesses some variety: depressions, undulations, valleys and hummocks. The climate is generally mild and precipitation is moderate, with frequent fog on the North Sea coast.

Economy: Denmark is a leading exporter of dairy products, eggs and bacon. Two-thirds of the land is arable and crop yields are very high. Fishing is also important. Shipbuilding, engineering, electronic machinery and sophisticated specialized products are important features of the economy, while the pharmaceutical industry is second only to that of Switzerland.

Recent history: Denmark was a founder member of NATO in 1949, and joined the European Economic Community in 1973. Queen Margrethe came to the throne in 1972, the first queen to rule Denmark for 600 years.

DJIBOUTI

Official name: Republic of Djibouti (formerly French Territory of the Afars and Issas). Location: East Africa, at the head of the Gulf of Aden. Area: 23,000 sq. km (8,880 sq. miles). Form of government: Presidential democracy. Estimated population (1974): 125,000. Official language: French. Official religion: None. Monetary unit: The franc = 100 centimes. Capital: Djibouti (estimated population 62,000).

DOMINICAN REPUBLIC

Official name: Dominican Republic. Location: Occupies the eastern two-thirds of the island of Hispaniola in the Caribbean Sea. Area: 48,442 sq. km (18,704 sq. miles). Form of government: Military-civilian rule. Estimated population (1972): 4,304,900. Official language: Spanish. Official religion: None; over half the population is Roman Catholic. Monetary unit: The peso = 8 reales = 100 centavos. Principal towns and their population (1970 census): Santo Domingo (capital) 671,402; Santiago de los Caballeros 155,151; San Francisco de Macorís 43,941.

EAST GERMANY:

See Germany, East.

ECUADOR

Official name: Republic of Ecuador. Location: West coast of South America. The Galápagos Islands form one of the provinces of the country. Area: 283,561 sq. km (109,483 sq. miles; Galápagos 8,006 sq. km (3,090 sq. miles). Form of government: Military-civilian rule. Population (1974 census): 6,500,845. Official language: Spanish, but Indian languages are common. Official religion: None; about 90 per cent of the population is Roman Catholic. Monetary unit: The sucre = 100 centavos. Principal towns and their population (1974 census): Quito (capital) 557,113; Guayaquil 814,064; Cuenca 104,667; Ambato 77,062; Machala 68,379.

EGYPT

Official name: Arab Republic of Egypt. Location: North-eastern part of Africa. Area: 1,002,000 sq. km (386,900 sq. miles). Form of government: Constitutional dictatorship. Estimated population (1973): 33,619,000. Official language: Arabic; English and French are widely spoken by educated classes. Official religion: Islam. Monetary unit: The pound = 100 piastres = 1,000 millièmes.

Principal cities and their estimated population (1973): Cairo (capital) 5,517,000; Alexandria 2,210,000; Giza 650,900; Port Said 284,500; Suez 284,000.

Land and climate: Over 90 per cent of Egypt is desert. The most important physical feature is the long, winding Nile valley, to the west of which is a cultivated strip with desert on a gentle gradient farther out; to the east the desert links up with a series of mountains. The climate is remarkably uniform throughout the country: generally arid, with hot summers and mild winters.

Economy: The economic life of Egypt hinges on the Nile which, with the aid of a series of barrages, provides water for several crops a year. In particular the Aswan High Dam now retains one of the largest man-made lakes in the world. In addition desert

Arab Republic of Egypt: Nearly 5,000 years old, the Sphinx was buried under sand until modern times.

land is being reclaimed. The main crops are cereals, cotton and rice. Egypt is not rich in mineral resources, but oil is produced and exported, and natural gas has been discovered under the Nile delta.

Recent history: For 15 years until his death in 1970 President Nasser tried to establish unity in the Arab world, although his policies towards Israel were disastrous, involving Egypt in the 'Six-Day War' of 1967. The administration of his successor, President Sadat, led to another war in 1973. The cease-fire proposed by the UN Security Council after this, and accepted by Egypt, seemed to be of a more lasting nature. There was a further dramatic peace bid in 1977 when President Sadat visited the President of Israel for discussions. This development was welcomed in the West, but did not have the full support of other Arab nations.

The Suez Canal, which had been blocked during the 1967 war, was reopened in 1975. An ambitious modernization programme to allow bigger ships to use it is in hand.

EIRE:
See Ireland.

EL SALVADOR
Official name: Republic of El Salvador. Location: Pacific coast of isthmus of Central America. Area: 20,975 sq. km (8,098 sq. miles). Form of government: Presidential democracy. Estimated population (1972): 3,760,450. Official language: Spanish. Official religion: Roman Catholicism. Monetary unit: The colón = 100 centavos. Principal towns and their estimated population (1972): San Salvador (capital) 378,900; Santa Anna 58,000; San Miguel 60,000; Mejicanos 55,000.

ENGLAND:
See United Kingdom.

EQUATORIAL GUINEA
Official name: Republic of Equatorial Guinea.

Location: West coast of Africa. Formerly Spanish Guinea, the territory consists of the islands of Fernando Póo (renamed Macias Nguema Byogo), Corisco, Great Elobey and Small Elobey, and the mainland of Mbini (formerly Rio Muni). Area: 28,051 sq. km (10,831 sq. miles). Form of government: Presidential democracy. Estimated population (1976): 250,000. Official language: Spanish. Official religion: None. Monetary unit: The peseta = 100 centimos. Principal towns and their estimated population: Malabo (formerly Santa Isabel, capital) 38,000; Bata 28,000.

ETHIOPIA
Official name: The Empire of Ethiopia. Location: North-east Africa, extending inland from the Red Sea coast. Area: 1,221,900 sq. km (471,778 sq. miles). Form of government: Military junta. Estimated population (1974): 27,800,800. Official language: Amharic; Arabic is spoken in Eritrea province. Official religion: none; the Ethiopian Coptic Church has a wide following and Islam is also widely practised in the south and east. Monetary unit: The dollar = 100 cents.

Principal towns and their estimated population (1974): Addis Ababa (capital) 1,083,420; Asmara 296,050; Dire Dawa 67,000; Dessie 50,000.

FIJI
Official name: Fiji. Location: Over 800 islands (100 inhabited) in south central Pacific. Area: 18,274 sq. km (7,055 sq. miles). Form of government: Parliamentary state. Estimated population (1976): 585,000. Official language: English. Official religion: None; 50 per cent of the population is Christian; 40 per cent Hindu. Monetary unit: The dollar = 100 cents. Capital: Suva (1975 estimated population 96,000).

FINLAND
Official name: Republic of Finland. Location: Northern Europe, bounded by Norway, Sweden and the USSR. Area (including inland waters): 337,032 sq. km (130,129 sq. miles). Form of government: Parliamentary democracy. Population (1975 census): 4,720,300. Official language: Finnish (93 per cent of

Fiji: Wearing 'grass' skirts and garlands of flowers, a group of men perform a traditional dance on the beach, against the dramatic background of a Pacific sunset.

population) and Swedish (7 per cent). Official religion: None; the majority belong to the National Lutheran Church. Monetary unit: The markka (Finnmark) = 100 pennia. Principal towns and their population (1975 census): Helsinki (capital) 496,872; Tampere 165,928; Turku 163,981; Espoo 121,307; Vantaa 118,307.

FORMOSA:
See Taiwan.

FRANCE
Official name: French Republic. Location: Western Europe. Area: 543,998 sq. km (210,039 sq. miles). Form of government: Presidential democracy. Population (1975 census): 52,655,802. Official language: French; small minorities speak Breton or Basque. Official religion: None; 90 per cent of the population is Roman Catholic. Monetary unit: The franc = 100 centimes.

The people: Basically the people of France are the ancestors of the invading armies of ancient Gaul: Germanic in the north east; Norse in Normandy; and Roman in the south. Many groups from various parts of Europe and North Africa have settled in France in more modern times.

French Republic: The Christian shrine of Mont Saint-Michel in Normandy is built on a rock surrounded by sands often covered by the sea.

Political divisions: France is divided into 96 departments. These are organized into 22 regional constituencies which administrate national development work, planning and budgeting policy.

Principal cities and their net population (1975 census): Paris (capital) 2,290,252; Marseilles 907,854; Lyons 456,674; Toulouse 373,670; Nantes 344,451; Strasbourg 252,959; Bordeaux 223,131; St Etienne 219,722; Le Havre 219,173; Rennes 197,399; Nîmes 187,635; Lille 175,477.

The land: High mountains, plateaux and wide river basins give France a diversity of landscape. The most extensive and loftiest of the plateaux is the Massif Central, which stands in the middle of the country; it is tilted from the south east and reaches 1,675 m (5,500 ft) in the Cévennes. In contrast with the plateaux are the great river basins of the Seine and the Garonne, and the wide valley of the Rhône and Saône. The highest land is in the Alps in the south east, which contain the highest peak in Europe (Mont Blanc, 4,810 m, 15,781 ft), and in the Pyrenees in the south which form a natural frontier with Spain.

The climate: The French climate is transitional between the northern and western cool temperate type and the warm temperate type of the south. The Alpine and Pyreneean regions receive over 125 cm (50 in) precipitation a year; the Paris region has less than 75 cm (30 in), but nowhere in France is it below 50 cm (20 in).

Natural resources: The fertility of its soil and the mildness and diversity of its climate enable France to produce a wide variety of crops. Wheat is grown almost everywhere, barley, sugar beet and grapes are also important; there is intensive livestock and dairy activity, as well as fishing. Coal is produced in the north, and hydro-electricity in the Alps, Massif Central, Pyrenees, and on some of the large rivers. Iron ore resources are the largest in Europe and the country is also the largest European producer of bauxite.

Industry and exports: France is self-sufficient in temperate foodstuffs and an exporter of many of them, including wheat, barley, wine, meat and dairy products. The automobile and aircraft industries are flourishing, and there is also intense activity in shipbuilding, railway rolling stock, textiles, chemicals and glass.

Recent history: General de Gaulle resigned as President of the Fifth Republic, which he created in 1969, to be followed by Georges Pompidou. This led to a rapprochement with Britain, which was welcomed to the Common Market, and to close co-operation between the two countries in various projects such as the development of the Concorde aircraft.

FRENCH SOMALILAND:

See Djibouti.

GABON

Official name: Gabon Republic. Location: West coast of Africa. Area: 267,667 sq. km (103,347 sq. miles). Form of government: Presidential democracy. Estimated population (1974): 950,000. Official language: French; Bantu dialects are widely spoken. Official religion: None; over half the population is Christian. Monetary unit: The franc = 100 centimes. Principal towns and their estimated population (1974): Libreville (capital) 251,400; Port-Gentil 77,000; Lambaréné.

THE GAMBIA

Official name: Republic of the Gambia. Location: Narrow territory around basin of Gambia river in West Africa. Area: 11,569 sq. km (4,467 sq. miles). Form of government: Parliamentary democracy. Population (1973 census): 494,279. Official language: English; principal vernacular languages used are Mandinka, Fula and Wollof. Official religion: None. Monetary unit: The dalasi = 100 butut. Principal towns and their population (1973 census): Banjul (capital, formerly known as Bathurst) 39,476; Kombo St Mary 38,934.

GERMANY, EAST

Official name: German Democratic Republic. Location: Eastern Europe, bounded by West Germany, Czechoslovakia and Poland, and with a coastline on the Baltic. Area: 108,178 sq. km (41,768 sq. miles). Form of government: Socialist republic. Population (1975): 16,820,249. Official language: German. Official religion: None; about half the population is Protestant and one-tenth Roman Catholic. Monetary unit: The Mark = 100 Pfennige.

Principal cities and their population (1975): East Berlin (capital) 1,098,174; West Berlin is an enclave of the German Federal Republic; Leipzig 566,630; Dresden 509,331; Karl-Marx-Stadt (formerly Chemnitz) 305,113; Madgeburg 277,656.

Land and climate: East Germany consists mainly of the northern plain, with a southern fringe of higher ground. The central lowlands provide good pasture and excellent conditions for intensive farming. Rainfall is relatively low in the northern plain, but considerably higher in the uplands. Winters become very cold and summers very hot, with averages of $-3°C$ (26°F) and 23°C (74°F) respectively in Berlin.

Economy: Almost half the land is arable and about one quarter forested. Cattle, pigs, sheep and poultry play an important part in the economy of the country, and there is also a surplus of sugar made from sugar beet. East Germany is the world's largest producer of lignite and there are also large deposits of potash. Four-fifths of the external trade is with countries in the Eastern Communist bloc, principally the USSR.

Recent history: East

German Democratic Republic: Stone gate in the city of Rostock in the north of the country on the Mecklenburg Bay of the Baltic Sea.

Germany was ruled from its foundation in 1949 by Walter Ulbricht until his death in 1973. In that year the country was admitted, together with West Germany, to the United Nations, an indication that the division of the historic nation was accepted not only by each other but by the rest of the world. The office of president was abolished in 1960 and replaced by a Council of State.

WEST GERMANY

Official name: Federal Republic of Germany. Location: Western Europe. Area: 248,882 sq. km (96,094 sq. miles). Form of government: Federal republic. Estimated population (1975): 61,644,600 (including West Berlin). Official language: German. Official religion: None; about 50 per cent of the population belong to the Evangelical Church and 45 per cent to the Roman Catholic Church. Monetary unit: The Mark = 100 Pfennige.

The people: German-speaking tribes occupied a large part of Europe east of the Rhine and north of the Danube in Roman times. They later moved eastwards to colonize formerly Slav lands, but political unity was not achieved until 1871 under the leadership of Prussia.

Political divisions: The republic is divided into ten states (*Länder*), each of which has its own diet and considerable local autonomy. In addition West Berlin is also given Länder status in the federal constitution.

Principal cities and estimated population (1975): Bonn (capital) 283,800; West Berlin 1,984,837; Hamburg 1,717,400; Munich 1,314,900; Cologne 1,073,800; Essen 677,600; Düsseldorf 664,400; Frankfurt-on-Main 636,200; Dortmund 630,600; Stuttgart 600,500.

The land: The physical features of West Germany are very diverse, varying from the lowlands of the North German plains to minor Alpine ranges. The largest physical section consists of uplands rising from 300 to 1,500 m (1,000–5,000 ft), stretching from the northern plain right down to the Danube. Forests still cover most of it. The important rivers, largely because of the traffic they carry, are the Rhine, the Main and the Elbe, the latter forming the frontier with East Germany.

Climate: The climate is temperate, with an average annual temperature of 9°C (48°F). To the south the effect of greater height tends to offset the effect of latitude, so that the Bavarian Alps have a much colder winter than the lowlands and with a lot more snow.

Natural resources: The industrial development of Germany was based on its large mineral resources, especially of coal in the Ruhr, Saar and Aachen districts. Lignite is produced in the Cologne area, and natural gas has been found in the north west. Nuclear power stations are springing up along the major rivers. West Germany is richly endowed with regularly navigable rivers, all linked by canals.

About one-third of the land is arable and a large part is still forested, mostly with conifers which are being exploited.

Industry and exports: West Germany produces about four-fifths of its total food requirements; the main crops are cereals and root vegetables, and animal husbandry is also important. The country is the leading European steel producer; much of the heavy engineering (apart from shipbuilding) is concentrated in the Ruhr, but lighter engineering is more scattered. The country is the largest producer and

Federal Republic of Germany: The Neuschwanstein Castle is one of many such romantic buildings typical of the beautiful countryside of Bavaria.

exporter of automobiles in Europe; other industries include electrical engineering, chemicals, dyestuffs, pharmaceuticals and petrochemicals. Foreign trade until the 1970s was largely with western Europe, the United States and Japan, but there has now been a rapid growth with eastern Europe and the USSR.

Recent history: The policies of West Germany's first Chancellor, Konrad Adenauer, and his successor Ludwig Erhard made the country the strongest member, both financially and industrially, of the European Economic Community. A treaty was signed with East Germany in 1972 agreeing the basis of relations between the two countries, and in 1973 West Germany was admitted to the United Nations.

GHANA

Official name: Republic of Ghana. Location: West coast of Africa, between the Ivory Coast and Togo. Area: 238,539 sq. km (92,100 sq. miles). Form of government: Military regime. Population (1976): 9,600,000. Official language: English; there are also eight major national languages in use. Official religion: None; about 40 per cent of the population is Christian. Monetary unit: The new cedi = 100 pesewas. Principal towns and their population (1970 census): Accra (capital) 738,498; Kumasi 345,117; Takoradi 160,868; Tamala 83,653.

Colony of Gibraltar: This 'island fortress' has played an important strategic role in world politics for many centuries.

GIBRALTAR
Official name: Colony of Gibraltar. Location: Southern Europe, a narrow peninsula running southward from the south-west coast of Spain. Area: 5.8 sq. km (2.25 sq. miles). Political status: British colony. Estimated population (1975): 29,950. Official language: English; most of the population is bilingual in English and Spanish. Official religion: None; 70 per cent of the population is Roman Catholic. Monetary unit: The pound = 100 pence.

GILBERT ISLANDS
Official name: Colony of Gilbert Islands (formerly Gilbert and Ellice Islands). Location: Three groups of islands in south-western Pacific Ocean, straddling the equator. Area: 685 sq. km (264 sq. miles). Political status: Parliamentary republic.
Population (1973): 51,929. Official language: English. Official religion: None. Monetary unit: The Australian dollar = 100 cents. Capital: Tarawa (1973 population 17,188).

GREAT BRITAIN:
See United Kingdom. Page 244.

GREECE
Official name: Hellenic Republic. Location: Southern Europe; a mountainous peninsula between the Mediterranean and the Aegean, and numerous islands to south, east and west, the largest of which is Crete. Area: Mainland 106,778 sq. km (41,216 sq. miles); Crete

Hellenic Republic: Greek soldiers at the Acropolis show off their traditional full-sleeved costumes, complete with long-tasselled hats and shoes with pompons.

8,331 sq. km (3,216 sq. miles); other islands 16,877 sq. km (6,515 sq. miles); total 131,896 sq. km (50,912 sq. miles). Form of government: Presidential parliamentary republic. Population (1971 census): Mainland 7,475,599; Crete 456,642; other islands 836,400; total 8,768,641. Official language: Greek. Official religion: Eastern Orthodox Church of Christ. Monetary unit: The drachma = 100 leptae. Principal towns and their population (1971 census): Athens (capital) 867,023; Salonika 345,799; Piraeus 187,458; Patras 112,228; Iraklion (Crete) 78,209.

GREENLAND
Official name: Greenland. Location: North America. Area: 2,175,600 sq. km (840,000 sq. miles). Political status: Integral part of Danish realm. Population (1976) 49,666. Official language: Danish; Eskimo

languages are also used. Official religion: Evangelical Lutheran Church. Monetary unit: The krone = 100 øre. Capital: Godthåb.

GRENADA
Official name: State of Grenada. Location: Caribbean Sea; the most southerly of the Windward Islands, West Indies. Area: 344 sq. km (133 sq. miles). Political status: Republic. Estimated population (1975): 107,800. Official language: English. Official religion: None; the majority of the population is Christian. Monetary unit: The dollar = 100 cents. Capital: St George's (1972 estimated population 23,000).

GUATEMALA
Official name: Republic of Guatemala. Location: Central America. Area: 108,889 sq. km (42,042 sq. miles). Form of government: Military dictatorship. Estimated population (1976): 6,300,000. Official language: Spanish; Indian dialects are widely spoken. Official religion: Roman Catholicism. Monetary unit:

The quetzal = 100 centavos. Principal towns and their population (1973): Guatemala City (capital) 717,322; Escuintla 65,573; Quezaltenango 65,733; Totonicapán 52,599.

GUINEA

Official name: Republic of Guinea. Location: West Coast of Africa. Area: 245,857 sq. km (94,925 sq. miles). Form of government: Republic. Population (1972): 5,143,284. Official language: French, pending the introduction of one of the national languages as the official language. Official religion: None; the majority of the population is Moslem. Principal towns and their population (1972): Conachry (capital) 525,670; Siguiri 12,700; Labé 12,500; Kissi 8,600.

GUINEA-BISSAU

Official name: Republic of Guinea-Bissau (formerly Portuguese Guinea). Location: West coast of Africa. Area: 36,125 sq. km (13,948 sq. miles). Form of government: Popular republic. Estimated population (1972): 568,000. Official language: Portuguese. Official religion: Roman Catholicism. Monetary unit: The escudo = 100 centavos. Capital: Bissau (1971 estimated population 65,000).

GUYANA

Official name: Cooperative Republic of Guyana. Location: North coast of South America, between Venezuela and Surinam. Area: 214,970 sq. km (83,000 sq. miles). Form of government: Republic. Estimated population (1975): 780,000. Official language: English; Hindi, Urdu and Amer-indian dialects are also spoken. Official religion: None. Monetary unit: The dollar = 100 cents. Principal towns and their estimated population (1970): Georgetown (capital) 195,000; Linden 31,000; New Amsterdam 25,000.

HAITI

Official name: Republic of Haiti. Location: West coast

of island of Hispaniola, Caribbean Sea. Area: 27,750 sq. km (10,714 sq. miles). Form of government: Dictatorship. Population (1975 census): 4,583,785. Official language: French; a creole dialect is generally spoken. Official religion: Roman Catholicism; voodoo is widely practised. Monetary unit: The gourde = 100 centimes. Principal towns and their population (1975 census): Port-au-Prince (capital) 458,675; Cap Haitien 30,000 (1970); Les Cayes 14,000 (1970).

HONDURAS

Official name: Republic of Honduras. Location: Central America. Area: 112,088 sq. km (43,277 sq. miles). Form of government: Military regime. Population (1974 census): 2,752,000. Official language: Spanish. Official religion: None; Roman Catholicism is the predominant religion. Monetary unit: The lempira = 100 centavos. Principal towns and their population (1974 census): Tegucigalpa (capital) 270,645; San Pedro Sulla 133,730; Puerto Cortés 29,981; Tela 19,658.

HONG KONG

Official name: Crown Colony of Hong Kong.

Crown Colony of Hong Kong: Hundreds of families live on junks, sampans and barges.

Location: Eastern Asia, off the south coast of China. Area: 1,045 sq. km (404 sq. miles). Political status: British colony. Estimated population (1975): 4,380,000. Official language: English; Cantonese is also widely spoken. Official religion: None; the main religion is Buddhism. Monetary unit: The dollar = 100 cents. Capital: Victoria.

HUNGARY

Official name: Hungarian People's Republic. Location: Eastern Europe. Area: 93,032 sq. km (35,920 sq. miles). Form of government: Communist republic. Estimated population (1976): 10,672,000. Official language: Magyar. Official religion: None; Roman Catholicism is the largest single religious denomination. Monetary unit: The forint = 100 fillér. Principal towns and their estimated population (1975): Budapest (capital) 2,065,000; Miskolc 199,000; Debrecen 187,000; Pécs 163,000; Györ 119,000.

ICELAND

Official name: Republic of Iceland. Location: Northern Europe; island near the Arctic Circle in the North Atlantic. Area: 102,846 sq. km (39,699 sq. miles). Form of government: Parliamentary democracy. Population (1975): 219,033.

Official language: Icelandic. Official religion: Evangelical Lutheran Church. Monetary unit: The króna = 100 aurar. Principal towns and their population (1975): Reykjavik (capital) 84,856; Kópavogur 12,570; Akureyí 11,970; Hafnarfjörour 11,599.

INDIA

Official name: Union of India. Location: Subcontinent in southern Asia, with the Himalayas to the north, and flanked by the Arabian Sea to the west and the Bay of Bengal to the east. Area: 3,280,483 sq. km (1,266,602 sq. miles). Form of government: Federal republic. Estimated population (1976): 605,000,000. Official languages: Hindi and English. Official religion: None; over 80 per cent of the population is Hindu and about 10 per cent Moslem. Monetary unit: The rupee = 100 paisa.

The people: The people of India belong to all the major racial groups, but the majority (over 90 per cent) are Caucasian. This group includes the taller, lighter-skinned Indo-Aryans in the north and the shorter, darker-skinned in the south. The rest belong to tribes such as the Bhils, Nagas, Santals and Todas, and Mongoloid tribes from cental Asia are found along the northern borders.

The land: India falls naturally into three parts: the greater part, known as the Deccan, consisting of a tableland; the northern plain; and the Himalayas. The Deccan is highest in the west and slopes eastwards, with a narrow coast plain in the west and a broader but more undulating one in the east. The northern plain extends over 2,000 miles from the Arabian Sea to the Bay of Bengal and provides fertile lowland. The main river systems are the Indus (with tributaries Chenab, Jhelum, Sutlej, Beas and Ravi); Ganges (with its chief tributary the Yamuna); Brahmaputra (flowing into the Ganges delta); Marmada and Tapti in northern Deccan;

Union of India: The River Ganges has an important religious significance to the largely Hindu population and also serves as a social meeting place.

Godavari and Krishna in central Deccan. The Himalayas, the highest mountain system in the world, form an unbroken range, pierced in only two places: by the Indus in the west and the Dihang (Brahmaputra) in the extreme east.

Climate: A country so large and with such diverse physical features provides great variations of climate. There are three well-defined climatic seasons: The cool season (October–February) which provides temperate climate in the Ganges valley, though rather warm in the south; the hot season (March–June) which averages a temperature of 32°C (90°F); and the monsoon season (June–September) which causes some areas to have an average annual rainfall of between 200 and 300 cm (80 and 120 in).

Political divisions: The country is divided into 22 self-governing states, each having a governor appointed by the President of India. Each state has its own legislative, executive and judicial machinery. In addition there are nine union territories, administered by chief commissioners, lieutenant-governors or administrators appointed by the President.

Principal cities and their population (1971 census): Delhi (capital) 3,647,023; Calcutta 7,031,382; Greater Bombay 5,970,575; Madras 3,169,930; Hyderabad 1,769,339; Ahmedabad 1,741,522; Bangalore 1,653,779; Kanpur 1,275,242; Poona 1,135,034; Nagpur 930,459; Lucknow 813,982.

Natural resources: Agriculture is still the basis of the economy. Of the total area about 45 per cent is cultivated and 22 per cent forest. Forest resources are large and include high-value timber. Although in some areas the average yields per acre are very high, due partly to their producing several crops a year, the average yields are generally low; however they are increasing as a result of irrigation developments. Grain is the main crop, particularly rice, and there is a large production of sugar cane, oilseeds and groundnuts. Also India is the world's largest tea producer.

Coal and oil are produced in limited quantities, but there are vast reserves; there is an offshore oilfield in the Bay of Cambay. The country is particularly rich in iron and manganese ores, and bauxite is exploited on a small scale. Only a small proportion of the hydro-electricity potential is ·

exploited, but it is growing rapidly as new schemes come into use.

Industry and exports: The largest traditional industry is the spinning and weaving of cotton, providing one-fifth of the national income. The iron and steel industry has been given high priority in economic planning and large state enterprises have been established. Tea accounts for about 10 per cent of India's exports, and the country is the leading exporter of manganese ore and mica. Engineering, chemical, electrical and cement industries are growing rapidly.

Recent history: India gained her independence in 1947 and in 1950 the republic was inaugurated. There were military clashes with China in 1959 and 1962, and with Pakistan in 1965 and 1971; the defeat of Pakistan was decisive in establishing the state of Bangladesh. The ever-present problems of over-population and inadequate food supplies since independence have been a constant source of unrest among the people and a threat to political leaders.

After 11 years' continuous premiership Indira Gandhi was utterly defeated in the 1977 elections, thus ending the Congress Party's continuous rule since independence.

INDONESIA

Official name: Republic of Indonesia. Location: Group of islands between South-east Asia and Australia. Area: 2,027,087 sq. km (782,663 sq. miles). Form of government: Military-civilian dictatorship. Estimated population (1975): 132,000,000. Official language: Bahasa Indonesian. Official religion: None; over 90 per cent of the population is Moslem. Monetary unit: The rupiah = 100 sen. Principal towns and their estimated population (1972): Jakarta (capital) 6,100,000; Surabaja 1,400,000; Bandung 1,200,000; Semarang 635,000; Medan 622,000; Palembang 616,000; Makasar 499,000.

IRAN

Official name: Iran. Location: South-western Asia. Area: 1,648,000 sq. km (636,296 sq. miles). Form of government: Islamic republic. Estimated population (1975): 33,010,000. Official language: Persian (Farsi). Official religion: Islam. Monetary unit: The rial = 100 dinars. Principal towns and their estimated population (1973): Teheran (capital) 4,000,000; Isfahan 520,000; Meshed 510,000; Tabriz 465,000; Shiraz 325,000; Abadan 300,000.

Iran: The importance of oil in the world economy has brought immense wealth and industrial development to Iran.

IRAQ

Official name: Republic of Iraq. Location: South-western Asia; an almost land-locked state with a narrow outlet to the Persian Gulf. Area: 438,446 sq. km (169,240 sq. miles). Form of government: Military-civilian dictatorship. Estimated population (1976): 11,505,300. Official language: Arabic. Official religion: Islam. Monetary unit: The dinar = 5 riyals = 20 dirhams = 1,000 fils. Principal towns and their estimated population (1970): Baghdad (capital) 2,696,000; Basrah 430,150; Mosul 353,100.

IRELAND

Official name: Irish Republic. Location: The most westerly part of Europe, occupying 83 per cent of the area of the whole of the island of Ireland. Area: 68,893 sq. km (26,600 sq. miles). Form of government: Parliamentary democracy. Population (1971 census): 2,978,248. Official language: Irish, but English is universally spoken. Religion: 95 per cent Roman Catholic. Monetary unit: The pound = 100 pence.

Principal towns and their population (1971 census): Dublin (capital) 567,866; Cork 128,645; Limerick 57,161; Waterford 31,968; Galway 27,726.

Land and climate: The island consists of a central plain surrounded by a broken fringe of highlands; much of this plain is drained by the River Shannon, the longest river in the British Isles. The lowlands have excellent pasture and farmland, and some of the country's largest peat bogs. The highest mountains around the edge rise in the north and near the west coast.

Ireland has a mild climate with a lot of rain. Temperatures average 5°C (40°F) in winter and 16°C (60°F) in summer. Annual rainfall averages between 100 cm and 150 cm (40–60 in) according to the altitude.

Economy: The economy is mainly based on agricultural resources, particularly livestock, and there is a valuable catch of fish. Lead-zinc ores are being mined; copper ore is also worked and copper concentrates exported. Manufacturing processes are mostly concerned with the processing of agricultural produce, especially dairy products. Brewing and distilling is also important.

Recent history: Ireland became a full member of the European Economic Community (together with Britain) following a national referendum.

The 1973 general election resulted in a coalition government with Liam Cosgrave of Fine Gael as prime minister, but there was a reversion to a Fianna Fail majority in the 1977 election, Jack Lynch replacing Cosgrave as prime minister.

IRELAND, NORTHERN:

See United Kingdom.

State of Israel: Israel has now become the spiritual and actual home of Jews from many countries.

ISRAEL

Official name: State of Israel. Location: South-western Asia, at the eastern end of the Mediterranean Sea. Area: 20,700 sq. km (7,992 sq. miles). Form of government: Parliamentary democracy. Estimated population (1976): 3,400,000. Official languages: Hebrew and Arabic; many European languages are also spoken. Official religion: None; Judaism is the religion followed by the great majority. Monetary unit: The pound = 100 agorot.

Principal towns and their estimated population (1975): Jerusalem 344,200; Tel-Aviv/Jaffa 357,600; Haifa 225,000; Ramat Gan 120,200; Bat-Yam 114,000; Holon 110,300; Petach Tikva 103,000.

Land and climate: Israel can be divided into three regions, all running parallel to the Mediterranean coast: a low coastal strip in the west consisting of fertile level alluvium; the central highlands forming a flat-topped plateau cut by deep wadis; and a trough in the east formed by the Jordan valley stretching down to the Gulf of Aqaba, but interrupted in the centre

by part of Jordan.

The climate is typically Mediterranean; all areas are dry from May to September, later in the south. Annual rainfall averages 68 cm (25 in) on the coastal plain, more in the northern hills and much less in the south.

Economy: Israel is one of the world's chief exporters of citrus fruit, and there is a growing market for wine. The most important mineral products are diamonds, which account for over a third of the total revenue from exports. Potash salts and bromine are also an important part of the economy. Manufactures include chemicals, cement, precision instruments, textiles, glass and ceramics.

Recent history: There has been a continuing dispute with the Arab states since Israel was established which led to wars in 1956 and 1967. Parts of the Jordanian and Syrian territories were occupied, and also the Sinai peninsula as far as the Suez Canal. Fighting broke out again in 1973 with Egyptian and Syrian forces, but a tenuous ceasefire was eventually negotiated with Egypt as a result of American intervention.

Ephraim Katzir was elected president in 1973 and General Yizhak Rabin succeeded Golda Meir as prime minister in 1977.

ITALY

Official name: Italian Republic. Location: Southern Europe; boot-shaped peninsula extending into the Mediterranean Sea. Area: 301,253 sq. km (116,314 sq. miles). Form of government: Presidential democracy. Estimated population (1973): 55,152,750. Official language: Italian; many regions have their own dialect. Official religion: Roman Catholicism. Monetary unit: The lira.

The people: The original races of Italy were of diverse origin and how they came to settle there is still obscure. The country was more or less united by the Romans, and the later incursions by northern races in the 5th and 7th centuries AD had little lasting impact.

Political divisions: The country is divided into 20 autonomous regions and subdivided into 92 provinces. Five of the regions (Sicily, Sardinia, Aosta, Trento-Alto Adige and Friulu-Venezia Giulia) have their own parliamentary governments.

Main cities and their population (1975): Rome (capital) 2,874,838; Milan 1,722,637; Naples 1,220,732; Turin 1,199,348; Genoa 804,204; Palermo 666,165; Bologna 489,642; Florence 465,312; Catania 399,419; Bari 379,654; Venice 364,550.

The land: The Italian peninsula is for the most part mountainous, but between the Apennine range, which forms the backbone of the country, and the east coast are large, fertile plains. The northern plain forms about one-seventh of the total area and drains into the River Po. Further north the Italian Alps average a height of 1,300 m (4,300 ft) with 11 peaks rising to over 3,950 m (13,000 ft). This area also has many lakes of glacial origin. As well as the long boot-shaped peninsula, the country consists of two major islands: Sicily and Sardinia.

Climate: The great differences in latitude and

altitude are responsible for a contrast in climates. The western side of the Apennines is more humid than the Adriatic slopes, while the Alps offer protection from cold northerly winds. The differences in temperature are only slight in the summer months but considerable in winter, varying from an average of 1°C (34°F) in the north to 10°C (50°F) in Sicily. The Alpine areas may have an annual precipitation as high as 300 cm (120 in), the northern and coastal plains between 60 and 75 cm (24–30 in), while Apulia in the south has less than 40 cm (16 in).

Natural resources: In spite of the high proportion of mountainous area, Italy has a comparatively generous area of arable land. Cereals are grown extensively especially in the northern plain, and vines are widespread.

There is only a small output of coal, and other deposits mined in limited quantities are iron ore, bauxite and sulphur. Italy

Italian Republic: Gondolas on the Grand Canal in Venice attract thousands of foreign tourists every year.

is responsible for about one-fifth of the world production of mercury.

About 40 per cent of the electricity produced is from hydrostations, most of them situated in the Alps.

Industry and exports: The traditional textile and clothing industries, located mainly in the north, have now been expanded by the development of synthetic fibres. Specialized foods, such as pasta and conserves, also form a sizable feature in the balance of payments. The major industry, however, is undoubtedly automobile manufacture and assembly. Italian firms also play a leading part overseas in constructional engineering. The tourist industry has been lavishly encouraged by state-subsidized agencies and the value of this trade plays an important part in Italian economy.

Recent history: Economic recovery, due largely to the development of the tourist industry, the automobile and other engineering activities, made Italy an equal partner in economic terms with other founder nations of the European Economic Community.

However, internal political instability, evidenced by over 35 governments in 30 years, was brought to a critical level in the 1976 election when the Communist Party only just failed to receive more votes than the Christian Democrat Party.

IVORY COAST

Official name: Republic of Ivory Coast. Location: West coast of Africa. Area: 322,463 sq. km (124,471 sq. miles). Form of government: Presidential rule. Population (1975 census): 6,673,013. Official language: French. Official religion: None; about 12 per cent of the population is Christian, the remainder follow traditional beliefs. Monetary unit: The franc = 100 centimes. Principal towns and their estimated population (1976): Abidjan (capital) 850,000; Bouaké 220,000; Daloa 130,000.

JAMAICA

Official name: Jamaica. Location: Island in Caribbean Sea, 150 km (90 miles) south of Cuba. Area: 10,991 sq. km (4,244 sq. miles). Form of government: Parliamentary state.

Jamaica: The traditional method of carrying fruit gives grace and poise.

Estimated population (1975): 2,060,300. Official language: English. Official religion: None; the majority of the population is Christian of various denominations. Monetary unit: The dollar – 100 cents. Capital: Kingston (1971 population 111,879).

JAPAN

Official name: Nippon Koku —Land of the Rising Sun. Location: Crescent-shaped archipelago forming the eastern margin of the Asian continent; Area: 372,488 sq. km (143,818 sq. miles). Form of government: Constitutional monarchy. Population (1975 census): 111,930,000. Official language: Japanese. Official religion: None; the major religions are Shinto and Buddhism. Monetary unit: The yen = 100 sen.

The people: Some of the first settlers in Japan were the Ainu, a white race that has gradually been absorbed into other races that came from the Asian mainland and the South Pacific. Generally speaking the Japanese today are a mixture of Ainu, Malay and Mongol.

Political divisions: Japan is divided into 47 prefectures, each governed by an elected governor and assembly.

Principal cities and their estimated population (1975): Tokyo (capital) 8,643,000; Osaka 2,779,000; Yokohama 2,622,000; Nagoya 2,080,000; Kyoto 1,461,000; Kobe 1,361,000; Sapporo 1,241,000;

Nippon Koku: Formal movement complements the elaborate make-up and elegant silk kimono with gracefully tied obi of this lovely Japanese dancer.

Kita-Kyushu 1,058,000.

The land: The four main islands of Japan, Hokkaido, Honshu, Shikoku and Kyushu, form a great arc fringed by a multitude of minor islands and reefs. Mountains occupy over three-quarters of the area, and many of the valleys are green and rocky. One of the mountain ranges forms a longitudinal spine through the whole arc of islands, which in Honshu, the largest island, forms the so-called Japanese Alps. The highest point is the volcanic cone of Mount Fuji (3,776 m; 12,388 ft); many other volcanic features are found as well as hot springs. Plains are limited in extent and are mostly coastal, the largest being the Kanto Plain on which stands Tokyo. The mountains streams are short and swift.

Climate: The greater part of Japan is in sub-tropical latitudes, but there are great differences in winter temperatures between north and south. Cold ocean currents from the north and a warm one from the south influence the climate, but conditions are largely determined by the monsoon wind system of eastern Asia. The range of summer temperatures is much smaller, varying from 16°C (61°F) in the north to 27°C (80°F) in the south. Most districts have over 100 cm (40 in) of rain, distributed throughout the year, but reaching a maximum in the summer. All parts of the country have snow in winter.

Natural resources: Japan has large reserves of coal, but it provides only some 20 per cent of the energy requirements: hydro-electricity provides another 10 per cent. There are also small amounts of oil and natural gas. Lead, zinc, manganese, chrome, copper and iron ore resources are also available in limited quantities, but not enough to keep the highly industrialized economy supplied. Japan is self-sufficient in sulphur and there is a surplus of mercury.

The dominant crop is rice, but there is now a conscious expansion in the production of other agricultural foodstuffs, such as sugar beet, vegetables and fruit. Japan has one of the world's biggest fish catches and it is one of the countries still operating a whaling fleet.

Industry and exports: Metallurgical, metal-working and engineering industries form the basis of Japanese economy. About half the world's tonnage of new ships is built there (a large part of which is made up of supertankers) and the automobile industry is second only to that of the United States. The enormous amounts of oil, iron ore, coal and other materials these industries demand have led to a large commercial fleet.

The traditional export of textiles (including natural silk) has now easily been overtaken by cars and shipping, precision instruments such as cameras, electronic products and computers. The largest single export market is the United States, but a quarter of the exports go to South-east Asia, and western Europe also offers a valuable market.

Recent history: The monarchy (Emperor Hirohito) was restored in 1952 and a vast and coordinated national effort in building up the economy has since been made with spectacular results. This has been accompanied by great social advantages to the individual, and political stability has been shown by the return for nearly three decades up to 1976 of the Liberal Democrat Party.

JORDAN
Official name: The Hashemite Kingdom of the Jordan. Location: South-western Asia; almost land-locked state separated from the Mediterranean by Israel. Area: 95,594 sq. km (36,909 sq. miles). Form of government: Constitutional monarchy. Estimated population (1976): 2,752,000. Official language: Arabic. Official religion: Islam. Monetary unit: The dinar = 1,000 fils. Principal towns and their estimated population (1974): Amman (capital) 615,000; Zarka 232,000; Irbid 116,000.

KAMPUCHEA:
See Cambodia.

KENYA
Official name: Republic of Kenya. Location: On the equator on the east coast of Africa. Area: 582,646 sq. km (224,961 sq. miles). Form

Republic of Kenya: Tall and graceful, the Masai continue their tribal existence relatively unchanged by the 20th century.

of government: One-party
democracy. Estimated
population (1975):
13,400,000. Official language:
Swahili; English, Kikuyu
and Luo are also widely
spoken. Official religion:
None; a quarter of the
population is Christian, 6
per cent Moslem, and the
rest follow traditional
beliefs. Monetary unit: The
shilling = 100 cents.
Principal towns and their
estimated population (1975):
Nairobi (capital) 700,000;
Mombasa 340,000; Kisumu
149,000; Nakuru 66,000;
Eldoret 30,000.

KHMER REPUBLIC:
See Cambodia.

KOREA, NORTH
Official name: Democratic
People's Republic of Korea.
Location: Eastern Asia,
northern part of Korean
peninsula. Area: 121,200 sq.
km (46,800 sq. miles). Form
of government: Communist
republic. Estimated
population (1975): 16,000,000.
Official language: Korean.
Official religion: None;
Buddhism, Confucianism,
Taoism, Shamanism and
Chundo are all practised.
Monetary unit: The won =
100 jon. Principal towns and
their estimated population
(1975): Pyongyang (capital)
1,500,000; Chongjin 200,000;
Heungnam 150,000.

KOREA, SOUTH
Official name: Republic of
Korea. Location: Eastern
Asia, southern part of
Korean peninsula. Area:
98,477 sq. km (38,022 sq.
miles). Form of government:
Presidential democracy.
Population (1975 census):
34,708,542. Official language:
Korean. Official religion:
None; Buddhism is the
principal religion. Monetary
unit: The won = 10 hwan =
100 chun. Principal towns
and their population (1975
census): Seoul (capital)
6,889,470; Pusan 2,454,051;
Taegu 1,311,078; Inchon
799,982; Kwangchu 607,058;
Taejon 506,703; Masan 371,937.

KUWAIT
Official name: State of
Kuwait. Location: South-
western Asia; north west of
extreme of Persian Gulf.

Area: 24,280 sq. km (9,375
sq. miles). Form of
government: Semi-
constitutional monarchy.
Population (1975 census):
990,380 including about
400,000 non-Kuwaitis.
Official language: Arabic;
English is widely used.
Official religion: Islam.
Monetary unit: The dinar =
1,000 fils. Principal towns:
Kuwait City (capital);
Hawalli; Salmiya.

LAOS
Official name: People's
Democratic Republic of
Laos. Location: Small
land-locked country in
South-east Asia. Area:
236,800 sq. km (91,400 sq.
miles). Form of government:
People's republic. Estimated
population (1976): 2,900,000.
Official language: Laotian;
French is also widely
spoken. Official religion:
Buddhism. Monetary unit:
The kip = 10 bi = 100 at.
Principal towns and their
population (1973 census):
Vientiane (capital) 176,637;
Savannakct 50,690; Pakse
44,860; Luang Prabang
44,244.

LEBANON
Official name: Republic of
Lebanon. Location:
South-western Asia, at
eastern end of
Mediterranean. Area:
10,230 sq. km (3,950 sq.
miles). Form of government:
Presidential democracy.
Estimated population (1974):
2,780,000. Official language:
Arabic; French and English
are also widely used. Official
religion: None; there are
almost equal numbers of
Moslems and Christians.
Monetary unit: The pound
= 100 piastres. Principal
towns and their estimated
population (1976): Beirut
(capital) 702,000; Tripoli
175,000; Zahlé 46,800; Saida
(Sidon) 24,800; Tyre 14,000.

LESOTHO
Official name: Kingdom of
Lesotho (formerly the
British High Commission
Territory of Basutoland).
Location: Southern Africa,
completely surrounded by
the Republic of South
Africa. Area: 30,340 sq. km
(11,716 sq. miles). Form of
government: Constitutional

monarchy. Estimated
population (1975): 1,180,000.
Official languages: English
and Sesotho. Official
religion: None; about 70 per
cent of the population is
Christian. Monetary unit:
The South African rand =
100 cents. Capital: Maseru
(1975 estimated population
30,000).

LIBERIA
Official name: Republic of
Liberia. Location: West
coast of Africa. Area:
111,400 sq. km (43,000 sq.
miles). Form of government:
Constitutional democracy.
Population (1974 census):
1,496,000. Official language:
English; many tribal
languages and dialects are
also used. Official religion:
None. Monetary unit: The
dollar = 100 cents. Capital:
Monrovia (1974 population
171,680).

LIBYA
Official name: Libyan Arab
Republic. Location: North
Africa, along Mediterranean
coast. Area: 1,759,540 sq.
km (679,358 sq. miles). Form
of government: Islamic
people's republic. Population
(1973 census): 2,257,037.
Official language: Arabic;
English and Italian are
widely spoken. Official
religion: Islam. Monetary
unit: The dinar = 1,000
dirhams. Principal towns and
their population (1973
census): Tripoli (capital)
551,477; Benghazi 282,192;
Misurata 103,302.

LIECHTENSTEIN
Official name: Principality
of Liechtenstein. Location:
Western Europe, between
Austria and Switzerland.
Area: 160 sq. km (61.8 sq.
miles). Form of government:
Constitutional monarchy.
Population (1975 census):
23,947. Official language:
German; Alemannish (a
German dialect) is widely
spoken. Official religion:
Roman Catholicism.
Monetary unit: The Swiss
franc = 100 rappen
(centimes). Capital: Vaduz
(1975 population 4,472).

LUXEMBURG
Official name: Grand Duchy
of Luxemburg. Location:
Western Europe, between

France and Germany. Area:
2,586 sq. km (999 sq. miles).
Form of government:
Constitutional monarchy.
Estimated population (1975):
357,000. Official languages:
French and German; the
spoken language is
Letzeburgish (a German
dialect). Official religion:
None; the population is
predominantly Roman
Catholic. Monetary unit:
The franc = 100 centimes.
Principal towns and their
estimated population (1975):
Luxemburg (capital) 78,400;
Esch-Alzette 27,800;
Differdange 18,300;
Dudelange 14,700.

MADAGASCAR
Official name: Democratic
Republic of Madagascar.
Location: Island 500 km
(300 miles) off the coast of
Mozambique, southern
Africa. Area: 586,486 sq. km
(266,444 sq. miles). Form of
government: Military
government. Estimated
population (1977): 8,000,000.
Official languages:
Malagasy and French.
Official religion: None;
about 40 per cent of the
population is Christian and
10 per cent Moslem.
Monetary unit: The franc =
100 centimes. Principal
towns and their estimated
population (1972):
Tananarive (capital)
366,500; Majunga 67,500;
Tamatave 59,500;
Fianarantsoa 58,800;
Diégo-Suarez 48,000.

MALDIVES
Official name: Republic of
Maldives. Location:
Consists of some 2,000
islands (220 of which are
inhabited) in the Indian
Ocean, about 650 km (406
miles) south west of Sri
Lanka. Area: 298 sq. km
(115 sq. miles). Form of
government: Presidential
democracy in an elective
republic. Estimated
population (1976): 140,000.
Official language: Divehi.
Official religion: Islam.
Monetary unit: The rupee =
100 larees. Capital: Malé
(1976 estimated population
17,000).

MALI
Official name: Republic of
Mali. Location: Inland state

in West Africa. Area:
1,240,142 sq. km (478,822 sq.
miles). Form of government:
Military-civilian rule.
Estimated population (1976):
5,600,000. Official language:
French; a number of African
languages are widely
spoken. Official religion:
None; about 65 per cent of
the population is Moslem.
Monetary unit: The franc =
100 centimes. Principal
towns and their estimated
population (1976): Bamako
(capital) 215,700; Ségou
36,400; Kayes 34,100; Mopti
32,400; Sikasso 26,000.

MALAWI

Official name: Republic of
Malawi (formerly the
British Protectorate of
Nyasaland). Location:
Inland state in southern
central Africa. Area:
118,484 sq. km (45,747 sq.
miles). Form of government:
One-party democracy.
Estimated population (1976):
5,175,000. Official language:
English. Official religion:
None; the majority of the
population follows
traditional beliefs.
Monetary unit: The
kwacha = 100 tambala.
Principal towns and their
estimated population (1975):
Lilongue (capital) 102,000;
Blantyre 193,000; Zomba
(capital until 1975) 19,700;
Mzuzu 14,700.

MALAYSIA

Official name: The
Federation of Malaysia.
Location: South-eastern
Asia; consists of
peninsular Malaysia on the
mainland, and Sabah and
Sarawak in northern
Borneo. Area: 329,736 sq.
km (127,316 sq. miles). Form
of government: Federal
parliamentary democracy.
Estimated population (1976):
peninsular Malaysia
10,131,000; Sabah 795,700;
Sarawak 1,115,900; total
12,042,600. Official language:
Bahasa Malaysia, but
English is widely used.
Official religion: Islam.
Monetary unit: The dollar =
100 cents. Principal towns
and their population (1970
census): Kuala Lumpur
(federal capital) 451,810;
Kota Kinabalu (capital of
Sabah, formerly known as
Jesselton) 42,000; Kuching

(capital of Sarawak) 63,535;
Georgetown 269,247; Ipoh
247,969; Johore Bharu
136,229.

MALTA

Official name: Republic of
Malta. Location: Southern
Europe; islands (including
the islands of Como and
Comino) in central
Mediterranean. Area: 316
sq. km (122 sq. miles). Form
of government:
Parliamentary democracy.
Estimated population (1974):
297,622. Official languages:
Maltese and English.
Official religion: Roman
Catholicism. Monetary unit:
The pound = 100 cents.
Capital: Valetta (1975
population 14,048).

MARTINIQUE

Official name: Department
of Martinique. Location:
Windward Islands in
Caribbean Sea. Area: 1,116
sq. km (431 sq. miles).
Political status: French
overseas department.
Estimated population (1974):
342,000. Official language:
French. Official religion:
None. Capital: Fort-de-
France (1974 estimated
population 97,000).

*Department of Martinique:
Peasants on a mule transport
freshly harvested sugar cane, a
major Caribbean crop.*

MAURITANIA

Official name: Islamic
Republic of Mauritania.
Location: West coast of
Africa. Area: 1,030,700 sq.
km (397,950 sq. miles). Form
of government: One-party
democracy. Estimated
population (1976): 1,500,000.
Official languages: Arabic
and French; most people
speak Arabic or Hassaniya.
Official religion: None, but

the population is almost
entirely Moslem. Monetary
unit: The ougiyas = 5
khoums. Principal towns
and their estimated
population (1976):
Nouakchott (capital) 70,000;
Nouadhibou 130,000; Kaédi
13,000; Atar 13,000; Rosso
13,000.

MAURITIUS

Official name: Mauritius.
Location: Eastern Africa;
island in Indian Ocean.
Area: 1,865 sq. km (720 sq.
miles). Form of government:
Parliamentary democracy.
Estimated population (1976):
867,200. Official language:
English; French is also
widely spoken, and Creole,
Hindi, Urdu and Chinese
are spoken by minority
groups. Official religion:
None; most Europeans and
Creoles are Roman
Catholic, the Indians are
either Moslem or Hindu.
Monetary unit: The rupee =
100 cents. Principal towns
and their estimated
population (1976): Port
Louis (capital) 139,600; Beau
Bassin/Rose Hill 79,000;
Curepipe 58,000.

*United Mexican States: There
are many of these spectacular
relics of the bygone Aztec
civilization of Mexico. This
'Pyramid of the Sorceror' is
located on the Yucatan
Peninsula.*

MEXICO

Official name: United
Mexican States. Location:
Latin American state in
southern part of North
America. Area: 1,972,547 sq.
km (761,600 sq. miles). Form
of government: Federal
one-party democracy.
Estimated population (1976):
62,329,000. Official language:
Spanish. Official religion:
None; over 90 per cent of
the population is Roman
Catholic. Monetary unit:
The peso = 100 centavos.

Principal cities and their
estimated population (1976):
Mexico City (capital)
9,000,000; Guadalajara
2,000,000; Monterrey
1,500,000; Ciudad
Netzahualcóyotl 680,000;
Ciudad Juárez 570,000;
León 557,000; Puebla de
Zaragoza 516,000; Mexicali
390,400; Chihuahua 386,000;
Culiacán 358,800.

Land and climate: The
core of Mexico consists of a
broad plateau, bounded on
the east and west by a rim
of mountains. To the south
is a high volcanic zone
where high snow-covered
conical peaks dominate the
landscape. Most of the
drainage of the plateau is
towards inland basins, but
the Rio Grande (Rio Bravo
in Mexican) drains the
northern part.

In the south the coastal

Kingdom of Morocco: Narrow streets are typical of Marrakesh.

lowlands are always hot, the southern plateau may be 10°C (21°F) cooler, and the higher peaks are permanently covered in snow. The rainfall is equally varied, ranging from less than 25 cm (10 in) a year in the north of the plateau to 150 cm (60 in) in the south.

Economy: Cotton was formerly the main export, but this has now dropped sharply, giving way to cattle products, fish (tuna) mostly to the United States, and hard fibres. Silver is found in many places, often in association with lead-zinc ores. Copper, iron ore, manganese ore, sulphur and fluorite all contribute to the economy. Oil and natural gas supply 90 per cent of the country's energy needs. The textile and clothing industries are important, while iron and steel production feed the foundries, rolling mills and engineering workshops.

Recent history: Mexico achieved a considerable degree of economic stability during the Second World War and after as a result of financial help from the United States. Heavy unemployment, much land expropriation and a rapid depreciation of the peso after 22 years of stability marked the last six months of the presidency of Gustavo Diaz Ordaz who was succeeded in 1976 by José López Portillo.

MONACO

Official name: Principality of Monaco. Location: Western Europe; on French Mediterranean coast. Area: 1.89 sq. km (0.73 sq. miles). Form of government: Constitutional monarchy. Estimated population (1971): 23,500. Official language: French. Official religion: Roman Catholicism. Monetary unit: The French franc = 100 centimes. Capital: Monte Carlo (estimated population 1971, 10,000).

MONGOLIA

Official name: Mongolian People's Republic. Location: Central Asia, with the USSR to the north, and China to the south, east and west. Area: 1,565,000 sq. km (604,000 sq. miles). Form of government: Communist republic. Estimated population (1974): 1,380,000. Official language: Mongol; Kazakh is spoken in one state. Official religion: None; traces of Buddhism and Lamaism survive. Monetary unit: The tögrög (tughrik) = 100 möngö. Principal towns and their estimated population (1976): Ulan Bator (capital) 320,000; Darkhan 35,000.

MOROCCO

Official name: Kingdom of Morocco. Location: Extreme north west of Africa. Area: Officially given as 458,730 sq. km (177,070 sq. miles). Form of government: Absolute monarchy. Estimated population (1973): 16,310,000. Official language: Arabic, but a large minority speak Berber; Spanish and French are also used widely. Official religion: Islam. Monetary unit: The franc = 100 dirham. Principal cities and their estimated population (1973): Rabat (capital) 702,600 (including Sale); Casablanca 1,894,400; Marrakesh 1,642,600; Kenitra 1,415,600; Agadir 1,220,600; Fez 1,137,800; Safi 942,600.

MOZAMBIQUE

Official name: People's Republic of Mozambique. Location: East African coast, opposite Madagascar. Area: 784,961 sq. km (302,995 sq. miles). Form of government: Popular republic. Estimated population (1977): 9,000,000. Official language: Portuguese. Official religion: None. Monetary unit: The escudo = 100 centavos. Capital: Maputo (formerly known as Lourenço Marques), estimated population (1977): 442,000.

NAURU

Official name: Republic of Nauru. Location: Small island in Central Pacific. Area: 21.25 sq. km (8.2 sq. miles). Form of government: Presidential democracy. Population (1976): 8,007 about half of whom are Nauruans. Official language: English. Official religion: Nauruan Protestant Church. Monetary unit: The Australian dollar = 100 cents.

NEPAL

Official name: Kingdom of Nepal. Location: Land-locked state in central Himalayas, southern Asia. Area: 140,798 sq. km (54,362 sq. miles). Form of government: Semi-constitutional monarchy. Estimated population (1973): 11,700,000. Official language: Nepali, spoken in varying dialects. Official religion: None; half the population is Hindu and the rest mainly Buddhist. Monetary unit: The rupee = 100 paisa. Principal towns and their estimated population (1973): Kathmandu (capital) 195,300; Patan 135,250; Bhadgaon 84,240.

THE NETHERLANDS

Official name: Kingdom of the Netherlands. Location: Western Europe, facing the North Sea. Area: 41,160 sq. km (15,892 sq. miles). Form of government: Constitutional monarchy. Estimated population (1975): 13,733,600. Official religion: None. Monetary unit: The guilder = 100 cents.

Principal towns and cities and their estimated population (1976): Amsterdam (constitutional capital) 752,500; The Hague (seat of government) 479,369; Rotterdam 614,767; Utrecht 250,887; Eindhoven 192,562; Haarlem 164,672; Groningen 163,357; Arnhem 126,051.

Land and climate: The highest point in the Netherlands is 322 m (1,057 ft), but about two-fifths of the country lies below sea-level; it is protected

Kingdom of the Netherlands: Modern Holland is still a picturesque country of canals, flat countryside and windmills.

from tidal inundation by dunes and dykes. Much of the remainder consists of sandy regions which are only rarely about 90 m (300 ft). The country is intersected by a network of waterways, both natural and man-made, and reclamation of land is still continuing. The principal river is the Rijn (Rhine) with its tributaries the Ijssel, Lek and Waal; the Maas (Meuse) and Scheldt also reach the North Sea through the Netherlands. The weather is changeable, with frequent westerly winds. Average July and January temperatures are 17°C (62°F) and 5°C (41°F) respectively.

Economy: Over 70 per cent of the land is cultivated; cereals are the main crop. The country is the world's largest exporter of potatoes, cheese, eggs and pork. Intensive horticulture also provides much exportable produce. The food processing and fishing industries are both flourishing. The coal industry has been phased out but oil and natural gas provide alternative sources of power; natural gas is exported to neighbouring countries and there is a large refining industry based on imported crude oil. The many other important industries include steel production, shipbuilding, chemicals (especially superphosphates) and textiles.

Recent history: Queen Wilhelmina abdicated after a reign of 50 years in 1948 and was succeeded by her daughter Juliana. The Netherlands was one of the original six founder members of the European Economic Community established in 1958.

NEW ZEALAND

Official name: New Zealand. Location: South-west Pacific, 1,900 km (1,200 miles) from Australia. Area: 268,676 sq. km (103,736 sq. miles). Form of government: Parliamentary state. Population (1976 census): 3,129,383. Official language: English. Official religion: None. Monetary unit: The

New Zealand: Mount Ngauruhoe in Tongariro National Park on the North Island is a spectacular sight. The volcano is still active.

dollar = 100 cents.

The people: About 90 per cent of New Zealanders are descendants of British stock and a small proportion originate from European countries other than the British Isles. Earlier settlers, the Maoris, came to New Zealand in the 14th century from Polynesia; they now number about 250,000.

Political divisions: New Zealand is divided into counties, some of which are subdivided into ridings.

Principal towns and their population (1976): Wellington (capital) 349,628; Auckland 797,406; Christchurch 325,710; Hamilton 154,606; Dunedin 120,426.

The land: New Zealand has three main islands: North, South and Stewart; in addition there are a large number of small islands forming a wide arc around the main islands. The plateau at the southern end of South Island slopes southwards and the rest of the island is dominated by the Southern Alps, with the highest point at Mount Cook. The only true plains are the lowlands built by river deposits; these include the Canterbury Plains and the plains formed by the Clutha river which is the swiftest of many

fast-flowing rivers in New Zealand.

The mountain ranges in the main part of North Island are a continuation of the Southern Alps, and the northern part forms a narrow peninsula with rolling hills and low mountains, The longest river is the Waikato, and the thermal region near Rotorua has geysers and hot springs.

Climate: The climate is temperate, maritime with moderate temperatures, high humidity and abundant sunshine. Winters are mild and in general rainfall is reliable and well-distributed. Average temperatures in Auckland range from 23°C (73°F) in January to 10°C (50°F) in August. Comparable figures for Dunedin are 19°C (66°F) and 3°C (37°F).

Natural resources: The economy of New Zealand is basically agricultural, dependent on grassland, and serious efforts are being made to develop the potentialities of the fisheries and forests. Black sands, which can produce a high yield of iron, are found in both North and South Island. A vast field of natural gas has been discovered and will eventually supply quantities far in excess of the country's needs, but hydro-electricity is at present the greatest energy source.

Industry and exports: Of New Zealand's total exports

90 per cent are agricultural, the chief being meat (lamb and beef), dairy produce and wool; an important by-product of the butter production is the large export of casein. The chief manufactured products include aluminium, flour, machinery and textiles. Formerly the bulk of the exports went to Britain, but since Britain's entry into the Common Market New Zealand has sought other markets, and now has a growing trade with the United States and Japan.

Recent history: In 1951 New Zealand signed a mutual defence pact with Australia and the United States (ANZUS), and in 1954 became a member of the South-East Asia Treaty Organization.

NICARAGUA

Official name: Republic of Nicaragua. Location: Central American isthmus. Area: 128,875 sq. km (49,759 sq. miles). Form of government: Military dictatorship. Estimated population (1976): 2,253,100. Official language: Spanish; English is widely understood. Official religion: None; the dominant religion is Roman Catholicism. Monetary unit: The córdoba = 100 centimes. Principal towns and their estimated population (1974): Managua (capital) 449,600; León 61,650; Matagalpa 61,400; Granada 24,200.

NIGER

Official name: Republic of Niger. Location: Land-locked state in West Africa. Area: 1,186,408 sq. km (458,075 sq. miles). Form of government: Military junta. Estimated population (1974): 4,239,000. Official language: French; numerous indigenous languages are also spoken. Official religion: None; about 85 per cent of the population is Moslem. Monetary unit: The franc = 100 centimes. Principal towns and their estimated population (1974): Niamey (capital) 102,000; Zinder 39,000; Maradi 37,000; Tahoua 31,000.

NIGERIA

Official name: Federation of Nigeria. Location: West coast of Africa, within the Gulf of Guinea. Area: 923,773 sq. km (356,669 sq. miles). Form of government: Federal military government. Estimated population (1973) 79,800,000. Official language: English; Hausa, Ibo and Yoruba are also spoken. Official religion: None; northern Nigeria is mainly Moslem and southern Nigeria predominantly Christian. Monetary unit: The nairo = 100 kobo. Principal towns and their estimated population (1973): Lagos (capital) 665,250; Abuja is the capital designate; Ibadan 627,400; Ogbomosho 320,000; Kano 295,500; Oshogbo 209,000; Abeokuta 187,300; Port Harcourt 179,500.

NORWAY

Official name: Kingdom of Norway. Location: The western part of Scandinavia in northern Europe. Area: 323,883 sq. km (125,051 sq. miles). Form of government: Constitutional monarchy. Estimated population (1976): 4,017,100. Official language: Norwegian. Official religion: Evangelical Lutheran Church. Monetary unit: The krone = 100 øre.

Principal towns and their estimated population (1976): Oslo (capital) 463,022; Bergen 213,594; Trondheim 134,889; Stavanger 86,643; Kristiansand 59,477.

Land and climate: The south consists of a high plateau, deeply dissected in the west by fjord valleys; in the east the valleys are broader and more gentle, and the rivers here, which rise near the Atlantic coast, are longer. Farther north the country narrows (at one point to less than 8 km (5

Kingdom of Norway: Both the man's costume and the harness of his tame reindeer are richly embroidered.

miles)) and although the countryside appears to be more mountainous, the peaks are generally lower.

The climate is dominated by the passage of cyclones and much affected by the warm North Atlantic drift. Temperatures are moderate but precipitation considerable, particularly along the exposed western slopes. There is a lot of snow in the winter months, but frosts are not severe in the lowlands.

Economy: Forests cover 20 per cent of the area, farmland about 3 per cent, mostly under grass for hay, and with barley and potatoes. Dairy cattle and sheep are an important element of the farm economy, and there are also specialized fur farms. Fisheries are varied and valuable, concentrating on herring and cod, most of which is exported, either fresh, frozen, dried or as processed fillets.

Norway's great asset for industrial activities is the availability of hydro-electric power, used mostly for electro-chemical and electro-metallurgical purposes. The most important products are aluminium (second only to Canada) and ferro-alloys. The large fleet of merchant ships makes a significant contribution to overseas earnings.

Recent history: Norwegian political life has for a long time been fairly stable. A Labour government has been in power most of the time during the past 40 years, and King Olav V acceded to the throne in 1957. The country became a member of NATO in 1949 and applied for membership to the European Economic Community in 1972. However, in a referendum held later that year 53.5 per cent of the electorate voted against entry.

OMAN

Official name: Sultanate of Oman. Location: Extreme south east of Arabian peninsula. Area: 272,500 sq. km approx. (105,000 sq. miles). Form of government: Absolute monarchy. Estimated population (1974): 750,000. Official language: Arabic; English is widely used in business circles. Official religion: Islam. Monetary unit: The rial = 1,000 baiza. Principal towns and their estimated population (1974): Muscat (capital) 7,500; Matrah 15,500.

PAKISTAN

Official name: Islamic Republic of Pakistan. Location: Southern Asia; bordering on to India to the east. Area: 796,095 sq. km (307,374 sq. miles). Form of government: Presidential regime enforcing martial law. Estimated population (1977): 74,955,000. Official language: Urdu; English and Bengali are also extensively used. Official religion: Islam. Monetary unit: The rupee = 100 paisa.

Principal cities and their estimated population (1972): Islamabad (capital) 235,000; Karachi 3,469,000; Lahore

2,148,000; Lyallpur 820,000; Hyderabad 624,000; Rawalpindi 615,000; Multan 544,000; Peshawar 273,000.

Land and climate: Pakistan consists of: an eastern zone of largely alluvial lowland containing the delta, valley and many headwaters of the Indus river; a northern high mountain region formed by the Himalayas; and an arid plateau in the west surrounded by a ring of mountains.

The climate is notable for its aridity and in the southern half, which is mostly desert, there are only a few inches of rain a year and the summer heat is excessive. Rainfall increases towards the Himalayas but this is due mostly to the monsoons. Here again summers are hot but winters are cool, with some frost.

Economy: The agricultural development of Pakistan followed the building of canals which irrigate the southern plain. The chief commercial crops are wheat, cotton and rice. Cotton is the most important export. The chief fuel is natural gas, and some of the dams, originally built for irrigation, now produce hydro-electricity.

Recent history: Political unrest in 1969 led to President Ayub Khan's resignation. His successor Yahya Khan declared martial law, but a brief war broke out with East Pakistan which, with the active support of India, was seeking autonomy. Pakistan troops were defeated and the new independent republic of East Pakistan (under the name of Bangladesh) was declared. It was not until 1974 that Pakistan recognized the new republic.

Zulfiqar Ali Bhutto, who succeeded Yahya Khan, tried to deal with the internal unrest but failed, and he increasingly assumed a style of personal rule. The general election in 1977 overwhelmingly supported him but the opposition claimed the results had been rigged; the army again took over control, for the third time in 19 years.

PANAMA

Official name: Republic of Panama. Location: Southern end of Central American isthmus. Area: 75,650 sq. km (29,201 sq. miles) excluding Panama Canal Zone. Form of government: Military junta in all but name. Estimated population (1975): 1,678,000. Official language: Spanish. Official religion: Roman Catholicism. Monetary unit: The balboa = 100 centésimos. Principal towns and their estimated population (1975): Panama City (capital) 441,100; Colón 95,300.

PAPUA NEW GUINEA

Official name: Papua New Guinea (formerly Trust Territory of New Guinea). Location: Eastern half of island of New Guinea and the adjacent islands in south-western Pacific. Area: 462,840 sq. km (178,656 sq. miles). Form of government: Parliamentary democracy. Estimated population (1975): 2,760,000. Official language: English. Official religion: None. Monetary unit: The kina = 100 toea. Principal towns and their population (1971 census): Port Moresby (capital) 76,500; Lae 38,700; Rabaul 26,600; Madang 16,900.

PARAGUAY

Official name: Republic of Paraguay. Location: Land-locked state in central South America. Area: 406,752 sq. km (157,048 sq. miles). Form of government: Military-civilian dictatorship. Estimated population (1975): 2,650,000. Official language: Spanish; Guaraní is also spoken. Official religion: Roman Catholicism; there is a small Protestant minority. Monetary unit: The guaraní = 100 céntimos. Capital: Asunción (1972 population 392,753).

PERU

Official name: Republic of Peru. Location: Pacific coast of South America. Area: 1,285,216 sq. km (496,093 sq. miles). Form of government: Revolutionary junta. Estimated population (1977): 15,500,000. Official

Republic of Peru: A fruit and vegetable market in this Andean village provides a scene of rich colours.

language: Spanish; Quechua and Aymará are spoken by many of the Indian population. Official religion: Roman Catholicism; there is a small Protestant minority. Monetary unit: The sol = 10 dineros = 100 centavos. Principal towns and their estimated population (1972): Lima (capital) 3,317,648; Callao 336,500; Arequipa 194,700; Trujillo 157,500; Chiclayo 141,900; Piura 112,500; Cuzco 109,800.

PHILIPPINES

Official name: Republic of the Philippines. Location: Archipelago (over 7,000 islands) in Pacific Ocean, South-east Asia. Area: 300,000 sq. km (115,830 sq. miles). Form of government: Martial law. Estimated population (1976): 43,940,000. Official language: Philippino; English is also widely spoken, and also some Spanish. Official religion: None; 90 per cent of the population is Christian, the large majority Roman Catholics. Monetary unit: The peso = 100 centavos. Principal cities and their population (1975 census): Manila (capital) 1,454,352; Quezon City (ancient capital) 960,341; Davao 482,233; Cebu 408,173; Zamboanga 261,978; Bacolod 222,735; Pasay 186,920.

POLAND

Official name: Polish People's Republic. Location: Eastern Europe. Area: 312,677 sq. km (120,693 sq. miles). Form of government:

Communist republic. Estimated population (1976): 34,100,000. Official language: Polish. Official religion: None; most of the population is Roman Catholic. Monetary unit: The zloty = 100 groszy. Principal towns and their estimated population (1976): Warsaw (capital) 1,436,000; Lódź 798,000; Cracow 685,000; Breslau 576,000; Poznan 516,000; Danzig 421,000.

PORTUGAL

Official name: Portuguese Republic. Location: South-western Europe, on Atlantic coast of Iberian peninsula. Area (including islands): 91,631 sq. km (35,370 sq. miles). Form of government: Democratic republic. Estimated population (1971): 8,869,800. Official language: Portuguese. Official religion: Roman Catholicism. Monetary unit: The escudo = 100 centavos. Principal towns and their population (1970 census): Lisbon (capital) 760,150;

Portuguese Republic: Oxen are used to haul a fisherman's boat ashore at the fishing centre of Nazaré.

Oporto 301,655; Coimbra 55,985; Setubal 49,670.

PUERTO RICO

Official name: Commonwealth of Puerto Rico. Location: Outer Caribbean. Area: 8,897 sq. km (3,435 sq. miles). Political status: Commonwealth in association with the United States. Estimated population (1976): 3,196,100. Official languages: Spanish and English. Official religion: None; the vast majority is Roman Catholic. Monetary unit: The US dollar = 100 cents. Principal towns and their estimated population (1975): San Juan (capital) 471,400; Bayamón 180,800; Ponce 176,100; Carolina 142,750; Caguas 111,650.

QATAR

Official name: State of Qatar. Location: Peninsula on west coast of Persian Gulf. Area: 11,400 sq. km (4,400 sq. miles). Form of government: Absolute monarchy. Estimated population (1972): 180,000. Official language: Arabic; English is usually spoken for business purposes. Official religion: Islam. Monetary unit: The riyal = 100 dirhams. Capital: Doha (1972 estimated population 130,000).

ROMANIA

Official name: Socialist Republic of Romania. Location: South-east Europe. Area: 237,500 sq. km (91,699 sq. miles). Form of Government: Communist republic. Population (1975): 21,250,000. Official language: Romanian. Official religion: None; most Romanians belong to the Romanian Orthodox Church. Monetary unit: The leu = 100 bani. Principal towns and their population (1975): Bucharest (capital) 1,588,592; Cluj-Napoca 222,429; Iaşi 216,206; Timişoara 213,054; Braşov 202,761; Constanta 198,429.

RUSSIA:

See Union of Soviet Socialist Republics.

RWANDA

Official name: Republic of Rwanda. Location: Land-locked state in Central Africa, just south of the equator. Area: 26,338 sq. km (10,169 sq. miles). Form of government: Military junta. Population (1970 census): 3,736,000. Official languages: French and Kinyarwanda, the native language. Official religion: None. Monetary unit: The franc = 100 centimes. Capital: Kigali (1970 population 54,403).

SAMOA:

See Western Samoa.

SAN MARINO

Official name: Republic of San Marino. Location: Central Italy, southern Europe. Area: 61 sq. km (24 sq. miles). Form of government: Democratic republic; executive power vested in two regents and congress of state. Population (1974): 19,168. Official language: Italian. Official religion: None; Roman Catholicism is the predominant religion. Monetary unit: Both Italian and Vatican City currency is in general use. Capital: San Marino (1974 population 4,512).

SÃO TOMÉ E PRÍNCIPE

Official name: Democratic Republic of São Tomé e Príncipe. Location: Islands in the Gulf of Guinea, West Africa. Area: 964 sq. km (372 sq. miles). Form of government: Republic. Estimated population (1973): 76,450. Official language: Portuguese. Official religion: Roman Catholicism. Monetary unit: The escudo = 100 centavos. Capital: São Tomé (1973 estimated population 3,200).

SAUDI ARABIA

Official name: Kingdom of Saudi Arabia. Location: Western Asia; occupies the greater part of the Arab peninsula. Area: 2,400,000 sq. km approx. (927,000 sq. miles). Form of government: Absolute monarchy. Estimated population (1976): 9,156,500. Official language: Arabic. Official religion: Islam. Monetary unit: The riyal = 20 qursh = 100 halalah.

Principal cities and their population (1974 census): Riyadh (royal capital) 666,840; Jidda (administrative capital) 561,104; Mecca 366,801; Taif 204,857; Medina 198,186; Buraida 69,940.

Land and climate: A narrow coastal plain extends along the Red Sea coast; parallel to it and rising sharply to 1,220 m (4,000 ft) are the Hejaz mountains with a few high peaks in the north. To the east is the central plateau, which slopes gently to the Persian Gulf, broken by several escarpments. The heart of Saudi Arabia is the Nedj, with the Nefud desert in the north and the Empty Quarter in the south east, the most arid area in the world. North of the Nefud is largely a projection of the Syrian Desert.

Rainfall is very low except in the western uplands, and temperatures may rise to 55°C (130°F) in the interior.

Economy: Petroleum is Saudi Arabia's most important resource, providing over 80 per cent of the country's considerable revenue. In 1976 it was the second largest oil-producing country (after the USSR) with 15 per cent of world production. Efforts are being made to diversify the economy, especially in connection with water resources, road transport and the exploration for minerals. Most of the area is unsuitable for any form of agriculture, cultivation

Kingdom of Saudi Arabia: Many people still follow the nomadic way of life unchanged by the vast economic developments oil has brought to the country. Although they wear decorative bangles, the women keep their faces veiled.

being confined to oases, part of the Red Sea coastal plain and the highlands.

Recent history: King Faisal, who officially came to the throne in 1964, was successful in abolishing slavery, curbing corruption and establishing reform programmes. He was murdered in 1975 and succeeded by his brother.

SCOTLAND:

See United Kingdom.

SENEGAL

Official name: Republic of Senegal. Location: West coast of Africa. Area: 197,722 sq. km (76,320 sq. miles). Form of government: Parliamentary democracy. Estimated population (1977): 4,500,000. Official language: French; many native languages are also used. Official religion: None; over 80 per cent of the population is Moslem. Monetary unit: The franc = 100 centimes. Principal towns and their estimated population (1977): Dakar (capital) 581,000; Kaolack 96,250; Thiès 90,500; Saint-Louis 81,200.

SEYCHELLES

Official name: Republic of the Seychelles (formerly British Crown Colony). Location: Group of islands in Indian Ocean. Area: 444 sq. km (171 sq. miles). Form of government: Republic. Estimated population (1976): 59,000. Official languages: English and French. Official religion: None. Monetary unit: The rupee = 100 cents. Capital: Victoria (on island of Mahé), 1976 estimated population 14,500.

SIAM:

See Thailand.

SIERRA LEONE

Official name: Republic of Sierra Leone. Location: West coast of Africa. Area: 72,362 sq. km (27,925 sq. miles). Form of government: Presidential democracy. Population (1974 census): 3,002,426. Official language: English; native languages are widely used. Official religion: None; there are Moslem and Christian minorities. Monetary unit:

The leone = 100 cents. Capital: Freetown (estimated population 274,000).

SINGAPORE

Official name: Republic of Singapore. Location: One main island and several offshore islands at southern extremity of Malay peninsula in south-eastern Asia, just north of the equator. Area: 597 sq. km (230 sq. miles). Form of government: Parliamentary democracy. Estimated population (1976): 2,278,200. Official languages: Malay, Chinese (Mandarin), Tamil and English. Official religion: None. Monetary unit: The dollar = 100 cents. Capital: Singapore.

SOMALIA

Official name: Somali Democratic Republic. Location: East coast of Africa. Area: 637,660 sq. km (246,201 sq. miles). Form of government: Military dictatorship. Estimated population (1976): 3,221,000. Official language: Somali; English, French and Arabic are also widely used. Official religion: Islam.

Monetary unit: The shilling = 100 centesimi. Principal towns and their estimated population (1976): Mogadiscio (capital) 350,000; Hargeisa 50,000; Kisimayu 30,000.

SOUTH AFRICA

Official name: Republic of South Africa. Location: Southern extremity of African continent. Area: 1,221,042 sq. km (471,322 sq. miles). Form of government: Limited democracy. Population (1970 census): 3,726,540 whites; 17,675,930 non-whites. Official languages: Afrikaans and English; the principal African languages are Xhosa, Zulu and Sesotho. Official religion: None; the population is mainly Christian, over half the white population belonging to the Dutch Reformed Church. Monetary unit: The rand = 100 cents.

The people: The first white settlers were the Boers who came from the

Republic of South Africa: The cloud-capped Table Mountain dominates the view across Capetown.

Netherlands, starting in the seventeenth century. Other European settlers came from Britain, France and Germany. The non-whites include the Bantus (Zulus, Basutos, Xhosas, Pondos, etc), the coloureds (of mixed blood), and the Asians who are descendants of labourers brought from India in the 19th century.

Political divisions: There are four provinces: Cape of Good Hope, Natal, the Transvaal and the Orange Free State, each with a provincial council and an administrator appointed by the State President-in-Council. The state of Lesotho is an independent enclave within South Africa. The Transkei territory (homeland of the Xhosa nation) was granted self-government in 1976, but no other country has recognized the status of independence. South Africa also administrates South West Africa (Namibia) although according to the United Nations the mandate has now lapsed.

Principal cities and their population (1970 census):

Cape Town (legislative capital) 1,096,597; Pretoria (administrative capital) 561,703; Bloemfontein (judicial capital) 180,176; Johannesburg 1,432,643; Durban 843,327; Port Elizabeth 468,577; Germiston 139,472.

The land: Tablelands at different levels occupy most of the country. Only a narrow coastal fringe lies below 180 m (600 ft), and more than half the country is above 900 m (3,000 ft). A great saucer-shaped plateau dominates the interior, rising in the east and south; the eastern escarpment forms the Drakenberg mountains, the highest peak of which is 3,475 m (11,400 ft) in altitude. There are no great rivers but the more important ones flow towards the interior and across the central tableland; one of these, the Orange river, flows westwards towards the Atlantic but in its lower course it suffers heavy losses through evaporation, so that, except when sudden storms occur, no river water reaches the sea. The north of the country drains via the Limpopo river to the Indian Ocean.

Climate: Rainfall is unreliable over the greater part of the country, especially inland and in the north. Areas of high rainfall are limited, and only the east and south receive over 75 cm (30 in) of rain a year. The atmosphere on the plateau is dry, and temperatures cover a wide range, frost occurring between April and October. Summers are everywhere hot, with temperatures ranging between 24°C (75°F) and 30°C (85°F). A limited area in the south west experiences a Mediterranean climate, with hot dry summers and mild wet winters.

Natural resources: South Africa's greatest source of wealth is the mines; there are a variety of minerals, gold and diamond representing the most important of them. But there are also large reserves

of platinum, copper, iron ore, manganese, antimony and chrome, and also asbestos. A useful by-product from gold mining is uranium oxide. There is no domestic oil supply, but much of the coal is processed into oil. The two most important agricultural activities are stock raising and the cultivation of maize and sugar cane. Citrus fruit, grapes (for wine) and tobacco are also important crops where conditions permit. The country is noted for its fine wool and fishing, mostly in Atlantic waters.

Industry and exports: The output of steel and steel products is increasing, and ferro-manganese, stainless steel and ferro-chrome are produced where fuel is plentiful and cheap. The country is now virtually self-sufficient in machinery and consumer goods; raw materials for the growing engineering and electrical industries are supplied locally, while imported materials such as rubber are processed in the country for their own needs; in addition a large petrochemical complex has been built and is now making general chemicals and fertilizers. There is a large export of fishmeal, and canned and frozen fish; of the wines produced in South Africa only sherry is a major export.

Recent history: South Africa left the Commonwealth in 1961 and became an independent republic. In 1966 the doctrinaire apartheid prime minister Hendrik Vervoed was assassinated, and was replaced by John Vorster who continued strict apartheid policies, in spite of the most bitter repercussions and condemnation at international level.

The objection to the use of Afrikaans was the sparking off point of violent riots by coloured students in 1976, sweeping many coloured townships. Confrontations with security forces and riot squads resulted in many casualties which shocked

the white population but hardened the government's policy of separate development.

SOUTHERN YEMEN
Official name: The People's Democratic Republic of Yemen. Location: Southern shore of Arabian peninsula. Area: 160,300 sq. km (61,875 sq. miles). Form of government: Presidential council. Estimated population (1975): 1,663,200. Official language: Arabic. Official religion: Islam. Monetary unit: The dinar = 1,000 fils. Principal towns and their estimated population (1975): Aden (capital) 250,000; Shaikh Othman 30,000; Mukalla 25,000.

SOUTH WEST AFRICA (NAMIBIA)
Official name: South West Africa (called Suidwes Afrika in Afrikaans but Namibia by UN resolution of 1966). Location: West coast of southern Africa. Area: 824,296 sq. km (318,178 sq. miles). Political status: Mandated territory administered by South Africa, although the mandate according to the UN has lapsed. Estimated population (1974): 852,000. Official languages: Afrikaans and English. Official religion: None. Monetary unit: The South African rand = 100 cents. Capital: Windhoek (national); Swakopmund (summer).

SOVIET UNION:
See Union of Soviet Socialist Republics.

SPAIN
Official name: Spanish State. Location: South-west Europe; forms more than four-fifths of the Iberian peninsula. Area: 504,750 sq. km (194,885 sq. miles). Form of government: Constitutional monarchy. Estimated population (1972): 34,364,000. Official language: Spanish; Catalan is spoken in the north east and Basque in the north. Official religion: Roman Catholicism. Monetary unit: The peseta = 100 céntimos.

Principal cities and their population (1970 census): Madrid (capital) 3,146,071;

Barcelona 1,745,142; Valencia 653,690; Seville 548,072; Saragossa 479,843; Bilbao 410,490; Málaga 374,452.

Land and climate: The greater part of the Iberian peninsula is plateau (the Meseta), averaging 610 m (2,000 ft) in altitude and rising in the north, the centre and in the south west. The Pyrenees form a frontier with France. Along the Mediterranean coast in the south east is another range of mountains which contain the highest peak in Spain (3,477 m, 11,407 ft). Apart from a narrow strip along the east coast, the only lowlands are the valleys formed by the main rivers, which flow mainly in an east-west direction into the Atlantic and the Mediterranean.

There is a great range of temperature, severe winters and very hot summers in the Meseta, but the northern mountains have moderate temperatures and mild rainy winters. There is heavy winter rainfall in the south, but drought conditions in the summer.

Economy: Spain has considerable metal wealth: iron ore is mined in the north and non-ferrous ores in the south. Pyrites and mercury are particularly important and both are exported. Coal is also mined in the north, offshore natural gas fields are being exploited and there is a small production of oil. Hydro electricity stations are another important source of power and more are being built.

The main agricultural products which provide a surplus for export are cereals, wine (including sherry), olive oil, and oranges. Recent development in manufacturing industries, particularly steel, means that these now employ over a third of the workforce. Important also are textiles, shipbuilding and chemicals, but by far the most lucrative of the activities is the tourist trade.

Recent history: After ruling Spain for 36 years in which he achieved a long period of stability, Franco died in 1975 and was succeeded by King Juan Carlos I. Democracy returned to Spain with general elections held in 1977 and the opening of the Cortès (parliament).

SRI LANKA

Official name: Democratic Socialist Republic of Sri Lanka (formerly Ceylon). Location: Southern Asia; island 50 miles east of southern tip of India. Area: 65,610 sq. km (25,332 sq. miles). Form of government: Presidential rule. Estimated population (1974): 13,870,000. Official language: Sinhala; Tamil and English are also widely used. Official religion: None; about two-thirds of the population is Buddhist. Principal towns and their population (1971 census): Colombo (capital) 562,160; Jaffna 107,663; Kandy 93,602; Galle 72,720.

SUDAN

Official name: Democratic Republic of the Sudan. Location: Northern Africa; the largest country on the continent. Area: 2,505,813 sq. km (967,500 sq. miles). Form of government: Military-civilian dictatorship. Estimated population (1977): 17,760,000. Official language: Arabic; English is widely understood. Official religion: None; the predominant religion is Islam. Monetary unit: The pound = 100 piatres = 1,000 millièmes. Principal towns and their population (1971): Khartoum (capital) 280,431; Omdurman 273,268; Khartoum North 138,014; Port Sudan 116,366.

SURINAM

Official name: Republic of Surinam (formerly Dutch Guiana). Location: North east of South American continent. Area: 163,820 sq. km (63,234 sq. miles). Form of government: Presidential democracy. Estimated population (1976): 414,000. Official language: Dutch; many European and Asian languages are also used, as well as a vernacular. Official religion: None;

Kingdom of Sweden: Fishermen's boats are moored on the small island of Smogen on the west coast.

Moslems and Hindus form the majority. Monetary unit: The guilder = 100 cents. Capital: Paramaribo (1971 population 151,500).

SWAZILAND

Official name: Kingdom of Swaziland. Location: Southern Africa. Area: 17,364 sq. km (6,703 sq. miles). Form of government: Absolute monarchy. Estimated population (1976): 490,000. Official languages: siSwati and English. Official religion: None; over half the population is Christian. Monetary unit: The South African rand = 100 cents. Principal towns and their estimated population (1972): Mbabane (administrative capital) 15,800; Lobamba (royal and legislative capital); Manzini 7,000.

SWEDEN

Official name: Kingdom of Sweden. Location: Eastern half of Scandinavian peninsula, north-west Europe. Area: 449,964 sq. km (173,686 sq. miles). Form of government: Constitutional monarchy. Population (1975 census): 8,208,544. Official language: Swedish; Lapp and Finnish minorities retain their own language. Official religion: Swedish State Church. Monetary unit: The krone = 100 öre.

Principal towns and their population (1975 census): Stockholm (capital) 665,202; Gothenburg 444,651; Malmö 243,591; Uppsala 138,116; Norrköping 119,169.

Land and climate: Long rivers rise in the mountain range along the Norwegian border, all flowing more or less parallel into the Gulf of Bothnia. South of latitude 60° are the central lowlands, broken by large lake basins and an impoverished upland (Småland). The southern tip

and the islands of Öland and Gotland yield fertile clay soils.

Sweden is relatively dry, with a semicontinental climate; annual precipitation, mostly in the form of snow in the winter months, is less than 52.5 cm (25 in), and about 75 cm (30 in) along the west coast where winters are relatively mild. In the northern part, which is above the Arctic Circle, winters are long and cold.

Economy: The north is rich in its resources of forest, grazing, water power and minerals; more minerals are found in the south, which also has most of the arable land and manufacturing activities. Lakes and waterfalls provide abundant hydro-electric power and the country is able to export electric power to Denmark. Wood and woodpulp are an important part of the economy, and there is also a large output of iron and steel, especially stainless steel. Engineering products, however, form by far the largest item exported—these include electrical equipment, domestic equipment, armaments, locomotives, ships, aircraft and automobiles.

Recent history: King Gustaf VI's reign was characterized by the reconciliation of the country's various currents of political opinion. He was succeeded in 1973 by his grandson Carl XVI Gustaf. The Social Democrat Party, which greatly developed the social welfare system during 44 years in office, was defeated in a general election in 1976.

SWITZERLAND

Official name: Swiss Confederation. Location: Western Europe. Area: 41,293 sq. km (15,943 sq. miles). Form of government: Federal parliamentary democracy. Estimated population (1975): 6,400,000. Official languages: French, German, Italian and Romansch. Official religion: None; population more or less equally divided between Roman Catholic and Protestant Churches. Monetary unit: The franc (Franken) = 100 centimes (Rappen).

Principal towns and their estimated population (1975): Bern (capital) 149,800; Zürich 389,600; Basel 192,800; Geneva 155,800; Lausanne 134,300.

Land and climate: There are three major regions: the Swiss Alps, the Mittelland, and the Swiss Jura. The Alps include the highest peaks in Europe, with deep (often flat-floored) valleys and glacial lakes. The gently undulating landscape in the Mittelland plateau is diversified by wooded ridges which partly encircle lakes at the foot of the Alps. The Jura mountains rise to over 1,800 m (6,000 ft). Both the Rhône and the Rhine rise in Switzerland, and also feeders of the Danube and the Po.

The climate is mid-European, modified by elevation. The high peaks receive over 250 cm (100 in) precipitation yearly, mainly as snow, but the Rhône valleys only 60 cm (24 in). In winter cold air collects above the valleys and temperature inversions occur.

Economy: A quarter of the area of Switzerland is unproductive due to altitude, a quarter forested, another quarter pastureland, and the remainder farmland. Agriculture is concerned mostly with dairy farming, and nearly half the cheese production is exported. Hydro-electricity provides about half the energy requirements. A high level of prosperity has been reached by the development of efficient industries requiring a high degree of technology and precision, and a dynamic marketing programme. Invisible exports such as banking and tourism also contribute to the Swiss economy and prosperity.

Recent history: The policy of strict but armed neutrality has led the Swiss government to avoid all military alliances, including membership of the UN and NATO. The country is however a member of various UN agencies, some of which have their headquarters in Swiss cities. The President of the Confederation is elected annually for one calendar year.

SYRIA

Official name: Syrian Arab Republic. Location: Eastern shore of the Mediterranean, south-western Asia. Area 185,680 sq. km (71,672 sq. miles). Form of government: Military-civilian dictatorship. Estimated population (1977): 7,200,000. Official language: Arabic; Kurdish is a minority language. Official religion: Islam. Monetary unit: The pound = 100 piastres. Principal towns and their population (1970): Damascus (capital) 836,668; Aleppo 639,631; Homs 215,526; Hama 137,589; Lattakia 121,570; Deir-ez-Zor 66,143.

TAIWAN

Official name: Republic of China. Location: Island 320 km (200 miles) off Chinese mainland, plus the islands of Quemoy and Matsu, south-eastern Asia. Area: 35,981 sq. km (13,892 sq. miles). Form of government: Presidential rule. Estimated population (1975): 16,150,000. Official language: Mandarin Chinese. Official religion: None; the predominant religion is Buddhism.

Syrian Arab Republic: The ancient tombs of Palmyra are located in the central region of Syria.

Monetary unit: The dollar = 100 cents. Capital: Taipi (1974 estimated population 2,000,000).

TANZANIA

Official name: United Republic of Tanzania. Location: Eastern Africa; consisting of the former territory of Tanganyika and the islands of Zanzibar and Pemba. Area: 945,203 sq. km (364,848 sq. miles). Form of government: One-party democracy. Estimated population (1975): 15,000,000. Official languages: Swahili and English. Official religion: None. Monetary unit: The shilling = 100 cents. Capital: Dar-es-Salaam (1975 estimated population 396,700).

THAILAND

Official name: Kingdom of Thailand. Location: South-east Asia. Area: 514,000 sq. km (198,404 sq. miles). Form of government: Indirect military rule. Population (1973 census): 39,950,306. Official language: Thai. Official religion: Hinayana Buddhism. Capital: Bangkok (1973 metropolitan population 3,967,081).

TOGO

Official name: Republic of Togo. Location: West African coast. Area: 56,000 sq. km (21,616 sq. miles). Form of government: Military-civilian dictatorship. Estimated population (1975): 2,197,900. Official language: French. Official religion: None. Monetary unit: The franc = 100 centimes. Capital: Lomé (1975 estimated population 135,000).

TONGA (FRIENDLY ISLANDS)

Official name: Kingdom of Tonga. Location: About 150 islands in south-west Pacific. Area: 699 sq. km (270 sq. miles). Form of government: Absolute monarchy. Estimated population (1975): 100,100. Official languages: Tongan and English. Official religion: None; the majority of the population are Wesleyan Protestants. Monetary unit: The pa'anga

(Tongan dollar) = 100 seniti. Capital: Nuku'alofa (1975 estimated population 25,000).

TRINIDAD AND TOBAGO

Official name: Trinidad and Tobago. Location: Southernmost part of the Caribbean islands. Area: 5,128 sq. km (1,980 sq. miles). Form of government: Republican democracy. Estimated population (1974): 1,073,800. Official language: English. Official religion: None; most of the population are Christian, with Roman Catholics as the largest single group. Monetary unit: The dollar = 100 cents. Principal towns and their population (1970 census): Port-of-Spain (capital) 62,680; San Fernando 36,879; Arima 11,636.

TUNISIA

Official name: Republic of Tunisia. Location: North Africa, on Mediterranean coast. Area: 164,150 sq. km (63,362 sq. miles). Form of government: One-party democracy. Estimated population (1975): 5,770,000. Official language: Arabic; French is also widely used. Official religion: Islam. Monetary unit: The dinar = 1,000

Republic of Tunisia: Colourful pottery is displayed in the market at Nabeul.

millimes. Principal towns and their estimated population (1976): Tunis (capital) 944,000; Sfax 475,000; Sousse 255,000; Bizerta 62,000; Kairouan 54,000.

TURKEY

Official name: Republic of Turkey. Location: South-eastern Europe and south-western Asia. Area: 23,764 sq. km (9,173 sq. miles) in Europe; 755,855 sq. km (291,760 sq. miles) in Asia; total 779,619 sq. km (300,933 sq. miles). Form of government: Parliamentary democracy. Estimated population (1975): 40,200,000. Official language: Turkish; Arabic and Kurdish are spoken on eastern borders. Official religion: None; the large majority of the population is Moslem. Monetary unit: The lira = 100 kurus = 4,000 paras. Principal towns and their population (1970 census): Ankara (capital) 1,208,791; Istanbul 2,247,630; Izmir 520,686; Adana 351,655; Bursa 275,917; Gaziantep 225,881; Eskisehir 216,330; Konya 200,760.

UGANDA

Official name: Republic of Uganda. Location: Equatorial country in East Africa. Area: 236,860 sq. km (91,428 sq. miles). Form of

government: Provisional revolutionary government. Population (1974): 11,171,900. Official language: English; the most important local language is Luganda. Official religion: None. Monetary unit: The shilling = 100 cents. Capital: Kampala (1969 estimated population 330,700).

UNION OF SOVIET SOCIALIST REPUBLICS

Official name: Union of Soviet Socialist Republics. Location: Extends from the Baltic Sea in the west to the Pacific Ocean in the east. Area: 22,402,200 sq. km (8,647,249 sq. miles). Form of government: Communist republic. Estimated population (1976): 254,380,000. Official language: Russian; some 120 languages are spoken in the country as a whole. Official religion: None. Monetary unit: The rouble = 100 kopeks.

The people: There are said to be over 100 nationalities in the Soviet Union, indentified mainly by the language they use. Most groups are Caucasoid and the remainder Mongoloid, although there has been a lot of interbreeding.

Three-quarters of the population belongs to the Slavic group, which includes the Russians, the Ukrainians and the Byelorussians. The group next in importance are the Turkic peoples, which include the Uzbeks, Kazakhs, Kirghiz, Turkmen, Tuvinians and Yakuts. Other groups include the Finno-Ungric peoples near the Baltic, the Armenians and Georgians in the Caucasus region and the Tadzhiks in central Asia.

Political divisions: There are 15 union republics in the USSR, within certain of which are 20 autonomous republics, 8 autonomous regions, and 10 *okrugs* (national areas). Each of the union republics has a supreme soviet, members of which are elected for a four-year term, and a presidium. The largest of the union republics, the Russian

Soviet Federal Socialist Republic, contains about half the population and stretches over three-quarters of the territory.

Capitals of the union republics and their estimated population (1976): Moscow (USSR and Russian SFSR) 7,734,000; Kiev (Ukrainian SSR) 2,013,000; Tashkent (Uzbek SSR) 1,643,000; Baku (Azerbaizhan SSR) 1,406,000; Minsk (Byelorussian SSR) 1,189,000; Tbilisi (Georgian SSR) 1,030,000; Yerevan (Armenian SSR) 928,000; Alma-Ata (Kazakh SSR) 851,000; Riga (Latvian SSR) 806,000; Frunze (Kirghiz SSR) 498,000; Kishinev (Moldavian SSR) 471,000; Dushanbe (Tadzhik SSR) 448,000; Vilnius (Lithuanian SSR) 447,000; Tallinn (Estonian SSR) 408,000; Ashkhabad (Turkmen SSR) 297,000.

The land: The six main land regions from west to east are: (1) the European plain which averages 180 m (600 ft) above sea-level, although it rises to 5,500 m (18,000 ft) in the Caucasus mountains between the Black Sea and the Caspian Sea in the south; (2) the Ural mountains which form a natural boundary between Europe and Asia with an average height of 610 m (2,000 ft); (3) Soviet central Asia which consists of desert and low plateaux, part of them below sea-level, but rising to 7,495 m (24,590 ft), the highest peak in the country being in the Pamir mountains in the south; (4) the flat west Siberian plain which is the largest level region in the world; (5) the central Siberian plateau which stretches from the Arctic Ocean down to a range of mountains fringing the Mongolian border; and (6) the east Siberian uplands, a wild region of mountains and plateaux, with an offshore chain of volcanoes, the highest of which is Klyuchevskaya (4,750 m, 15,584 ft).

The Caspian Sea, the largest lake in the world, is entirely in the USSR except for its southern shore. Other

in the communist bloc.

Recent history: A visit of the American President Nixon to the USSR in 1972 led to a promising development of détente, and the following year the First Secretary of the Communist Party, L. I. Brezhnev, visited the United States, as well as European countries and India. Ways of promoting trade, peace, and cultural and scientific exchanges were explored, and agreements were signed. The Middle East conflict in 1973 threatened good relations with Western countries, and efforts to maintain a common approach were not helped by the repression of intellectual dissidents in the USSR and the resumption of purge-type trials.

UNITED ARAB EMIRATES

Official name: United Arab Emirates (consisting of the seven emirates formerly known as the Trucial States). Location: South-western Asia, along the Persian Gulf. Area: 83,657 sq. km (32,300 sq. miles).

Form of government: Absolute monarchy with separate emirates. Official language: Arabic. Official religion: None; the majority is Moslem. Monetary unit: The dirham = 10 dinar = 100 fils.

Estimated populations (1976): Abu Dhabi 235,700; Ajman 21,600; Dubai 206,900; Fujairah 26,500; Ras al Khaimah 57,300; Sharjah 88,200; Umm al Qaiwain 16,800.

Land and climate: The only high ground is on the eastern border, otherwise the federation is mainly desert, with short water courses of very irregular regime. In the higher area rainfall may be as much as 20 cm (8 in) in a good year, but everywhere else the country depends on underground water. Summer day temperatures average 33°C (74°F), though with comparatively cold nights.

Economy: The emirates are experiencing boom conditions as a result of the

Union of Soviet Socialist Republics: The spectacular architecture of the cathedral in Moscow's famous Red Square is a great attraction to visitors.

lakes are the Aral Sea, Lake Baykal, Lake Balknash, and Lake Ladoga. The larger European rivers include the Dnieper which flows into the Black Sea, the Volga and the Ural into the Caspian Sea, the Don into the Sea of Azov, and the Dvina. The Asiatic section is drained by the Ob, the Yenisei and the Lena which flow into the Arctic Ocean, and the Amur flowing into the Pacific.

Climate: About half the country has permanently frozen soil beneath the ground surface and is covered in snow for half the year. Western and eastern Siberia may receive up to 1 m (4 ft) of snow in the year. North-eastern Siberia is a land of extreme

temperatures: −68°C (−90°F) and 38°C (100°F) have been recorded in January and July respectively. Summers are short except in the southern deserts. The heaviest rainfall is in the Caucasus region which may receive up to 250 cm (100 in) a year.

Natural resources: Vast stretches of the USSR are unproductive agriculturally, being desert land, forest, tundra, or merely too dry for crops. Only 13 per cent of the total area is cultivated, and even then crops vary considerably from year to year according to the weather. In spite of this the country is the world's leading producer of rye, oats, potatoes, sugar beet, cotton, flax, hemp and butter, and the world's largest timber producer.

Russia is probably better endowed with minerals than any other country; large

deposits of these are in remote areas which have as yet never been exploited. Even so production of almost every kind of mineral, except tin and cobalt, is sufficient to meet the country's needs and more. Output of natural gas and oil are respectively one-fifth and one-sixth of the world total, while hydro-electricity is provided by gigantic reservoirs regulating the flow of the large lowland rivers.

Industry and exports: The USSR is the largest producer of crude steel and wool yarn, and also important are the cotton and cement industries. In spite of vast natural resources and industrial activity, international trade has not been developed on a large scale. Machinery and vehicles account for about one quarter of exports, over half to European countries

discovery of oil in Abu Dhabi, Dubai and Sharjah, so much so that Abu Dhabi, the largest of the seven emirates, has within ten years become one of the richest powers in the world in proportion to the population. This new prosperity has been shared among all members of the federation by building large projects such as deep water harbours and dry docks, and by subsidizing the four northern emirates who have not yet struck oil.

Recent history: Politically the UAE remain among the most conservative of the Arab states. The federation was formed in 1971 when British responsibility for defence and foreign relations ended, though Ras al Khaimah joined only the following year.

UNITED KINGDOM

Official name: United Kingdom of Great Britain and Northern Ireland. Location: Separated from the European continent by the English Channel to the south and the North Sea to the east. Area: England 130,357 sq. km (50,331 sq. miles); Wales 20,761 sq. km (8,016 sq. miles); Scotland 78,749 sq. km (30,405 sq. miles); Northern Ireland 14,146 sq. km (5,460 sq. miles); total 244,013 sq. km (94,212 sq. miles). Form of government: Constitutional monarchy. Estimated population (1975): England and Wales 49,219,000; Scotland 5,206,000; Northern Ireland 1,540,000; total 55,965,000. Official language: English; Welsh is spoken extensively in Wales. Official religion: Church of England; other main Christian denominations are Roman Catholicism, Presbyterianism, Methodism, Congregationalism and the Baptist Church. Monetary unit: The pound = 100 pence.

The people: Little is known of the original inhabitants, but in the 6th century BC the Celts brought their culture to England, though the Picts in Scotland may have preceded them. There were

United Kingdom of Great Britain and Northern Ireland: Colourful and picturesque, heraldic trumpeters are part of Britains ever-popular pageantry.

further invasions by the Celts and others: by the Romans in the 1st century BC who remained 500 years, by the Anglo-Saxons and Jutes from the European continent, and by the Normans in 1066. All these groups are the ancestors of the present inhabitants. It is estimated that Commonwealth immigrants and their families now number about 1,800,000.

Political divisions: Since the reorganization of local government that came into effect in 1974–75, England is divided into 39 non-metropolitan counties and 7 metropolitan counties (Greater London, Greater Manchester, Merseyside, South Yorkshire, Tyne and Wear, West Yorkshire and West Midlands). Within these are 332 districts. Wales has 8 counties divided into 37 districts. The Scottish mainland is divided into 9 regions (further subdivided into 53 districts), and in addition there are 3 island areas. Northern Ireland has a single tier system of 26 district councils. The Isle of Man and the Channel Islands are not part of the

United Kingdom inasmuch as they are not represented in the Westminster parliament.

Principal cities and their estimated population (1974). England: London (capital) 7,282,000; Birmingham 1,005,000; Liverpool 575,000; Manchester 540,000; Sheffield 513,000; Leeds 502,000; Bristol 423,000. Wales: Cardiff (capital) 278,000; Swansea 174,000. Scotland: Edinburgh (capital) 470,100; Glasgow 1,105,650; Aberdeen 210,400; Renfrew 208,900; Dundee 194,800. Northern Ireland: Belfast (capital) 364,000; Londonderry 53,000.

The land. England and Wales: The Pennines, a mountain range known as the 'backbone' of England, rarely exceed 600 m (2,000 ft); they are flanked on both sides by lowlands which infrequently exceed 180 m (600 ft). In the west, the Cotswolds, and in the south, the South Downs, are uplands but of insufficient altitude to justify their exclusion from the lowlands; in some areas in the east and south east the land is at or below sea-level. Other mountainous areas in England are the Lake District in the north west with high peaks and deep valleys often filled with lakes, and the granite

uplands, of which Dartmoor is the largest, in the south-western peninsula. Wales is predominantly mountainous, although in the south and south west there are lowlands where agriculture has been developed. The longer rivers in England and Wales flow towards the North Sea; the Thames, Trent, Tees, Wear, Tyne and those that drain into the Wash. The only important river flowing west is the Severn which has a particularly circuitous course.

Scotland: The largest of the geographical areas is the Highlands, a large plateau which has a number of peaks exceeding 1,200 m (4,000 ft) and the principal Scottish lakes. The central lowlands are broken by a series of hills and are drained by the three main Scottish rivers: the Forth, the Tay and the Clyde. Another plateau area is the southern uplands with heights of over 800 m (2,600 ft). The rivers in the western part drain southwards and those in the eastern part flow to the North Sea.

Northern Ireland: The Sperrin mountains in the north are a continuation of the Scottish Highlands, while those in the south (the Mourne mountains) are similar to the southern

244

uplands. In between, the lowland that runs westwards from Belfast Lough is an extension of the Scottish lowlands. Great outpourings of volcanic rock have formed the hills in the north-east, including the famous Giant's Causeway.

Climate: In spite of the comparatively northern latitude, the climate is mild —largely attributable to the Gulf Stream which brings warm water to the coasts. The sea winds bring plenty of rain, the heaviest being in Northern Ireland, the west coast of Scotland, North Wales and the Lake District. The annual average is 100 cm (40 in), though some regions have as much as 250 cm (100 in).

Part of the country is subject to severe cold, particularly in Scotland and the eastern counties of England. Snow often falls in the Pennine Chain, Snowdonia in Wales and the Scottish Highlands. Average temperatures are 3.5°C (38°F) in winter and 17°C (63°F) in summer. Another hazard is fog, which in industrial cities forms a noxious mixture with smoke.

Natural resources: Coal

United Kingdom of Great Britain and Northern Ireland: Bioda Buidhe in Skye is a view of breathtaking beauty.

and iron have been the mainstay of the country's development as a leading industrial nation. Coalfields in Tyneside, in the Midlands, South Wales and the lowlands of Scotland have large reserves, and since many of the principal iron ore deposits are found near they partly provide the raw materials for the steel industry. Deposits of lead, zinc and tin are found in the west, and bauxite in Northern Ireland. The principal farming areas for grain crops are in the eastern regions, but sheep, cattle and dairy farming activities take place in most other areas, especially in Wales, western England, the Scottish lowlands and Northern Ireland.

Large reservoirs of natural gas were found in the 1960s in the North Sea, and in the early 1970s rich reserves of oil were discovered off Scotland; these are now being rapidly exploited. Coal is still the predominant fuel for electric power although the capacity is supplemented by oil-fired and nuclear power stations, and in Scotland by hydro-electricity.

Industry and exports: The major occupations are manufacturing and trade, both of which provide valuable exports. Among

United Kingdom of Great Britain and Northern Ireland: Many fans of Shakespeare visit Stratford-upon-Avon each year.

the principal industries are those producing iron and steel and heavy engineering. Shipbuilding continues, especially in Scotland and Northern Ireland, though on a declining scale. Newer forms of engineering include the manufacture of aero-engines and automobiles. The chemical and petrochemical industries have been highly developed, and various consumer industries have been encouraged. Linen is still an important export for Northern Ireland, but many of the firms manufacturing it have turned to synthetic fibres.

Agricultural surplus in Northern Ireland is mostly shipped to England, while Scotland's biggest export is whisky. Manufactured goods made from basic imported materials such as cotton, wool, rubber, chemicals and tobacco, are re-exported. Commercial oil production from the large fields discovered in the North Sea began in 1975 and self-sufficiency is expected by 1980. Important features of the British economy are invisible exports such as shipping, insurance and tourism.

Recent history: The United Kingdom was not a founder member of the European Economic Community in 1957 and did not succeed in joining until

1973. There was a general rise in prosperity and security under successive governments, both Conservative and Labour, in the 1950s and 1960s. But the Labour government that came to power in 1974, with Harold Wilson as prime minister followed by James Callaghan in 1976, had principally to concern itself with inflation, the problems of balance of trade and the rise of unemployment. These economic difficulties were increased in the late 1960s by the troubles in Northern Ireland. Units of the British army were brought into the province to keep the peace between Protestant and Roman Catholic extremists, but the position continued to deteriorate. The future of the government in Northern Ireland still remains unsolved.

In the mid-1970s there was more pressure by Scottish and Welsh Nationalist MPs and regional groups to gain a greater degree of autonomy for their respective countries. Queen Elizabeth II celebrated the silver jubilee of her accession to throne in 1977.

UNITED STATES

Official name: United States of America. Location: The North American continent between Canada and Mexico. Area: 9,363,123 sq. km (3,615,122 sq. miles). Form of government: Presidential democracy. Estimated population (1976):

213,630,000. Official language: English. Official religion: None; Christianity is the predominant religion. Monetary unit: The dollar = 100 cents.

The people: The Indians, Eskimos and Hawaiians were the first peoples to settle in the United States, but even they originally came from other lands. The first European settlers came from Britain, but even before the American War of Independence large numbers came from other countries such as the Netherlands, Germany, France, Italy and Spain, quite apart from the Negro slaves who were brought from Africa. Immigrants from Europe continued to arrive, attracted by the rich rewards of a new country or else to escape persecution, until the early 1900s, and again after the Second World War.

Political divisions: The country is divided into 50 states, two of which, Alaska and Hawaii are non-conterminous. Alaska lies to the north west of Canada and Hawaii is an island in the central Pacific. Each of the member states exercises a measure of self government, and elects two Senators to the Federal Senate. The Governor of each state is responsible for the administration of the law and has command of the

4,877,500; Detroit 4,488,900; Boston 3,417,000; San Francisco 3,131,800; Nassau-Suffolk 2,597,300; St Louis 2,399,800; Pittsburgh 2,395,900; Dallas 2,380,000; Baltimore 2,125,000; Newark 2,082,000; Cleveland 2,045,500; Houston 2,000,000; Minneapolis-St Paul 1,995,800; Atlanta 1,683,600; Anaheim-Santa Ana-Garden Grove 1,527,300; San Diego 1,443,100; Milwaukee 1,423,100; Seattle 1,399,600; Cincinnati 1,391,400; Buffalo 1,353,100; Miami 1,331,100; Denver 1,309,200; Kansas City 1,303,600; St Petersburg 1,189,000; San Bernardino Riverside 1,178,500; Indianapolis 1,128,000; San Jose 1,126,700; New Orleans 1,076,000; Columbus 1,057,700; Phoenix 1,053,000; Portland 1,036,300.

The land: The Atlantic Plain extends from the coast to the Appalachian highlands, the chief mountain range in the east, which rise to over 1,500 m (5,000 ft), the highest peak being Mount Mitchell (2,037 m, 6,684 ft). The surface of this region is a

United States of America: The seemingly endless plains of Kansas stretch as far as the eye can see.

series of parallel ranges divided by fertile valleys. The Rocky mountains, the other important mountain system in the United States, lie in the west from the Canadian border and beyond down to New Mexico. There are many volcanoes or extinct volcanoes in this area, and the highest peak is Mount Whitney in California (4,418 m, 14,495 ft). In the west part of the southern Rockies is the Basin of Colorado which is intersected by deep canyons. The Pacific mountains, nearer the coast, consist of three further ranges: The Sierra Nevada, the Cascade Range and the Coast Range.

Rivers of the Atlantic Plain rise in the Appalachians; the chief ones are the Hudson, the Delaware, the Susquehanna, the Potomac, the James and the Savannah. They are comparatively short and in many cases too rapid for navigation. The great Central Plain, which lies between the Appalachians and the Rockies, is drained by the Mississippi–Missouri river system, the basin of which covers half the area of the country. It flows into the Gulf of Mexico, as do the Mobile

and Rio Grande. Rivers flowing into the Pacific are also comparatively short; the only important ones are the Columbia, and the San Joaquin and Sacramento which unite to join the sea at San Francisco.

Of the Great Lakes on the Canadian border, only Lake Michigan lies entirely in US territory. Together they comprise the greatest inland body of fresh water in the world. The largest lake in the country apart from the Great Lakes is the Great Salt Lake in Utah.

Climate: On the Atlantic coast rapid weather changes occur with changes in wind direction, but generally speaking there is a marked contrast between New England in the north, where winters are severe and stormy, and Florida in the south, where average winter temperatures lie between 13°C (55°F) and 21°C (70°F). Along the Pacific coast the climate ranges from mild and rainy in the north, through a summer-dry climate in California, to desert conditions in the south. Rainfall in the Gulf states is heavy and chiefly monsoonal, falling mainly in the summer.

The mountain ranges in

military forces of the state; he is chosen by direct vote of the people for a term varying from two to four years.

Populations of metropolitan areas of cities with over one million inhabitants (1972 estimates): Washington D.C. (capital) 2,998,900; New York 9,943,800; Chicago 7,084,700; Los Angeles 6,999,600; Philadelphia

the west receive considerable rain and snow, the Rockies and Coastal Ranges having perpetual snow. The climate of the Central Plain is rendered colder in winter by a lack of shelter from northern winds, and it has heavy snowfalls in winter. Mean July temperatures in the Central Plain range between 18°C (65°F) in the north and 30°C (85°F) in the south where thunderstorms are frequent and tornadoes sometimes experienced.

Natural resources: The United States has a wide variety of mineral resources, particularly metallic ores. Iron ore is mined in large quantities near Lake Superior and in Alabama. Copper, uranium ores, molybdenum and silver are found in the Rockies; the largest output of zinc is from Tennessee, that of lead from Missouri, and that of bauxite from Arkansas. Non-metallic minerals include phosphate rock (mainly from Florida), salt (from Louisiana and Texas), and sulphur (also from Louisiana and Texas).

The most intensively cultivated area is the Prairie States of the Middle West—the 'Corn Belt'. Soya beans, wheat and hay are grown in rotation with the corn (maize), thus providing feed stock for intensive cattle and pig farming. In the south cotton is the chief commercial crop; citrus fruit are grown in California and Florida; and in the east tobacco and peanuts are grown in Virginia and North Carolina. About 40 per cent of the world's woodpulp production comes from the United States, and there is also a substantial output of softwoods and hardwoods. The most valuable fish are salmon and tuna caught in Alaska and southern California respectively.

The chief coalmining areas lie in the Appalachian plateaux, Illinois and numerous smaller coalfields in the Rockies. In 1975 the United States took second place to the USSR as the world's

largest producer of oil. Output is mainly from Texas, Oklahoma, California and Alaska. Natural gas is found in the same areas. The western mountain ranges, Niagara Falls and the Tennessee Valley are the main site of hydro-electric power stations.

Industry and exports: A complete range of industrial activity takes place in the United States resulting from the abundance of raw materials and power. Iron and steel and heavy engineering was concentrated around the Pennsylvania coalfields and the iron ores of Minnesota, but has now spread to Pittsburgh and the cities around the Great Lakes. There are also heavy industries in Alabama. Electronic and aerospace industries flourish in southern California in the west and Florida in the east.

The United States is the leading producer of a wide range of manufactured goods, including paper, rayon and fertilizers, while it produces about one-third of the world's total output of automobiles, which together with machinery and aircraft, account for nearly half the total exports of the country. Other important exports are foodstuffs such as grains and fruit, and also cotton, tobacco and chemicals. Canada and Western Europe are the main export markets, although trade with Japan is increasing rapidly.

Recent history: President Richard Nixon's term of office, although cut short by political scandal and corruption, was successful in terminating the Vietnam war and in effecting a rapprochement with Soviet Russia and Communist China. The President's obstructive handling of investigations into domestic affairs led to a growing clamour for his impeachment. Finally in 1974 he resigned, to be succeeded by his Vice-President, Gerald Ford. In the presidential elections of

1976 a Democrat, James Carter, was returned to the White House with a popular vote of 40,263,599 against 38,512,666.

UPPER VOLTA

Official name: Republic of Upper Volta. Location: Land-locked state in West Africa. Area: 274,002 sq. km (105,765 sq. miles). Form of government: Republic. Population (1975 census): 6,144,013. Official language: French. Official religion: None. Monetary unit: The franc = 100 centimes. Principal towns and their population (1975 census): Ouagadougou (capital) 124,779; Bobo-Dioulasso 102,059.

URUGUAY

Official name: Oriental Republic of Uruguay. Location: East coast of South America, with Brazil to the north and Argentina to the west. Area: 186,926 sq. km (72,153 sq. miles). Form of government: Presidential rule. Estimated population (1975): 2,764,000. Official language: Spanish. Official religion: None; Roman Catholicism is the predominant religion. Monetary unit: The peso = 100 centésimos. Principal towns and their estimated population (1975): Montevideo (capital) 1,229,750; Salto 80,000; Paysandú 80,000; Mercedes 53,000.

VENEZUELA

Official name: Republic of Venezuela. Location: North coast of South America, bordered by Colombia, Guyana and Brazil. Area: 921,417 sq. km (355,667 sq. miles). Form of government: Presidential democracy. Estimated population (1975): 11,500,000. Official language: Spanish. Official religion: None; the majority of the population is Roman Catholic. Monetary unit: The bolivar = 2 reales = 100 céntimos. Principal towns and their population (1971 census): Caracas (capital) 1,764,000; Maracaibo 651,574; Barquisimeto 330,815; Valencia 367,154; Maracay 255,134; San

Cristóbal 152,239.

VIETNAM

Official name: Socialist Republic of Vietnam. Location: South-eastern Asia. Area: 335,767 sq. km (129,606 sq. miles). Form of government: Communist republic. Estimated population (1974): 23,787,000. Official language: Vietnamese. Official religion: None; the principal religion is Buddhism. Monetary unit: The dong = 100 has. Capital Hanoi (1974 estimated population 1,378,300); other towns: Ho Chi Minh City (formerly Saigon); Haiphong; Da Nang; Hué.

WALES:

See United Kingdom.

WESTERN SAMOA

Official name: Western Samoa. Location: Two large islands (Sava'i and Upolu) and seven small ones in South Pacific. Area: 2,842 sq. km (1,097 sq. miles). Form of government: Constitutional monarchy. Estimated population (1974): 155,000. Official languages: Samoan and English. Official religion: None. Monetary unit: The tala (dollar) = 100 sene (cents). Capital: Apia (1970 population 28,880).

WEST INDIES ASSOCIATED STATES

Location: Group of Caribbean islands. Form of government: Self government in association with Britain which remains responsible for defence and foreign affairs. Official language: English. Official religion: None. Monetary unit: The dollar = 100 cents.

ANTIGUA AND BARBUDA—Area: 440 sq. km (170 sq. miles). Estimated population (1975): 69,700. Capital: St John's (1975 population 13,000).

DOMINICA—Area: 750 sq. km (289.5 sq. miles). Estimated population (1976): 78,000. Capital: Roseau (1976 population 10,150).

ST CHRISTOPHER (KITTS), NEVIS AND ANGUILLA—Area: 396 sq.

km (153 sq. miles).
Estimated population (1976):
54,500. Capital: Basseterre
(1976 population 15,900).

ST LUCIA—Area: 616 sq.
km (238 sq. miles).
Estimated population (1975):
114,000. Capital: Castries
(1975 population 45,000).

ST VINCENT—Area: 389
sq. km (150.3 sq. miles).
Estimated population (1975):
100,400. Capital: Kingstown
(1975 population 22,000).

YEMEN

Official name: Yemen Arab
Republic. Location:
South-west corner of
Arabian Peninsula. Area:
200,000 sq. km approx.
(77,200 sq. miles). Form of
government: Constituent
assembly. Estimated
population (1975):
6,500,000. Official language:
Arabic. Official religion:
Islam. Monetary unit: The
riyal = 40 buqsha.
Principal towns and their
estimated population (1975):
San'a (capital) 150,000;
Hodeida 100,000; Ta'iz
100,000.

YEMEN (ADEN):

See Southern Yemen.

YUGOSLAVIA

Official name: Socialist
Federal Republic of
Yugoslavia. Location:
Balkans, eastern Europe.
Area: 255,804 sq. km
(98,740 sq. miles). Form of
government: Federal
Communist Republic.
Estimated population (1975):
21,352,000. Official
languages: Serbo-Croat,
Macedonian and Slovene.
Official religion: None;
about a third of the
population belongs to the
Roman Catholic Church,
and the majority of the
remainder to the Serbian
Orthodox Church. Monetary
unit: The dinar = 100 para.
Principal towns and their
population (1976): Belgrade
(capital) 1,209,360; Zagreb
602,205; Skopje 388,962;
Sarajevo 292,263;
Ljubljana 257,647.

ZAIRE

Official name: Republic of
Zaïre. Location: West
central Africa. Area:
2,345,409 sq. km (895,348 sq.
miles). Form of government:
Military junta. Estimated
population (1976):
25,600,000. Official language:
French; over 400 Sudanese
and Bantu dialects are
spoken. Official religion:
None. Monetary unit: The
zaïre = 100 makuta = 10,000
sengi. Principal towns and
their population (1976):
Kinshasa (capital, formerly
Leopoldville) 1,990,717;
Kananga (formerly
Luluabourg) 595,954;
Lubumbashi (formerly
Elisabethville) 401,612;
Mbuji-Mayi (formerly
Bakwanga) 234,725;
Kisangani (formerly
Stanleyville) 297,829.

ZAMBIA

Official name: Republic of
Zambia. Location: Southern
central Africa. Area:
752,618 sq. km (290,586 sq.
miles). Form of government:
One-party presidential
democracy. Estimated
population (1974): 4,751,000.
Official language: English;
Bantu dialects are spoken.
Official religion: None; 80 per
cent of the population is
Christian. Monetary unit:
The kwacha = 100 ngwee.
Principal towns and their
estimated population (1974):
Lusaka (capital) 415,000;
Kitwe 350,000; Ndola 240,000;
Chingola 202,000; Mufulira
136,000.

ZIMBABWE

Official name: Zimbabwe-
Rhodesia. Location: Land-
locked state in south-central
Africa. Area: 390,622 sq. km
(150,780 sq. miles). Form of
government: Illegal republic.
Estimated population (1976):
6,420,000. Official language:
English; the main African
languages are Sindebele and
Chishona. Official religion:
None. Monetary unit: The
dollar = 100 cents. Principal
towns and their estimated
population (1972): Salisbury
(capital) 490,000; Bulawayo
296,000; Gwelo 54,000; Umtali
52,000.

ACKNOWLEDGMENTS

The publishers would like to thank the following organisations and individuals for their kind permission to reproduce the photographs in this book:

Adespoton Film Services 180–181, 199; Ampliaciones Y Reprodacciones MAS 112–113; Heather Angel 68–69, 79 above left and below right, 81 above and below, 83 below, 84, 89 below, 90 above and below, 91 above left and right, 92 centre and below, 93 below and centre right, 96; Architectural Association, London 142–143; University of Arizona, Lunar and Planetary Laboratory 16; Courtesy of the Art Institute of Chicago 207; J. Arthur Dixon 20; Baroness International 171 below; B.B.C. Copyright Photographs 166, 179; Bibliothèque Nationale, Paris 123; Boeing Engineering and Construction Company 184–185; G. C. Bridge 67 above right; Paul Brierley 49 above, 163, 172; The Trustees of the British Museum 118 (M. Holford) 104 above, 104–105; Camera Press (Almasy/RBO) 217, (N. Faridani) 229 right, (P. Lichfield) 231 above, (J. Messerschmidt) 234 right, (F. Peer) 239, (Silberstein) 231 below, (L. Skoogfors) 138, (W. Swann) 225, (B. Williams) 227 below; California Institute of Technology and Carnegie Institute of Washington 10–11, 18–19, 23, 28–29, 30–31, 34–35 (Jet Propulsion Laboratory) 40–41; M. Carter 83 above; John Cleare/Mountain Camera 67 below; Stephanie Colasanti 4–5; Bruce Coleman (G. Cox) 71 centre right and below right, (L. Lee Rue II) 91 below, (Prato) 89 above, (H. Reinhard) 85 right, 93 below, (J. Shaw) 86; Colorific Photograph Library (J. Moss) 246; Douglas Dickens 228, 244, 248–249; Robert Estall 220, 226 below; Mary Evans Picture Library 126–127; Photographie Giraudon 109, 124 (Lauros) 130–131; Glaxo Operations U.K. Limited 162; Hale Observatories, California 24, 25, 32, 33, 34; Sonia Halliday 110; R. Harding 198, 219 above; The Health Education Council 187; Michael Holford 98–99, 106; Angelo Hornak 209; David Hosking 85 left; Hosokawa Collection, Japan 119; Robert Hunt 137; Alan Hutchison Library 2–3, (K. Hillman) 66 above right, (V & A Wilkinson) 66 below; I.B.M. 171 above; I.C.L. 170; A. F. Kersting 122; Keystone Press Agency 53, 135, 152; Kings College Hospital 192 inset; Laser Images Incorporated, California/London Planetarium 212–213; Leimbach Films and Fotos, Endpapers, 154–155; Lick Observatory Photographs 15; S. Lousada 192; Microcolour (Gene Cox) 71 above right; Margaret Murray 148–149, 153, 156–157, 196–197; The National Maritime Museum, London 111, 112; Natural Science Photos (B. Wood) 102; NERC Copyright, reproduced by permission of the Director, Institute of Geological Sciences, London 44 below, 49 below; Novosti Press Agency 132–133, 182; Picturepoint 42–43, 46, 58, 180, 218, 226 above, 229 left, 230, 232 above, 235 below, 236; Popperfoto 139; Practical Electronics 164–165; Rapho (Mopy) 185, (Duroy) 145, (Serraileir) 224; Rex Features 47, 175; Captain T. Rigg 67 centre; G. R. Roberts 50; SCALA (Napoli National Museum) 116–117; Science Museum, London (E. Tweedy) 12; Seaphot (P. David) 92 above; Spectrum Colour Library 146; Stedelije Museum/Amsterdam 206; The Tate Gallery, London 210–211; E. R. Thomas 67 above left; E. Tweedy 114, 115; U.K.A.E.A. 159, 161; University College, London, Department of Physics 21; Mireille Vautier (de Nanxe) 200; Dr. Waechter 100, 103; Winterhur Museum 129; Woods Hole Oceanographic Institute 60; Zefa 125, 144, 147, 150–51, 168–169, 174, 177, 190–191, 195, 201, 202, 204–205, 216, 219 below, 222, 227 above, 232 below, 234 left, 235 above, 237, 238 below, 240, 242, 243, 245, 247 above and below, 249.